Zaire
a country study

Federal Research Division
Library of Congress
Edited by
Sandra W. Meditz
and Tim Merrill
Research Completed
December 1993

On the cover: Traditional wooden mask

Fourth Edition, First Printing, 1994.

Library of Congress Cataloging-in-Publication Data

Zaire, a country study / Federal Research Division, Library of
   Congress ; edited by Sandra W. Meditz and Tim Merrill. — 4th ed.
      p.   cm. — (Area handbook series, ISSN 1057-5294)
   (DA pam ; 550-67)
      "Research completed December 1993."
      Rev. ed. of: Zaire, a country study / American University
   (Washington, D.C.). Foreign Area Studies. 3rd ed. 1979.
      Includes bibliographical references (pp. 343-363) and index.
      ISBN 0-8444-0795-X
      1. Zaire. I. Meditz, Sandra W., 1950-   . II. Merrill, Tim,
   1949-   . III. Library of Congress. Federal Research Division.
   IV. American University (Washington, D.C.). Foreign Area
   Studies. Zaire, a country study. V. Series. VI. Series: DA Pam ;
   550-67.
   DT644.Z3425   1994   94-25092
   [Z663.275]   CIP
   967.51—dc20

Headquarters, Department of the Army
DA Pam 550-67

Reprinted without alteration
on acid-free paper

Bernan
Lanham, Maryland
December 1994

Foreword

This volume is one in a continuing series of books prepared by the Federal Research Division of the Library of Congress under the Country Studies/Area Handbook Program sponsored by the Department of the Army. The last two pages of this book list the other published studies.

Most books in the series deal with a particular foreign country, describing and analyzing its political, economic, social, and national security systems and institutions, and examining the interrelationships of those systems and the ways they are shaped by cultural factors. Each study is written by a multidisciplinary team of social scientists. The authors seek to provide a basic understanding of the observed society, striving for a dynamic rather than a static portrayal. Particular attention is devoted to the people who make up the society, their origins, dominant beliefs and values, their common interests and the issues on which they are divided, the nature and extent of their involvement with national institutions, and their attitudes toward each other and toward their social system and political order.

The books represent the analysis of the authors and should not be construed as an expression of an official United States government position, policy, or decision. The authors have sought to adhere to accepted standards of scholarly objectivity. Corrections, additions, and suggestions for changes from readers will be welcomed for use in future editions.

Louis R. Mortimer
Chief
Federal Research Division
Library of Congress
Washington, DC 20540–5220

Acknowledgments

The authors wish to acknowledge their use and adaptation of information in the 1979 edition of *Zaire: A Country Study,* edited by Irving Kaplan. The authors are also grateful to numerous individuals in various government agencies and private institutions who generously shared their time, expertise, and knowledge about Zaire. These people include Ralph K. Benesch, who oversees the Country Studies/Area Handbook Program for the Department of the Army.

The authors also wish to thank those who contributed directly to the preparation of the manuscript. These include Marilyn Majeska, who managed editing and book production; Catherine Schwartzstein, who edited the chapters and performed the final prepublication editorial review; Andrea T. Merrill, who reviewed all tabular and graphic materials; Joshua Sinai and Laverle Berry, who updated portions of the manuscript; Barbara Edgerton, Janie L. Gilchrist, and Izella Watson, who did the word processing; Joan C. Cook, who compiled the index; and Linda Peterson of the Printing and Processing Section, Library of Congress, who prepared the camera-ready copy under the supervision of Peggy Pixley.

David P. Cabitto, the firm of Greenhorne and O'Mara, and Harriett R. Blood provided invaluable graphics support. David P. Cabitto prepared the illustrations for the book's cover and each of the chapter title pages, as well as some of the charts. He also reviewed and finalized all of the maps, which were drafted by Tim Merrill and Laverle Berry. Greenhorne and O'Mara prepared some charts and all of the maps except the topography and drainage map, which was prepared by Harriett R. Blood.

Finally, the authors would like to acknowledge the generosity of the individuals and public and private organizations who allowed their photographs to be used in this study. They are indebted especially to those who contributed work not previously published.

Contents

Chapter 4. Government and Politics 201
Thomas Turner

List of Figures

Preface

This study replaces *Zaire: A Country Study,* which was completed in 1978, during the height of the personalistic regime of Mobutu Sese Seke, president since 1965. Since 1990, following an ostensible move toward multiparty democracy, Mobutu has presided over a nation in political, economic, and social disarray. This edition of *Zaire: A Country Study* focuses primarily on the Zaire of the early 1990s, during which time the Mobutu regime has appeared to be on the verge of collapse and yet has clung tenaciously to power, using its continued control of key military and security forces to obstruct the functioning of the transitional government, to intimidate the opposition, and to promote instability throughout the country.

Like its predecessor, this study is an attempt to treat in a concise and objective manner the dominant historical, social, economic, political, and national security aspects of contemporary Zaire. Sources of information included scholarly books, journals, and monographs; official reports of governments and international organizations; foreign and domestic newspapers; the authors' previous research and observations; and numerous periodicals. Chapter bibliographies appear at the end of the book; brief comments on some of the more valuable sources suggested as possible further reading appear at the end of each chapter.

Place-names follow the system adopted by the United States Board on Geographic Names (BGN). Place-names in Zaire present a particular problem to the reader in that most, including the name of the country itself, have been subject to change. At independence in 1960, the former Belgian Congo adopted the name Republic of the Congo. This name was changed in August 1964 to Democratic Republic of the Congo, and then in 1971 to Republic of Zaire. In all cases, this country is to be distinguished from its neighbor, the Republic of the Congo, formerly the People's Republic of the Congo. At times in the past, the two have been differentiated by indicating the names of their capital cities, as in Congo-Kinshasa (now Zaire) and Congo-Brazzaville. Most place-names in Zaire were changed between 1966 and 1972 as part of a campaign to eliminate vestiges of colonialism. The older place-names are used in this volume in historical contexts. To assist the reader in tracking the changes, former and new names of major cities are given in Table B. In addition, a comparison of fig. 1 and fig. 4 will help the reader to attain a clearer understanding of the relationship between the old provinces and the new regions that replaced them in 1972.

Most personal names in Zaire also changed as part of the authenticity (see Glossary) campaign. For example, Mobutu Sese Seko was formerly Joseph-Désiré Mobutu. By the 1990s, however, many Zairians had resumed the use of their given forename, including, for example, opposition leader Étienne Tshisekedi wa Mulumba. In general, the authors have used the name by which individuals are (or were) most commonly known. In second references to individuals, only the surname is given. In the case of Zairian names, readers should note that the first name is the surname. Thus, Mobutu Sese Seku becomes Mobutu after the first use.

All measurements in this book are given in the metric system; a conversion table is provided to assist those readers who are unfamiliar with metric measurements (see table 1, Appendix). A glossary is also included to explain terms with which the reader may not be familiar.

The body of the text reflects information available as of December 1993. Certain other portions of the text, however, have been updated: the Introduction discusses significant events that have occurred since the information cutoff date; the Country Profile and Chronology include updated information as available; and the Bibliograhy lists recently published sources thought to be particularly helpful to the reader.

Table A. Chronology of Important Events

Period	Description
EARLY HISTORY	
ca. 10,000 B.C.	Late Stone Age cultures start to flourish in southern savannas.
first millennium B.C.	In long series of migrations, lasting well into first millennium A.D., Bantu-speaking peoples from north of the Congo Basin disperse throughout Zaire, bringing an economy based on yam and palm farming.
ca. late first millennium B.C.	Non-Bantu speakers arrive in northern grasslands, then penetrate forest area, intermingling with Bantu speakers who preceded them; Central Sudanic speakers introduce cattle herding and cultivation of cereals into northeastern Zaire.
ca. A.D. 100	Related food complex based on cereals and hunting separately introduced into southeastern Zaire from East Africa.
first millennium A.D.	Bananas introduced from East Africa; iron and copper implements come into use; smelting introduced.
FOURTEENTH CENTURY	
late 1300s	Kongo Kingdom established, beginning expansion that continues until mid-seventeenth century.
FIFTEENTH CENTURY	
	Luba Empire "founded" in late fifteenth century by legendary figures, Nkongolo and Ilunga Kalala; other Luba chiefs settle among neighboring peoples, including Lunda, and introduce Luba concepts of state organization; Luba state based on patrilineal farming villages governed by divine king whose authority derived from *bulopwe*—an inherited, supernatural power conferring the right to kingly office and title. Luba noted for artistic achievements in sculpture, praise poetry, and polyphonic music. Lunda chiefdoms unite to form Lunda Kingdom.
1483	Portuguese explorers reach Congo River, beginning long-term relationship between Portugal and Kongo Kingdom that lasts until destruction of Kongo in early eighteenth century.
SIXTEENTH CENTURY	
	Lunda kingdom comes under Luba influence; legendary founders of Lunda include Kinguri, Chinyama, and Mwaant Yaav; Kinguri and Chinyama migrate west and found Lunda-like states in Angola; Mwaant

Table A.—Continued

Period	Description
	Yaav's name becomes perpetual title in and royal name for central Lunda kingdom; beginning in sixteenth century, and continuing to eighteenth century, Lunda expand west, east, and south, creating series of related kingdoms governed jointly by kings and councils of titled officials; Lunda expansion facilitated by devices of positional succession and perpetual kinship, which made it possible to incorporate non-Lunda into the Lunda administrative system; hunting important among the matrilineal Lunda; despite their political genius, their culture, in general less developed than that of Luba.
ca. 1500	Zande appear in northern Zaire and found a number of agriculturally based kingdoms.
early 1500s	Kongo king Affonso requests technical help from Portugal, agreeing to make payment in copper, ivory, and slaves; Affonso declares Roman Catholicism Kongo state religion.
mid-1500s	Corn introduced to Kongo by Portuguese, followed by cassava shortly after 1600 and tobacco by late seventeenth century.
SEVENTEENTH CENTURY	
ca. 1630	Kuba Kingdom founded by King Shyaam aMbul aNgoong; a highly centralized agricultural and trading state, it reached its zenith in mid-eighteenth century and remained stable into nineteenth century.
EIGHTEENTH CENTURY	
	Europeans in west and Arabs in east become heavily involved in slave trade.
ca. 1750	Kazembe Kingdom founded in Luapula Valley as Lunda offshoot following Lunda expansion to control salt pans and copper mines in Katanga; loosely part of Lunda Empire but autonomous in practice.
NINETEENTH CENTURY	
1840–72	David Livingstone explores Congo River basin.
1871	Livingstone and Henry Morton Stanley, journalist commissioned to search for him, meet on eastern shore of Lake Tanganyika.
1874–77	Stanley commissioned by New York and London newspapers to continue Livingstone's explorations; Stanley completes descent of Congo River in 1877.

Table A.—Continued

Period	Description
1878	King Léopold II forms consortium of bankers to finance exploration and colonization of Congo.
1878–87	Under auspices of consortium, Stanley sets out to establish trading posts and make treaties with local chiefs, eventually returning with 450 treaties in hand.
1884–85	At Conference of Berlin, November 1884–February 1885, major European powers acknowledge claim of Léopold II's International Association of the Congo; colony named Congo Free State.
1890s	Construction of transportation network and exploitation of mineral resources begin; forced labor used extensively to harvest rubber, ivory, and other commodities; mutinies within Force Publique in 1895 and 1897.
1890–94	Belgian military campaign expels Afro-Arab traders from Zaire and ends slave trade.
TWENTIETH CENTURY	
1908	In response to growing criticism of treatment of African population, Belgian parliament annexes Congo Free State and renames it Belgian Congo.
1914–17	Units of Belgian colonial forces see action alongside British forces in German East Africa.
1921	Simon Kimbangu founds Kimbanguist Church.
1920s–30s	Early nationalistic aspirations expressed by Kimbanguist Church and Kitawala religious movement.
1940–45	Production of goods and minerals greatly increased to finance Belgian effort in World War II; large-scale social and economic changes occur as many rural Africans relocate to urban areas; demands for political reforms grow.
1952–58	Legal reforms enacted permitting Africans to own land, granting them free access to public establishments, and the right to trial in all courts of law as well as some political participation.
1956	Alliance of the Kongo People (Alliance des Bakongo—Abako) issues manifesto calling for immediate independence.
late 1950s	Calls for independence of Katanga grow, and separatist party, Confederation of Katanga Associations (Confédération des Associations du Katanga—Conakat), headed by Moïse Tshombe organized.

Period		Description
1957	March	Statute passed allowing urban Africans to elect local communal councils; Abako wins majority of seats in urban elections.
	May	Appointed rural councils established.
1959	January	Belgian authorities disperse crowd of Abako members at political meeting; widespread rioting follows; Belgium recognizes total independence as goal for Belgian Congo.
	July	Congolese National Movement (Mouvement National Congolais—MNC), which had emerged as standard-bearer of independence movement in 1958–59, splits into two camps: radicals headed by Patrice Lumumba and moderate wing led by Joseph Ileo, Cyrille Adoula, and Albert Kalonji.
1960	January	Round Table Conference held in Brussels to discuss independence.
	May	In national legislative elections, MNC-Lumumba wins largest number of votes; Belgian authorities name MNC's Patrice Lumumba prime minister; colonial government promulgates Loi Fondamentale (Fundamental Law) to guide nation to independence and to serve as first constitution.
	June	Abako leader Joseph Kasavubu elected president; Congo becomes independent and First Republic established June 30.
	July	Army mutinies against its European officers, July 4–5; officer corps Africanized and Joseph-Désiré Mobutu (later Mobutu Sese Seko) named chief of staff, July 6–9; mutiny spreads to Équateur and Katanga, and Belgium sends in paratroopers; Moïse Tshombe declares Katanga an independent state and Belgian naval forces bombard Matadi on July 11; Lumumba and Kasavubu request United Nations (UN) military assistance in face of Belgian aggression and Katangan secession, July 12; UN Security Council resolution calls for Belgian withdrawal and authorizes UN intervention, July 14; first UN troops arrive in Congo, July 15, begin military intervention against Katanga in support of central government.
	August	South Kasai headed by Albert Kalonji secedes, August 8.
	September	President Kasavubu and Prime Minister Lumumba formally break and fire each other from their posts; Kasavubu names Joseph Ileo as new prime minister on September 5; on September 14, Mobutu steps in

Period		Description
		and assumes power while keeping Kasavubu as nominal president; government to be run by the so-called College of Commissioners; United Nations and most Western nations recognize Kasavubu government.
	November	Antoine Gizenga leaves for Stanleyville to establish rival national regime. Lumumba, under house arrest since dismissal by Kasavubu, leaves to join Gizenga, but is arrested and transferred to Katanga.
1961	January	Lumumba killed on January 17, but death not announced until February.
	February	College of Commissioners dissolved, and provisional government formed, headed by Joseph Ileo.
	July	Continuing deliberations undertaken at three conferences earlier in 1961, parliament meets close to Léopoldville to work out framework for a reunified Congo; deputies from all provinces attend; secession of South Kasai ends.
	August	Cyrille Adoula named prime minister, August 2.
1963	January	After two and a half years of conflict, Tshombe concedes defeat, and Katanga secession ends, January 14; Tshombe arrested and sent into exile.
1964	January	Led by Pierre Mulele, rebellion breaks out in Kwilu area around Kikwit.
	May	Second rebellion, headed by Gaston Soumialot, begins in east and rapidly spreads.
	July	Tshombe recalled from exile and replaces Adoula as prime minister.
	August	First postindependence constitution adopted.
	December	Eastern rebellion put down and Soumialot sent into exile.
1965	November	Rivalry between Prime Minister Tshombe and President Kasavubu leads to government paralysis; Mobutu leads successful coup, November 24, dismisses Kasavubu and Tshombe, names himself as president, and appoints figurehead prime minister, Colonel Léonard Mulamba; these actions mark end of First Republic.
	December	Kwilu uprising ends, and Mulele goes into exile in Brazzaville; he later (1968) returns to Congo under amnesty but is executed.

Period		Description
1966	July	Former Katangan gendarmes mutiny in Kisangani.
	December	Cities with European names gradually given African names, in process that continues until 1972.
1967	January	Upper Katanga Mining Union (Union Minière du Haut-Katanga—UMHK) nationalized.
	April	Popular Revolutionary Movement (Mouvement Populaire de la Révolution—MPR) created, April 17.
	May	In Manifesto of N'Sele, Mobutu proclaims official ideologies.
	June	Second postindependence constitution proclaimed, removing virtually all political power from provinces and allowing president to rule by decree.
	July	Former Katangan gendarmes again mutiny in Kisangani.
1969	June	About thirty Lovanium University students killed in clashes with security forces.
1970	November	Mobutu elected president in first presidential election, having already held office for five years.
1971–72		Country's name changed to Zaire, October 1971; under policy of authenticity, all colonial or Christian names changed to Zairian ones, 1972; provinces now called regions and given non-European names.
1973	November	Policy of Zairianization proclaimed; foreign-owned businesses and property expropriated and distributed to Zairian government officials, resulting in increasing economic chaos.
1974	August	Revised version of 1967 constitution promulgated, making MPR synonymous with state.
1975	November	Policy of retrocession announced, returning much expropriated property to foreign owners.
1977	March	Shaba I: Zairian insurgency group invades Shaba Region from Angola and is defeated, only with help from France and Morocco, by May.
	October	Legislative elections held.
	December	Mobutu reelected president, running unopposed.
1978	February	Constitution revised; military establishment purged following discovery of coup plot.

Table A. —Continued

Period		Description
	May	Shaba II: Same insurgent group launches another invasion of Shaba from Zambia and is again defeated only with help of French and Belgians.
	June	Pan-African peacekeeping force installed in Shaba and stays for over a year.
1982	September	Legislative elections held; multiple candidates allowed for first time; more than three-quarters of incumbents voted out; thirteen parliamentarians attempt to form second party and are arrested.
1984	July	Mobutu reelected without opposition.
	November	Rebel forces occupy Moba in Shaba Region for two days before town recaptured by Zairian forces.
1985	June	Zaire celebrates twenty-five years of independence; on eve of celebration, guerrillas briefly occupy Moba again.
1987	September	Legislative elections held.
1989	February	Student disturbances break out in Kinshasa and Lubumbashi and result in violent clashes with armed police.
1990	April	Third Republic declared on April 24; Mobutu promises national multiparty elections the following year.
	May	Protesting students at University of Lubumbashi massacred by government forces; as a result, Belgium, European Community, Canada, and United States ultimately cut off all but humanitarian aid to Zaire.
	December	Legislation permitting political parties to register finally passed.
1991	April–May	Security forces intervene violently against demonstrators.
	August	National conference on political reform convened with ostensible mandate to draft new constitution as prelude to new elections; conference suspended, August 15.
	September	Unpaid paratroopers mutiny in Kinshasa and go on rampage; looting and violence spread; France and Belgium send troops to restore order and evacuate foreign nationals.
	October	Opposition leader Étienne Tshisekedi named prime minister in early October but fired by Mobutu a week later, spurring violent demonstrations; France joins

Period	Description
	other Western nations in cutting off economic aid to Zaire; Mobutu appoints Bernardin Mungul-Diaka to succeed Tshisekedi.
November	Mobutu names another opposition leader, Nguza Karl-i-Bond, prime minister.
December	National conference reconvenes.
1992	National conference activities periodically suspended by Mobutu; economy continues to deteriorate; Western nations call for Mobutu to step down, but he clings to power.
February	Peaceful demonstrations by Christian groups violently broken up by security forces; up to forty-five killed and 100 injured.
April	National conference meets, declares itself to have sovereign powers not only to draw up new constitution but also to legislate multiparty system; Transitional Act passed establishing new, transitional government; these actions constitute a direct challenge to Mobutu, who does not accept conference's authority.
August	Newly named Sovereign National Conference elects Tshisekedi prime minister, precipitating violent confrontations in Shaba Region between supporters of Tshisekedi and Nguza; conflict between Tshisekedi and Mobutu over who runs government continues.
1993 January	Soldiers riot and loot following refusal by merchants to accept new Z5 million notes with which military personnel paid; in ensuing violence, dozens of soldiers killed by elite army unit loyal to Mobutu; French ambassador killed while watching violence from office window.
March	Mobutu dismisses Tshisekedi and names Faustin Birindwa prime minister of so-called government of national salvation; Birindwa names cabinet in April; Zaire now has two rival, parallel governments.
October	More rioting and looting occur when opposition parties promote boycott of new currency issue used to pay troops.

Table B. City Name Changes, 1966–72

Former Name	New Name
Albertville	Kalemie
Bakwanga	Mbuji-Mayi
Banningville	Bandundu
Baudoinville *	Moba
Coquilhatville	Mbandaka
Élisabethville	Lubumbashi
Léopoldville	Kinshasa
Luluabourg	Kananga
Stanleyville	Kisangani
Thysville	Mbanza-Ngungu

New Name	Former Name
Bandundu	Banningville
Kalemie	Albertville
Kananga	Luluabourg
Kinshasa	Léopoldville
Kisangani	Stanleyville
Lubumbashi	Élisabethville
Mbandaka	Coquilhatville
Mbanza-Ngungu	Thysville
Mbuji-Mayi	Bakwanga
Moba *	Baudoinville

* The city now called Moba was known as Virungu for some time after its name was changed from the colonial Baudoinville.

Country Profile

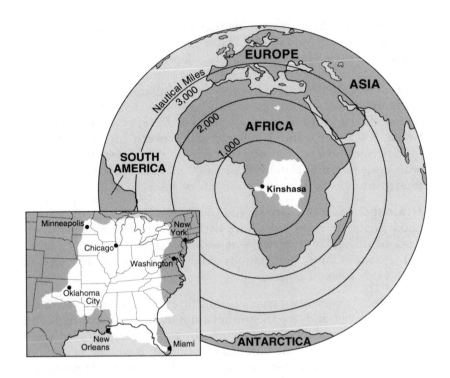

COUNTRY

Formal Name: Republic of Zaire.

Short Form: Zaire.

Term for Citizen(s): Zairian(s).

Capital: Kinshasa.

Date of Independence: June 30, 1960, from Belgium.

National Holidays: June 30, Independence Day; November 24, celebrating establishment of Second Republic on November 24, 1965.

Geography

Size: Second largest country in sub-Saharan Africa; about 2,344,885

NOTE—The Country Profile contains updated information as available.

square kilometers, roughly size of United States east of Mississippi River.

Topography: Major geographic regions include central Congo Basin, uplands north and south of basin, and eastern highlands. Core region is central Congo Basin, large depression with average elevation of about forty-four meters, constituting about one-third of Zaire. North and south of basin lie higher plains and hills covered with mixtures of savanna grasses and woodlands. Southern uplands region also constitutes about one-third of Zaire, with elevations between 500 meters and 1,000 meters. Eastern highlands region highest and most rugged portion, bounded by Great Rift Valley, with some mountains more than 5,000 meters. Eastern border extends through valley and its system of lakes.

Drainage: Most of Zaire served by Congo River system. Congo and its tributaries provide Zaire with Africa's most extensive network of navigable waterways as well as vast hydroelectric potential. Flow of Congo unusually regular because tributaries feed in from both sides of equator.

Climate: Ranges from tropical rain forest in Congo River basin to tropical wet-and-dry in southern uplands to tropical highland in eastern areas above 2,000 meters. In general, temperatures and humidity quite high, but with much variation; many places on both sides of equator have two wet and two dry seasons. Average annual temperature 25°C. Average annual rainfall between 1,000 millimeters and 2,200 millimeters, highest in heart of Congo River basin and highlands west of Bukavu.

Society

Population: Estimated at 39.1 million in 1992; annual growth rate estimated at 3.3 percent. Estimated at 42.7 million in 1994, with estimated annual growth rate of 3.2 percent.

Language: About 250 languages spoken. French remains primary language of government, formal economy, and most education. Four indigenous languages also have official status: Kikongo, Tshiluba, Lingala, and Kiswahili.

Ethnic Groups: As many as 250 different groups, mostly Bantu-speaking. Largest Bantu-speaking groups are Luba, Kongo, Mongo, and Lunda.

Religion: Majority of population Christian: 46 to 48 percent Roman Catholic, 24 to 28 percent Protestant, up to 16.5 percent members of indigenous Kimbanguist Church. About 1 percent of population Muslim. Most other people practice traditional African religions.

Education and Literacy: Numbers of schools, teachers, and pupils have increased, but enrollment ratios relatively low—78 percent for primary school and 23 percent for secondary school in 1990. Only 56 percent of primary school-aged children reach fourth grade. Pervasive and accelerating qualitative decline at all levels. In early 1990s, most state-run schools reported to have closed. Adult literacy rate estimated at 72 percent (84 percent for males, 61 percent for females) in 1992.

Health and Welfare: Life expectancy at birth in 1991 estimated at fifty-two for males and fifty-six for females. In 1994 overall life expectancy estimated at forty-seven years, forty-nine for females and forty-six for males. Infectious and parasitic diseases—including malaria, trypanosomiasis (sleeping sickness), onchocerciasis (river blindness), and schistosomiasis—major health threat. Measles, diarrheal diseases, tetanus, diphtheria, pertussis, poliomyelitis, tuberculosis, and leprosy also prevalent. Majority of population also infected with intestinal worms. Acquired immune deficiency syndrome (AIDS) and other sexually transmitted diseases spreading rapidly. State-run health care system in virtual collapse in early 1990s. Private sources of health care reach only 50 percent of population. Only 14 percent of population has access to safe water. Malnutrition widespread, especially among children.

Economy

General Character: Since colonial times, dependent on exports of few commodities, particularly copper, cobalt, and coffee. Heavy government participation in and ownership of enterprises in all sectors, especially mining; management often inefficient, corrupt. Postindependence development undermined by misguided, overambitious economic policies. Key sectors and infrastructure neglected. In early 1990s, economy on verge of collapse despite vast mineral resources; formal sector barely operational; most activity in informal economy.

Gross Domestic Product (GDP): GDP growth negative since 1989, estimated at − 8.0 percent in 1992. Statistics rough approximations, do not include large informal economy, estimated to be three times size of official economy.

Currency and Exchange Rate: Consistently overvalued zaire (Z) leading to huge discrepancy between official and black-market exchange rates. Dramatic decline in value since 1985. Exchange rate in 1985: Z50 = US$1; rate in December 1993 estimated at Z110,000,000 = US$1.

Budget: Government regularly overspent since independence. Financial administration characterized by widespread mismanagement, corruption, and poor budgetary control. Budget deficit Z703,632 million in 1992, projected to total Z1,097,909,000 million in 1993. Government generally regarded as bankrupt in early 1990s.

Debt: Massive foreign debt, estimated at US$10,705 million in 1991. Debt-service ratio 15.4 percent in 1990. In 1992 Zaire essentially terminated debt repayment, paying only US$79 million of US$3,450 million due. Main bilateral and multilateral lenders froze financial aid programs in early 1990s, regarded as unlikely to agree to reschedule or cancel existing debt or to approve further borrowing.

Agriculture: Main economic sector, employing 65 percent of work force, accounting for approximately 32 percent of GDP throughout 1980s. Potential to be net exporter of agricultural produce, but greatly underutilized; as little as 1 percent of land under cultivation. Zaire not self-sufficient in food production in 1990s. Sector neglected, suffered from nationalizations in 1970s, lack of investment funds, and inadequate infrastructure for transport of produce. Major food crops cassava, corn, rice, and plantains, followed by bananas, beans, peanuts, millet, sorghum, yams, potatoes, and fruits. Main staple food cassava. Principal cash crops coffee, palm oil and palm kernel oil, sugar, cocoa, rubber, and tea. Coffee most important cash crop; prices, exports, and quotas tightly controlled by government. Estimated 30 to 60 percent of coffee crop smuggled out of country.

Mining: Mining, mineral processing, and petroleum extraction 17 percent of GDP in 1990. Mineral exports, principally copper, cobalt, diamonds, and gold, provided nearly 75 percent of export earnings in 1990. Sector major source of government revenues. Traditionally world's largest producer of cobalt, fifth largest copper producer, second or third largest producer of industrial diamonds. Copper mining mainstay of economy, but had virtually collapsed from many years of neglect and from economic chaos in 1990s.

Industry: Manufacturing sector accounted for only 1.7 percent of GDP in 1988. Concentrated in Kinshasa and mining area of Shaba, consists largely of consumer goods, mainly food processing, textile manufacturing, beer, cigarettes, metalworking, woodworking, and vehicle assembly. Manufacturing in formal economy virtually at standstill by 1992 in wake of general economic chaos and military-led looting and rioting. Many enterprises in informal sector.

Energy: Sector largely government-controlled, but lacks coordination and planning. Tremendous hydroelectric potential, estimated at 100,000 megawatts. Installed capacity estimated at 2,486 megawatts in 1987, with 95 percent hydropower. Largest hydroelectric site at Inga dams on lower Congo River supplies mining center, main power consumer, in Shaba Region via 1,725-kilometer high-voltage transmission line. Operational status of line precarious in early 1990s because of lack of maintenance. Fuelwood and charcoal primary household energy sources and used by small industries, contributing to deforestation. Offshore oil production since 1975, onshore since 1979. Reserves estimated at 140 million barrels in early 1990s, likely to be depleted unless new exploration successful. Domestic production heavy crude that cannot be refined domestically; all production (9.9 million barrels in 1991) exported for refining. Petroleum imported for refining to meet domestic need for fuel and other finished petroleum products.

Foreign Trade and Balance of Payments: Copper, cobalt, crude petroleum, diamonds, coffee, and gold most significant exports. Primary imports machinery and other capital goods for mining industry as well as fuels, consumer goods, and foodstuffs. Belgium, United States, and other West European countries main partners. Trade balance positive in 1980s but dropped by 1991 because of decrease in world commodity prices, drops in production, and rises in import prices. Current account balance consistently negative because of massive increase in external debt service. Overall balance of payments generally negative; net capital transfers insufficient to cover current account deficit. Cross-border smuggling widespread.

Foreign Aid: Multilateral aid and bilateral aid from West, especially Belgium, France, Germany, Italy, and United States, once significant. All but humanitarian assistance (primarily food aid) cut off in 1990–91 because of Zaire's economic chaos and human rights abuses.

Fiscal Year: Calendar year.

Transportation and Telecommunications

Roads: Network of approximately 145,000 kilometers, but only

2,500 kilometers paved. Vast interior virtually devoid of roads. Entire network in serious disrepair in early 1990s.

Railroads: 5,138 kilometers in three discontinuous lines: one linking Kinshasa and Matadi, another in northeastern Zaire, and another in southeastern Zaire to export minerals. National Route (Voie Nationale) combines rail and river transport network between copper-mining region of Shaba and principal port of Matadi. Entire rail system in desperate need of repair in early 1990s.

Inland Waterways: Traditionally important, but limited in early 1990s because barges old and in short supply and marking of navigable channels neglected. Congo River most significant waterway for passengers and freight between Kinshasa and Kisangani. In late 1993, riverboats between Kinshasa and Kisangani said to have ceased operating because of lack of fuel and spare parts.

Ports: Ports limited because Zaire has tiny Atlantic coastline of about forty kilometers. Matadi on lower Congo River principal port, but not accessible by large vessels, also Atlantic port at Boma and inland ports at Kinshasa and at Ilebo on Kasai River.

Air Transport: Principal airport at Kinshasa badly damaged by looting in late 1991, subsequently used by few foreign airlines. Travelers could fly to Brazzaville in Congo and continue to Kinshasa by ferry across Congo River. Domestic air services deteriorated in 1980s and 1990s. National carrier, Air Zaire, virtually bankrupt.

Telecommunications: In 1990 about 32,000 telephones, most in Kinshasa. Adequate international service, domestic service limited. In early 1990s, entire system dysfunctional. Residents of most larger towns could receive radio and television programming. In 1990 estimated 40,000 television sets and 3.7 million radio receivers, but system in poor condition. Only reliable national radio network said to be that run by Roman Catholic Church.

Government and Politics

Government: Republic with strong presidential authority dominated since 1965 by Mobutu Sese Seko. Personalistic regime often described as "presidential monarchy," in which Mobutu has run government as personal fiefdom, using national treasury as checkbook and disbursing rewards and punishments at will. Corruption, nepotism, and cronyism pervasive. Administrative structure effectively fused with sole legal political party, Popular Revolutionary

Movement (Mouvement Populaire de la Révolution—MPR).

Regime ostensibly changed in April 1990 with announcement of move toward multiparty democracy. In mid-1991 national conference, ultimately known as Sovereign National Conference (Conférence Souveraine Nationale—CSN) convened to oversee drafting of new constitution and smooth political transition. Transitional Act adopted August 1992 to serve as provisional constitution, provided for parliamentary system with figurehead president, High Council of the Republic (Haut Conseil de la République—HCR) provisional legislature, and first state commissioner (prime minister) head of government. Étienne Tshisekedi wa Mulumba elected head of two-year transitional government, recognized by Western powers, unable to govern because of Mobutu's continued control of key military and security forces, treasury, media, and administrative facilities. Mobutu also reconvened former legislature, National Legislative Council (Conseil National Législatif—CNL), attempted to obtain more favorable draft constitution, and, in March 1993, appointed rival government under Prime Minister Faustin Birindwa. Since then, government stalemate, with two parallel governments vying for political supremacy. Agreement reportedly reached in October 1993 on new transitional constitution, transitional parliament, and electoral schedule, but no action taken by mid-1994.

Politics: From 1967 until 1990, MPR sole legal political party. Formal registration of political parties allowed December 1990, and numerous parties sprang up. Principal opposition party Union for Democracy and Social Progress (Union pour la Démocratie et le Progrès Social—UDPS) led by Tshisekedi. Also Union of Federalists and Independent Republicans (Union des Fédéralistes et des Républicains Indépendants—UFERI) led by Jean Nguza Karl-i-Bond, Democratic and Social Christian Party (Parti Démocrate et Social Chrétien—PDSC) led by Joseph Ileo Nsongo Amba, Congolese National Movement-Lumumba (Mouvement National Congolais-Lumumba—MNC-Lumumba) led by Christophe Gbenye, and Unified Lumumbist Party under Antoine Gizenga. Major opposition parties united in Sacred Union (Union Sacrée) during 1991–92. In November 1991, Nguza and UFERI formed Alliance of Patriotic Forces as rival opposition force within CSN. Other schisms occurred in opposition. In September 1993, Tshisekedi formed another coalition called Democratic Forces of the Congo-Kinshasa. Pro-Mobutu forces, led by MPR, worked together in coalition known as United Democratic Forces (Forces Démocratiques Unies—FDU). MPR retained the same abbreviation and same political orientation, reportedly changed name to

Popular Movement for the Revival (Mouvement Populaire pour le Renouveau).

Administrative Divisions: Administratively, country divided into ten regions plus capital of Kinshasa. Highly centralized system with little autonomy at regional or local level.

Foreign Relations: Foreign policy orientation officially nonaligned but generally pro-Western under Mobutu. Mobutu regime traditionally perceived as enjoying, and depending on, support of Belgium, France, and United States. Because of Zaire's size, mineral wealth, and strategic location, as well as Mobutu's willingness to support Western foreign policy goals (e.g., in Angola and Chad), Mobutu able to capitalize on Cold War tensions to garner support and substantial economic and military assistance. Until early 1990s, Western powers mostly disregarded growing evidence of human rights abuses and corruption of Mobutu regime. But following end of Cold War and chaotic events in Zaire in early 1990s, Belgium, France, and United States terminated all but humanitarian aid to Zaire, have increasingly pressured Mobutu to improve human rights record and institute multiparty democracy. All three nations have voiced support for transitional government under Tshisekedi, have refused to recognize rival, Mobutu-appointed Birindwa government, but have stopped short of adopting stronger measures against Mobutu, such as confiscating his assets abroad or imposing economic sanctions.

Regional relations significant because Zaire borders on nine other states. But relations with neighbors often tense because of refugees, smuggling, mutual harboring of antigovernment rebels, and border violations by security forces.

International Agreements and Memberships: Member of many international and regional organizations, including United Nations (UN) and its specialized agencies, World Bank, International Monetary Fund, General Agreement on Tariffs and Trade, International Criminal Police Organization (Interpol), International Telecommunications Satellite Organization (Intelsat), Nonaligned Movement, Organization of African Unity (OAU), African Development Bank, Economic Community of Central African States (Communauté Économique des États de l'Afrique Centrale—CEEAC), and Economic Community of the Great Lakes Countries (Communauté Économique des Pays des Grands Lacs—CEPGL).

National Security

Armed Forces: Zairian Armed Forces (Forces Armées Zaïroises—

FAZ) consisting of army, navy, air force, and paramilitary gendarmerie, which also functions as nation's primary police organization. Total FAZ strength estimated at 49,100 in 1993, including 25,000 army, 1,300 navy, 1,600 air force, and 21,000 gendarmerie personnel. In addition, 10,000-member Civil Guard, not technically part of the FAZ, performs integral national security and police role. Official FAZ mission is to defend country against all internal and external threats, but in practice primary task has been suppressing perceived internal threats to the Mobutu regime.

Major Military Units: Army most significant military force; most capable and trusted unit is elite Special Presidential Division (Division Spéciale Présidentielle—DSP). In chaotic political and security situation of early 1990s, DSP only military unit regularly paid, and thus loyal and effective instrument of control.

Military Equipment: Wide variety of poorly maintained equipment, mostly of United States, French, and Chinese origin. Most equipment not operational because of shortages of spare parts, poor maintenance, and theft.

Foreign Military Relations: Since independence, country has benefited from variety of foreign military assistance, especially from Belgium, France, United States, and Israel, also China and Democratic People's Republic of Korea (North Korea). But Western nations terminated military assistance in early 1990s because of widespread human rights abuses and prevailing nationwide chaos.

Internal Security Forces: Two national organizations performing police and internal security functions: 21,000-member National Gendarmerie and 10,000-member Civil Guard, both ineffective, suffering from poor training, discipline, and equipment, and unreliable pay. Many members contribute to lawlessness by practicing banditry and extortion.

Figure 1. Administrative Divisions of Zaire, 1993

Introduction

ZAIRE HAS LONG BEEN CONSIDERED SIGNIFICANT because of its location, its resources, its potential, and (perhaps paradoxically) because of its weakness. The country has been at the center of a number of crises over the years, most notably following independence, during the Congo crisis of the 1960s, when there was a threat of the Cold War spilling over and heating up in Central Africa. Again in the 1990s, Zaire is threatening to become a source of international instability.

Zaire's importance is to some extent geopolitical. It borders on no fewer than nine other states. These countries range from Arab-dominated Sudan in the north, to Angola in the south. Hence, in defending its borders Zaire can—and has—become entangled in political rivalries extending all the way from Libya and Egypt to South Africa, i.e., the length of the continent. During the 1990s, Zaire's borders with Angola and especially Rwanda have been international flash points.

Zaire's minerals add to the country's importance. Although the value attached to them by outsiders has varied over the years, the country's resources remain impressive. In recent years, Zaire has been the world's largest producer of cobalt, second or third largest producer of industrial diamonds, and fifth largest producer of copper. Zinc, tin, manganese, gold, tungsten-bearing wolframite, niobium, and tantalum also are found in Zaire. In addition, the Atlantic coast contains important oil reserves, and the country also has some coal deposits. Also intriguing, in terms of Zaire's development prospects, is the country's immense agricultural and hydrolectric potential, believed to be sufficient to feed and power the entire continent. Obviously, however, the potential represented by these resources has yet to result in any significant benefit for the vast majority of Zaire's impoverished population. For example, failure to reinvest in the mining sector, since the mid-1980s at least, has diminished Zaire's ability to profit from its mineral resources. By 1994 it appeared that copper and cobalt production had declined to the point that diamonds were Zaire's most import export.

Indigenous developments laid the groundwork for what has become Zaire. Well before Europeans arrived in the fifteenth entury, the indigenous peoples had developed iron-working and long-distance trade. Large states had emerged, notably among the Kongo and Luba peoples of the southern savannas. Artistic traditions that have become world renowned had begun, particularly in the areas of sculpture, weaving, and music.

For the last five centuries, the area of present-day Zaire has also been influenced by the outside world. The Portuguese navigator Diogo Cão reached the estuary of the Congo River in 1483. Shortly thereafter commercial and diplomatic relations were established between Portugal and the coastal Kongo Kingdom; the slave trade soon came to dominate the relationship, however. Over the centuries, a larger and larger portion of the Congo Basin was drawn into trade networks connected to the Atlantic Coast. By the founding of the Congo Free State in 1885, most of its territory was linked to one of these Atlantic networks or to two newer ones that tied the country to the Nile Valley and the Indian Ocean.

"Traditional" culture in Zaire has been substantially modified by these precolonial contacts with the outside world. The so-called traditional diet of many Zairian communities, for example, includes crops from the Western Hemisphere introduced by the Portuguese (notably cassava, or manioc as it is called in Zaire) and rice, introduced from the East coast of Africa by the Afro-Arabs in the nineteenth century.

The colonization of what became Zaire took place in an atmosphere of intense international competition. The Scottish missionary, David Livingstone, first brought the Congo to the attention of the Western world through his explorations of the Congo River basin, beginning in the mid-nineteenth century. Then, in 1878 journalist Henry Morton Stanley was commissioned by Léopold II, king of Belgium, to undertake additional explorations and to establish Belgian sovereignty along the Congo. In 1884–85, Léopold's claims to the Congo River basin were recognized by the major powers at the Conference of Berlin, and the Congo Free State was established under his personal rule. In 1908, following international criticism of the brutalities tolerated by Léopold, Belgium assumed direct control of the colony, which henceforth was called the Belgian Congo.

Once Léopold's personal fiefdom had been replaced by a more orthodox arrangement, the Belgian Congo largely disappeared from international view. However, Belgium remained very nervous regarding the intentions of the major powers toward the colony and with good reason. Germany planned to link its colonies in West and East Africa by annexing the Belgian Congo, had it won World War I. Adolf Hitler had designs on the Belgian Congo during World War II. Moreover, in the late 1930s, the British apparently considered trying to buy Hitler's good will by giving him the Belgian

Congo. In both cases, the colony's strategic position as well as its minerals made the acquisition appealing.

France had only recognized Léopold's sovereignty over the lion's share of the Congo Basin with a reservation, namely a right of first refusal should Léopold give up the territory. The French raised this supposed right when Belgium took over the Congo Free State and again in 1960 when Belgium proposed to grant independence to the colony.

The legacy of nervousness regarding the threat to its colony helps to explain the ambiguity of Belgium's response to the Katanga (now Shaba) secession of 1960—i.e., supporting the secessionist regime while denying it the official recognition that might have enabled it to consolidate its independence. Had the Katangan leaders achieved full independence, they might have opened the door to non-Belgian investors in Katangan minerals, as indeed occurred during the 1970s.

Bula matari ("he who breaks rocks" in Kikongo, the language of the Kongo people) became the name of the Léopoldian state at its very beginning and is still used to refer to the state, for example in radio broadcasts in indigenous languages. The name graphically symbolizes the brutal form of extortion—extracting ivory and natural rubber from the Congolese—by which Léopold attempted to pay the cost of penetration of the territory and development of infrastructure.

The Belgian Congo was run on a somewhat different basis. Philosophically, "paternalism" served to guide and justify the actions of the administration. But coercion or the threat of coercion never was far from the surface. The brutality of colonial rule, particularly in its early years, left a double legacy. On the one hand, it created strong resentments on which nationalist movements could draw. At the same time, it generated a mood of fear and hopelessness that deterred the appearance of nationalist movements.

The state shared responsibility for administration and development with the Roman Catholic Church and business interests involved in mining and plantations. State, church, and business thus constituted what was called, even by Belgian officials, the "colonial trinity." It was not simply a question of the state's taking care of administration, the church of evangelization, and the business community of economic development. Rather, the tasks of the three overlapped and reinforced one another. In the postcolonial era, particularly after 1965 under Mobutu, finding a new equilibrium among the members of the "trinity" and sorting out the areas of responsibility of each would pose major problems, particularly with regard to education and management of the economy.

The troubled role of the military in Zairian politics also has its roots in the colonial era. Since the days of the Congo Free State, the Zairian state has had a strong military dimension. The Force Publique, or colonial army, was essentially used to subdue and control the indigenous population, although it served outside the colony during the two world wars. Many of the Free State's administrative personnel were military officers, drawn not only from Belgium but also from the United States, Canada, and European countries ranging from Norway to Turkey. Although courses were set up to train civilian administrators, the Force Publique remained the backbone of the Congo Free State and the Belgian Congo.

The first rank-and-file troops were foreigners from the coasts of East Africa and West Africa, but as the Free State began to recruit Congolese, it tended to rely on what were seen as "martial races," first people of the middle reaches of the Congo River (the so-called Ngala or Bangala) and then the Tetela from southeastern Zaire. Although later quotas spread recruitment more evenly across the colony, there is some reason to think that the early imbalances were perpetuated by differential re-enlistment and promotion. During decolonization, military men of Ngala and Luba-Kasai backgrounds, in particular, played major roles in the fall and murder of the first prime minister, Patrice Lumumba.

After a series of revolts had demonstrated the danger of ethnically defined units, the Belgians made sure that all units down to the lowest levels were ethnically mixed. The Force Publique supposedly was the most "national" institution of the Belgian Congo, as well as the guarantor of the Pax Belgica. But with the benefit of hindsight, it is evident that both the Pax Belgica and the national quality of the Force Publique were somewhat mythical.

The unity of the Force Publique was also mythical, or at least exaggerated. Certainly, by the time independence arrived in 1960, various politicians had established contact with adjutants from their respective ethnic groups. These contacts laid the groundwork for division of the army into warring camps in the tense atmosphere surrounding accession to independence and for the Force Publique mutiny of July 1960. The mutiny obviously was directed at the Belgian officers; less obviously, it was directed at Prime Minister Lumumba, instigated in particular by soldiers whose ethnic affinities led them to sympathize with Lumumba's rivals such as President Joseph Kasavubu, Albert Kalonji, and Jean Bolikango.

Failed decolonization was to a large extent responsible for the Congo crisis of the early 1960s. Considerable economic development took place under Belgian rule, but within a highly paternalistic framework in which Africans were confined to the lowest ranks of the administration and the economic enterprises. Although opposition to Belgian rule became manifest in the late 1950s, Belgium made no preparations for decolonization. Rioting in Léopoldville (now Kinshasa) in January 1959, however, forced Belgium's hand and led to an agreement whereby the colony gained independence as the Republic of the Congo on June 30, 1960, and the First. Republic was established.

Independence was followed immediately by crisis, dramatized by the mutiny of the Force Publique on July 5 and the secession of the country's richest province, Katanga, on July 11, soon followed by a similar move in southeastern Kasai Province (now Kasai-Oriental Region and Kasai-Occidental Region). The crisis was further compounded by the power struggle between Prime Minister Lumumba and President Kasavubu, ultimately culminating in Lumumba's assassination in January 1961 at the hands of Katangan secessionists, and also, according to most accounts, with the connivance of Mobutu and others in Kinshasa as well as the United States and Belgian governments.

From its inception, the Congo crisis had an international dimension. The chaos that followed on the heels of independence was caused not only by conflict among Congolese but also by foreign interference. Politics in the First Republic involved numerous rivalries among political leaders on behalf of various Congolese constituencies, ethnic or otherwise. At the same time, however, outside forces clearly intervened in Congolese politics and decisively determined outcomes. The Force Publique mutinied in large part because Belgium had persistently refused to Africanize the officer corps, even following independence. In response to the mutiny, Belgium sent in troops, ostensibly to protect Belgian lives, but the intervention was seen by many Congolese as an act of unwarranted aggression, perhaps even an attempt by Belgium to reoccupy the Congo. Belgium also played a role in the secession of Katanga. Moïse Tshombe was backed by Belgian settlers and financial interests when he declared the independence of Katanga.

The crisis acquired a broader international dimension when a multinational United Nations (UN) force was sent in, at the invitation of President Kasavubu and Prime Minister Lumumba, to restore peace and bring Katanga back into the fold. Lumumba's own actions then inexorably drew the fledgling nation into the Cold War and, ultimately, sealed Lumumba's own fate.

The conflict between President Kasavubu and Prime Minister Lumumba had several dimensions, including a personality clash, different bases of support, and diametrically opposed conceptions of the ultimate character of the Congolese polity. But international factors helped precipitate the crisis between the two—specifically, Lumumba's policies toward Belgium, the UN, and the secessionists, including his insistence on converting the newly arrived UN forces into a military instrument for bringing Katanga and Kasai back under the control of the central government. Lumumba's greatest mistake, however, was his decision to accept substantial Soviet aid in order to attack secessionist areas. This move brought to a climax the issue of communist influence, which had been a source of growing concern to the West and to more moderate Africans alike.

Indeed, historical accounts of the Congo crisis almost uniformly place it in a Cold War context. In particular, United States policy toward the Congo is seen as a response to a perceived threat of Soviet involvement in the region. (More recently some scholars have also attempted to demonstrate the involvement of American mining interests in the shaping of United States policy toward the Congo.) Certainly, United States opposition to Lumumba and consistent support over the years for his eventual successor, Mobutu Sese Seko, were dictated by Cold War concerns.

The secession of Katanga was finally suppressed in January 1963 by UN forces, but the next year the nation's viability was threatened by "Lumumbist" rural insurgencies in Kwilu and in the east that soon controlled about half of the national territory. Once again, international assistance proved pivotal in the survival of the nation. The rebellion was defeated by the national government only because of support from Belgium and the United States.

In 1965, when the tide had turned against the Lumumbist rebellion but the threat was not over and national politics was again paralyzed by a rivalry between the president and the prime minister, army commander General Joseph-Désiré Mobutu (later Mobutu Sese Seko) seized power. He abolished parties, then established a single party, the Popular Revolutionary Movement (Mouvement Populaire de la Révolution—MPR). The logic of single-party rule was pushed to its limits in the 1974 constitution, when all public institutions (including the army and the university) became subsidiaries of the MPR. Despite the rhetoric of party rule, however, most observers agree that what emerged was a personalisitic dictatorship, dominated by Mobutu and a clique of close associates.

The chaos of the First Republic obviously provided a justification for Mobutu's coup of 1965, and for his subsequent establishment of a single-party dictatorship. However, as Zairians struggle to establish multiparty democracy in the 1990s, it is important to remember that the legacy of the First Republic was not all negative. When political debate was opened after 1990, a number of politicians invoked the 1964 Constitution of Luluabourg (Luluabourg is now called Kananga) as a model for a new federalist constitutional order.

Once in power, Mobutu reversed the process of territorial fragmentation that had begun in 1960. From twenty-one *provincettes* in 1965, the number of administrative divisions was cut first to twelve provinces (known as regions after 1972), then to eight, plus Kinshasa, representing a nearly complete restoration of the colonial boundaries. (In the early 1990s, the most populous region, Kivu, was divided into three regions—Nord-Kivu, Sud-Kivu, and Maniema, corresponding to the three *provincettes* of the 1960s.) Under Mobutu the regions, once quasi-federal political units with their own governments, were reduced to administrative subdivisions of the unitary state. Not until 1984, when Mobutu accepted suggestions from external aid donors that he carry out political ''liberalization,'' were the regions given legislative assemblies and a degree of politico-administrative autonomy. The extreme centralization of power under Mobutu, and the abuses that followed from that centralization, led to a push for decentralization once political debate emerged after 1990. The push for democratization is attributable, above all, to the courage of opposition groups and of ordinary Zaïrians. Yet external linkages were important, notably the publicity given to the Union for Democracy and Social Progress (Union pour la Démocratie et le Progrès Social—UDPS) in Europe and North America.

Mobutu's style of governance reflects both continuity and change. Much analysis has focused on the changes wrought by Mobutu, but outside observers often fail to understand an important area of cultural continuity from which the Mobutu regime has derived much of its power and legitimacy. Mobutu is a president, not a king. He travels in jet aircraft and appears on television. Yet some of his ideas, and some of the ideas that his subjects have about him, are based on traditional Zairian sources and uses of power.

First, it is important to distinguish between the ideology and the practice of leadership. Ideologically, a precolonial Congolese ruler (emperor, king, or chief) was seen as a father to his people. He had a priestly function, as intermediary between the material and spiritual worlds. The symbols of rule expressed his uniqueness; only the ruler could wear the skin of the leopard or the feathers of the eagle, for these beasts were kings of their respective spheres of the animal world.

At the same time, and particularly in the vast equatorial forest (Mobutu's home area), the ruler was an entrepreneur. He built up wealth, which he used on his own behalf, but also on behalf of his people. The successful "big man" (*mokonzi* in Lingala) built up a community of blood relatives, allies, clients, dependents, wives, slaves, and others. Copper, the symbol of wealth in precolonial Zaire, adorned the chiefs and elders. However—and this point was missed by many analysts until recently—the community was described in terms of genealogy, the ruler being presented (and his rule justified) in terms of his being the head of the family.

This model of the ruler as father (ideologically) and entrepreneur (behaviorally) has carried over into postcolonial Zaire. For example, in reconstructing the army after the mutinies and secessions of the early 1960s, Mobutu behaved very much as the "big man." He tied other officers to him by means of resources, often from his foreign backers, which he channeled to them, meaning that troops loyal to Mobutu were more likely to be paid, and to be paid on time, than other troops.

After 1965, and especially after 1970, Mobutu's relationship with his principal political associates—government ministers, advisers, and high-ranking military personnel—also was based on the "big man" model. Indeed, the term *presidential monarch* has been used, appropriately, to describe Mobutu. Acting as "Father of the Nation," his self-awarded title, Mobutu presided over a political system that had the formal trappings of a republic but was in reality the personal fiefdom of the president, who used the national treasury as his personal checkbook and disbursed both rewards and punishments at will. Cabinet ministers, for example, were routinely shuffled in and out and political allies exiled or "recuperated," as political fortunes rose and fell—or as Mobutu's whims dictated.

The Mobutu regime also sought legitimacy through ideology. The MPR initially espoused a doctrine of nationalism, borrowed from Lumumba's Congolese National Movement (Mouvement National Congolais—MNC) and other parties of the early postindependence era. By 1971 it was promoting authenticity (see Glossary), espousing "authentic" Zairian nationalism and rejecting foreign cultural influences. The most dramatic symbol of this Zairianization (see Glossary) process was the change of the country's name to Zaire in October 1971 and the gradual renaming of its cities and provinces (later regions). By 1974 the official ideology had metamorphosed into Mobutism (see Glossary), in which the acts and sayings of the leader were glorified, increasingly to a ridiculous degree. To "Founder-President" were added ever more extravagant praise-names: "Guide of the Revolution," "Helmsman" (borrowed from Mao Zedong), "Mulopwe" (emperor, or even god-king), and finally "Messiah." At this point, the ideology of the regime had become so overblown that many Zairians and most foreign observers found it impossible to take seriously. But many of the themes in the Mobutist ideology—the yearning for cultural and economic autonomy and for strong, paternalistic leadership—resonated with deeply held opinions on the part of Zairians, among both the elite and the general poulace. Nevertheless, it is difficult to avoid the conclusion that this ideology served to justify the domination of the political system by a self-serving ruling class.

Cultural nationalism inevitably brought the Mobutu regime into conflict with the Roman Catholic Church, which, along with the state and the business community, made up the "colonial trinity." But the church, whose active following includes 46 to 48 percent of the population of Zaire, possesses worldwide links and a resilient institutional infrastructure and thus was able to withstand the regime's pressures. Roman Catholic institutions, for example, particularly schools and health services were—and remain—comparable in extent and vastly superior in quality to those of the state.

Although the church had welcomed the Mobutu regime, the hegemonic ambitions of the MPR aroused suspicion, and a conference of bishops in 1969 privately noted "dictatorial tendencies" in the regime. The following year, Joseph Cardinal Malula expressed fears about the regime's intentions at a mass celebrating the tenth anniversary of independence. In the presence of both King Baudouin of Belgium and Mobutu, he denounced political elites for "a fascination with the triumphant and the superficial, and a hunger for the lavish."

The Roman Catholic Church also viewed as an affront the absorption of the jewel of its educational system, Lovanium University, into the secular National University of Zaire (Université Nationale du Zaïre—UNAZA) in August 1971. Even more serious was the regime's announcement in December 1971 that party youth branches had to be established in the seminaries.

Another battle took place over the concept of authenticity. The regime's stress on "mental decolonization" and "cultural disalienation" could be seen as a disguised attack on Christianity as an import from the West. One symbolic accoutrement of the authenticity campaign, the 1972 elimination of Christian forenames, was treated by the church as a particular affront. The church's opposition to the name changes led to a dramatic riposte. Cardinal Malula, archbishop of Kinshasa, became the target of attacks as a "renegade of the revolution"; he was evicted from the residence the regime had built for him and was forced to leave the country for three months in 1972.

In late 1972, the regime moved to monopolize the socialization process, banning all religious broadcasts and dissolving church-sponsored youth movements. The zenith of this campaign came at the end of 1974 when the religious school networks were nationalized, celebration of Christmas as a public holiday was ended, and the display of religious artifacts was limited to the interior of churches. (The school networks were, however, returned to the churches eighteen months later when the state proved unable to operate them effectively.)

Over the following years, the Roman Catholic bishops in Zaire continued to criticize the Mobutu regime. In 1976 Monsignor Kabanga, archbishop of Lubumbashi, issued a pastoral letter denouncing a system under which, "Whoever holds a morsel of authority, or means of pressure, profits from it to impose on people and exploit them, especially in rural areas. All means are good to obtain money, or humiliate the human being. . . ." It was small wonder, then, that the Roman Catholic Church maintained moral standing in the eyes of the population and that Monsignor Laurent Monsengwo Pasinya, archbishop of Kisangani, was chosen president of the national conference that was convened in the early 1990s to oversee a transition to a democratic, multiparty political system.

Despite the importance of cultural nationalism, over which church and state battled, the primary component of Zairian nationalism was economic and was designed to wrest control of the economy from foreign interests and place it firmly in Zairian hands. As early as 1967, this desire had led to a clash with Belgium over control of Zaire's major industrial concern, the Upper Katanga Mining Union (Union Minière du Haut-Katanga—UMHK), which mined copper and cobalt. Eventually, a compromise was reached under which a state-owned mining company, General Quarries and Mines (Générale des Carrières et des Mines—Gécamines), was created. The settlement proved lucrative to UMHK and brought unanticipated costs to Zaire.

The linkage between politics and the economy became increasingly clear in the 1970s. In 1973 the government seized 2,000 economic enterprises owned by foreigners (but not those owned by Americans) and turned them over to Zairians, mainly members of the political elite. Mobutu was the leading beneficiary. Within a few months, the scope of the disaster of this Zairianization was clear, but instead of turning back, Mobutu plunged forward into the "radicalization of the revolution," apparently inspired by his visit to China and North Korea. "Radicalization" supposedly included the nationalization of trade and the mobilization of agricultural brigades to relieve food shortages. But in its application, the new measure became an assault on the primarily Belgian-owned

xliv

industrial sector. The effect was to extend the chaos of Zairianization to virtually all spheres of the economy.

As the Zairian economy went into a tailspin, Mobutu finally came to realize the magnitude of the catastrophe ushered in by Zairianization and radicalization. In November 1975, he introduced a new policy of retrocession (see Glossary), under which a substantial portion of Zairianized enterprises were returned to their original owners. Meanwhile, however, almost irreparable damage had been inflicted upon the economy.

The economic disaster resulting from Zairianization was compounded by the regime's insistence on undertaking large-scale industrialization, in the process squandering the country's mineral wealth and neglecting the agricultural sector. To fund its grandiose industrial projects, the regime resorted to heavy foreign borrowing. When the prices of commodities (especially copper), on which Zaire was heavily dependent, dropped drastically and the cost of vital imports, such as petroleum products, skyrocketed in the mid-1970s, export earnings and government revenues dropped sharply, and Zaire faced a grave economic and financial crisis.

Since 1975, Zaire's massive foreign debt has had a major impact on policy, both foreign and domestic. Some causes of the huge debt, such as the rise in the price of petroleum imports and the fall in the price of copper exports, were beyond Zaire's control. Others were not, notably Zairianization and radicalization, the squandering of funds on prestige projects, and their diversion into overseas bank accounts by the president and the elite.

As a consequence of the debt, foreign creditors became major actors in the Zairian political process—and in economic development, thus making a mockery of Mobutu's much-vaunted quest for economic independence. In 1976 the first of a series of economic stabilization programs was adopted under the guidance of the International Monetary Fund (IMF—see Glossary) and other external forces. During the next eighteen years, Zairian authorities alternately cooperated with and struggled against the international financial institutions. In 1994 this era came to an end (for a time, at any rate) as the World Bank (see Glossary) closed its office in Kinshasa, and Zaire was expelled from the IMF.

In line with the IMF's economic orthodoxy, the "Mobutu Plan" of 1976 and each successive plan was supposed to reduce corruption, rationalize and control expenditures, increase tax revenues, limit imports, boost production, improve the transportation infrastructure, eliminate arrears on interest payments, ensure that principal payments were made on time, and improve financial management and economic planning. But ultimately all efforts at reform or significant change were undercut by the patrimonialism (see Glossary) and rampant corruption that characterized the regime.

Zaire's public and publicly insured debt was rescheduled by the Paris Club (see Glossary) at least seven times between 1976 and 1987. Zaire's private creditors also rescheduled their part of the debt in 1980 and at various times thereafter, and numerous meetings of World Bank and Western aid consortia were held to generate further official assistance, starting in 1979.

When the first two standby agreements with the IMF yielded meager results, the IMF and the World Bank decided in the early 1980s to send their own teams of experts to run key posts in the Bank of Zaire (the country's central bank), the Customs Office, and the Ministries of Finance and Planning. The head of the Bank of Zaire team, Erwin Blumenthal of the Federal Republic of Germany (West Germany), cut off credit and exchange facilities to firms of members of the political elite and imposed very strict foreign exchange quotas. However, Mobutu and his colleagues were able to evade many of the restrictions and to wear down Blumenthal and the other experts. After Blumenthal's departure, the international teams were careful to avoid what one member called the "political hotspots," and the regime continued on its self-destructive course.

In 1981 Zaire began to cooperate with the IMF, laying off large numbers of civil servants and teachers. In 1983 it agreed to devalue its currency by 80 percent and to liberalize the economy. In response, the IMF agreed to a fifth standby agreement, and the Paris Club agreed to roll over more than US$1 billion of debt, with a maturity of eleven years, in contrast to the eight years normally approved for debtor nations. In 1985 and 1987, the Paris Club rescheduled Zaire's debt for ten years and fifteen years, respectively, making it clear that the greater leniency being shown to Zaire was a reward for following IMF guidelines.

Although Zaire appeared to be following the IMF guidelines, benefits were slow to appear in terms of improved economic activity within the country, not to mention improved living conditions. Mobutu, said to be one of the ten wealthiest men in the world, continued to enrich himself at the expense of the people, whose living standards continued to decline.

During the years when lenders and Western governments were somewhat successful in controlling the financial practices of Zaire's rulers, they paid dearly for their success in that they were forced to provide the regime with additional support to compensate for the withdrawn financial opportunities. Belgium, France, Israel, and the United States, among others, provided both symbolic and instrumental backing in the form of military assistance. In the case of the United States, the military relationship increased when the two countries found themselves supporting the same faction in the Angolan civil war in 1975. In 1986–87 Mobutu reportedly agreed to allow the United States to ship arms to Angolan rebels via Zaire and to refurbish the air base at Kamina (in southeastern Zaire), in exchange for increased aid as well as United States pressure on the IMF to treat Zaire leniently. Mobutu and his regime thus benefitted substantially from the perceived United States need to assure a stable Zaire and to garner Zairian support for United States strategic interests in sub-Saharan Africa.

Over the years, the Western powers rewarded Mobutu both economically and militarily and for the most part maintained silence in the face of increasing evidence of his regime's abuses. Only since the end of the Cold War has support for Zaire become more conditional. By early in the 1990s, the West had terminated most aid to the Mobutu regime and was putting increasing pressure on Mobutu to improve his human rights record and institute multiparty democracy.

In the early years of his regime, many Zairians gave Mobutu credit for restoring order and securing the country's borders. Increasingly, however, the forces of order have become sources of disorder within the country. Rather than protecting the Zairian people, the armed forces and security forces prey upon them and are perceived, justifiably, as instruments of repression. Examples of their excesses abound. One of the most egregious instances occurred in Bandundu in 1978, when the security forces summarily executed about 500 people following a minor uprising set off by a self-proclaimed prophet. Another occurred in 1981, when perhaps 100 diamond miners were killed in Kasai-Oriental. The incident that gained the greatest international attention and that had the most serious repercussions for the Mobutu regime was the May 1990 massacre of students at the University of Lubumbashi. Up to 100 students were killed in the incident, ultimately prompting most multilateral and bilateral donors to terminate all but humanitarian aid to Zaire.

Just as they have failed to provide internal order, so, too, have the armed forces failed to secure Zaire's borders. In 1977 and 1978, Shaba Region was invaded by Angola-based rebels, who had to be repulsed by foreign troops. In 1984 and again in 1985, another opposition group briefly held the town of Moba on the shore of Lake Tanganyika, again demonstrating the Zairian military's lack of capability—and the government's lack of control of its territory. In 1993 there were reports that the Zairian army had clashed with troops of yet another opposition group, this time along the Uganda border. In 1994 Zaire's border with Rwanda also became a major source of insecurity, as over one million refugees fled from perceived danger in their home country.

In 1977, following the first Shaba invasion, Mobutu responded to Western pressure for reform by paying lip service to the notion of democracy in Zaire. Competitive elections among multiple candidates for the legislature were permitted—but only within the single-party framework, which is to say that the system still offered no real political choice. All electoral choice, or competition, took place solely within the MPR. Nevertheless, by 1980, some of the deputies elected in 1977—The Thirteen, as they were called—had challenged Mobutu's system of rule through an open letter cataloging regime abuses. The Thirteen ultimately evolved into an internal opposition party, the UDPS. Despite being banned, with its leaders largely exiled or under internal house arrest, the UDPS was to prove remarkably resilient and formed the core of opposition to the regime when a political opening occurred in the early 1990s.

In April 1990, Mobutu radically transformed the political environment by announcing the establishment of the Third Republic, ostensibly a new, multiparty system of government. The initiative was presented as a magnanimous gesture on the part of the president, but in fact Mobutu was bowing to renewed pressure for change from Western governments and international financial institutions. In addition, his move was a calculated attempt to quell growing domestic discontent.

It soon became clear that Mobutu's announcement had unleashed volatile forces that he would be hard-pressed to contain. And, in fact, Mobutu proceeded to embark on a checkered course of half-hearted moves toward democratization, interspersed with periodic brutal crackdowns on dissent.

The immediate result of Mobutu's announcement was the unleashing of efforts to publicize existing organizations and to found new ones. Although Mobutu backpedaled furiously, attempting to constrict the political space he had appeared to open up, by December 1990, independent political parties were permitted to register. By mid-1991, over 200 political parties had been recognized. Most significant among them was the UDPS, which had emerged as the main opposition party. Other major opposition parties were the Democratic and Social Christian Party (Parti Démocrate et Social Chrétien—PDSC) led by Joseph Ileo and the Union of Federalists and Independent Republicans (Union des Fédéralistes et des Républicains Indépendants—UFERI) led by Jean Nguza

Karl-i-Bond. Opposition activities were spearheaded by a multiparty coalition, the Sacred Union (Union Sacrée).

In August 1991, Mobutu also convened a long-promised national conference ultimately known as the Sovereign National Conference (Conférence Nationale Souveraine—CNS), which was ostensibly designed to oversee the drafting of a new constitution and to manage the transition to a democratic, multiparty political system. But inevitably conflicts arose between a conference determined to assert its sovereign powers and a president equally determined not to cede control of the government, and the conference was very much an on-again-off-again institution throughout 1991 and most of 1992.

Nevertheless, the conference, encompassing over 2,800 delegates, did meet—intermittently—to debate the country's political future from August 1991 until it finished its work in December 1992. In August 1992, the conference passed a Transitional Act to serve as a provisional constitution. That act established a parliamentary system with a figurehead president, a 453-member High Council of the Republic (Haut Conseil de la République—HCR) to serve as a provisional legislature, and a first state commissioner (prime minister) to serve as head of government. Mobutu and the conference also agreed to abide by the Comprehensive Political Agreement (Compromis Politique Global), which included ten principles, the most significant being that no institution or organ of the transition should use its constitutional powers to prevent any other institution from functioning. In essence, all parties agreed to share power and to abide by the constitutional provisions embodied in the Transitional Act.

UDPS leader Étienne Tshisekedi wa Mulumba was duly elected as the transitional prime minister by the CNS on August 15, 1992. On August 30, he appointed a transitional government of "national union," including various Mobutu opponents, but no Mobutu supporters. In December 1992, the CNS dissolved itself and was succeeded by the HCR, headed by Archbishop Monsengwo. As the supreme interim legislative authority, the HCR was authorized to formulate and adopt a new constitution and to organize legislative and presidential elections. But Mobutu refused to accept the authority of the HCR or the legitimacy of any constitution it might formulate, instead reconvening the former legislature, which had been suspended, and entrusting it with drafting a rival constitution more to his liking. In March 1993, Mobutu further undermined the Tshisekedi transitional government when he convened a special "conclave" of political forces to chart the nation's future, including devising a new constitution. Mobutu then

xlix

dismissed the Tshisekedi government, although according to the Transitional Act he did not have the authority to do so. At his urging, the conclave then named Faustin Birindwa as prime minister of a so-called government of national salvation.

Since that time, Zaire has had two parallel, rival governments vying for domestic and international acceptance. The Birindwa government did not receive international recognition. But the Tshisekedi government, although recognized internationally, has from the beginning lacked the power or resources to govern. Indeed, it has never been able to govern effectively because of its inability to limit Mobutu's powers except on paper. The result of this situation is government stalemate, which has worked to Mobutu's advantage.

Mobutu has been able to cling to power because of three main factors. First, he has maintained control of key institutions, including the central bank, state radio and television facilities, the security police, and the military, particularly the elite Special Presidential Division (Division Spéciale Présidentielle—DSP). In fact, control of key military units has been critical to Mobutu's continued exercise of power. He has used those units to obstruct the functioning of the transitional government, to intimidate critical opposition leaders and the media, to promote anarchy and chaos, to disperse popular demonstrations, and to incite ethnic violence. Mobutu has also retained control over the network of diplomatic representatives abroad, in particular Zaire's delegations to the UN and its specialized agencies. Likewise, he apparently has maintained control over the network of regional, subregional, and local administrators in the interior of the country.

Mobutu's position also has been strengthened by his ability—and that of his allies—to incite ethnic violence, thereby promoting instability, fostering anarchy, weakening the opposition, and undermining mass political mobilization against his regime. Officially instigated cases of ethnic violence clearly occurred in Shaba, where, beginning in August 1992, attacks on Luba-Kasai—Tshisekedi's ethnic group—were incited by Nguza and other former opposition figures, including the governor of Shaba, Gabriel Kyungu wa Kumwanza. Officials may also have played a role in ethnic violence in Nord-Kivu, where indigenous local people attacked immigrants from Burundi and Rwanda, collectively known in Zaire as the Banyarwanda. Both instances of ethnic tension reflect a history of enmity and resentment. But most observers believe that the recent violence is less historical than the result of deliberate government manipulation designed to divert popular resentment of the Mobutu regime. In the Nord-Kivu case, Mobutu also was able

1

to demonstrate his control of the use of force, sending in the DSP to quell the violence.

In Shaba, however, Mobutu stood aside and let events proceed without interference, no doubt because they appeared to be working to his advantage. In addition to instigating the ethnic cleansing campaign in Shaba, Nguza and Kyungu have raised the specter of Shaban autonomy, at times threatening to pursue it if Tshisekedi were to be "forced on" the nation as prime minister in a political settlement. Observers note that both issues have been used to the detriment of Tshisekedi and the UDPS and to the benefit of Mobutu, who can thus present himself as the only political figure who can hold Zaire together, including Zaire's most vital region, mineral-rich Shaba.

A final factor in Mobutu's ability to retain power is his consummate political skill. Over and over again, he has succeeded in dividing the opposition and in co-opting key opponents. For example, in October 1991, Mobutu appointed Tshisekedi as prime minister of a transitional coalition government, but fired him just one week later following a dispute over the apportionment of ministerial portfolios. When the Sacred Union refused to choose a successor, Mobutu named Bernardin Mungul-Diaka, leader of a small opposition party, as prime minister. Then, in late November 1991, Mobutu formed another transitional government, this time under Nguza. The appointment of Nguza proved to be highly beneficial to Mobutu, in that it brought Mobutu the support of Nguza and his followers while at the same time fracturing the opposition. At the time, Nguza was a Tshisekedi rival in the Sacred Union, but he subsequently left the Sacred Union, after other members termed his nomination as prime minister a "betrayal." He then created a rival political coalition within the CNS, the Alliance of Patriotic Forces. Encompassing some thirty parties, led by UFERI, the Alliance ostensibly remained committed to political change but rejected "extremist" stands.

Mobutu's appointment of Birindwa as prime minister in March 1993 further undercut opposition forces. Birindwa proved to have little difficulty in recruiting ministers for a government. Political expediency aside, co-optation of political figures by Mobutu and Birindwa was facilitated by the disastrous economic situation. In June 1993, six political leaders from the Sacred Union joined the Birindwa government and then left the Sacred Union, claiming that the Sacred Union had become too extremist. They then formed their own coalition, which they called the Restored Sacred Union (Union Sacrée Rénovée). Having joined the Mobutu-appointed Birindwa government, the six could no longer be regarded as ardent proponents of political change. The same could be said of Nguza, given his acceptance of a position as first deputy prime minister in charge of defense in the Birindwa government.

In 1994 Mobutu's tactics of stalling and dividing the opposition bore further fruit. Birindwa resigned as prime minister of the rival, Mobutu-appointed government. The selection of a successor then fell to the new 780-member legislature created in late 1993. That body, the High Council of the Republic (Haut Conseil de la République—HCR)-Parliament of the Transition (Parlement de la Transition—PT), or HCR–PT, encompassed both the HCR and Zaire's former, pro-Mobutu legislature. After five months of political vacuum, in June 1994 the HCR–PT finally elected a candidate from the moderate opposition, Léon Kengo wa Dondo, to replace Birindwa. The election was an affront and setback for Tshisekedi. Although continuing to assert his claim to be the sole legitimate head of government, Tshisekedi was not among the seven candidates for the job of government leader. Instead, he simply called upon members of the HCR–PT to "confirm" his position as prime minister.

Kengo was a founder of the Union of Independent Democrats (Union des Démocrates Indépendants—UDI) in 1990. Although denounced at its founding as "MPR II," the UDI in fact represented a claim to an independent future by politicians and businessmen formerly close to Mobutu. Kengo had been premier twice before, in the 1980s, and was considered an advocate of fiscal austerity as promoted by the IMF. His candidacy in 1994 was put forward by the Union for the Republic and Democracy (Union pour la République et la Démocratie—URD), a coalition including the UDI and other moderate groups within the Sacred Union. The radical wing of the Sacred Union, driven primarily by the UDPS, termed Kengo's selection "illegal and anticonstitutional" and continued to regard Tshisekedi as the country's only legitimate prime minister.

For its part, the HCR–PT claimed to be acting in accord with popular sentiment. But observers note that the HCR–PT's claim to represent popular feeling is questionable, given the swelling of its ranks by members of the pro-Mobutu parliament. In fact, nobody can say whether or to what extent the Mobutists and their allies in Kengo's UDI as well as the other moderate parties really represent a majority of the Zairian people.

Political unrest continued as Tshisekedi attempted to assert his authority and pro-Mobutu forces strove to discredit Tshisekedi. On June 5, Tshisekedi, speaking publicly for the first time in three months in front of a large crowd in Kinshasa, threatened to paralyze the diamond extraction industry if Mobutu continued to refuse him the job of prime minister. He called on diamond workers to go on indefinite strike to halt production and exports of diamonds. The threat was regarded as credible because Tshisekedi has continued to enjoy broad support from the working class, especially in his home region of Kasai-Oriental, where diamond mining is centered. If successful, such a strike would have a major impact on the Mobutu regime, which has come to rely on the diamond industry for revenue since the demise of Gécamines and the copper industry.

One response to Tshisekedi's threat was further harassment and the concoction of what he termed, credibly, "a plot" against him. A week after his speech, Tshisekedi was arrested and detained for ten hours. According to the official version of events, Tshisekedi had been driving within a military camp near the presidential residence at N'Sele, east of Kinshasa, in a car containing arms and ammunition. In protest of Tshisekedi's arrest, demonstrators burned cars and set tires alight in a Kinshasa suburb. During the demonstration, one of Tshisekedi's advisers was arrested by the Civil Guard and allegedly tortured. The demonstration was just one sign that the task confronting Kengo—guiding the country through the transition toward the Third Republic—is a daunting one given the extremely confused political situation in the country and the general state of collapse at all levels. As he said in a brief speech after his election, his priority will be to restore the authority of the state. He also promised to promote "national harmony, reconciliation, tolerance, democracy, and the exercise of freedom." It appeared to most observers, however, that these goals would be extremely difficult to achieve, considering the economic and social situation.

While the struggle between Mobutu and the opposition has dragged on, the nation's economic and financial situation has continued to deteriorate. The country remains heavily indebted and impoverished. A large proportion of its population lives outside of the formal economy, eking out a marginal existence through subsistence agriculture and informal trade or barter. The standard of living for most of the population has continued to decline.

The export-oriented Zairian economy has been in a free fall for a number of years, suffering the effects of monumental, institutionalized corruption, neglect, and mismanagement. The economic crisis was worsened by the rampant looting and rioting by unpaid troops in late 1991 and again in early 1993, which in turn led to the mass exodus of the foreign technicians who had kept the economy going—in particular copper production and economic infrastructure.

Throughout the 1990s, Zaire's economy has been described in only the direst of terms. It has been characterized as desperate, in ruins, dysfunctional. In fact, the formal economy has almost ceased to function. The banking system has collapsed because of the rampant hyperinflation and the drastic fall in the value of the currency. The central bank, which in the past served as Mobutu's personal piggy bank, is for all practical purposes bankrupt. Most other banks have closed, and those that have remained open deal in cash transactions only. The state takes in few revenues: the tax collection system is defunct, few if any customs revenues are collected, most foreign aid has been cut off, and copper production, long the mainstay of the economy and the main source of government revenues, has dropped off significantly. The government has been able to pay its bills only by printing new currency.

The effects of the economic chaos on Zairian society are enormous: unemployment and poverty are widespread, the economic infrastructure has decayed, state institutions have ceased to function, and most state-run hospitals and schools have closed. Civil servants, teachers, and health-care workers have largely ceased working because they have not been paid, and medical equipment and medicine are scarce. As a result, diseases once eradicated have begun to reappear. Acquired immune deficiency syndrome (AIDS), sleeping sickness, and malnutrition have become increasingly prevalent. Malnutrition is particularly common among children, as the price of food exceeds the financial resources of more and more Zairian families. The availability of safe drinking water also has become problematic.

Most observers of Zaire's deplorable economic and social conditions marvel at how a land of such superlative natural endowments—enormous mineral deposits, immense forests, mighty rivers, and abundant fertile soils—could have sunk so low. By rights, Zaire should have become one of sub-Saharan Africa's most developed and wealthiest states. But instead it is an impoverished nation in a rich land, with its economy and society in total disarray and most of its citizens (80 percent by some estimates) living in absolute poverty. When ethnic conflict—which has resulted in the internal displacement of several hundred thousand Zairians in the early 1990s—is taken into account as well, Zaire's characterization as "an African horror story" in a recent article by Bill Berkeley in the *Atlantic Monthly* appears well founded.

And yet, as press accounts continue to emphasize, Zairians have somehow survived, their ability to do so a reflection of their ability to fend for themselves. In the absence of a functioning government, economy, or social services sector, enterprising individuals have resorted to the informal economy to make a living and to obtain the goods and services they need. In essence, government services—such as health care, schools, road maintenance—have been "privatized." Moreover, a de facto decentralization of government power has occurred. Recognizing the weakness of the central government, which can no longer project its power or offer its services much beyond the capital city, regions and local communities have stepped into the void to provide what order and services they can. For example, local businesses may pay for maintenance of local infrastructure, and local merchants may band together to pay local military and security forces to provide peace and protection.

A less positive result of the individual Zairian's quest for survival is, of course, the widespread corruption that has resulted. Recent travelers to Zaire note the proliferation of "enterprising" individuals and "facilitators" who prey on those entering the country, attempting to extract payment for a multitude of services. Similarly, anyone traveling in Zaire encounters frequent roadblocks set up by security officials who then extort money in exchange for the right to pass.

On a larger scale, the massive official corruption and greed characterizing the Mobutu regime have had disastrous results for the country and its people. In an August 1994 article in the *Washington Post*, "An African Giant Falls under Its Own Weight," Keith Richburg examines the causes of Zaire's desperate state in the 1990s. He notes that Zaire has not broken up into civil war like Liberia or been overcome by tribal slaughter like neighboring Rwanda. Rather, it has crumbled under the weight of years of rampant corruption, greed, incompetence, neglect, and decay.

Since the end of the Cold War, Africa has appeared to lose much of its significance to the developed world, and African nations generally make headlines only when their situation has become catastrophic. Throughout the mid-1990s, Zaire has occasionally been featured in the Western media, attention focusing on the mystery of how the nation could continue to operate and how Mobutu could continue to survive. But as the status quo continued in Zaire, international attention largely shifted elsewhere.

Zaire entered the spotlight, indirectly, in July 1994 as over 1 million refugees fleeing ethnic violence in neighboring Rwanda crossed the border into Goma in eastern Zaire. In August there were fears of an additional mass exodus from Rwanda into Bukavu, Zaire, when the French withdrew their troops from Rwanda. The number of new refugees into Bukaku remained much lower than expected, however, estimated at about 70,000 at the end of August (but the area as a whole was inundated by a total refugee population of about 400,000).

That Zaire could appear as a safehaven is supremely ironic given the condition of Zaire's economy, society, and polity in 1994. The irony of the situation was further dramatized by the behavior of Zairian border and security forces, who allowed the flood of refugees to pass, but not before robbing them of whatever food, weapons, and other valuables they had managed to bring with them. In addition, there were reports of attempts by Zairian officials to extort cash payoffs to permit international relief flights to land (or to depart), although such flights are supposed to be exempt from landing charges. Zairian soldiers reportedly also helped themselves to relief supplies.

The massive influx of Rwandan refugees poses enormous problems for Zaire, a country already gripped by anarchy and lawlessness and demonstrably unable to meet the needs of its own population, including the many internally displaced Zairians. The area is quite inaccessible and is served by a very limited transportation infrastructure in very poor condition. This situation hampers the ability of international relief organizations, the UN, and foreign governments to deliver the food, clean water, and health care supplies and personnel that are so desperately needed. In addition, security has become a major problem as well. The refugee camps are beset by common thievery as well as attacks by Hutu extremists, loyal to the deposed Rwandan government, seeking Tutsi spies. Maintaining control in the camps is the responsibility of Zairian military and security forces, but doing so is beyond their capability, despite the presence of several thousand troops in the area, including 400 elite troops dispatched to Goma in response to the Rwandan refugee crisis. Moreover, the security forces themselves have contributed to the lawlessness in the region by preying on both the local populace and the refugees. A popular protest erupted in one of the camps in Goma after a soldier killed a money-changer who apparently refused to comply with a demand for money.

The squalid, disease-ridden refugee camps that have proliferated in the scenic areas surrounding Goma and Bukavu on Lac Kivu represent public health hazards, as witness the cholera epidemic among refugees in Goma. In addition, some individual refugees, eschewing the camps, reportedly have flooded the towns, pitching tents in the streets, chopping down trees for firewood, using sidewalks as toilets, and grazing livestock on lawns and open spaces. Even if the toll on Zairians were not so great, it should come as no surprise that local Zairians have not welcomed the refugees.

To understand why, one need only recall the ethnic violence against the Banyarwanda—earlier immigrants from Rwanda and Burundi—that spread throughout Nord-Kivu in the early 1990s.

Given all of these factors, the refugee influx appears likely to add unbearably to the existing chaos in Zaire. Moreover, some analysts fear the prospect of regional conflict if Zaire were to permit Rwandan Hutu refugees to set up an exile government or stage commando raids into Rwanda. Mobutu apparently met with the new Rwandan government and pledged not to permit such anti-regime activities, but there is substantial room for skepticism. Contributing to this skepticism is Mobutu's love of meddling, as demonstrated by his involvement in the Angolan civil war. In addition, Mobutu supported the Rwandan regime ousted in 1994. The Zairian opposition also has accused Mobutu of complicity in ethnic violence in Rwanda in May 1994. Mobutu allegedly allowed arms to be sent to Hutu hardliners who attacked both Tutsis and Hutu moderates; those same Hutu extremists are among the refugees who have now fled to Zaire.

There are also indications that Mobutu might somehow turn the crisis to his advantage. Before the crisis, Mobutu had become a pariah in the eyes of the West. But as the likelihood of Mobutu's overthrow receded, and in the face of the overwhelming human tragedy in Rwanda, Western leaders appear to have become reconciled to the idea of working with Mobutu. Mobutu reportedly played a role in facilitating the French intervention in Rwanda in support of the collapsing Hutu regime, and there are reports that Birindwa's replacement by Kengo was brokered by the French, who wanted to ensure Mobutu's compliance with its Rwanda policy. The United States, too, has been forced to deal with Mobutu and has at last replaced its ambassador, long absent from Kinshasa as a sign of official United States displeasure with the Mobutu regime.

Thus, as the summer of 1994 drew to a close, Mobutu appeared to have profited from the Rwandan refugee crisis, consolidating his political position domestically and rehabilitating his image internationally. Despite the deterioration of Zaire and the deplorable conditions in which most Zairians live, Mobutu appears so strongly entrenched that many observers believe he might succeed in winning the presidential election set for 1995—even if he does not rig the election. Unfortunately, such an electoral result will only bring more stagnation and disintegration to Zaire.

September 9, 1994   Thomas Turner and Sandra W. Meditz

Chapter 1. Historical Setting

Wooden figurine

THIRTY YEARS AFTER ITS BIRTH as an independent state, Zaire still bore the imprint of its colonial past. Behind the omnipresent apparatus of control forged by President Mobutu Sese Seko since 1965 lurked the shadow of King Léopold II of Belgium, whose absolute and arbitrary sovereignty found symbolic expression in the Kikongo (language of the Kongo people) phrase *bula matari* ("he who breaks rocks"), a name also applied to the colonial armed forces, the Force Publique, and generally evocative of brute force. The modern version of the *bula matari* state was nowhere more evident than in the Mobutu regime's extreme centralization of authority, highly personalized style of governance, and readiness to use force whenever the circumstances seemed to require it.

The Mobutist state is, however, the product of a complex concatenation of forces that go far beyond the years of Léopoldian autocracy. Between the formal proclamation of the Congo Free State in 1885 and Mobutu's second seizure of power in 1965, a number of events occurred that had a profound and lasting effect on the Zairian polity and on society. The first occurred in 1908, when the Belgian parliament assumed full administrative and political responsibility for the colony, which until independence in 1960 would be known as the Belgian Congo. The second involved the rise of organized nationalist activity, symbolized by the 1956 manifesto of the Alliance of the Kongo People (Alliance des Bakongo—Abako) calling for immediate independence. The crisis of decolonization, dramatized by the mutiny of the Force Publique in July 1960, constituted the third, and by far the most consequential, event. The final stage in Zaire's precipitous leap to independence began with the proclamation of the First Republic immediately after independence, extended through the convulsive aftereffects of regional secessions and rural insurgencies, and reached a plateau of sorts after the proclamation of the Second Republic in 1965.

In Zaire, as elsewhere in Africa, both indigenous and Western influences have been significant. The impact of the West has been felt most strongly through the import of institutions, policies, and culture that were radically new to the area. Zairian traditions are represented by many different ethnic groups with historically different beliefs, loyalties, and tensions. Whatever their exposure to these various historical influences, modern-day Zairians are alike in being repressed or neglected by a small and highly centralized political elite.

Human Origins

Archaeological evidence of and research on past societies in Zaire are scanty, in no small part because of the tropical climate and the rain forest covering most of the northern half of Zaire and encompassing much of the Congo River basin. Nonetheless, equatorial Africa has been inhabited since at least the middle Stone Age. Late Stone Age cultures flourished in the southern savanna after ca. 10,000 B.C. and remained viable until the arrival of Bantu-speaking peoples during the first millennium B.C. Evidence suggests that these Stone Age populations lived in small groups, relying for subsistence on hunting and gathering and the use of stone tools. Some of these groups may have remained long enough in one vicinity to be considered permanent residents, but others moved, following game along the extensive river network and through the rain forest.

The development of food-producing communities in Zaire is associated with the expansion of Bantu-speaking peoples. In a long series of migrations beginning ca. 1000 B.C. and lasting well into the mid-first millennium A.D., Bantu speakers dispersed from a point west of the Ubangi-Congo River swamp across the forests and savannas of modern Zaire. A northern group moved northeastward around the swamp and across the northern regions of Zaire and settled in the forest zone. Meanwhile, other groups moved south and southwest, the former then migrating up the Congo as well as into the inner part of the Congo Basin, while the southwestern Bantu-speakers spread into modern Gabon, Congo, and lower Zaire.

It was apparently after these movements that Bantu speakers spread south and southeastward across the southern Zairian savannas as far as present-day Angola and Zambia, thereafter continuing to expand into eastern and southern Africa. These migrating groups generally brought with them a technology superior to that of the existing inhabitants. The Bantu speakers were better able to exploit an area's resources through the practice of agriculture, based on yam and oil palm cultivation, and, as time went on, by adopting iron tools and technology.

Bantu-speaking peoples settled in the rain forests and southern savannas. Non-Bantu-speaking peoples are found in the grasslands north of the forest. Information on the settlement dates and routes of migration of these peoples remains vague at best, but they seem to have dwelt at first in the northern grasslands and only later penetrated the forest. Since perhaps late in the first millennium B.C., they have intermingled with the Bantu-speaking groups who preceded them, in the process creating a complex ethnic mosaic (see Ethnic Groups, ch. 2).

The significance of some of these peoples extends beyond purely linguistic considerations. The peoples speaking Central Sudanic languages brought with them a new food complex involving cereal cultivation and herding. A related food pattern based on cereals and hunting was separately introduced to southeastern Zaire from East Africa after ca. A.D. 100. Cereal cultivation, hunting, and herding were much better adapted to conditions in the savannas than the oil palm and yam farming that the Bantu speakers had brought with them, and, hence, spread rapidly, especially in the southern grasslands. The banana, another important food crop, was introduced, apparently, from southern Asia into East Africa in the early centuries of the present era and thereafter diffused across Central Africa. These new food sources allowed for greater settlement and population growth in the grasslands; they also contributed in no small way to the growth of trade and to increasingly complex social and political organization among those peoples who dwelt in the savannas.

Early Historical Perspectives

Zaire's precolonial past is characterized by considerable complexity. A diversity of social aggregates developed in Zaire, ranging from the small, autonomous groups of hunters and gatherers of the Ituri Forest in the northeast to the centralized chiefdoms and large-scale state systems of the savannas, from the settled village communities of the interior to the predominantly Muslim and Arab trading communities of the eastern region. In order to bring a measure of coherence to our understanding of this otherwise confusing mix of peoples and cultures and to appreciate their enduring political, economic, and social legacies, it is important to specify the broad criteria by which they can best be differentiated from each other. One criterion is the size and scope of the societies concerned; another concerns the ways in which power was distributed between rulers and ruled; a third focuses on the different impact of early Westernizing influences on their traditional social systems.

State Systems Versus Segmentary Societies

The first and most obvious distinction to be made between the various peoples who first populated the area of Zaire is between the small-scale, segmentary societies of the rain-forest zone and the state systems of the savannas. Segmentary societies, which may be defined as societies that are divided into a number of units, such as lineage (see Glossary) or clan (see Glossary) groups, which are structurally similar and functionally equivalent, were widely distributed across the interior north and south of the great bend of the Congo River. Most of the peoples of the rain-forest area were organized into village communities, under the leadership of chiefs or of dominant clans or lineages. Some of these communities were able to absorb or conquer neighboring villages and thus develop into sizable chiefdoms. In specific instances, as among the Mangbetu, these expanding societies provided the basis for a common sense of identity among otherwise unrelated peoples. Elsewhere, however, social fragmentation remained one of the most salient characteristics of the rain-forest peoples.

A classic example of such fragmentation is offered by the various communities loosely referred to as the Mongo people, who occupied most of the central basin. Divided as they were into congeries of smaller communities (Ntomba, Mbole, Kutu, etc.), they had nothing resembling a unifying political focus. Their social boundaries were generally coterminous with village groups. The same applies to the so-called *gens d'eau* (water people), a generic term coined to designate the Bobangi, Lobala, Ngiri, and neighboring groups who lived along water courses to the north of the Congo River. Most of the peoples between the Congo and Ubangi, however, such as the Ngbandi, Ngbaka, Banda, and Ngombe, possessed lineage-based systems that were more hierarchical than those found farther south. Finally, to emphasize the great diversity among the peoples and their social organization in this region, the Zande and the Mangbetu, who lived in the far northeast, were organized into states.

A different picture emerges from the history of the southern savannas, the traditional habitat of several large-scale societies with centralized political systems, variously described as kingdoms, empires, and chiefdoms, that emerged between 1200 and 1500 A.D. (see fig. 2; fig. 3). These include the Kongo, Lunda, Luba, and Kuba state systems, all of which shared certain common features, such as a centralized structure of authority identified with a single ruler, more often than not enjoying the attributes of divine kingship; a corpus of oral traditions tracing the birth of the state to a mythical figure; and a tendency to incorporate and assimilate smaller neighboring societies. Cultural assimilation went hand in hand with political conquest. As recent historical research suggests, territorial expansion of the original nuclear kingdom involved various methods, ranging from armed raids and military occupation to more peaceful forms of interaction. Yet in each case, the end result was the creation of large-scale political entities that were far more capable of concerted action than the segmentary societies of the rain-forest zone.

Rulers and Ruled

Unlike the societies of the rain-forest zone, where power was diffused among a group of elders or else centered upon a clan head or a village chief, the kingdoms of the southern savannas developed elaborate political structures, buttressed by the symbolic force of monarchy as well as by military force. Despite significant variations in the extent to which kings could be said to exercise an effective monopoly of power, relations between rulers and ruled were structured along hierarchical lines. Typically, power emanated from the central seat of authority to the outer provinces through the intermediation of appointed chiefs or local clan heads. Relations between center and periphery, however, were by no means free of ambiguity. Ensuring the loyalty of subordinate chiefs was the critical problem faced by African rulers throughout the southern savanna zone.

Although the origins of these kingdoms are shrouded in myths, their capacity to expand and conquer was directly related to their internal political structure. Thus, the expansion of the Lunda Kingdom, which probably began in the late sixteenth century and resulted in the so-called Lunda Empire that flourished in the seventeenth and eighteenth centuries, was critically related to what historian Jan Vansina calls "the twin mechanisms of perpetual succession and positional kinship." That is, each succeeding officeholder, monarch or otherwise, assumed the name, title, and personal identity of the original occupant (founder) of the office (perpetual succession). At the same time, the new officeholder adopted all kin relationships of the founder of the office as his own (positional kinship). In this manner, the personalized identity and kin ties of each founding official were perpetuated over time. These mechanisms were extremely useful in that they divorced the political structure from the actual descent structure. In so doing, they freed the processes of political recruitment from the constraints of kinship and facilitated the recruitment of new officials from within Lunda society and from the ranks of recently conquered peoples.

By the same token, the Lunda governed through a hierarchy of subordinate chiefs, a form of indirect rule, in newly occupied lands, a practice that facilitated the adaptation of the political kingdom beyond its original homeland. This custom shows how the Lunda Kingdom differed in some fundamental ways from the Luba kingdoms (fifteenth to nineteenth centuries) from which it split off, probably in the fifteenth century. Although both evolved out of

7

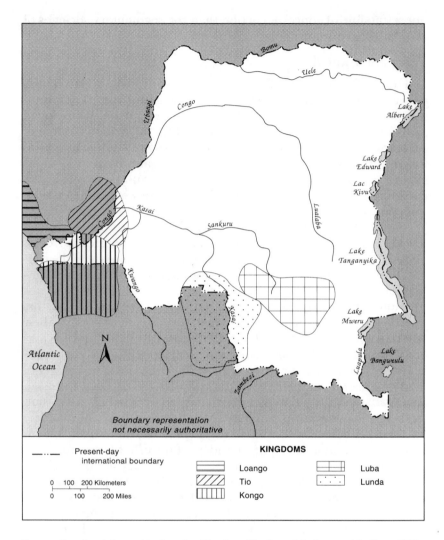

Source: Based on information from Jan Vansina, *Kingdoms of the Savanna*, Madison, 1968;
and Jan Vansina, *Paths in the Rainforests: Toward a History of Political Tradition in
Equatorial Africa*, Madison, 1990.

Figure 2. Major Kingdoms in Central Africa, Sixteenth Century

preexisting chiefdoms and shared many of the same political symbols, including the notion of divine kingship, only the Lunda were
able to expand substantially beyond their core area. During the
seventeenth century, the Lunda expanded toward the west and northwest into present-day Angola, initially to escape Luba domination,

and to the south and east, initially in search of copper and salt and control of the trade associated with these desirable commodities, and later in pursuit of ivory. In the course of that expansion, the Lunda established a number of subsidiary states, including an eastern branch known as the Kazembe Kingdom of the Luapula Valley in the mid-eighteenth century. That kingdom successfully controlled the ivory trade in the area and set up a tributary organization of subordinate chiefs.

The absence among the Luba of anything like positional succession or perpetual kinship proved a major handicap. The rise and fall of at least three different Luba dynasties in the seventeenth century testifies to the relative weakness of the Luba monarchy. Competition for control of the throne led to incessant civil wars, and by the late nineteenth century, the kingdom had become easy prey for the Chokwe (often spelled Cokwe) people.

The Chokwe were originally a seminomadic, Bantu-speaking people living near the headwaters of the Kwango and Kasai rivers. They were primarily hunters, although their movements permitted them to trade successfully in such commodities as wax. By the start of the nineteenth century, the Chokwe were still largely unknown. They expanded dramatically in the second half of the century, however, largely at the expense of the Lunda, whose territories they invaded and occupied. Chokwe warriors, armed with rifles, wreaked havoc among the Lunda, looting and burning villages and either absorbing the local population or selling captives into slavery. After about 1885, the Chokwe began to attack the Luba as well, but by the end of the century, the Lunda had managed to defeat the Chokwe and to drive them back southward.

Chokwe political structure was similar to that of the Lunda, under whose chiefs they had originally lived. This structure enabled the Chokwe to absorb people organized into small lineages over a wide area and to gain military superiority over the indigenous population of the lands into which they moved. Once they conquered a people, the Chokwe rapidly assimilated them into their own social structure. The reason for their expansion seems to have been the rich trade in wax, ivory, slaves and, later, rubber; the avenues of Chokwe expansion were along the lines of preexisting trade routes.

External Pressures

By the late 1800s, new sets of players appeared on the African scene, the Arabs in the east and the Europeans in the west, both deeply involved in slave-trading activities. The tactical alliance between the Luba king, Kasongo Kalombo, who ascended to the Luba

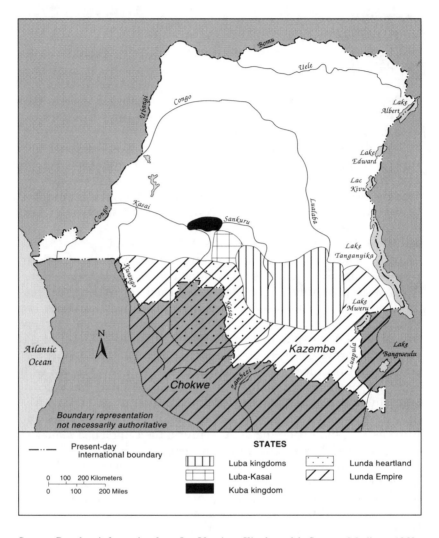

Source: Based on information from Jan Vansina, *Kingdoms of the Savanna,* Madison, 1968.

Figure 3. Major States in the Southern Savannas, Mid-Nineteenth Century

throne in the 1860s, and Arab traders did little to prevent the disintegration of his kingdom. As elsewhere through the savannas, externally inspired local revolts accelerated the process of fragmentation instigated by competition for the monarchy, causing outlying provinces to break away and set themselves up as more or less independent political entities.

From the inception of Portuguese penetration into the old Kongo

Kingdom in the late fifteenth century, and well into the beginning of the scramble for colonies in the nineteenth century, the Kongo monarchy was a major pawn in international struggles. These conflicts pitted the Vatican against the Portuguese crown for control of African souls, the Dutch (who began arriving on the west coast of Africa in the seventeenth century) against the Portuguese for control of the slave trade, and ultimately Spain against Portugal for sovereignty over the Portuguese Empire.

The Kongo Kingdom was the first state on the west coast of Central Africa to come into contact with Europeans. Portuguese sailors under Diogo Cão landed at the mouth of the Congo River in 1483. Cão traveled from Portugal to Kongo and back several times during the 1480s, bringing missionaries to the Kongo court and taking Kongo nobles to Portugal in 1485. In the 1490s, the king of Kongo asked Portugal for missionaries and technical assistance in exchange for ivory and other desirable items, such as slaves and copperwares—a relationship, ultimately detrimental to the Kongo, which continued for centuries.

Competition over the slave trade had repercussions far beyond the boundaries of Kongo society. Slave-trading activities created powerful vested interests among both Africans and foreigners— the Portuguese and later the Dutch, French, British, and Arabs. A new source of instability was thus introduced into the coastal areas of Central Africa and its hinterland, which greatly hastened the decline of the kingdoms. Nowhere is this more evident than in the history of the Kongo Kingdom, which was a centralized state system ruled by an absolute monarch.

In the late fourteenth century, a group of Kongo, led by the son of a chief from the area of present-day Boma, moved south of the Congo River into northern Angola, conquered the territory, and established Mbanza Kongo Dia Ntotila (Great City of the King) as the capital of their kingdom (the capital was later moved to São Salvador). By the middle of the fifteenth century, the Kongo king ruled the lands in northern Angola and the north bank of the Congo. By the early sixteenth century, the kingdom was divided into six provinces, each under a subchief or governor, who also held a religious title and authority. The last really effective years of the Kongo monarchy were from 1641 to 1661, although the kingdom endured into the next century. By the eighteenth century, however, most of the kingdom's provinces (Mbamba, Mbata, Mpemba, and Soyo) had become self-governing principalities. The king, though claiming a divine right to the monarchy, had little authority beyond his capital, and internal bickerings that had surrounded his throne and further diminished his power also contributed to the weakening of the provincial chiefdoms.

The dynamics of internal fragmentation were directly linked to commercial activities. Just as the ownership of slaves became a major source of wealth and prestige, both in turn made it possible for the slave owners to challenge the authority of the king. Here, as elsewhere in the savannas, the competition for slaves introduced a major source of instability, creating a permanent state of social unrest and civil war. The history of the old Kongo Kingdom encapsulates many of the crises experienced by several other states of the savannas in their efforts to cope with the challenge of the new economic forces.

The area of the Congo was one of the principal sources of slaves for markets in Arabia, the Middle East, and the New World. The trade had devastating effects on both Kongo and non-Kongo communities for almost 400 years. By the late seventeenth century, up to 15,000 slaves a year were sent out of the lower Congo River area. The European slave traders were usually the final link in a chain of African and Arab merchants who brought slaves down to coastal trading posts. The slave trade in the eastern part of present-day Zaire was dominated by Arabs and continued until the late nineteenth century. All European nations had abolished the trade by the mid-nineteenth century, and the end of the American Civil War in 1865 finally extinguished another main market. Besides the obvious depopulation, the slave trade in the Congo area had caused many local rebellions and increased ethnic warfare.

On the eve of the Belgian conquest in the late nineteenth century, Congolese societies had reached a degree of internal dislocation that greatly lessened their capacity to resist a full-scale invasion. Resistance to outside forces was further hampered by the devastating raids and civil wars that followed in the wake of the slave trade, by the subsequent improvement in the capacity of Africans to destroy each other through the use of firearms, and ultimately by the divisions between "collaborators" and "resisters" and between the allies of the Arabs and the allies of the Europeans. In addition, a more enduring cleavage had emerged out of the varying exposure of Zairian societies to Western influences and early trade activities. Long before the conquest of the vast hinterland, the coastal communities had had centuries of contact with Europeans; by the time the Conference of Berlin began in 1884, on the other hand, most of the societies of the interior had yet to experience the full impact of European rule. Out of these different historical experiences emerged different self-images and cultural dispositions. That the Kongo peoples were the first Zairian people to challenge the legitimacy of the colonial state is perhaps not unrelated to their long and dramatic experience of European hegemony.

The Colonial State

From 1840 to 1872, the Scottish missionary, David Livingstone, engaged in a series of explorations that brought the Congo to the attention of the Western world. During these travels, Livingstone was out of touch with Europe for two years. Henry Morton Stanley, a journalist, was commissioned by the *New York Herald* to conduct a search for him. The two met at Ujiji, on the eastern shore of Lake Tanganyika, in 1871. Three years later, Stanley was commissioned by the *New York Herald* and London's *Daily Telegraph* to continue the explorations begun by Livingstone. With three British companions, Stanley began the descent of the Congo from its upper reaches, completing his journey in 1877. Returning to Europe, he tried to interest the British government in further exploration and development of the Congo but met with no success. His expeditions did, however, attract another European monarch.

Stanley's adventures brought the Congo to the attention of Belgium's King Léopold II, a man of boundless energy and ambition. The European occupation of Africa was well under way, but the Congo River basin remained for the most part unknown to Europeans. With no great powers contesting its control, the area appeared to present an ideal opportunity for Belgian expansion.

Recruiting Stanley to help him from 1878, Léopold II founded the International Association of the Congo, financed by an international consortium of bankers. Under the auspices of this association, Stanley arrived at the mouth of the Congo in 1879 and began the journey upriver. He founded Vivi, the first capital, across the river from present-day Matadi and then moved farther upriver, reaching a widening he named Stanley Pool (now Pool de Malebo) in mid-1881. There he founded a trading station and the settlement of Léopoldville (now Kinshasa) on the south bank. The north bank of the river had been claimed by France, leading ultimately to the creation of the colony of French Congo. The road from the coast to Vivi was completed by the end of 1881, and Stanley returned to Europe. He was back in Africa by December 1882 and sailed up the Congo to Stanleyville (now Kisangani), signing more than 450 treaties on behalf of Léopold II with persons described as local chieftains who had agreed to cede their rights of sovereignty over much of the Congo Basin. In 1884 Stanley returned to Europe.

At the Conference of Berlin, held in 1884–85 to settle disputes among the European nations and in essence to partition Africa among them, thirteen powers, following the example set by the United States, separately recognized Léopold II's International Association of the Congo, which had already adopted its own flag, as an independent entity. Shortly afterward the association became the Congo Free State. By the General Act of Berlin, signed at the conclusion of the conference in 1885, the powers also agreed that activities in the Congo Basin should be governed by certain principles, including freedom of trade and navigation, neutrality in the event of war, suppression of the slave traffic, and improvement of the condition of the indigenous population. The conference recognized Léopold II as sovereign of the new state.

Shortly thereafter, in order to meet the conference's legal requirement of "effective occupation," Léopold II proceeded to transform the Congo Free State into an effective instrument of colonial hegemony. Indigenous conscripts were promptly recruited into his nascent army, the Force Publique, manned by European officers (see The Colonial Period, ch. 5). A corps of European administrators was hastily assembled, which by 1906 numbered 1,500 people; and a skeletal transportation grid was eventually assembled to provide the necessary links between the coast and the interior. The cost of the enterprise proved far higher than had been anticipated, however, as the penetration of the vast hinterland could not be achieved except at the price of numerous military campaigns. Some of these campaigns resulted in the suppression or expulsion of the previously powerful Afro-Arab slave traders and ivory merchants. Only through the ruthless and massive suppression of opposition and exploitation of African labor could Léopold II hold and exploit his personal fiefdom.

The Léopoldian Legacy

"Without the railroad," said Léopold II's agent, Henry Morton Stanley, "the Congo is not worth a penny." Without recourse to forced labor, however, the railroad could not be built; nor could the huge concessions made to private companies become profitable unless African labor was freely used to locate and transport rubber and ivory; nor could African resistance in the east be overcome without a massive recruitment of indigenous troops. The cruel logic of the revenue imperative left the Léopoldian system with no apparent option but to extract a maximum output of labor and natural resources from the land (see From Colonial Times to Independence, ch. 3).

At the heart of the system lay a perverse combination of rewards and penalties. Congo Free State agents and native auxiliaries (the so-called *capitas*) were given authority to use as much force as they

14

Waterfalls, such as this one on the Kasai River, hampered early European exploration of the interior.

deemed appropriate to meet delivery norms, and because their profits were proportional to the amount of rubber and ivory collected, the inevitable consequence was the institutionalization of force on a huge scale. Although native chiefs were expected to cooperate, the incessant and arbitrary demands made on their authority were self-defeating. Many chiefs turned against the colonial state; others were quickly disposed of and replaced by state-appointed "straw chiefs." Countless revolts ensued, which had an immediate effect on the scale and frequency of military expeditions. As the cost of pacification soared, Léopold II declared a state monopoly on rubber and ivory. The free-trade principle that had once been the cornerstone of the Congo Free State thus became a legal fiction, aptly summed up in this pithy commentary of the time: "Article one: trade is entirely free; article two: there is nothing to buy or sell."

Protestant missionaries were the first to alert international public opinion to the extent of cruelties visited upon the African population, and with the creation of the Congo Reform Association in 1904, the public outcry against the Congo Free State reached major proportions. Not until 1908, however, did the Belgian parliament vote in favor of annexation as the most sensible solution to the flood of criticisms generated by the reform movement. The Colonial

Charter provided for the government of what was thereafter known as the Belgian Congo. This charter permitted the king to retain a great deal of authority and influence over affairs in the colony through power of appointment and legislative authority, but his power was constitutional rather than personal and, therefore, limited. The main purpose of the charter was to prevent the establishment of a royal autocracy in the colony similar to the one that had existed in the Congo Free State.

For almost the entire period of the Congo Free State (1885–1908), the peoples of present-day Zaire were subjected to a staggering sequence of wars, repression, and regimentation. The impact of this colonial experience was so devastating, and its aftereffects so disruptive, because the initial shock of European intrusion was followed almost immediately by a ruthless exploitation of human and natural resources. In terms of its psychological impact, the *bula matari* state left a legacy of latent hostility on which subsequent generations of nationalists were able to capitalize; on the other hand, the sheer brutality of its methods generated a sense of fear and hopelessness, which, initially at least, discouraged the rise of organized nationalist activity.

Belgian Paternalism: Underlying Postulates

Reduced to its essentials, Belgian paternalism meant that basic political rights could be withheld indefinitely from Africans as long as their material and spiritual needs were properly met. Paternalism drew its rationale from a vision of Africans as essentially "big children," whose moral upbringing required a proper mixture of authority and dedication. Its essence is perhaps best captured in the opening sentence of a celebrated work by a former colonial governor general, Pierre Ryckmans: "Dominer pour servir (Dominate in order to serve. . . . This is the only excuse for colonial conquest; it is also its complete justification.).''

Putting into effect the social welfare postulate of paternalism was largely the responsibility of parastatal organizations, semipublic corporations enjoying a substantial measure of autonomy in organizing and dispensing social services. Their names became identified with a wide spectrum of social welfare activities ranging from medical services to housing projects, from education and health care programs to family allowances and social centers (*foyers sociaux*) for African women. An extensive network of social welfare programs thus reached out to the governed to ensure their material well-being "from the womb to the tomb." Roman Catholic and Protestant missions, meanwhile, assumed full responsibility for their spiritual well-being, the former being more numerous in the endeavor. Through their teaching and evangelical activities, and with the help of generous subsidies from the state, missions thus formed a major element in the armature of paternalism.

The darker side of this paternalism was the political control and compulsion underlying Belgian colonial policies. Extensive restrictions affected Africans in their everyday life—ranging from prohibition of the purchase of liquor (until 1955) to stringent police surveillance and curfew regulations in the urban centers, and from compulsory crop cultivation to various forms of administrative and social regimentation in the countryside.

Part of the Belgian goal was to teach Africans to work, not in the "childish" pursuits of their own culture, but in organized, rational routines of productive wage labor in the European manner, for European employers. Such labor was considered to exercise a civilizing influence. A profitable by-product was the provision of cheap labor. The Colonial Charter had declared that no one could be compelled to work, and by 1912 the forced delivery of rubber and other natural products had come to a stop, but until the depression of the 1930s, mining and agricultural companies resorted to recruiting methods little different from forced labor.

The colonial government believed that Africans could be "civilized" through agricultural as well as industrial labor. Agricultural programs began as early as 1917, when the administration first required Africans to raise certain designated crops. The crops most often raised were cotton for export or food crops for towns and mines within the colony, neither of which threatened European interests, nor did either ensure the health and well-being of the indigenous population.

To help boost production, Belgium set up a national institute that introduced improved agricultural technology to the colony during the 1930s. But a program that had greater influence on African life eventually was the establishment of native farming settlements (*paysannats indigènes*). African peasants were resettled on them in order to intensify the cultivation of cash crops or export crops, to conserve the fertility of the soil, and to facilitate the introduction of modern farming methods. The settlements were generally successful but represented another European intrusion into African culture. As such, most of the settlements collapsed after independence.

In the political realm, Belgian policy was theoretically to respect the authority of African chiefs and political leaders, permitting Africans to be ruled by their own customs unless these customs were judged disruptive of public order or harmful to development. Colonial administrators divided the entire Belgian Congo into chiefdoms (*chefferies*), later grouped into sectors. Chiefs, salaried by the state and given administrative and police powers, were expected to provide the link between Africans and the colonial administration. But the Belgian division of its territory into chiefdoms often did not reflect ethnic boundaries or indigenous political units, and Belgian authorities were generally ignorant of African custom. Moreover, the Belgian colonial system did not encourage indigenous involvement in the colony's political life. By placing the inculcation of colonial moral principles above political education, and social welfare benefits above the apprenticeship of social responsibility, Belgian policies inevitably ruled out the introduction of institutions and procedures designed to nurture political experience and responsibility.

Not until 1957, with the introduction of a major local government reform, were Africans given the opportunity to elect local communal councils (see Postwar Reforms, this ch.). Important as this step was in laying the foundation for local self-government and a major departure from the postulates of paternalism, it was heavily mortgaged by previous decades of enforced political passivity. When independence began to seem imminent in the late 1950s and the future Zairians could make a limited use of their political freedom, few had acquired the necessary practical experience to guide their first steps toward democracy.

The Apparatus of Control

State, church, and business formed the trinity of powers upon which the royal hegemony rested during most of the colonial era. By virtue of their special relationship with the state, formalized by the 1906 Concordat between the Vatican and Belgium, Catholic missions were the privileged instrument of primary and vocational education for the colony's people; the operating costs of their educational and missionary activities were almost entirely covered by state subsidies. According to some estimates, the mission establishment had virtually as many personnel as the state and three times as many outposts. The business corporations, involved in plantations and mining, were given virtually a free hand to recruit African labor, to organize food production for the labor camps, and to provide social services for African workers and their families. Both missionary and business interests were given direct access to the state through the appointment of representatives to advisory organs, such as the Government Council in Léopoldville and the Colonial Council in Brussels. The result was a close and, most of the time, mutually supportive relationship between the state on the one hand and the church and business interests on the other.

18

*Traditional tombs
in Bas-Zaïre Region
Courtesy Zaire National
Tourism Office*

The colonial state was, of course, the pivotal element in this coalition of interests, because of its unchallenged monopoly of force and highly visible administrative presence. From the time of its creation in 1888 until its dissolution in the wake of the 1960 mutiny, the Force Publique provided the colonial state with a formidable instrument of coercion, whose reputation for brutality was well established. The everyday tasks of administration were mostly performed by a corps of colonial civil servants whose density on the ground was without equivalent elsewhere on the continent. By independence there were some 10,000 European civil servants and officers serving in the Belgian Congo. From the territorial administrators to the district commissioners and provincial governors, the network of colonial functionaries reached out from remote areas of the colony to its administrative nerve center in Léopoldville, where the governor general held court. Except for the 1957 local government reform, the grid of administrative control fashioned by Belgium remained virtually unchanged throughout the colonial era.

Adding to the weight of the European hegemony, a system of native tribunals and local councils was introduced in the 1920s to enlist local chiefs in administration of the colony. Few of the chiefs, however, claimed as much as a glimmer of legitimacy, as most of them acted as the agents of the colonial state. The machinery of African participation in local government was a far cry from the

19

native authority systems established in British colonies, for example. Ultimate control over local affairs always rested with European administrators.

Equally restrictive of African participation was the system of administration prevailing in urban sectors, the so-called *centres extra-coutumiers*. Under the arrangement introduced in 1931, urban areas were administered by a special sector chief (*chef de centre*) assisted by a separate sector council (*conseil de centre*) appointed by the local district commissioner; urban centers were in turn divided into zone councils (*conseils de zone*), headed by appointed authorities, called zone chiefs (*chefs de zone*). As the system proved increasingly ineffective, however, the tendency, especially after World War II, was to resort to a more direct form of administration, in which European territorial agents ran the affairs of the so-called native townships (*cités indigènes*) as they deemed fit.

Not until the postwar years was this complex system of interlocking structures among the colonial state, the church, and big business much called into question. The decisive factor then was the intrusion of metropolitan politics into the colonial arena, following the election in 1954 of a Socialist-Liberal cabinet in Brussels whose anticlerical program had a profound effect on colonial policies.

Postwar Reforms

World War II marks a watershed in the history of the Belgian colony. Profound social and economic changes stirred up the collective consciousness of Africans both in the rural and urban sectors. The heavy demands made upon the rural milieus by the war effort accelerated the flow of migrants to the towns; a new class of educated, French-speaking Africans called *évolués* (sing., *évolué*— see Glossary) came into being, increasingly vocal in their demands for reforms; and the frequency of labor disputes and strikes in the industrial centers of Katanga Province (now Shaba Region) drew attention to the changing attitude of African mine workers. Nor were the changes limited to the domestic arena. Anticolonial sentiment was quickly emerging as a fundamental reality of the international scene, and the United Nations (UN) was becoming a major forum for promoting the aspirations of the colonized. No longer could the Belgian Congo be kept in a state of splendid isolation. These pressures and challenges on Belgian officials resulted in the idea of a Belgo-Congolese community, articulated for the first time in 1952. Rather than a radical change in the constitutional relationship, what the Belgians envisioned was a polity in which Africans and Europeans would learn to live in harmony with each other, share the same interests, and ultimately become equal participants in the political life of the Belgian Congo.

As a first step toward this goal, the 1952 decree on immatriculation (see Glossary) provided for the juridical assimilation (i.e., transferring the persons concerned from the jurisdiction of customary law to that of European law) of Africans who were able to show "by their upbringing and way of life" that they had reached an adequate "state of civilization." The decree, which reasserted the provisions for immatriculation in the Colonial Charter, was followed by a series of measures designed to break down the barrier of racial discrimination between Africans, whether matriculated or not, and Europeans. A decree of February 1953 allowed Africans to own land in urban and rural areas, and in 1955 they were allowed free access to public establishments and authorized to buy alcoholic beverages. Several years later, in 1958, substantial changes were introduced in the judicial system of the colony. From then on, offenses committed by Africans could be tried in all courts of law instead of just in native tribunals.

The really critical step toward political participation came with the March 26, 1957, introduction of the urban statute, a move intended to give urban Africans a meaningful share of power at the local level. In each of the several communes included in the major towns, Africans were given the opportunity to elect communal councils, to be headed by burgomasters nominated by the councils from among their members. At the city level, a town council would be appointed by the provincial governor from among the members of the communal councils and headed by a first burgomaster. A May 10, 1957, decree introduced equally significant changes in rural administration. The most noteworthy involved the establishment of rural councils (*conseils de secteur*), whose members were to be appointed "after taking into account the preferences of the inhabitants." The highly ambiguous phrasing of the decree meant that considerable leeway would be allowed to the provincial authorities in designating council members.

The psychological impact of these reforms on the political consciousness of Africans cannot be overstated. For the first time in the history of the colony, the basic premises of paternalism were openly called into question: a legitimate alternative to the status quo had come into view; new opportunities suddenly materialized for genuine political participation at the local level. From this perspective, the 1957 urban reform must be seen as the decisive factor behind the crystallization of aspirations for political independence. On the other hand, the official ban on the organization of political parties, combined with the growth of ethnic self-awareness in the urban sectors, meant that electoral competition was structured along ethnic lines.

Ethnic distinctions among the inhabitants of the Congo area had always been fluid: the concept of who was or was not a member of a specific ethnic group had never been as rigid as Europeans believed. Yet the Belgian administration acted as if rigid distinctions did exist. The identity cards of Congolese listed the ethnic group to which they belonged, and they were required to supply this information in filling out forms. The European emphasis on ethnic identity helped reinforce the concept of such an identity among the Congolese.

Another critical factor that contributed to the increase in ethnic awareness was the process of urbanization. Congolese migrated to population centers to look for work. Once in the cities and towns, they came into contact on the one hand with other individuals with whom they shared language, culture, and history and on the other with quite different peoples. To promote their culture and to offer mutual support, these people formed ethnically based associations, the benefits of which they communicated to family and friends who had remained behind in rural areas.

The formation of ethnic associations reinforced ethnic lines between groups and at the same time made more apparent their relative size and social, economic, and political status. If members of one ethnic group were perceived as having the best jobs, whether or not this was so, indignation among the others might be aroused. One of the most notable examples of this response was in Léopoldville, where the Kongo people, who believed that they had always been the leading ethnic group in the Belgian Congo, felt threatened by the influx of people from far upriver. It was in large measure in response to this perceived threat to their position that some of the Kongo formed in 1950 the Association for the Maintenance, Unity, and Expansion of the Kikongo Language (Association pour le Maintien, l'Unité, et l'Expansion de la Langue Kikongo). This organization later became the Alliance of the Kongo People, or Alliance des Bakongo, known as Abako (see Nationalist Awakenings, this ch.).

Thus, in most instances, and particularly in Léopoldville and Élisabethville (now Lubumbashi), electoral processes had a catalytic effect on the rise of ethnic sentiment. Almost everywhere ethnic associations served as the main vehicles of political mobilization, and in some regions ethnic conflict reached alarming proportions. The flurry of ethno-nationalist activity generated by the 1957 decrees brought further pressure to bear upon the Belgian authorities to accelerate the pace of political reforms.

Nationalist Awakenings

Congolese resistance to Belgian rule has a long history, traceable to the countless uprisings against Belgian rule instigated by local chiefs—as among the Babua in 1903, 1904, and 1910, and the Budja in 1903 and 1905—and the mutinies of the Force Publique in 1895 and 1897. To these early "primary resistance" movements must be added the various independent African religious movements that flourished in the 1920s and 1930s. The Kimbanguist Church, founded by Simon Kimbangu in 1921, upheld a vision of spiritual salvation that attracted thousands of followers among the Kongo people and that the Belgians perceived as a threat (see The Kimbanguist Church, ch. 2). Much the same kind of messianic message was conveyed through other indigenous African religions, such as the Kitawala movement, which first appeared in the urban centers of Katanga in the 1920s. Although immediate measures were taken by Belgian officials to repress activities of these groups and to exile their members to distant areas, there can be little doubt that each of these early, proto-nationalist movements played an important role in forcing social protest into religious channels, and, in the case of Kimbanguism, into a powerful ethno-religious framework that helped structure and legitimize the nationalist aspirations of subsequent generations of Kongo politicians.

The Rise of Militant Ethnicity: Abako

Because of its long exposure to the West and rich heritage of messianic unrest, the lower Congo region, homeland of the Kongo people, was the first area to emerge as a focal point of militantly anti-Belgian sentiment and activity. The spearhead of ethnic nationalism there was the cultural association headed by Joseph Kasavubu, known as Abako, which in 1956 issued a manifesto calling for immediate independence. The move came about as a response to a far more conciliatory statement by a group of non-Kongo intellectuals identified with the editorial committee of a Léopoldville newspaper, *Conscience Africaine*. In it they gave their full endorsement to the ideas set forth by Professor A.A.J. Van Bilsen in his newly published *Thirty-Year Plan for the Political Emancipation of Belgian Africa*. Far more impatient in tone and radical in its objectives, the Abako manifesto stated: "Rather than postponing emancipation for another thirty years, we should be granted self-government today."

The metamorphosis of Abako into a major vehicle of anticolonial protest unleashed considerable unrest throughout the lower Congo.

In the capital city, the party emerged as the dominant force: the urban elections of December 1957 gave Abako candidates 133 communal council seats out a total of 170, thus vesting unfettered control of the African communes in the hands of the partisans of "complete independence." While the Abako victory at the polls greatly strengthened its bargaining position vis-à-vis the administration, in the countryside its local sections quickly proliferated, creating a de facto power structure almost entirely beyond the control of the colonial civil servants. In Léopoldville, meanwhile, the situation was rapidly getting out of hand. The turning point came on January 4, 1959, when Belgian administrators took the fatal step of dispersing a large crowd of Abako supporters gathered to attend a political meeting. Widespread rioting throughout the city immediately followed, resulting in the wholesale plunder of European property. When order was finally restored, at the price of an exceedingly brutal repression, forty-nine Congolese were officially reported killed and 101 wounded. A week later, on January 13, the Belgian government formally recognized independence as the ultimate goal of its policies. "It is our firm intention," King Baudouin I (1951–93) solemnly announced, "without undue procrastination, but without fatal haste, to lead the Congolese forward to independence in prosperity and peace." Although no precise date was set for independence, the tide of nationalist sentiment could not be stemmed. A year later, the Belgian Congo would be hurtling toward independence (see The Crisis of Decolonization, this ch.).

Its anti-Belgian orientation notwithstanding, Abako was first and foremost a Kongo movement. Its concentration on the past splendors of the Kongo Kingdom and on the cultural values inherent in the Kikongo language was entirely consonant with its proclaimed objective of working toward the reconstruction of the Kongo polity, and, at one point, of advocating secession as the quickest way of achieving this all-consuming goal. Thus, while inspiring other groups of Congolese to emulate its demands for immediate independence, another consequence of Abako militancy was to structure political competition along ethnic lines. Kongo elements in Léopoldville came into conflict with a group of Lingala-speaking upriver people; in 1959 and 1960, the rivalry became a major trial of strength between the forces of ethno-regionalism and the claims of territorial nationalism.

The Challenge of Territorial Nationalism: Lumumba and the MNC

In the welter of political formations that appeared after the Belgian declaration of January 13, 1959, at least one party stood as the standard-bearer of pan-territorial nationalist aspirations: the Congolese National Movement (Mouvement National Congolais—MNC). Technically, the MNC was formed in August 1956. Its declared objective was to "pursue the political emancipation of the Congo," while fostering among its members "a consciousness of their national unity and responsibilities." Although the party never disavowed its commitment to national unity, not until the arrival of Patrice Lumumba in Léopoldville in 1958 did it enter its militant phase.

There can be little doubt that the MNC owed a great deal of its success to Lumumba's charisma, to his uncanny ability to galvanize crowds, never more impressive than when venting the collective grievances of his followers against Belgian colonialism. His undeniable talent as a political organizer and an activist, coupled with his passionate commitment to the idea of a united Congo—perhaps reflective of his Tetela origins, the Tetela being a relatively small group located in Kasai—were critical factors as well behind the rapid extension of the MNC in at least four of the Belgian Congo's six provinces (see fig. 4). On the other hand, his well-known propensity to arrogate to himself unfettered control over the affairs of the party led to serious frictions within its leadership. Internal dissension came to a head in July 1959 when Joseph Ileo, Cyrille Adoula, and Albert Kalonji decided to set up their own moderate wing, from then on known as the MNC-Kalonji. The result was to deprive the main part of the party of some of its most capable leaders and to considerably narrow its bases of support in Kasai and Katanga.

In spite of these handicaps, the MNC-Lumumba was to claim the largest number of votes (though not a majority) in the May 1960 national elections, leaving the Belgian authorities no choice but to formally recognize Lumumba as prime minister of the new country. The subsequent election of the Abako leader, Joseph Kasavubu, as president in June 1960 institutionalized in particularly awkward fashion a latent conflict between the two radically different brands of nationalism. Behind the constitutional crisis that developed in the weeks following independence, on June 30, 1960, loomed a more fundamental crisis of legitimacy, reflecting diametrically opposed conceptions of the Congolese polity (see The Center No Longer Holds, this ch.).

Settler Politics in Katanga

The major challenges posed to the MNC in its early years were the rise of ethno-nationalism and the threat of regional separatism in Katanga. Settler interests played a determining role in manipulating

Figure 4. Provinces at Independence, 1960

the regional balance of power to the advantage of secessionist forces.

Because of its industrial base and comparatively large European population, Katanga differed in some essential ways from other regions. By 1956 it claimed a non-African population of approximately 34,000, about 31 percent of the total European population of the colony. Many Europeans became active members of the Union for the Colonization of Katanga (Union pour la Colonisation du Katanga—Ucol-Katanga), a settler organization founded in 1944 for the specific purpose of "securing for the white population of Katanga the liberties granted by the Belgian constitution, and to promote, by all available means, the growth of European colonization." Yet, as it became increasingly clear that self-government under settler rule was not a viable option, and as the extension of the vote to Africans in 1957 brought into existence a new constellation of political forces, settler politics took on a radically different objective. The aim was no longer to prevent Africans from gaining power, but to work toward a close political collaboration with those Africans who shared both the settlers' distrust of centralized control and their separatist goals.

The most likely catalyst for this collaborative partnership was the Confederation of Katanga Associations (Confédération des Associations du Katanga—Conakat), headed by Moïse Tshombe. Describing themselves as "authentic Katangese," Conakat supporters were essentially drawn from the Lunda and Yeke peoples of southern Katanga, that is, from those elements who were most resentful of the presence of Luba immigrants from Kasai, many of whom found employment in the mining centers. The decisive victory scored by these "strangers" during the 1957 urban council elections sharply intensified the animus of Conakat leaders toward immigrants from Kasai, while bringing into clearer focus the common aspirations of European settlers and "authentic Katangese."

As time went on, however, another threat to Conakat emerged from the north, not from Luba-Kasai but from Luba elements indigenous to northern Katanga. Led by Jason Sendwe, they eventually set up their own political organization, the Association of the Luba People of Katanga (Association des Baluba du Katanga—Balubakat), soon to enter into an alliance with Lumumba's branch of the MNC. Despite strong cultural affinities between the two groups, the Luba-Kasai went their own way, directing their loyalties to the Federation of Kasai (Fédération Kasaïenne—Fédéka). Their political aloofness was in large part motivated by the rift in Kasai between the MNC-Lumumba and the MNC-Kalonji, identified, respectively, with Lulua and Luba elements in the Kasaian arena. Thus, the alliance of Balubakat with the MNC-Lumumba made it highly unlikely that a similar rapprochement would ever materialize between Balubakat and Fédéka. The split between Kasaian and Katangese Luba thus played directly into the hands of Conakat and its European partners.

The victory of the MNC-Lumumba in the May 1960 national legislative elections transformed the alliance between European settlers and Conakat into an increasingly close partnership, and Conakat's relationship with Balubakat into a protracted trial of strength. The conflict with Balubakat began with the provincial elections of May 1960, when Conakat won twenty-five seats, Balubakat twenty-two, and independents the remaining thirteen. Although Balubakat appealed the results, the Belgian magistrate rejected the appeal, and after the thirteen independents joined Conakat, the latter emerged with a solid majority in the Katangan provincial assembly. On June 1, the Balubakat deputies walked out of the assembly, depriving it of the necessary quorum to start its deliberations. At this point, the provincial governor, yielding to the urgings of European settlers, appealed to Brussels to promulgate an amendment to the constitution, the Fundamental Law (Loi Fondamentale), which had been enacted on May 19. On June 15, despite the prophetic warning of Balubakat that "the promulgation of (the amendment) would inevitably lead to civil war after June 30," the Belgian parliament nevertheless enacted the amendment, thus making it legally possible for Conakat to gain full control of the provincial institutions. On July 11, Tshombe formally declared Katanga an independent state (see The Secession of Katanga, this ch.).

The Crisis of Decolonization

The crisis that suddenly burst upon the Republic of the Congo, as the new nation was called, in the wake of independence, on June 30, 1960, has several dimensions: the mutiny of the Force Publique on July 5; the secession of the country's richest region, Katanga, on July 11, soon followed by a similar move in southeastern Kasai Province (now Kasai-Oriental Region), which declared itself the Independent Mining State of South Kasai on August 8; and the role of the United Nations, first as a peacekeeping force and ultimately as the chosen instrument for bringing Katanga back into the fold of the central government. The crisis was further compounded by the trial of strength at the center between President Kasavubu and Prime Minister Lumumba, culminating in Lumumba's assassination at the hands of the Katangan secessionists in January 1961.

The Road to Independence

The rioting that swept across Léopoldville in early January 1959, did more than induce the Belgian government to recognize independence formally as the ultimate goal of its policies; it also set in motion a decolonization plan designed to lay the foundation for major constitutional reforms. The Colonial Council, renamed the Legislative Council, would include twelve indigenous Congolese members and provide the embryo of an upper chamber; the Government Council and provincial councils would be transformed into advisory bodies to monitor the decisions of the Belgian governor general and provincial governors. By late 1959, local councils would be elected to serve as an electoral college for the establishment of provincial councils. No provision was made, however, for the transfer of executive or administrative power to non-Europeans. And the few Congolese selected for membership in the new advisory organs could scarcely be seen as representative of their countrymen's interests.

In view of its omissions and ambiguities, it is easy to see why the Belgian plan fell short of the expectations of most politically conscious Congolese. Even before it began to be put into effect, the Belgian blueprint had been largely outstripped by the pace and intensity of nationalist activity. Faced with an impasse, the Belgian government finally agreed to the Round Table Conference, held in Brussels in January 1960, involving the participation of a broad spectrum of nationalist organizations. At the conference, June 30, 1960, was agreed upon as the date of independence. Elections would be held in May, on the basis of universal suffrage, for the election of a bicameral parliament and provincial councils. Finally, a special commission was appointed to frame a new constitutional system, which became the Fundamental Law.

The constitutional formula adopted by the Round Table Conference was a carbon copy of the Belgian constitution. Its essential feature was a threefold division of powers, between the central government and the provinces, between the Senate and the Chamber of Representatives, and between the head of state and the prime minister. The duality of executive powers meant in theory that the president would be cast in the role of the Belgian king, acting largely as a figurehead, with effective executive power vested in the hands of the prime minister. In the context of the newly emergent Congolese polity, however, this system incorporated within itself the seeds of a major conflict of jurisdiction between the president and the prime minister.

The national legislative elections of May 1960 and the setting up of national and provincial executives almost completed the process of decolonization. At the national level, Lumumba's MNC was able to control a slim majority of seats in both chambers, thanks to its alliance with smaller parties. Lumumba thus became the country's first prime minister, but the presidency went to Abako leader Kasavubu. At the provincial level, there emerged a more complex situation. Only in Orientale (now Haut-Zaïre Region) did the MNC win a solid majority. Katanga was split between separatists (identified with Tshombe's Conakat) and unitarists. Kasai was about to become the scene of a major ethnic confrontation between Lulua and Luba elements. And in Léopoldville Province, Abako failed to win a majority of seats, thus paving the way for serious tensions between Kongo and upriver deputies. In at least three provinces

29

out of six, the political arenas were fraught with incipient ethno-regional conflicts, and these in turn quickly generated a vicious circle at the center.

The Mutiny of the Force Publique

Maintaining stability in the provinces would have been difficult enough with the help of a reliable security apparatus; the mutiny of the Force Publique rendered the Lumumba government utterly impotent (see The Congolese National Army, ch. 5). The first acts of indiscipline were recorded in the capital on July 4; as other units were called in from Thysville (now Mbanza-Ngungu) to attend to the situation, they turned against their European officers. On July 5, bands of mutineers could be seen roaming through the streets of the capital, causing panic among both Africans and Europeans.

This extraordinary situation was, in large part, caused by Force Publique commander Lieutenant General Janssens, who had persistently refused to Africanize the officer corps, and who, on the very day that the mutiny broke out flatly declared that the Force Publique would continue as before. But with the mutiny in full swing, urgent and sweeping changes were needed to restore a measure of order. On July 6, Lumumba dismissed General Janssens, and the following day the entire officer corps was Africanized, with only a small number of European officers retained as advisers. Shortly thereafter, the decision was made to promote all enlisted men to the next higher rank, thereby eliminating all privates from the army. On July 9 Lumumba promoted Victor Lundula to major general and commander in chief of the renamed Congolese National Army (Armée Nationale Congolaise—ANC), with Joseph-Désiré Mobutu (later Mobutu Sese Seko) as chief of staff.

Unrest nonetheless persisted. By July 9 the mutiny had reached Équateur and Katanga provinces; panic-stricken Europeans began to arrive in Léopoldville, telling their own grisly stories. Ostensibly to protect Belgian lives, Brussels sent in two companies of paratroopers, in turn causing Lumumba to denounce Belgian intervention as an unwarranted aggression. The troop landings—a breach of the Treaty of Friendship and Cooperation signed by the two countries the day before independence—convinced the Congolese authorities that Belgium was attempting to reoccupy the country. Meanwhile, on July 11 Belgian naval forces took the unfortunate step of bombarding Matadi, which by then had already been evacuated by Europeans. On the same day, Katanga formally proclaimed its independence, an act supported by Belgians in Katanga. As tension rapidly mounted between Brussels and Léopoldville, Lumumba and Kasavubu agreed for once to send a formal cable to the UN secretary general on July 12 to solicit "urgent UN military assistance" in the face of Belgian aggression and support of the secession of Katanga.

A United Nations Security Council resolution on July 14, 1960, responding to the Congo government's request for aid, called for the withdrawal of Belgian troops and authorized Secretary General Dag Hammarskjöld to take the necessary steps, in consultation with the Congo government, to provide military and technical assistance for the Congolese security forces. Although the first UN troops landed in Léopoldville the next day, Kasavubu and Lumumba were dissatisfied with the pace of UN action and threatened to request Soviet help unless Belgian troops were withdrawn in two days. By July 20, the UN force had several thousand troops under its command, and Lumumba withdrew the threat when Belgium agreed to remove its troops from Léopoldville.

The Center No Longer Holds

In this rapidly deteriorating situation, mistrust, suspicion, and bitterness increased between the Congolese and the Belgians and among different factions of Congolese. The new government, preoccupied with soliciting external aid, had been unable to attack the massive problems of organizing its administration, and administrative problems were compounded by the mass departure of Belgian civil servants and technicians. In the meantime, the Katangan secessionist regime was consolidating its position.

Between the outbreak of the Force Publique mutiny and the overthrow of the Lumumba government on September 14, a situation of near anarchy spread through much of the country, reflecting the total breakdown of authority at the center. Adding to the confusion created by the collapse of the security forces and the intervention of the Belgian paratroopers, the constitutional impasse arising from the fundamental opposition between president and prime minister brought the machinery of government to a virtual standstill.

Several factors lay at the root of the conflict between president and prime minister, including a personality clash, their different bases of support, and their diametrically opposed conceptions of the ultimate character of the Congolese polity. What precipitated the crisis was growing opposition to Lumumba's policies toward Belgium, the UN, and the secessionists in Katanga and Kasai. Particularly divisive were Lumumba's insistence on converting the newly arrived UN forces into a military instrument for bringing Katanga and Kasai back into the fold of the central government (despite the fact that the UN mandate did not permit the organization to interfere in the Congo's internal conflicts) and his eventual decision to use those units of the ANC that were loyal to him to launch a major offensive against both Katanga and Kasai. Although Congolese units never made it to Katanga, their attack on Kasai in August 1960 led to a large-scale massacre of the Luba.

Against the warning of a number of his colleagues, Lumumba made a trip abroad with a number of his officials from July 21 to August 8, a critical time for the country and the new government. After his return, Lumumba intensified his quarrel with the UN authorities, especially when he failed to secure UN aid to force the end of the secession of Katanga. In late August, amid more intense opposition, Lumumba declared martial law for six months and arrested a number of his political opponents.

Lumumba's greatest affront, however, was his decision to accept substantial Soviet aid in order to attack the secessionist areas. This move brought to a climax the issue of communist influence, which had been a source of growing concern to the West and to more moderate Africans alike. As a result, on September 5 President Kasavubu announced the dismissal of Lumumba, Vice Prime Minister Antoine Gizenga, Minister of Information Anicet Kashamura, and several others from the government. At the same time, Kasavubu also appointed Mobutu as head of the ANC. Joseph Ileo was chosen as the new prime minister and began trying to form a new government.

Lumumba and his cabinet responded by accusing Kasavubu of high treason and voted to dismiss him. Parliament refused to confirm the dismissal of either Lumumba or Kasavubu and sought to bring about a reconciliation between them. After a week's deadlock, Mobutu announced on September 14 that he was assuming power until December 31, 1960, in order to "neutralize" both Kasavubu and Lumumba.

Mobutu emphasized from the beginning that his action was not an army coup but was rather a "peaceful revolution" during which the country would be run by a group of technicians. Mobutu's first acts were an ultimatum demanding the departure within forty-eight hours of Soviet and East European diplomatic personnel and the release by troops loyal to him of political prisoners.

But the period of government by the so-called College of Commissioners (made up of recent university graduates, students, and a few members of Lumumba's cabinet under the leadership of Justin-Marie Bomboko), formally installed on September 29, was marked by constant political conflict. The legitimacy of the government was challenged by political factions within the Congo and by the more radical African nations and communist countries. Relations between the college and the UN became progressively worse. In the meantime, the inability of the central government to regain any significant amount of authority enabled the secessionists to strengthen their administrative arrangements and armies.

As the process of fragmentation set in motion by the secession of Katanga reached its peak, the former Belgian colony essentially had broken up into four separate fragments (see fig. 5). The "unitarists" found themselves divided into two separate political arenas. The Lumumbist radicals joined forces with Antoine Gizenga, who was head of the African Solidarity Party (Parti Solidaire Africain—PSA), who had moved his forces to Stanleyville (now Kisangani). The moderates rallied to the Mobutu government in Léopoldville. South Kasai and Katanga, headed, respectively, by Albert Kalonji and Moïse Tshombe, were left in the hands of ethno-regional separatists.

The major event leading to the move by the Lumumbists to establish themselves at Stanleyville, the area of Lumumba's strongest support, was the recommendation by the United Nations Credentials Committee on November 10 to seat the delegation to the UN appointed by Mobutu. Gizenga left for Stanleyville on November 13 to form a rival national government. Soon thereafter, Lumumba, who had been under house arrest since his dismissal by Kasavubu, also left for Stanleyville to join Gizenga. But Lumumba was arrested, transferred to Katanga, and assassinated in January 1961. The assassination, when announced on February 13, 1961, prompted anarchy in many areas. But the incident helped Gizenga consolidate his regime, and a number of African and East European countries accorded it official recognition. The Tshombe government, on the other hand, remained utterly isolated diplomatically. And yet it was in Élisabethville, not Stanleyville, that the central authorities and the UN encountered their most serious challenge.

During the prolonged crisis after Lumumba's arrest and death, a new government was finally established in Léopoldville. On February 9, 1961, the College of Commissioners was dissolved, and a provisional government formed by Joseph Ileo. The events of February had so weakened Léopoldville's position, however, that the provisional government was unable to exert its authority much beyond the provinces of Léopoldville and Équateur.

The Secession of Katanga

Katanga had always been a special case, administered until 1910

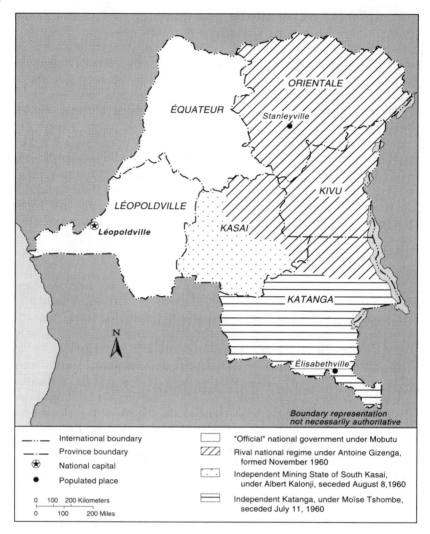

Source: Based on information from Hermann Kinder and Werner Hilgemann, *The Anchor Atlas of World History,* 2, Garden City, New York, 1978, 268.

Figure 5. Political Fragmentation and Territorial Control, 1960–61

by the privately owned Special Committee of Katanga (Comité Spécial du Katanga). In 1910 administration of Katanga was placed in the hands of a vice governor general, still separate from the rest of the Belgian Congo. The administrative reorganization of 1933, which brought Katanga administratively in line with the rest of the provinces under the central colonial authorities in Léopoldville, was strongly resented by Katangan residents, both local and foreign. The predominant role Katanga played in the country's economy reinforced this regional pride and sense of separateness. In the months preceding independence, pressure to restore Katangan autonomy grew.

The breakdown of central authority offered Tshombe an ideal pretext for proclaiming the long-planned independence of Katanga on July 11, 1960. Although Brussels withheld formal recognition, through the legal fiction that any province could receive Belgian technical assistance if it so desired, the Belgian government played a crucial role in providing military, economic, and technical assistance to the secessionist province.

Under Belgian supervision, immediate steps were taken to convert the Katangan Gendarmerie into an effective security force. Recruitment agencies were set up in Brussels for the enlistment of mercenaries. A variety of Belgian advisers surfaced in various administrative organs of the breakaway state. Professor René Clemens, of the University of Liège, was invited to draft the Katangan constitution.

That the secession lasted as long as it did (from July 11, 1960, to January 14, 1963) is largely a reflection of the efforts of Belgian civilian and military authorities to prop up their client state. Yet from the very beginning, the operation ran into serious difficulties. A major handicap faced by "authentic Katangese" stemmed from their inability to come to terms with the Balubakat-instigated revolt in the north. Despite the numerous military expeditions against northern "rebels," at no time was the Tshombe regime able to claim effective control of the Luba areas. Further discredit was cast on Tshombe when, in January 1961, Balubakat leaders proclaimed the secession of their own northern province, presumably out of loyalty to the principle of a united Congo. Balubakat seceding from the secessionists for the sake of unity was a painful logic for Conakat to assimilate.

Diplomatic isolation was another major weakness. In spite of countless demarches, overtures, bribes, and promises, the secessionist state never gained international recognition. Even Belgium never officially recognized Katanga. But perhaps the most serious diplomatic blow against the Tshombe regime came on February 21, 1961, when the UN Security Council passed a resolution urging the UN "to take immediately all appropriate measures to prevent the occurrence of civil war in the Congo, including arrangements for cease-fire, the halting of all military operations, the prevention of clashes, and the use of force, if necessary, in the last resort."

The UN Security Council's February resolution was an attempt to check the trend toward total anarchy in the Congo and to bring about international pressure for reintegration of the Congo. The resolution gave the UN forces greater authority to act in order to prevent civil war and called for the removal of foreign advisers and mercenaries attached to the Congo governments, the convening of parliament, and the reorganization of the ANC.

This entirely new construction of the UN mandate, allowing the use of force as a last resort, was the direct, though largely unanticipated, outcome of Lumumba's death. The worldwide commotion caused by Lumumba's death had an immediate repercussion in the UN General Assembly. The new mandate given to the UN forces in Zaire did little more than articulate in legal terms the sense of shock and anger of most developing nations in the face of the cold-blooded murder of the man who best symbolized the struggle of African nationalism against the forces of neocolonialism.

The UN Intervention

Ambiguous as it was, the phrasing of the UN February 21 resolution left little doubt about the sense of frustration felt by Secretary General Dag Hammarskjöld in dealing with the Katanga secession. Keeping the peace without meddling in the internal affairs of Katanga proved a contradiction; UN efforts to act as a mediator between Katanga and the central government met with repeated setbacks. As one reconciliation formula after another was tried and found wanting, it dawned on many people at the UN that the scope of permissible action had to be substantially broadened, which is what the February 21 resolution sought to achieve.

The new mandate provided the basis for Operation Rumpunch on August 28, 1961. As it became clear that Tshombe had no intention of complying with the UN request that mercenaries and European officers be withdrawn from Katanga—a move that he realized would cripple his security forces and quickly bring the collapse of his regime—UN troops at last sprang into action, securing the Katangan post office, radio, and residences of key European and Congolese officials and rounding up mercenaries and European officers. The operation, however, was suddenly halted when the Belgian consul in Léopoldville persuaded local UN officials that he would complete the operation by himself, a pledge that turned out to be a ruse as only regular Belgian officers and not mercenaries were expelled from the province.

Anger and frustration on both sides mounted rapidly. A new UN plan, Operation Morthor, following rapidly after Rumpunch and expected to go into effect on September 13, was no longer merely to rid the province of mercenaries and foreign advisers but to terminate the secession by force. Forewarned of the impending attack, the Katangan gendarmes put up a stiff resistance, while a lone jet fighter strafed the UN troops. News of UN attacks on civilian installations was received with indignation in European capitals. Morthor ended in a total fiasco. It was at this point, on September 17, that Hammarskjöld decided to give up force and once again try to arrive at a negotiated solution with Tshombe. Hammarskjöld never made it to the site of their meeting in Ndola, Northern Rhodesia (now Zambia), however; shortly before it was due to land, his aircraft crashed into a wooded hillside, killing all passengers.

The next and final phase in the Katangan imbroglio began with the so-called "U Thant Plan," made public on August 10, 1962, and ended with Tshombe's announcement, on January 14, 1963, that "the secession was now terminated." The plan, which offered yet another constitutional formula for reunification, at first met with Tshombe's approval; then equivocation ensued, and the work of the joint Léopoldville-Élisabethville commissions soon bogged down. As tensions mounted between UN troops and Katangan gendarmes, little was needed to trigger an explosion. It came on Christmas Eve, when UN troops accused the Katangan forces of shooting down a UN helicopter. On December 28 Tshombe called for a general uprising of the population, to which the UN responded by moving against key points. This time the tide moved decisively against the gendarmes. In the end, Tshombe had no alternative but to concede defeat. After two and a half years of conflict and crisis, the Katangan secession had finally come to an end. Many of the remaining Katangan gendarmes went into exile in Angola. Others were incorporated into the Congolese military.

The First Republic, 1960–65

Much of the history of the First Republic revolves around two critical issues: the abortive efforts of the central government to negotiate the end of the Katangan secession and the reentry of Katanga into the framework of a united Congo, and the threats posed to the survival of the republic by the 1964 outbreak of major rebellions in Kwilu (some 400 kilometers east of Léopoldville) and the eastern region. Not the least of the ironies brought to light in the course of this tormented era in the country's history is that the man who once stood as the standard-bearer of the secession of Katanga ended up as the key figure in the struggle of the central authorities against rebel forces. With the appointment of Tshombe as prime minister in July 1964, following the resignation of the government of Cyrille Adoula, the First Republic entered the last phase of its brief and tumultuous existence.

The Adoula Government, August 1961–July 1964

In the months preceding the investiture of the Adoula government, several conferences were held between the representatives of the central caretaker government and the Katangan authorities for the specific purpose of reaching agreement on the constitutional framework of a reunified Congo. These meetings included the Léopoldville Round Table (January–February 1961), the Tananarive Conference (in Madagascar in March), and the Coquilhatville Conference (Coquilhatville is now Mbandaka, April–May). The Tananarive Conference called for a confederated form of government, but the notion of confederation met with strong opposition in Léopoldville. By contrast, the Coquilhatville Conference recommended the establishment of a federal system as the future form of government. Tshombe opposed this plan.

Finally, after extensive negotiations, parliament met at Lovanium University outside Léopoldville on July 25, 1961, with the participation of deputies from all provinces, including Katanga and South Kasai (which ended its secession at that time). On August 2, Adoula was elected prime minister by a unanimous vote of confidence, thus bringing to an end the constitutional crisis triggered by the conflict between Lumumba and Kasavubu. There remained the more arduous task of resolving once and for all the Katangan secession, reducing the last vestiges of dissidence in Stanleyville, and elaborating the constitutional framework that would replace the Fundamental Law.

As noted earlier, not until January 1963, and only after a violent showdown with UN forces, was the secession of Katanga decisively crushed; and it took another year before the rival claimant to national power, the Stanleyville government, was brought to heel. Meanwhile, Adoula gave immediate priority to the task outlined in his inaugural declaration, "to take adequate measures permitting each region to administer itself according to its profound aspirations," and to initiate the constitutional revisions required by this objective. The result was the elimination of the former six provinces and their replacement by twenty-one smaller administrative entities, known as *provincettes*. The new formula proved thoroughly unworkable, however. Reducing the size of the provinces merely shifted the focus of ethnic conflict to a smaller arena, a phenomenon further encouraged by the sheer arbitrariness of their boundaries and the emergence of several bitterly contested areas. While sharply reinforcing ethnic animosities, the creation of the new *provincettes* was made more problematic still by the dearth of competent administrators, frequent recourse to force and skulduggery, and rampant corruption.

Despite its inauspicious beginnings, the new arrangement was formalized in the new constitution adopted by referendum in June and July 1964. And arrangements were made to change the country's name to Democratic Republic of the Congo with effect from August 1, 1964. By then, however, many of the *provincettes* were in a state of semi-anarchy, and at least three had fallen into the hands of rebel forces. The stage was set for yet another trial of strength between the central government and dissident forces.

Rural Insurgencies: The "Second Independence"

From January to August 1964, rural insurgency engulfed five *provincettes* out of twenty-one and made substantial inroads into another five, raising the distinct possibility of a total collapse of the central government (see fig. 6). The extraordinary speed with which the rebellions spread among the rural masses attests to the enormous insurrectionary potential that had been building up in previous years. Prolonged neglect of the rural sectors, coupled with the growing disparities of wealth and privilege between the political elites and the peasant masses, inefficient and corrupt government, and ANC abuses, created a situation ripe for major uprising. Further aggravating the frustration of the rural masses, the promise of a life more abundant made at the time of independence had remained unfulfilled. It seemed to many, especially disaffected youths, that nothing short of a "second independence" would bring them salvation.

Among the several factors that combined to precipitate rebellion, none was more consequential than the dissolution of parliament in September 1963, a move spurred by the incessant divisions and bickerings among deputies. The immediate result was to deprive the opposition of the only remaining legitimate avenue for political participation. Faced with this situation, several deputies affiliated with the MNC-Lumumba, among them Christophe Gbenye and Bocheley Davidson, decided to move to Brazzaville, in the former French Congo, and organize a National Liberation Council (Conseil National de Libération—CNL). In time the CNL became the central coordinating apparatus for the eastern rebellion.

Another major factor behind the insurrection was the anticipated withdrawal of the UN forces by June 30, 1964. The prospective elimination of the only reliable crutch available to the central government acted as a major incentive for the opposition to mobilize against Adoula.

39

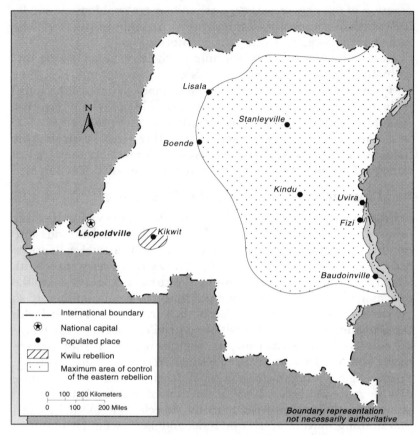

Source: Based on information from Hermann Kinder and Werner Hilgemann, *The Anchor Atlas of World History*, 2, Garden City, New York, 1978, 268.

Figure 6. Rural Insurgencies, 1964

Finally, with the arrival in the Kwilu area of Pierre Mulele in July 1963, a key revolutionary figure entered the arena. Once affiliated with Antoine Gizenga's PSA, Mulele traveled widely in Eastern Europe before reaching China, where he received sustained training in guerrilla warfare. Upon arriving in Kwilu, Mulele proceeded to recruit a solid phalanx of followers among members of his own ethnic group, the Mbunda, as well as among Gizenga's kinsmen, the Pende, both of whom had long been the target of government repression. The Kwilu rebellion began in January 1964, when Mulelist insurgents attacked government outposts, mission stations, and company installations. On January 22 and 23, four European missionaries were killed, and on February 5 the chief of staff of the ANC was ambushed and killed. Troops were immediately sent to the area, and by April a measure of stability had been restored. The Kwilu rebellion did not finally end until December 1965, however.

The central figure behind the eastern rebellion was Gaston Soumialot, who, in January 1964, was sent to Burundi by the CNL, with the mission of organizing the rebellion. With the full support of the Burundi authorities, and thanks to his own skill in exploiting local conflicts and working out tactical alliances with Tutsi exiles from Rwanda, Soumialot was able to recruit thousands of dedicated supporters in eastern Kivu, along the border with Burundi. On May 15, the town of Uvira fell to the rebels, and, shortly thereafter, so did Fizi. From then on, the rebels (now widely known as Simbas, from the Swahili for lions) made increasing use of magic to claim immunity to bullets. Panic-stricken, two heavily armed ANC battalions were routed by spear-toting Simbas believed to have been rendered invincible by their antibullet concoctions.

As the rebel movement spread, discipline became more difficult to maintain, and acts of violence and terror increased. Thousands of Congolese were executed, including government officials, political leaders of opposition parties, provincial and local police, school teachers, and others believed to have been Westernized.

In Kivu, Maniema, and north Katanga, the administrative vacuum caused by the utter failure of the *provincette* experiment was a key factor behind the initial success of the rebellion. In north Katanga, Baudoinville (later Virungu, now Moba) fell on July 19; Kindu, in Maniema, was taken on July 24; and in early August the Soumialot forces, now calling themselves the National Liberation Army (Armée Nationale de Libération—ANL), captured the Lumumbist stronghold of Stanleyville. Equipped with armaments left by the routed ANC units, the Simbas pushed on north and west of Stanleyville, eventually penetrating as far west as Lisala on the Congo River. On September 5, with the proclamation of a revolutionary government in Stanleyville, the eastern rebellion reached its high-water mark: almost half of Zaire and seven local capitals out of twenty-one were in rebel hands.

No less astonishing than the swiftness of rebel victories was the inability of the insurgents to consolidate their gains and establish an alternative system of administration to the one they had so easily destroyed. Corruption, administrative inefficiency, and ethnic favoritism turned out to be liabilities for the rebel leaders as much as they had been for previous provincial administrators. Heavy reliance on specific ethnic communities (Tetela-Kusu in the east, Pende and Mbunda in Kwilu) for manning the military and administrative apparatuses of the rebellions was seen by many as a reversion to tribalism. Further complicating ethnic tensions between the ANL leadership and the Simbas, serious conflicts erupted at the *provin-cette* level over who should get the lion's share of the property seized from the enemy. Finally, countless disputes disrupted the CNL leadership in exile, stemming from personality differences as well as disagreements over questions of tactics and organization.

The rapid decline of popular support for the eastern rebellion is in large part a reflection of the very inadequate leadership offered by the CNL and local cadres. The military setbacks suffered by the ANL in the fall of 1964 were not just the result of poor leader-ship, however; even more important in turning the tide against the insurgents was the decisive contribution made by European mercenaries in helping the central government regain control over rebel-held areas. Much of the credit for the government's success went to Tshombe, who in July 1964 had been recalled from exile and replaced Adoula as prime minister. A year and a half after his defeat at the hands of the UN forces, the most vocal advocate of secessionism had suddenly emerged as the providential leader of a besieged central government.

As he set about the task of quashing the rebellions, Tshombe could rely on two major assets denied to Adoula, i.e., the Katan-gan gendarmes, recalled from exile in Angola, and a few hundred battle-hardened white mercenaries. The former were immediately integrated into the ANC, with the latter providing the much-needed leadership for the conduct of military operations against rebel forces. Supported by air strikes, these units spearheaded attacks against rebel strongholds. As the white mercenaries took the offensive and, with their technical superiority and discipline, began to recapture rebel strongholds, the fighting grew progressively more brutal, and numerous atrocities were committed by all of those involved. Merce-nary elements played a decisive role in retaking Lisala on Septem-ber 15, Boende on October 24, and Kindu on November 6. By then, the revolutionary government in Stanleyville had decided to hold local European residents hostage, in the hope of using them as bargaining chips in negotiations with the central authorities. Their action resulted in the joint Belgian-American parachute rescue operation (code-named Dragon Rouge, or Red Dragon) on Stan-leyville, on November 24, scheduled to coincide with the arrival of ANC and mercenary units in the vicinity of the provincial capi-tal. The capture of Stanleyville dealt a devastating blow to the eastern rebellion. The two key rebel leaders, Gbenye and Soumi-alot, went into exile in Cairo; demoralization quickly set in among the Simbas; by the end of the year, the eastern rebellion was reduced to isolated pockets of resistance. Nonetheless, for months thereafter insecurity was widespread in the northeast, as well as along the Fizi-Uvira axis in Kivu.

Tshombe's popularity within the Congo and his prestige throughout Africa were severely damaged by the Belgo-American operation against Stanleyville, which had also provoked heated debates in the UN. Moreover, political opposition to Tshombe's conduct of the government greatly increased in the capital. In particular, Tshombe had antagonized both Kasavubu and Mobutu.

Mobutu's Second Coming

Mobutu's second coup, on November 25, 1965, occurred in circumstances strikingly similar to those that had led to his first takeover—a struggle for power between the incumbent president, Joseph Kasavubu, and Prime Minister Moïse Tshombe. The Kasavubu-Tshombe friction began to gain momentum during the legislative elections in the spring of 1965. The immediate task facing the new parliament was the election of a new president, whose role was defined by the constitution as the chief executive, leaving the prime minister in charge of the day-to-day tasks of government. Determined to seize the presidency from Kasavubu, Tshombe had organized a new party, the National Confederation of Congolese Associations (Confédération Nationale des Associations Congolaises—Conaco), which in effect was little more than a loose alliance of forty-nine, primarily southern, parties from among the more than 200 parties that mushroomed into existence to participate in the electoral process.

Although Conaco emerged triumphant from the March 1965 elections, with a total of 122 out of 167 parliamentary seats, Kasavubu decided to appoint Évariste Kimba, a leading figure of the anti-Tshombe forces, as prime minister-designate. Complex maneuverings followed the nomination of Kimba. When the time came for a vote of confidence, on November 14, the Tshombe coalition, with its clear majority in parliament, managed to block his investiture by a vote of 121 to 134. Another candidate, Victor Nendaka, then sought the investiture, only to be faced with further obduracy from Kasavubu, who went on to renominate Kimba. As in 1960, the constitutional impasse threatened the machinery of government with total paralysis.

The constitutional deadlock paved the way for Mobutu's second military takeover. On November 24, fourteen members of the ANC high command met in Léopoldville with Mobutu in an emergency session. The following day, the announcement was made that Kasavubu and Kimba had been removed from office as president and prime minister-designate, and that Mobutu had been named as chief of state by the army. Colonel Léonard Mulamba became prime minister of the new "government of national union." Parliament, meanwhile, approved by acclamation the new government, which announced that it could remain in office for five years under a state of emergency.

The new regime received considerable initial approval from other African states and from the United States. Indeed, United States support for the new regime was to prove remarkably durable (see Relations with the West, ch. 4).

The Second Republic, 1965–90: The Rebirth of *Bula Matari*

In retrospective justification of his 1965 seizure of power, Mobutu later summed up the record of the First Republic as one of "chaos, disorder, negligence, and incompetence." Rejection of the legacy of the First Republic went far beyond rhetoric. In the first two years of its existence, the new regime turned to the urgent tasks of political reconstruction and consolidation. Creating a new basis of legitimacy for the state, in the form of a single party, came next in Mobutu's order of priority. A third imperative was to expand the reach of the state in the social and political realms, a process that began in 1970 and culminated in the adoption of a new constitution in 1974. By 1976, however, this effort had begun to generate its own inner contradictions, thus paving the way for the resurrection of a *bula matari* ("he who breaks rocks") system of repression and brutality.

Mobutu, Self-Proclaimed Father of the Nation

Ever since 1965, Mobutu Sese Seko has dominated the political life of Zaire, restructuring the state on more than one occasion, and earning his self-appointed title of "Father of the Nation." Any discussion of Zaire's political structures and processes must therefore be based on an understanding of the man who literally gave the country its name.

Mobutu was born in the town of Lisala, on the Congo River, on October 4, 1930. His father, Albéric Gbemani, was a cook for a colonial magistrate in Lisala. Despite his birthplace, however, Mobutu belonged not to the dominant ethnic group of that region but rather to the Ngbandi, a small ethnic community whose domain lay far to the north, along the border with the Central African Republic.

Mobutu referred frequently both to his humble background as

the son of a cook and to the renown of his father's uncle, a warrior and diviner from the village of Gbadolite. Although officially known as Joseph-Désiré Mobutu, Mobutu was also given the name of his great-uncle, Sese Seko Nkuku wa za Banga, meaning "all-conquering warrior, who goes from triumph to triumph." When, under the authenticity (see Glossary) policy of the early 1970s, Zairians were obliged to adopt "authentic" names, Mobutu dropped Joseph-Désiré and became Mobutu Sese Seko Nkuku wa za Banga—or, more commonly, Mobutu Sese Seko (see Zairianization, Radicalization, and Retrocession, this ch.).

Mobutu, who had completed four years of primary school in Léopoldville, took seven more years to reach the secondary level, moving in and out of different schools. He had frequent conflicts with the Catholic missionaries whose schools he attended, and in 1950, at the age of nineteen, he was definitively expelled. A seven-year disciplinary conscription into the Force Publique followed.

Military service proved crucial in shaping Mobutu's career. Unlike many recruits, he spoke excellent French, which quickly won him a desk job. By November 1950, he was sent to the school for noncommissioned officers, where he came to know many members of the military generation who would assume control of the army after the flight of the Belgian officers in 1960. By the time of his discharge in 1956, Mobutu, had risen to the rank of sergeant-major, the highest rank open to Congolese. He also had begun to write newspaper articles under a pseudonym.

Mobutu returned to civilian life just as decolonization began to seem possible. His newspaper articles had brought him to the attention of Pierre Davister, a Belgian editor of the Léopoldville paper *L'Avenir*. At that time, a European patron was of enormous benefit to an ambitious Congolese; under Davister's tutelage, Mobutu became an editorial writer for the new African weekly, *Actualités Africaines*. Davister later would provide valuable services by giving favorable coverage to the Mobutu regime as editor of his own Belgian magazine, *Spécial*.

Mobutu thus acquired visibility among the emergent African elite of Léopoldville. Yet one portal to status in colonial society remained closed to him: full recognition as an *évolué* depended upon approval by the Roman Catholic Church. Denied this recognition, Mobutu rejected the church.

During 1959–60, politically ambitious young Congolese were busy constructing political networks for themselves. Residence in Belgium prevented Mobutu from taking the path of many of his peers at home, who were building ethno-regional clienteles. But their approach would have been unpromising for him in any case, since the Ngbandi were a small and peripheral community, and among the so-called Ngala (Lingala-speaking immigrants in Léopoldville) such figures as Jean Bolikango were potential opponents. Mobutu pursued another route, as Belgian diplomatic, intelligence, and financial interests sought clients among the Congolese students and interns in Brussels.

Fatefully, Mobutu also had met Patrice Lumumba, when the latter arrived in Brussels. He allied himself with Lumumba (whose school background, like that of Mobutu, inclined him to anticlericalism), when the Congolese National Movement (Mouvement National Congolais—MNC) split into two wings identified, respectively, with Lumumba and Albert Kalonji. By early 1960, Mobutu had been named head of the MNC-Lumumba office in Brussels. He attended the Round Table Conference on independence held in Brussels in January 1960 and returned home only three weeks before Independence Day, June 30. When the army mutinied against its Belgian officers, Mobutu was a logical choice to help fill the void. Lumumba, elected prime minister in May 1960, named as commander in chief a member of his own ethnic group, Victor Lundula, but Mobutu was Lumumba's choice as chief of staff.

During the crucial period of July–August 1960, Mobutu built up "his" national army by channeling foreign aid to units loyal to him, by exiling unreliable units to remote areas, and by absorbing or dispersing rival armies. He tied individual officers to him by controlling their promotion and the flow of money for payrolls. Lundula, older and less competitive, apparently did little to rival Mobutu.

After President Kasavubu dismissed Lumumba as premier on September 5 and Lumumba sought to block this action through parliament, Mobutu staged his first coup on September 14. On his own authority (but with United States backing), he installed an interim government, the so-called College of Commissioners, composed primarily of university students and graduates, which replaced parliament for six months in 1960–61.

During the next four years, as weak civilian governments rose and fell in Léopoldville, real power was held behind the scenes by the "Binza Group," a group of Mobutu supporters named for the prosperous suburb where its members lived.

When in 1965, as in 1960, the division of power between president and prime minister led to a stalemate and threatened the country's stability, Mobutu again seized power (again with United States backing). Unlike the first time, however, Mobutu assumed the presidency, rather than remaining behind the scenes.

Toward Political Reconstruction

From 1965 to 1967, the Mobutist state set out to establish its authority by gradually dismantling the institutions of the First Republic and at the same time bringing about a substantial measure of centralization around the president. Although parliament continued to meet occasionally, its legislative powers were reduced to a mere ritual because key decisions were taken through executive decrees (*ordonnances-lois*). All political parties were dissolved and political activities banned, in line with Mobutu's promise that "for five years there will be no political party activity." By 1966 the twenty-one *provincettes* had been reduced to twelve and then to eight provinces plus the capital, which were redesignated as regions in 1972 (see fig. 1). They were transformed into purely administrative entities whose officials were directly responsible to the central government and whose assemblies were consultative rather than legislative bodies. After the elimination of the office of prime minister in October 1966, the presidency became the fulcrum of all executive power.

Most of the remnants of the Tshombist opposition were quickly absorbed into the state through various patronage operations. Just as quickly, summary justice disposed of the more obdurate opponents of the regime. On May 30, 1966, four key personalities of the First Republic, including former Prime Minister-designate Évariste Kimba, were charged with conspiring against the state, tried in a parody of justice, and publicly hanged in Kinshasa (formerly Léopoldville). Threats to the regime nonetheless persisted. Pockets of insurgency continued to confront the regime with serious challenges to its authority in Kivu (since the early 1990s, divided into Nord-Kivu, Sud-Kivu, and Maniema) and Haut-Zaïre (formerly Orientale Province). Months went by before these residual areas of dissidence were brought under control.

Meanwhile, rumors that Tshombe was plotting a comeback from his Spanish retreat hardened into ominous certainty when in July 1966 some of Tshombe's former Katangan gendarmes, led by a handful of mercenaries, mutinied in Kisangani (formerly Stanleyville). Two months later, the gendarmes were finally brought to heel after French mercenary Bob Denard was persuaded to take the lead in crushing the mutiny. By July 1967, however, another major mutiny broke out in Kisangani, triggered by the news that Tshombe's airplane had been hijacked over the Mediterranean and forced to land in Algiers, where Tshombe was held prisoner. As the rebels were forced out of Kisangani by the ANC, they made their way to Bukavu, near the Rwandan border, which they held for three months. They unsuccessfully tried to fight back the attacks of the ANC, but by November, faced with imminent defeat, the entire group crossed the border into Rwanda where it surrendered to local authorities. The unexpectedly brilliant performance of the ANC in Bukavu gave the regime a renewed sense of pride and self-confidence. The time was ripe for consolidating its institutional legitimacy.

Already in January 1966, a major step toward political consolidation had taken place with the creation of the Corps of Volunteers of the Republic (Corps des Volontaires de la République—CVR), a loosely knit organization whose membership was mainly recruited from the students associated with the General Union of Congolese Students (Union Générale des Étudiants Congolais—UGEC). Many of the ideas set forth by the CVR came to reflect a brand of student radicalism in which the themes of nationalism, economic independence, and socialization received pride of place. Rather than a party, the CVR is better seen as a vanguard movement designed to mobilize popular energies behind Mobutu, ''our Second National Hero'' (after Lumumba). The very mixed record of the CVR as an agent of political mobilization, reflecting in part its excessive reliance on student activists, must have been an important consideration in prompting Mobutu to launch a more broadly based movement—a movement which, in Mobutu's words, ''will be animated by the Chief of State himself, and of which the CVR is not at all the embryo.''

The Quest for Legitimacy

By 1967 Mobutu had consolidated his rule and proceeded to give the country a new constitution and a single party. The new constitution was submitted to popular referendum in June 1967 and approved by 98 percent of those voting. It provided that executive powers be centralized in the president, who was to be head of state, head of government, commander in chief of the armed forces and the police, and in charge of foreign policy. The president was to appoint and dismiss cabinet members and determine their areas of responsibility. The ministers, as heads of their respective departments, were to execute the programs and decisions of the president. The president also was to have the power to appoint and dismiss the governors of the provinces and the judges of all courts, including those of the Supreme Court of Justice.

The bicameral parliament was replaced by a unicameral legislative body called the National Assembly. Governors of provinces were no longer elected by provincial assemblies but appointed by the central government. The president had the power to issue

*President
Mobutu Sese Seko
with the secretary general
of the United Nations,
Kurt Waldheim, 1979
Courtesy
The United Nations*

autonomous regulations on matters other than those pertaining to the domain of law, without prejudice to other provisions of the constitution. Under certain conditions, the president was empowered to govern by executive order, which carried the force of law.

But the most far-reaching change was the creation of the Popular Revolutionary Movement (Mouvement Populaire de la Révolution—MPR) on April 17, 1967, marking the emergence of "the nation politically organized." Rather than being the emanation of the state, the state was henceforth defined as the emanation of the party. Thus, in October 1967 party and administrative responsibilities were merged into a single framework, thereby automatically extending the role of the party to all administrative organs at the central and provincial levels, as well as to the trade unions, youth movements, and student organizations. In short, the MPR had now become the sole legitimate vehicle for participating in the political life of the country. Or, as one official put it, "the MPR must be considered as a Church and its Founder as its Messiah."

The doctrinal foundation was disclosed shortly after its birth, in the form of the Manifesto of N'Sele (so named because it was issued from the president's rural residence at N'Sele, sixty kilometers upriver from Kinshasa), made public in May 1967. Nationalism, revolution, and authenticity were identified as the major themes of what came to be known as Mobutism (see Glossary).

Nationalism implied the achievement of economic independence. Revolution, described as a "truly national revolution, essentially pragmatic," meant "the repudiation of both capitalism and communism. "Neither right nor left" thus became one of the legitimizing slogans of the regime, along with "authenticity." The concept of authenticity was derived from the MPR's professed doctrine of "authentic Zairian nationalism and condemnation of regionalism and tribalism." Mobutu defined it as being conscious of one's own personality and one's own values and of being at home in one's culture. In line with the dictates of authenticity, the name of the country was changed to the Republic of Zaire in October 1971, and that of the armed forces to Zairian Armed Forces (Forces Armées Zaïroises—FAZ). Many other geographic name changes had already taken place, between 1966 and 1971. The adoption of Zairian, as opposed to Western or Christian, names in 1972 and the abandonment of Western dress in favor of the wearing of the *abacost* (see Glossary) were subsequently promoted as expressions of authenticity.

Authenticity provided Mobutu with his strongest claim to philosophical originality. So far from implying a rejection of modernity, authenticity is perhaps best seen as an effort to reconcile the claims of the traditional Zairian culture with the exigencies of modernization. Exactly how this synthesis was to be accomplished remained unclear, however. What is beyond doubt is Mobutu's effort to use the concept of authenticity as a means of vindicating his own brand of leadership. As he himself stated, "in our African tradition there are never two chiefs . . . . That is why we Congolese, in the desire to conform to the traditions of our continent, have resolved to group all the energies of the citizens of our country under the banner of a single national party."

Critics of the regime were quick to point out the shortcomings of Mobutism as a legitimizing formula, in particular its self-serving qualities and inherent vagueness; nonetheless, the MPR's ideological training center, the Makanda Kabobi Institute, took seriously its assigned task of propagating through the land "the teachings of the Founder-President, which must be given and interpreted in the same fashion throughout the country." Members of the MPR Political Bureau, meanwhile, were entrusted with the responsibility of serving as "the repositories and guarantors of Mobutism."

Quite aside from the merits or weaknesses of Mobutism, the MPR drew much of its legitimacy from the model of the overarching mass parties that had come into existence in Africa in the 1960s, a model which had also been a source of inspiration for the MNC-Lumumba. It was this Lumumbist heritage which the MPR tried to appropriate in its effort to mobilize the Zairian masses behind its founder-president. Intimately tied up with the doctrine of Mobutism was the vision of an all-encompassing single party reaching out to all sectors of the nation (see The Party-State as a System of Rule, ch. 4).

The Expansion of State Authority

Translating the concept of "the nation politically organized" into reality implied a major expansion of state control of civil society. It meant, to begin with, the incorporation of youth groups and worker organizations into the matrix of the MPR. In July 1967, the Political Bureau announced the creation of the Youth of the Popular Revolutionary Movement (Jeunesse du Mouvement Populaire de la Révolution—JMPR), following the launching a month earlier of the National Union of Zairian Workers (Union Nationale des Travailleurs Zaïrois—UNTZA), which brought together into a single organizational framework three preexisting trade unions. Ostensibly, the aim of the merger, in the terms of the Manifesto of N'Sele, was to transform the role of trade unions from "being merely a force of confrontation" into "an organ of support for government policy," thus providing " a communication link between the working class and the state." Similarly, the JMPR was to act as a major link between the student population and the state. In reality, the government was attempting to bring under its control those sectors where opposition to the regime might be centered. By appointing key labor and youth leaders to the MPR Political Bureau, the regime hoped to harness syndical and student forces to the machinery of the state. Nevertheless, as has been pointed out by numerous observers, there is little evidence that co-optation succeeded in mobilizing support for the regime beyond the most superficial level (see Political Dynamics, ch. 4).

The trend toward co-optation of key social sectors continued in subsequent years. Women's associations were eventually brought under the control of the party, as was the press, and in December 1971 Mobutu proceeded to emasculate the power of the churches. From then on, only three churches were recognized: the Church of Christ in Zaire, the Kimbanguist Church, and the Roman Catholic Church (see Religion, ch. 2). Nationalization of the universities of Kinshasa and Kisangani, coupled with Mobutu's insistence on banning all Christian names and establishing JMPR sections in all seminaries, soon brought the Roman Catholic Church and the state into conflict. Not until 1975, and after considerable pressure from the Vatican, did the regime agree to tone down its attacks on the Roman Catholic Church and return some of its

51

control of the school system to the church. Meanwhile, in line with a December 1971 law, which allowed the state to dissolve ''any church or sect that compromises or threatens to compromise public order,'' scores of unrecognized religious sects were dissolved and their leaders jailed.

Mobutu was careful also to suppress all institutions that could mobilize ethnic loyalties. Avowedly opposed to ethnicity as a basis for political alignment, he outlawed such ethnic associations as the Association of Lulua Brothers (Association des Lulua Frères), which had been organized in Kasai in 1953 in reaction to the growing political and economic influence in Kasai of the rival Luba people, and Liboke lya Bangala (literally, ''a bundle of Bangala''), an association formed in the 1950s to represent the interests of Lingala speakers in large cities. It helped Mobutu that his ethnic affiliation was blurred in the public mind. Nevertheless, as dissatisfaction arose, ethnic tensions surfaced again.

Running parallel to the efforts of the state to control all autonomous sources of power, important administrative reforms were introduced in 1967 and 1973 to strengthen the hand of the central authorities in the provinces. The central objective of the 1967 reform was to abolish provincial governments and replace them with state functionaries appointed by Kinshasa. The principle of centralization was further extended to districts and territories, each headed by administrators appointed by the central government. The only units of government that still retained a fair measure of autonomy—but not for long—were the so-called local collectivities, i.e., chiefdoms and sectors (the latter incorporating several chiefdoms). The unitary, centralized state system thus legislated into existence bore a striking resemblance to its colonial antecedent, except that from July 1972 provinces were called regions.

With the January 1973 reform, another major step was taken in the direction of further centralization. The aim, in essence, was to effect a complete fusion of political and administrative hierarchies by making the head of each administrative unit the president of the local party committee. Furthermore, another consequence of the reform was to severely curtail the power of traditional authorities at the local level. Hereditary claims to authority would no longer be recognized; instead, all chiefs were to be appointed and controlled by the state via the administrative hierarchy. By then, the process of centralization had theoretically eliminated all preexisting centers of local autonomy.

The analogy with the colonial state becomes even more compelling if we take into account the introduction in 1973 of ''obligatory civic work'' (locally known as Salongo after the Lingala term for work), in the form of one afternoon a week of compulsory labor on agricultural and development projects. Officially described as a revolutionary attempt to return to the values of communalism and solidarity inherent in the traditional society, Salongo was intended to mobilize the population into the performance of collective work "with enthusiasm and without constraint." But, in fact Salongo was forced labor. The conspicuous lack of popular enthusiasm for Salongo led to widespread resistance and foot dragging, causing many local administrators to look the other way. Although failure to comply carried penalties of one month to six months in jail, by the late 1970s few were the Zairians who did not shirk their Salongo obligations. By resuscitating one of the most bitterly resented features of the colonial state, obligatory civic work contributed in no small way to the erosion of legitimacy suffered by the Mobutist state.

Zairianization, Radicalization, and Retrocession

The conquest of economic independence figured prominently on Mobutu's agenda from the outset. Government moves to establish greater control over foreign enterprises operating in the country brought about a confrontation with the Belgian-owned Upper Katanga Mining Union (Union Minière du Haut-Katanga—UMHK), which was nationalized in January 1967, and a new state-owned company formed (see Postindependence, ch. 3).

It was not until November 1973, however, that specific and more extensive measures were announced to restore the control of the economy to Zairian nationals. "Zaire is the country that has been the most heavily exploited in the world," Mobutu declared on November 30. "That is why," he added, "farms, ranches, plantations, concessions, commerce, and real estate agencies will be turned over to sons of the country." In this way began the campaign that became known as Zairianization (see Glossary; Zairianization, ch. 3).

At first, "the sons of the country" consisted essentially of high-ranking party members and government officials, in all approximately 300 people. Major plantations and ranches and large commercial business enterprises were given to the top political elite. Smaller enterprises were allocated to local notables. Army officers, judges, members of the regional administration, and ambassadors failed to qualify as potential recipients (*acquéreurs*).

The self-serving character of this decision caused immediate public indignation. Faced with mounting opposition to his Zairianization policies, Mobutu announced that the economic activities covered by the November 30 measures would be entirely taken over by the state. Those citizens who wished to acquire a plantation or a farm would have to buy it from the state. Considerable confusion followed in the wake of this announcement. For one thing, the criteria used for assessing individual qualifications—party militancy, integrity, commercial experience, solvency—could be interpreted in many different ways; for another, the screening procedure was at best arbitrary, and when a candidate failed to meet the stipulated conditions, a bribe (*matabiche*) was often the quickest way to clinch a favorable decision from the local authorities. As Crawford Young and Thomas Turner observed, "what transpired was a tumultuous, disorderly and profoundly demeaning scramble for the loot . . . . Success in the scramble was above all a measure of political influence and proximity to the ultimate sources of power."

Zairianization engendered economic disaster on an unprecedented scale. In a matter of months, commercial networks were utterly disrupted; massive layoffs were reported; and shortages of basic commodities became increasingly widespread, along with liquidations of assets. Asset stripping in the retail sector became a common practice. Efforts of the regime to introduce price controls did little to curb inflation. The plantation sector of the economy, meanwhile, was brought to a virtual standstill.

Confronted with a wholesale plunder of the Zairian economy, on December 30, 1974, Mobutu announced a ten-point "radicalization" program intended to bring about "a revolution in the revolution." Officially, major economic initiatives remained the exclusive domain of the state. The main thrust of radicalization was aimed at the self-serving attitude of the *acquéreurs*. Party leaders were expected to turn their properties over to the state and devote themselves to agricultural activities. Party cadres were chastised for their "mercenary behavior" and lack of civic sense. More importantly, the large-scale, Belgian-owned corporations that had been left untouched by the Zairianization decrees were now targeted for nationalization. Thus, the calamitous effects of Zairianization were extended to the commanding heights of the economy. While being constantly reminded of their revolutionary duties, members of the political class were given yet another opportunity to draw further benefits from their control of an even larger sector of the economy.

As the Zairian economy went into a tailspin, Mobutu finally came to realize the magnitude of the catastrophe ushered in by Zairianization and radicalization. In November 1975, he announced the creation of a stabilization committee in charge of examining a retrocession (see Glossary) formula designed to return a substantial

Presidential compound at Ngaliema on the Congo River near Kinshasa
Courtesy Zaire National Tourism Office

portion of Zairianized enterprises to their original owners. Agreement was reached on a return of 40 percent equity in both radicalized and Zairianized businesses; in time, however, foreign owners were allowed to regain as much as 60 percent in equity, with the remaining 40 percent remaining in Zairian hands.

Meanwhile, almost irreparable damage had been inflicted upon the economy, and the insatiable greed of the political class was made all the more intolerable by the conditions of acute penury now confronting the rural masses. The fall of copper prices and the sharp rise in the cost of oil imports in 1974 further propelled the economy into a period of prolonged stagnation (see Economic Decline, ch. 3). Zaire's growing dependence on foreign lending agencies made a mockery of Mobutu's insistence on the conquest of economic independence. And with the disparities of wealth and privilege between the political class and the populace only slightly diminished by ''retrocession,'' growing social turbulence became inevitable (see Opposition to the Regime prior to 1990, ch. 4; Public Order and Internal Security, ch. 5).

External Threats to Regime Stability

Further aggravating the economic fiasco of Zairianization were the military setbacks suffered by the Zairian army in the course of its intervention in the Angolan civil war. In late 1974, in order to counteract the growing influence of the neo-Marxist Popular Movement for the Liberation of Angola (Movimento Popular de Libertação de Angola—MPLA), Mobutu chose to throw his weight behind Holden Roberto's pro-Western National Front for the Liberation of Angola (Frente Nacional de Libertação de Angola—FNLA), and by July 1975, with Angolan independence just around the corner, units of the Zairian army made their way into Angola and joined the FNLA in an effort to seize control of the capital. But as the Zairian-FNLA forces approached the vicinity of Luanda, they encountered stiff resistance from the MPLA, acting in concert with remnants of the old Katangan gendarmes. Eventually, Cuban soldiers supporting the MPLA inflicted a devastating defeat upon the Zairian-FNLA units (see Involvement in Angola, ch. 5).

While the defeat of the Zairian troops in Angola cast grave doubts on their military capabilities, their performance during the 1977 and 1978 Shaba invasions proved equally disastrous. The FAZ not only failed to stop the invasions but showed its usual disposition to steal and loot civilian property. Only after the intervention of Moroccan troops in 1977, and of the French Foreign Legion in 1978, were the invaders forced back into Angola, accompanied by thousands of civilians fleeing their homeland for fear of retribution (see Shaba I; Shaba II, ch. 5).

The 1977 and 1978 invasions were spearheaded by the Front for the National Liberation of the Congo (Front pour la Libération Nationale du Congo—FLNC), the only Zairian opposition movement that at the time claimed a measure of credibility. The distant origins of the FLNC are traceable to Tshombe's Katangan gendarmes, many of whom had found refuge in Angola after the secession; others were incorporated into the Zairian army, and those few who survived the Kisangani mutinies of 1966 and 1967 fled to Rwanda. Of the few thousand who found a haven in Angola in 1963, many joined the irregular units then being assembled by the Portuguese (the so-called Black Arrows) to fight the Angolan insurgents. In 1968 the Black Arrows transformed themselves into the FLNC. Understandably mistrustful of Mobutu and the FNLA with which he was allied, when Portuguese rule was about to crumble in 1974, the FLNC threw its support to the MPLA.

After the independence of Angola, the FLNC returned to its original sanctuary, near the Shaba border. It was from this base area that the "rebels" launched their first invasion into Shaba, on March 8, 1977. The towns of Dilolo, Kisenge, and Kapanga, all in south and west Shaba, fell into their hands with little or no resistance from the FAZ. In mid-April, as the FLNC closed in on Kolwezi, a major mining town in south Shaba, Mobutu issued an urgent call for military assistance to France and Morocco, and shortly thereafter French transport airplanes proceeded to airlift Moroccan troops into Shaba. Unwilling to engage the Moroccans, the invaders quickly retreated into Angola. FAZ units then moved in to orchestrate a brutal "pacification campaign" that led to a massive exodus of the civilian population into Angola.

A year later, in May 1978, the FLNC launched another invasion into Shaba, this time from Zambia. Once again, the performance of the FAZ proved less than spectacular. Encountering virtually no resistance from the Zairian army, the attacking units moved into Kolwezi on May 13. Greeted as liberators by the young and the unemployed, many of whom bitterly resented the presence of a sizeable group of expatriates in this major industrial town, the FLNC leadership appeared utterly incapable of controlling its troops, much less those Zairians who had spontaneously cast in their lot with the invaders and who now took the law into their hands. Scores of Europeans were massacred, some by the FLNC, some by Zairian civilians, and many more, according to knowledgeable observers, by Zairian troops anxious to loot European property. As on previous occasions, the FAZ showed itself to be little more than a rabble. Not until May 19, after paratroops from the French Foreign Legion and Belgium were airlifted into Shaba, was Kolwezi recaptured. By then more than 100 European residents had lost their lives as well as large numbers of Kolwezi residents and FAZ and FLNC soldiers. Again hundreds of rebels withdrew into Angola, anticipating vengeance from Mobutu's FAZ.

Zairian allegations of joint Soviet-Cuban involvement in the Shaba invasions were instrumental in prompting a favorable response from Mobutu's friends (France, Belgium, and the United States) to his request for immediate military assistance. But the evidence in support of these allegations is scanty at best. Quite aside from the part played by the FLNC in spearheading the invasions, the sharp deterioration of the Zairian economy after 1975, coupled with the rapid growth of anti-Mobutist sentiment in the copper belt and elsewhere, were crucial factors behind the Shaba crises in 1977 and 1978. His impeccable anti-Soviet credentials nonetheless gave Mobutu guarantees of Western backing against his domestic foes, as well as substantial rewards in the form of United States development assistance and military aid. In later years, Mobutu converted the Kamina Base into a major link in the supply route for arms shipments to Jonas Savimbi's National Union for the Total Independence of Angola (União Nacional para a Independência Total

de Angola—UNITA). In so doing, he once again benefited from
the convergence of his regional foreign policy goals and United
States strategic objectives in southern Africa (see Regional Relations, ch. 4). Mobutu's endorsement of United States security objectives in southern Africa made it possible for his regime to benefit
financially from foreign aid while resisting domestic pressures for
economic, social, and political reforms.

The Durability of the Patrimonial State

Under Mobutu formal institutions have always been of little consequence in explaining how power is distributed; the informal networks of influence built around the president are the key to an
understanding of the patrimonial (see Glossary) underpinnings of
the regime (see Establishment of a Personalistic Regime, ch. 4).
In accordance with his chiefly role, Mobutu's rule was from the
outset based on bonds of personal loyalty between himself and his
entourage. His hegemony has been absolute, extending to every
level of government. In an effort to forestall the emergence of independent power centers, administrative and government personnel
have been constantly moved around; opposition members, alter-
natively rusticated and rehabilitated; and security forces dissolved
and restructured as the circumstances dictated.

Prior to 1990, what has been termed the "presidential brother-
hood" constituted the inner circle of Mobutu's clients, numbering anywhere from fifteen to twenty people. Included in this group
were the members of the Political Bureau of the MPR and certain
key personalities of the security forces. A somewhat larger and
shadowy entourage of courtiers and technocrats could be identified as the next most important group of clients, overlapping with
yet a third group represented by the provincial bosses. The boundaries separating one group from the other were highly fluid,
however, reflecting Mobutu's well-known disposition to constantly rearrange the structure and personnel of his government. What
held these clients together was their presumed loyalty to the patrimonial ruler, a loyalty nurtured by the anticipation of rewards
commensurate with their willingness and ability to comply with
presidential orders.

Penalties to the disloyal have always been just as important as
rewards to the faithful in sustaining the Mobutist state. The coercive
side of the patrimonial state is equally pertinent to an understanding
of how Mobutu has managed to stay on top. His real power base
lies in a wide array of paramilitary and intelligence-gathering agencies (see The Intelligence Apparatus and Security Forces, ch. 5).
The most important are the Special Presidential Division (Division

Spéciale Présidentielle—DSP), an elite force in charge of ensuring Mobutu's personal security; the Military Action and Intelligence Service (Service d'Action et de Renseignements Militaire—SARM), in charge of military intelligence; and SARM's civilian counterpart, the National Documentation Agency (Agence Nationale de Documentation—AND). Each agency has separate access to the president, and each has a history of rampant corruption and abuse of the civilian population. Agents are grossly underpaid, so bribery and extortion are common currency. Arresting innocent citizens and holding them captive until they pay the required amount is by no means unusual (see Popular Attitudes Toward the Civil Security Apparatus; Civil and Human Rights, ch. 5). Along with the sanctions facing all forms of organized opposition, the diffuse fear instilled among the masses by the security forces must be seen as the most obvious explanation for Mobutu's extraordinary record of political longevity.

Servicing the networks of the patrimonial state is Mobutu's own responsibility. In practice, substantial amounts of the government's money have been regularly diverted into the presidential slush fund to be allocated to the faithful in accordance with the presidential whim. Just as the patrimonial state can best be visualized as an extension of the ruler's household, the coffers of the state have long been almost indistinguishable from Mobutu's private wealth (said to amount to approximately US$5 billion). The siphoning off of state funds into private networks is one of the norms of political clientage institutionalized under Mobutu (see Patrimonial Politics and Corruption, ch. 3).

The opportunity costs arising from the exigencies of the system are readily apparent in such deficiencies as the populace's low standard of living, the utter neglect of the rural sectors, the absence of an investment budget for the development and maintenance of infrastructure, and the very modest amounts spent on education and health services (see Education; Health and Medical Services, ch. 2). Although Mobutu's personal style bears much of the blame for this dismal state of affairs, part of the explanation must also be found in the emergence in Zaire of a polity that combined some of the worst features of the absolutist, *bula matari* state with the inefficiency and corruption of a patrimonial regime.

* * *

There is an excellent body of literature available in English on Zaire from the precolonial era to the present. Jan Vansina's *Kingdoms of the Savanna, Paths in the Rainforests,* and ''The Peoples of the

Forest'' offer authoritative accounts of the development of Zaire's diverse peoples and kingdoms. For the colonial and early independence era, the best sources are the numerous works by Crawford Young and René Lemarchand as well as Ruth Slade's *King Léopold's Congo,* Neil Ascherson's *The King Incorporated,* Jules Gérard-Libais's *Katanga Secession,* and Ernest Lefever's *Crisis in the Congo: A United Nations Force in Action. Dominer pour servir,* a celebrated work by former colonial governor Pierre Ryckmans, is also of interest in understanding Belgian motivations and policies.

The Mobutist era is amply covered in a number of authoritative works. Most notable are Thomas Callaghy's *The State-Society Struggle: Zaire in Comparative Perspective,* Michael G. Schatzberg's *Politics and Class in Zaire* and *The Dialectics of Oppression in Zaire,* Crawford Young and Thomas Turner's *The Rise and Decline of the Zairian State,* and David Gould's *Bureaucratic Corruption and Underdevelopment in the Third World: The Case of Zaire.* (For further information and complete citations, see Bibliography.)

Chapter 2. The Society and Its Environment

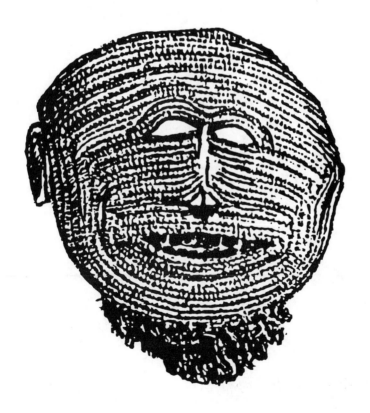

Traditional mask made of rope

ZAIRE'S ETHNIC DIVERSITY has frequently been stressed in discussions of its society and culture; as many as 250 different languages can be identified within its borders. But overemphasis on ethnicity would be misplaced in discussing the social realities of the 1980s and early 1990s. Zairians have shared a prolonged experience of state pauperization and oppression; the social polarization and strategies of survival that have evolved out of that experience shape them regardless of their individual ethnic identities.

Zairians have been increasingly divided into an elite class, most of whom are politically attached to the government of Mobutu Sese Seko (president, 1965–), and the mass of peasants, workers, and low-ranking civil servants. The former have used the state to advance their economic interests, although their dependence on political favor has left them insecure. The latter have seen their standard of living drop year after year, watching while as much as half their income is taken in fees, fines, and taxes to support the state and its elite.

Zairians' response to such deprivations has been differentiated not only by class but also by factors such as rural or urban status, gender, regionalism, and ethnicity. Villagers, for example, seeing road networks and educational and medical services collapse, have responded in part by fleeing to cities, increasing the country's rate of urbanization. Women have formed new alliances in both rural and urban areas to promote their interests and resist state exactions.

Most striking has been the creativity of ordinary Zairians in constructing an economic life outside the deteriorating formal economy. A major factor in the continuing survival and political quiescence of the population in the face of their pauperization has been the growth of the informal economy, whose size, according to most analysts, exceeds that of the formal national economy.

Notable, too, is the strength of institutions outside of or on the periphery of state control. Churches have continued to grow in membership, and their extensive networks of hospitals and schools have increased in importance since the collapse of state-run medical and education institutions.

Zaire is a land of superlative natural endowments—a vast territory encompassing enormous mineral deposits, immense forests, mighty rivers, and abundant fertile soils. It is said to have sufficient arable land and hydroelectric potential to feed and power the entire African continent. This situation, in combination with its legendary mineral wealth, should have made Zaire one of sub-Saharan Africa's most developed and wealthiest states. Instead, it is a poor nation in a rich land. Its economy and society are in disarray in the early 1990s, and most of its citizens (80 percent by some accounts) live in absolute poverty.

Zaire's public health and welfare system has collapsed. Most state-run hospitals and schools have closed. Medical equipment and medicine are scarce. Blood banks have closed, blood screenings are rare, and the rate of immunization among infants and children has declined drastically. Acquired immune deficiency syndrome (AIDS), tuberculosis, leprosy, trypanosomiasis, and malaria are widespread problems. Malnutrition has also become increasingly prevalent, particularly among children, as the price of food exceeds the financial resources of more and more Zairians. The availability of safe drinking water also has become problematic.

The impoverishment of Zairians can be attributed in large part to the monumental corruption and institutionalized theft characterizing the Mobutu regime. Nevertheless, the country's large population (39.1 million in 1992) and chronically high population growth rate (3.3 percent in 1992) have also played a role in the deterioration of economic and social conditions, in that population growth has consistently outpaced official economic growth. Ethnic and social tensions are also on the rise, as Zairians compete for increasingly scarce resources. One serious result of this ethnic conflict is that thousands of Zairians have been displaced by ethnic violence, creating a mass of internal refugees whose needs the state will not and cannot address.

Geography and Environment

The Republic of Zaire is the second largest country of sub-Saharan Africa, occupying some 2,344,885 square kilometers. It is roughly the size of the United States east of the Mississippi River.

Most of the country lies within the vast hollow of the Congo River basin. The basin has the shape of an amphitheater, open to the north and northwest and closed in the south and east by high plateaus and mountains. The edges of the basin are breached in the west by the passage of the Congo River to the Atlantic Ocean; they are broken and raised in the east by an upheaval of the Great Rift Valley (where lakes Mweru, Tanganyika, Kivu, Edward, and Albert are found) and by overflow from volcanos in the Virunga Mountains.

Rivers and Lakes

The Congo River and its tributaries drain this basin and provide the country with the most extensive network of navigable waterways in Africa. Ten kilometers wide at mid-point of its length, the river carries a volume of water that is second only to the Amazon's. Its flow is unusually regular because it is fed by rivers and streams from both sides of the equator; the complementary alternation of rainy and dry seasons on each side of the equator guarantees a regular supply of water for the main channel. At points where navigation is blocked by rapids and waterfalls, the sudden descent of the river creates a hydroelectric potential greater than that found in any other river system on earth.

Most of Zaire is served by the Congo River system, a fact that has facilitated both trade and outside penetration. Its network of waterways is dense and evenly distributed through the country, with three exceptions: northeastern Mayombé in Bas-Zaïre Region in the west, which is drained by a small coastal river called the Shilango; a strip of land on the eastern border adjoining lakes Edward and Albert, which is part of the Nile River basin; and a small part of extreme southeastern Zaire, which lies in the Zambezi River basin and drains into the Indian Ocean.

Most of Zaire's lakes are also part of the Congo River basin. In the west are Lac Mai-Ndombe and Lac Tumba, which are remnants of a huge interior lake that once occupied the entire basin prior to the breach of the basin's edge by the Congo River and the subsequent drainage of the interior. In the southeast, Lake Mweru straddles the border with Zambia. On the eastern frontier, Lac Kivu, Central Africa's highest lake and a key tourist center, and Lake Tanganyika, just south of Lac Kivu, both feed into the Lualaba River, the name often given to the upper extension of the Congo River. Only the waters of the eastern frontier's northernmost great lakes, Edward and Albert, drain north, into the Nile Basin.

Geographic Regions

Several major geographic regions may be defined in terms of terrain and patterns of natural vegetation, namely the central Congo Basin, the uplands north and south of the basin, and the eastern highlands (see fig. 7).

The country's core region is the central Congo Basin. Having an average elevation of about forty-four meters, it measures roughly 800,000 square kilometers, constituting about a third of Zaire's territory. Much of the forest within the basin is swamp, and still more of it consists of a mixture of marshes and firm land.

North and south of the basin lie higher plains and, occasionally, hills covered with varying mixtures of savanna grasses and woodlands. The southern uplands region, like the basin, constitutes about a third of Zaire's territory. The area slopes from south to north, starting at about 1,000 meters near the Angolan border and falling to about 500 meters near the basin. Vegetation cover in the southern uplands territory is more varied than that of the northern uplands. In some areas, woodland is dominant; in others, savanna grasses predominate. South of the basin, along the streams flowing into the Kasai River are extensive gallery forests. In the far southeast, most of Shaba Region (formerly Katanga Province) is characterized by somewhat higher plateaus and low mountains. The westernmost section of Zaire, a partly forested panhandle reaching the Atlantic Ocean, is an extension of the southern uplands that drops sharply to a very narrow shore about forty kilometers long.

In the much narrower northern uplands, the cover is largely savanna, and woodlands are rarer. The average elevation of this region is about 600 meters, but it rises as high as 900 meters where it meets the western edge of the eastern highlands.

The eastern highlands region is the highest and most rugged portion of the country. It extends for more than 1,500 kilometers from above Lake Albert to the southern tip of Shaba below Lubumbashi (formerly Élisabethville) and varies in width from eighty to 560 kilometers. Its hills and mountains range in altitude from about 1,000 meters to more than 5,000 meters. The western arm of the Great Rift Valley forms a natural eastern boundary to this region. The eastern border of Zaire extends through the valley and its system of lakes, which are separated from each other by plains situated between high mountain ranges.

In this region, changes in elevation bring marked changes in vegetation, which ranges from montane savanna to heavy montane forest. The Massif du Ruwenzori (Ruwenzori Mountains or Mountains of the Moon) between lakes Albert and Edward constitutes the highest range in Africa. The height and location of these mountains on the equator make for a varied and spectacular flora. Together with the Virunga Mountains north of Lac Kivu, site of several active volcanos, and together with the game park situated between them, they constitute Zaire's most important potential touristic resource.

Climate

Climate ranges from tropical rain forest in the Congo River basin to tropical wet-and-dry in the southern uplands to tropical highland in eastern areas above 2,000 meters in elevation. In general, temperatures and humidity are quite high. The highest and least variable temperatures are to be found in the equatorial forest, where daytime highs range between 30°C and 35°C, and nighttime lows rarely go below 20°C. The average annual temperature is about 25°C. In the southern uplands, particularly in southeastern Shaba, winters are cool and dry, whereas summers are warm and damp. The area embracing the chain of lakes from Lake Albert to Lake Tanganyika in the eastern highlands has a moist climate and a narrow but not excessively warm temperature range. The mountain sections are cooler, but humidity increases with altitude until the saturation point is reached; a nearly constant falling mist prevails on some slopes, particularly in the Ruwenzori Mountains.

The seasonal pattern of rainfall is affected by Zaire's straddling of the equator. In the third of the country that lies north of the equator, the dry season (roughly early November to late March) corresponds to the rainy season in the southern two-thirds. There is a great deal of variation, however, and a number of places on either side of the equator have two wet and two dry seasons. Rainfall averages range from about 1,000 millimeters to 2,200 millimeters. Annual rainfall is highest in the heart of the Congo River basin and in the highlands west of Bukavu and with some variation tends to diminish in direct relation to distance from these areas. The only areas marked by long four-month to five-month dry seasons and occasional droughts are parts of Shaba.

Environmental Trends

In the last decade, Africa's rain forests have been destroyed at a faster rate than anywhere else in the world, including the well-publicized Amazon region in South America; Nigeria, for example, is now 90 percent deforested. Environmental degradation has been less of a problem in Zaire than elsewhere in sub-Saharan Africa. Nevertheless, although still 86 percent intact in the early 1990s, Zaire's vast forests will be increasingly at risk. A major threat has been the signing of contracts with foreign logging corporations. Some 37 percent of the total exploitable area of Zaire's rain forest has already been designated as timber concessions.

The most intense logging to date has been in Bas-Zaïre Region in the hinterlands of the capital of Kinshasa. Logging itself disrupts the forest ecology; worse, logging roads carved out of forest to export felled timber have become avenues for immigration into the forest by poor farmers who clear and burn more forest for fields. In 1993 one analyst reported that there was virtually no primary rain forest left in Bas-Zaïre.

69

In the east, the appropriation of land for ranching and plantations in the Kivu highlands has simultaneously reduced forest hectarage and increased the intensity of use of the remaining land by
the existing population. The Ituri Forest of northeastern Zaire has
also experienced substantial recent immigration by growing populations in need of fertile soil for their crops. Extensive forest destruction has been reported as a consequence.

Population

Size and Growth

Zaire's population was estimated at 39.1 million in 1992, making the country among sub-Saharan Africa's most populous. This
figure represents a substantial increase over the 29.7 million inhabitants recorded in the last official census, taken in July 1984,
which in itself had indicated a near doubling of the 16.2 million
population at independence in 1960 (see table 2, Appendix).

Fluctuations in the country's population over time follow a clear
pattern, correlating to political and economic developments. Between 1880 and approximately 1920, a period of colonial conquest
and consolidation, Zaire suffered a drastic decline in population.
European and Arab penetration disrupted traditional agricultural
organization and introduced diseases such as smallpox, influenza,
and venereal diseases, devastating local populations and reducing
their numbers by roughly one-third to one-half. In the 1940s, population decline was also hastened by the conditions under which man-
datory labor was imposed by the colonial government during World
War II. Compulsory labor for porterage, road construction, mining, and the harvesting of rubber disrupted the planting and harvesting of food crops, provoking famine.

Only after 1948 did the country's population show rapid growth,
reflecting improved nutrition, health, and economic development.
Since that time, the average annual rate of population growth has
been consistently high even by African standards. It was estimated at just above 2 percent for most of the period from 1950 to 1970.
Thereafter, the rate has been near or above 3 percent. In 1992 the
annual population growth rate was estimated at 3.3 percent (see
table 3, Appendix). Moreover, the growth rate is projected to remain at or above 3 percent until at least 2015. Zaire is thus expected to continue to see its population grow at a faster rate than
its economy, exacerbating the economic and social deterioration
prevailing in the early 1990s. The United Nations (UN) estimates
that Zaire's population will total between 78.4 million and 100.9
million by 2025.

Zaire's high population growth rate is fueled by a high crude birth rate: forty-five births per 1,000 population in 1992, little changed from the forty-seven births per 1,000 population recorded in 1965 (see table 4, Appendix). The total fertility rate in 1992 was estimated to be 6.1 children born per woman. In the same year, the crude death rate was estimated at thirteen per 1,000 population, down substantially from the twenty-one per 1,000 noted in 1965 and thus another contributing factor to total population growth. The infant mortality rate, although substantially improved from the rate of 140 per 1,000 live births recorded in 1965, was, however, still high at ninety-seven per 1,000 live births in 1992. The under-five mortality rate was estimated at 150 per 1,000. Life expectancy was relatively low at fifty-two years for males and fifty-six for women in 1992.

The distribution of Zaire's population by age and sex is typical of that of a developing nation and quite dissimilar from that of the developed world. Most striking is the youthfulness of the population. In 1990 approximately 45 percent of the population was under the age of fifteen, 71 percent under the age of thirty, and 87 percent under the age of forty-five (see fig. 8). The number of males and females was nearly equal, estimated at 49 percent and 51 percent of the population, respectively, in 1990. Because of their greater longevity, females outnumbered males primarily in the older age-groups.

The size and composition of the population are also affected by uncontrolled and continuing immigration to Zaire. Both prior to and since independence, there have been periodic influxes of refugees from neighboring countries, such as Angola, Sudan, Uganda, Rwanda, and Burundi (people from the last two known collectively in Zaire as the Banyarwanda). Emigration of Zairians has offset only some of the population increases. In the 1960s, some sources indicate that Zaire gained 500,000 inhabitants through immigration. In May 1985, the number of refugees in Zaire was estimated at about 330,000.

In 1992 the U.S. Committee for Refugees estimated that Zaire was home to over 470,000 refugees: 310,000 from Angola, 104,000 from southern Sudan, 45,000 from Burundi, 10,000 from Uganda, and 1,300 from other African nations. Most of the Angolan refugees had been in Zaire for over twenty years and were self-supporting and socially integrated into Zairian society. About 80,000 were, however, more recent refugees, having fled to Zaire since 1985.

In late 1991, an estimated 20,000 foreigners, mostly European and United States citizens, left Zaire because of the country's

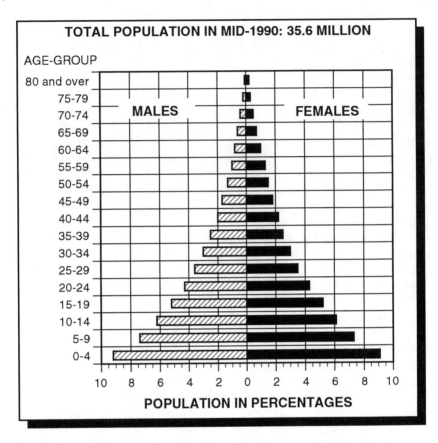

Source: Based on information from Federal Republic of Germany, Statistisches Bundesamt,
        Länderbericht Zaïre, 1990, Wiesbaden, 1990, 23.

Figure 8. Population by Age and Gender, 1990

political unrest and economic deterioration. A small number of Zairians are also reported to have fled from Zaire to Angola. However,
by contrast with the repatriation of 15,000 Angolan refugees and
the reduction of Western expatriates in Zaire during 1991, the number of refugees from Burundi and Sudan increased in the early 1990s.

In general, the Zairian government welcomed refugees, allowing
them to settle on empty land or seek employment. Further assistance
to displaced persons was provided by international relief agencies.

Population Distribution

Because of its large land area, Zaire as a whole is not overpopu-
lated, but population distribution is uneven, and some regions are

very densely populated. Although most of Zaire's land area is habitable, more than half of the country is still thinly populated, and some 10 percent almost totally uninhabited. Two-thirds of the population is estimated to live on one-quarter of the land area.

The population is least dense throughout the nation's center, in the Congo River basin. Two areas with relatively high densities (greater than twenty-five inhabitants per square kilometer) are found along the eastern border north of Lake Tanganyika and from Bas-Zaïre in the southwest intermittently throughout the southern savannas to Kasai-Oriental. The greater-than-average population density in the eastern highlands can be related to the superior soils and rainfall there, but no obvious natural reason accounts for the greater density of the southern savannas.

Average population density throughout Zaire was relatively low at 14.9 persons per square kilometer in 1990, but regional distribution was uneven (see table 5, Appendix). Kinshasa was by far the most densely populated region in the country (266.3 inhabitants per square kilometer in 1984), followed by Bas-Zaïre (36.5 inhabitants per square kilometer) and Kivu (since the early 1990s divided into Nord-Kivu, Sud-Kivu, and Maniema; 20.2 inhabitants per square kilometer overall—however, Nord-Kivu and Sud-Kivu are very densely populated, but Maniema is sparsely populated). Shaba was the least densely populated (7.8 inhabitants per square kilometer), exceeded only slightly, however, by Équateur and Haut-Zaïre (both 8.4 inhabitants per square kilometer in 1984).

In consonance with the high average annual growth rate of the total population, adjusted data from the five official censuses (1938, 1948, 1958, 1970, and 1984) clearly show a high rate of population increase in all regions after 1948. There are, nevertheless, substantial regional variations (see table 6, Appendix).

Internal migration to the capital city of Kinshasa has caused a spectacular rate of population growth for that area since 1938. Although the growth rate is declining, it measured 6.2 percent for the 1970–84 period. Growth rates in Kivu, Shaba, and Kasai-Oriental were also higher than the national average (i.e., over 3 percent) in the same period.

Immigration also accounts for some of the discrepancies in regional increases in population at various times. For example, refugees from the Angolan anticolonial struggle flooded parts of Bas-Zaïre between 1958 and 1970, swelling statistics. Substantial numbers of refugees from what are now Rwanda and Burundi fled to Kivu, first under Belgian colonial rule in the 1927–45 and 1949–55 periods, and later in response to domestic political unrest in the

1960s, in the 1970s, and in the early 1990s. Political unrest was also the major factor behind the entry of Sudanese and Ugandans into Haut-Zaïre in 1970 and 1984. In Shaba the rising growth rate from 1958 to 1970 can be attributed to both foreign immigration and internal migration, particularly from Kasai-Oriental to Shaba's thriving mining centers.

In the early 1990s, Zaire had to contend with an increasingly large population of internally displaced persons, the victims of ethnic conflict (see The Significance of Ethnic Identification, this ch.; Interest Groups, ch. 4). In 1992–93 several hundred thousand Luba-Kasai residing in Shaba (many whose families had been there for three to four generations) were forced from their homes and businesses. Most sought refuge in and around train stations (many literally living on station platforms), awaiting transport to the Kasai area. Because of their lack of funds and the unreliability of the country's dilapidated rail system, many never made it out of Shaba, and in mid-1993 there were reported to be 100,000 refugees trying to leave the region. There were also about 100,000 refugees in Kasai-Occidental and Kasai-Oriental who had succeeded in leaving Shaba but were awaiting resettlement in the "homeland" that many had never before visited.

In addition, densely populated Nord-Kivu had over 150,000 internal refugees displaced by violence against the so-called Banyarwanda, members of the Hutu and Tutsi ethnic groups originally from Rwanda and Burundi who had immigrated to Zaire over the years. Indigenous local groups, traditionally hunters, were locked in a struggle over land use with the more prosperous Banyarwanda, who were primarily farmers. The Banyarwanda, although numbering about 2 million and constituting about one-half the population of Nord-Kivu, were still widely regarded as "foreigners," and many of them had in fact been deprived of citizenship by a 1981 law that was finally invoked in 1991. Thus, they made convenient targets. Attacks began in March 1993; by August 1993, they had resulted in the deaths of over 7,000 Banyarwanda and the displacement of 150,000 people from both sides of the conflict.

The Zairian government is unable to deal with the social and health care needs of the displaced. Church groups and international organizations are in essence the only agencies delivering health care and other assistance to these internal refugees. Yet even their efforts are hampered by the near total collapse of the country's infrastructure, continuing corruption at all levels of officialdom, and widespread lawlessness and civil unrest.

Urbanization: Causes and Characteristics

Urbanization is a relatively recent phenomenon in Zaire, and in the early 1990s Zaire was still a predominantly rural nation. Since the 1940s, however, the population has increasingly shifted from rural to urban areas, especially Kinshasa. An estimated 39.5 percent of the population was classified as urban in 1990, up from 30.3 percent in 1970 and 34.2 percent in 1980. Between 1940 and 1970, all urban centers had grown in population by a factor of ten. Growth has continued at a relatively high rate since then. Indeed, the average annual urban population growth rate has been estimated at almost 4.7 percent for the 1985–90 period, as compared with an average annual rural population growth rate of less than 2.3 percent during the same period.

Kinshasa remains, overwhelmingly, the nation's largest city, with a population estimated at nearly 5 million in 1988. More than one-third of all city-dwellers lived in Kinshasa in 1988. There are, however, a number of other large cities as well, several of which (including Kananga, formerly Luluabourg, and Lubumbashi) had populations of nearly 1 million by 1985 (see table 7, Appendix).

The concentration of resources in the cities has long drawn migrants from the countryside. Civil strife following independence intensified the shift of population to urban areas. Most recently, the chaotic economic and social conditions of the late 1980s and early 1990s have aggravated existing disparities between urban and rural standards of living. Urban residence has thus grown increasingly attractive as the conditions of rural life have deteriorated even more rapidly than the conditions of urban life.

In the colonial era, influx controls kept large numbers of people from migrating to the cities. The controls also allowed more men (as workers) than women into the cities, resulting in a skewed urban sex ratio. But since independence, government attempts to discourage urban migration, including periodic roundups and deportations of the urban unemployed to the countryside, have failed. Ample evidence of the failure is provided by the numerous squatters' villages that have sprung up on the outskirts of Kinshasa and other cities.

Indeed, state policies over the years actually accelerated the rural exodus to the cities. State investment funds were almost entirely targeted toward cities and the mining areas, further aggravating the resource disparity between rural and urban areas. State-fixed prices for food crops produced by villagers were kept deliberately low in order to keep urban populations quiescent. The state also continued the colonial-era policies of compulsory agricultural

75

production quotas and of heavy direct and indirect taxation for cash crops such as cotton. When indirect taxes, such as turnover and export taxes, on cash crops are added to direct taxes, Zaire specialist Crawford Young has estimated that as much as 50 percent of real and potential village income is routinely extracted by the state or its representatives. Moreover, the exactions levied by the state and its agents generally increase in severity in proportion to distance from urban centers. Rural public employees and soldiers frequently use their official powers to live off the land, or for extortion, particularly when their salaries are either delayed or not paid by corrupt superiors. Given the scale of legal and illegal state exactions on the rural population, the flight of villagers to the cities is understandable.

Several particular aspects of the growing urban population are also noteworthy. Since independence, women have been particularly quick to migrate to cities and exploit the opportunities of urban life, especially the opportunity to engage in economic activity in the informal sector. In the 1990s, women generally equaled or outnumbered men in Zaire's urban centers, in sharp contrast to the colonial era. Migration of the young to Zaire's urban centers in search of postprimary education has also been a strong factor in urban growth.

Another striking feature of Zaire's urban populace has been the low number of wage earners in the formal economy relative to the total population. The most extreme known case is that of Kananga, which was reported to have only 10,000 wage earners out of a population of 429,000 in 1973. The survival of most urban households has been founded on activity outside of the formal economic sector. Much of the populace makes its living in the large and thriving informal sector (see The Informal Sector, this ch.; The Informal Economy, ch. 3).

Languages

Zaire has been cited as having as many as 250 languages spoken within its borders. In fact, the exact number is difficult to specify; it depends on whether or not a particular tongue is defined as a distinct language or merely as a dialect of a neighboring one.

Officially Recognized Languages

French, an inheritance from the Belgian colonial era, remains the primary language of government, of the formal economy, and of most educational instruction. Four indigenous languages have also been recognized as having official status since the colonial era, namely Kikongo, Tshiluba, Lingala, and Kiswahili. All have been used at various times in official documents, in religious works, in school instruction, and in various published works. Some of these languages have also been used in radio and television broadcasts.

Early missionaries attempted the standardization of orthography and grammar for these and other languages. Lomongo, for example, has seen wide use in much of the Congo River basin, in large part because of its use and promotion by missionary evangelists and educators. Sango, a trade language used along the northern border with the Central African Republic, was similarly promoted, although on a smaller scale and with less success as a result of competition with Lingala.

Of the four most widely used indigenous languages, two are identified with Zaire's two largest ethnic groups, namely, Tshiluba with the Luba-Kasai of south-central Zaire and Kikongo with the Kongo of southwestern Zaire. Tshiluba orthography has been relatively standardized. Kikongo, however, has long existed in several dialects, one of which evolved into a trade language called Fiote used in contact with Europeans. Its use by early Belgian colonial authorities led to its being called "state Kikongo." It is also known as Kituba or Monokutuba and has long been spoken across the border in Congo; radio broadcasts in the language are made in both countries.

Kiswahili penetrated Zaire from the east, imported by Arab slavers in the latter half of the nineteenth century. It spread over time throughout eastern Zaire and quickly established itself in the ethnically mixed population of the copper-belt towns. Once established, it endured; even the influx of large numbers of Tshiluba-speaking migrants to the copper towns failed to displace Kiswahili.

Since independence, the most prominent of the four principal indigenous languages has been Lingala. It first developed out of a trade language based on the Bangi tongue that was used on the lower Congo River between the Ubangi and Kasai tributaries in the late nineteenth century. Early European recruitment of soldiers from upriver regions necessitated selection of a language of command and of communication. Lingala was considered suitable, and its adoption by the military resulted in its spread wherever soldiers or veterans went. In addition, Lingala established itself early as the language of the capital. As with Kiswahili in the copper-belt towns, even the influx of large numbers of same mother-tongue immigrants, in this case of Kikongo-speakers (particularly in the post-World War II period), failed to displace Lingala.

The postindependence expansion of Lingala can be attributed to several additional factors. One is the enormous popularity of Zairian popular music, whose lyrics are mostly in Lingala. Lingala songs can be heard playing from radios in even the most remote villages throughout Zaire. Zairian music has reached an extremely wide area throughout sub-Saharan Africa and has established itself as one of the continent's most prestigious musical traditions. Another reason for Lingala's extensive penetration is its use by truck drivers and traders along most of the roads, railroads, and waterways in the country. On major routes, even through the heart of Kiswahili-speaking northeastern Zaire, travelers may use Lingala to order food and lodgings in small African restaurants and inns.

In some cities, Lingala's expansion has been quantified. Kisangani, for example, which is in Haut-Zaïre, sitting astride the east-west dividing line between Lingala- and Kiswahili-speaking areas and long harboring both Lingala- and Kiswahili-speaking communities, has seen two communities shift from Kiswahili-speaking majority to Lingala-speaking majority since independence. More significant is the fact that Lingala in Lingala-speaking areas has become, as has Kiswahili in Kiswahili-speaking areas, the first language of the children of urban interethnic marriages. This development has occurred despite the fact that neither language was ever the first language of any historical, prenineteenth-century Zairian community.

A map showing the distribution of major languages is only marginally useful, however, as a guide to which languages are spoken where. Even where one ethnic group predominates, multilingualism may be common. An individual Zairian may speak French in the workplace, a regional trade language such as Lingala in marketplace conversation, and the mother tongue of his or her ethnic group in the home or with other members of the ethnic group.

Choice of language may be a vehicle for establishing a particular relationship or even for making a political statement. A police officer or other low-level government official may begin a request for a favor (say a ride on a commercial truck) in French, switching quickly to the more comfortable Kiswahili or Lingala once the "official" tone implied by the use of French has been set. And on a larger scale, President Mobutu's deliberate use of Lingala in his public addresses, even speaking to Kiswahili-speaking crowds in Bukavu and elsewhere, has given political expression to his reported rejection of Kiswahili as an acceptable Zaire-wide trade language because of its association with Arab slavers. Lingala is, in fact, the only African language Mobutu uses in public.

Other Indigenous Languages

The vast majority of languages spoken in Zaire are Bantu

derivatives. Only in the north have other language groups been represented. Adamawa-Eastern languages are spoken in the entire northern portion of Zaire, interspersed in the east along the Uele River with Central Sudanic languages. In the far northeast (from Lake Albert north), the few Eastern Sudanic languages spoken in Zaire are heard, interspersed with Central Sudanic, Adamawa-Eastern, and an occasional Bantu language. Crude estimates of the number of speakers of these language divisions have cited 80 percent of the population as speakers of Bantu languages. The remaining 20 percent may be divided, in declining numbers of speakers, among people speaking Adamawa-Eastern, Central Sudanic, and Eastern Sudanic languages.

Ethnic Groups

Zaire's population is composed of as many as 250 different ethnic groups, most of which are Bantu speakers. The largest Bantu-speaking groups are the Luba, Kongo, Mongo, and Lunda. In 1992 some sources reported that the Luba, Kongo, and Mongo groups as well as the non-Bantu-speaking Zande and Mangbetu together made up about 45 percent of the population. Calculations of the number and relative sizes of ethnic groups in Zaire are at best approximations, however. These groups are neither fixed entities nor the sole or even primary points of reference for all Zairians. On the contrary, for most purposes and in most contexts, rural Zairians see themselves primarily as members of a local community or of a clan (see Glossary) or lineage (see Glossary). Ethnic identity has become salient only under certain conditions, and the precise boundaries of ethnic groups have shifted with circumstances. Ethnicity and regionalism (the latter based in part on ethnic considerations) were, and continue to be, of substantial importance in the political orientation of Zairians, but the units involved have always varied in composition, cohesion, and ideological self-awareness.

Given the difficulty of categorizing ethnic groups in such a way as to satisfy objective criteria on the one hand and the subjective standard of common identity on the other, and given the sheer number of named groups, only a brief survey of the major entities based on common (or closely similar) language and culture is attempted here. A mapping of clusters of related or culturally similar entities shows a limited correspondence to the major geographic regions of Zaire, and these provide a framework for the survey. The basic source on this subject is Jan Vansina's work from the 1960s, *Introduction à l'ethnographie du Congo*.

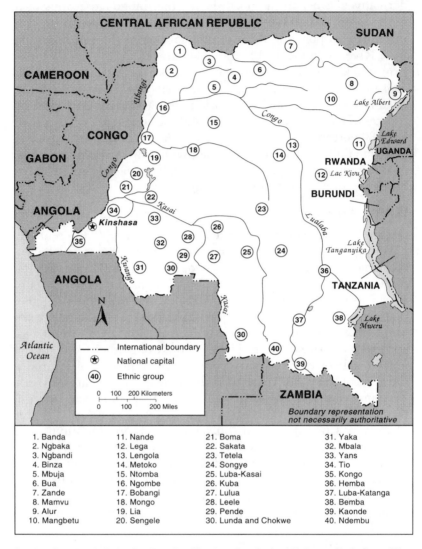

Source: Based on information from Jan Vansina, *Introduction à l'ethnographie du Congo*, Kinshasa, 1966.

Figure 9. Distribution of Principal Ethnic Groups

Non-Bantu Speakers of the Northern Savannas and Forest Fringe

Northwestern and north-central Zaire, more specifically the subregions of Ubangi and Mongala in Équateur Region, have been occupied by speakers of the eastern section of the Adamawa-Eastern language family since their arrival in the seventeenth or eighteenth century (see fig. 9). They are classed into three major ethnic groups, namely the Ngbandi, the Ngbaka, and the Banda-speaking groups (of which the Mbanja are the most important). Conflicts and migrations have dispersed these groups to some degree; the Mbanja in particular do not occupy a contiguous territory.

Northeastern Zaire, specifically in the subregion of Bas-Uele and the northern portions of Haut-Uele—both in Haut-Zaïre—is peopled by a heterogeneous group called the Zande, also speakers of the eastern section of the Adamawa-Eastern language family. The Zande are sometimes divided into two sections: to the east, the Vungara and to the west, the Bandiya. Each section has taken its name from the clan providing the ruling house in the areas included in it. The Vungara are the larger of the two, and the following sketch has been based on data from them.

The Zande emerged as a people in the eighteenth and nineteenth centuries when groups of hunters, probably divided into an aristocracy called the Vungara and commoners called the Mbomu, penetrated the area and subjugated the Bantu-speaking and Adamawa-Eastern-speaking peoples they found there. The dynamic of the conquest was influenced by the rules of succession to the monarchy among the Vungara. A man took his father's throne only when he had vanquished those of his brothers who chose to compete for it. One or more of the losing brothers, a prince or princes without land or people, then undertook to find and rule a previously unconquered people. This process continued through the nineteenth century until a large area and a wide assortment of peoples had been dominated by the Zande Vungara. The outcome was a rich mixture of the cultures of conqueror and conquered.

Most of the peoples speaking Central Sudanic languages entered the forest north and northeast of the Congo River basin. The Mangbetu and the Mamvu are the most important of these groups. Like the Zande, the Mangbetu established states incorporating other peoples and established distinctions between aristocrats and commoners. Also like the Zande, their influence extended beyond their realm to neighboring groups. The Mamvu, grouped by one source together with the Mangutu, Mvuba, and Balese into a larger Mamvu cluster, were characterized by small-scale political units; the Balese and the Mvuba are even said to have lacked chiefs.

In the far northeast, in the highlands area northwest of Lake Albert and bordered by Uganda and Sudan, live a collection of groups that speak languages from each of the four language families found in Zaire. In general, they traditionally constituted small-scale polities based on a system of patrilineal descent groups. The one exception are the Alur, the only significant group in Zaire to speak an Eastern Sudanic language. The Alur, most of whom live in Uganda, erected fairly large-scale states but with a simple administrative structure. Chiefs were seen as primarily religious figures controlling rain and interceding with the ancestors. Politically, their main task was moderating and limiting conflict between lineages. Their fertility and peacekeeping roles made them attractive to neighboring groups and helped the Alur to expand and dominate the commoner groups. The indigenous people came to think of Alur chiefs as capable of putting a stop to interlineage feuds and invited nearby chiefs to send them a ruler. It was largely in this way rather than by conquest (as with the Zande and Mangbetu) that Alur chieftainship expanded.

In general, the peoples stretching from the far northwest to the far northeast stood on the sidelines during the ethnically based competition that characterized the independence and postindependence periods. Remote from the chief urban centers and penetrated rather late by missions and modern education, they have only recently become engaged in the Zairian polity and economy. Although Mobutu is of Ngbandi origin, he is more commonly seen in Kinshasa and elsewhere as a man of Équateur Region, rather than as an ethnic Ngbandi or man of the far north.

Bantu Speakers of the Congo River Basin and Its Environs

Living just north and south of the Congo River, from Kisangani (formerly Stanleyville) in the east to the juncture of the Ubangi River with the Congo in the west, are a large number of diverse Bantu-speaking groups; a handful of groups speaking languages of the Adamawa-Eastern family are interspersed among them. The movement of groups within this region and the riverine trade characteristic of the area have made for considerable sharing of cultural elements.

This area typifies the house-village-district social structure that anthropologist Jan Vansina argues was the original tradition among Bantu speakers. Particularly among fishing and trading peoples such as the Bobangi, the basic social and political unit traditionally was the polygynous household. A cluster of such households formed the village. If the head of a household amassed sufficient wealth, through trade, the purchase of slaves, or acquisition of other clients, he could assume the title of chief. The wealthiest of the house chiefs headed the village. In some cases, a powerful chief unified several villages under his authority and thus created a district. Such trade and fishing villages were not based on actual or alleged kinship. Status and power depended on wealth rather than on personal seniority or on the seniority of the lineage to which one belonged.

Not all groups fit the above pattern. Most political units were small, but some specialized roles could be identified. Some groups had an official with special judicial powers in addition to a chief with largely ritual functions; still others had a war leader.

In the precolonial era, the potential for conflict between communities sharing the same language and culture was at least as great as that between those lacking such commonalities. Awareness of shared ethnic identity did not extend to villages far from one's own and certainly did not define the boundaries of war and peace. Only in the colonial era did such identity take shape when members of some of these groups migrated to the ethnically heterogeneous towns. And such identity was situational. For example, Ngombe living in Mbandaka (formerly Coquilhatville) saw themselves as Ngombe and were so seen by others. Ngombe who lived in Kinshasa, however, came to be defined as Ngala, or Lingala speakers, together with other upriver peoples.

Most of the Congo River basin and part of the lands stretching south to the Kasai and Sankuru rivers are inhabited by a large number of groups categorized under the name of a man from whom they claim descent, Mongo. Among most Mongo groups, the autonomous unit is the village, the core of which is a dominant lineage whose chief is also the chief of client lineages. Only among the Ntomba and some groups (the Lia, the Sengele, the Mpama, and perhaps others) in the southwestern subset of Mongo are hierarchical systems headed by a sacred chief and divided into provinces. A claim to common descent did not lead to a sense of common identity, at least not until Roman Catholic missionaries encouraged such a development.

Bantu Speakers of the Eastern Forest and Plain

To the south of the Central Sudanic-speaking groups and to some degree mixed in with them live a number of Bantu-speaking groups. While generally forest-dwelling, some groups have sited themselves in the more open plain leading to the eastern highlands, and a few have established themselves in the Ruwenzori Mountains. They have been grouped together primarily because they and their Central Sudanic-speaking neighbors share some significant cultural and organizational features and may be clearly distinguished from the neighboring highland Bantu speakers.

Here again, the village in which a localized lineage dwells is the significant political unit rather than any overarching descent group. Links between villages are provided by religious associations and initiation rites. Clan names are shared with adjacent Bantu-speaking groups as well as with some Central Sudanic-speaking communities. Lineage alliances found in some parts of the area also sometimes cross linguistic lines.

Farther south along both sides of the Lualaba River and extending east along its tributary, the Ulindi, another congeries of varied Bantu-speaking groups may be found. All but the Lengola and Metoko share closely related languages. Frequently, in this area of close intermingling, communities are known to have adopted the language and much of the culture of a neighboring, unrelated group. For example, groups of Lega origin, according to anthropologist Daniel Biebuyck, have adopted the culture of other entities and vice versa. Among most of these communities, hierarchically graded religious and political associations have served to tie together systems in which patrilineal lineages provide the bases.

Despite the absence of a centralized state among the Lega and despite the permeability of the borders between them and their neighbors, the Lega have a strong sense of their own historical and cultural unity. That sense was reinforced during the mid-1960s rebellions in eastern Zaire; rebel groups led by intrusive ethnic groups killed a number of Lega and thereby turned most of the others into supporters of the national army that fought and eventually defeated the rebels (see Rural Insurgencies: The "Second Independence," ch. 1; The Congolese National Army, ch. 5).

Bantu Speakers of the Eastern Highlands

From the northern end of Lake Tanganyika to Lake Edward are a number of groups that share cultural and political features among themselves and with the interlacustrine Bantu-speaking peoples of Rwanda, Burundi, southwestern Uganda, and northwestern Tanzania. Most live at an altitude of 1,400 meters or more with a handful sited in the lowlands. Whereas all are cultivators, those in the highlands proper also raise cattle, primarily for milk and milk products; the few lowland groups that are unable to raise cattle have turned, like their forest neighbors, to hunting and fishing.

The highland Bantu speakers have known, possibly as early as the fourteenth century, the presence of centralized states ruled by members of specific descent groups thought to have come from the interlacustrine states to the northeast. Traditionally, only one of their number, the Furiiru, were organized into a single, relatively small state. More often there were several states, for example, among the Shi, that despite their small size carried the heavy apparatus of royal family, court officials, and hierarchy of chiefs.

A degree of ethnic consciousness overriding membership in specific states developed during the late 1950s and early 1960s. The clearest example of the situational character of this consciousness came in 1964 when Shi irregulars joined the national army in opposing a rebel group passing through their territory because the rebels were perceived as outsiders led by Kusu.

Peoples of the Savannas: Southeastern Zaire

In eastern Shaba, stretching from the border with Tanzania and Zambia roughly to the Lualaba River, Vansina has distinguished three sets of communities: the Bemba cluster, the Hemba cluster, and the Haut-Katanga cluster encompassing peoples of Haut-Shaba Subregion (formerly Haut-Katanga). Settlement patterns are geographically fragmented so that representatives of one cluster live cheek by jowl with representatives of another or constitute an enclave in another group's territory.

The area has a long history of conquest and conflict. Most of the peoples of Haut-Shaba were subjects of the Kazembe Kingdom of Luapula, an offshoot of the Lunda Empire whose center was farther west. The Kaonde, the southwesternmost people in the Haut-Katanga cluster, living in present-day Lualaba Subregion (of Shaba Region), were ruled by still another Lunda king. After the middle of the nineteenth century, a group of long-distance traders, the Nyamwezi of central Tanzania, established the Yeke Kingdom, which lasted for thirty years. The introduction of new cultural elements by the Yeke and their trading activities both east and west had longer-range effects than the establishment of their political rule itself.

All of these kingdoms came to an end before the beginning of the twentieth century, leaving their people with polities of much smaller scale. The political pattern that preceded the institution of kingship and outlasted it was based on chiefs of the earth, basically ritual offices essential for maintaining fertility, and, occasionally, political chiefs.

Peoples of the Savannas: Lunda Region

Most of the inhabitants of western Shaba between the Lubilash and Kasai rivers and extending east to the town of Kolwezi are speakers of Lunda or closely related languages. Their distribution extends beyond this area to Angola, Zambia, southwestern Kasai-Occidental, and southeastern Bandundu. The vast scale of their distribution is the legacy of the Lunda Empire (see fig. 2; fig. 3).

Vansina has distinguished the northern Lunda from the southern Lunda and related peoples, in part on linguistic grounds, in part on the basis of differences in modes of inheritance and descent-group formation. The southern Lunda proper, the Chokwe (also seen as Cokwe), the Ndembu, and others are matrilineal; the northern Lunda (also called the Ruund) are marked by bilateral descent. Some contemporary conflicts between these groups, notably between Lunda and Chokwe, have their roots in the period of the breakup of the Lunda Empire in the late nineteenth century. Chokwe raiders from the periphery of the empire grew powerful enough to intervene in Lunda kingship succession disputes and briefly to seize the Lunda capital. Although the Chokwe were eventually ousted and their expansion halted, they succeeded in establishing themselves as competitors to Lunda power. The contemporary echoes of that competition have expressed themselves in the reluctance of Chokwe to support Lunda-led political action.

Peoples of the Southern Uplands: Kasai-Shaba

Extending across much of the southern savannas east of the middle reaches of the Kasai River are the Tshiluba- and Kiluba-speaking peoples. (Kiluba is the language of the Luba-Katanga as distinct from Tshiluba, the language spoken by the Luba-Kasai.) Vansina distinguishes three clusters: the Luba-Katanga—comprising the Luba-Katanga proper, the Kaniok, the Kalundwe, and the Lomotwa; the Luba-Kasai—comprising the Luba-Kasai proper, the Lulua, the Luntu, the Binji, the Mputu, and the North Kete; and the Songye—comprising the Songye proper and the Bangu-Bangu. Closely related to the Luba-Katanga and living to their east are the Hemba, separately distinguished chiefly because, unlike the others, they are matrilineal.

All of these peoples appear to have shared a tradition of chieftainship, but it was among the Luba-Katanga that more complex centralized states emerged as early as the fifteenth and sixteenth centuries. Elsewhere, the people and territory over which a chief ruled were much more restricted, and even among the Luba-Katanga, local chiefs had a substantial degree of autonomy.

Peoples of the Lower Kasai and Its Tributaries

This heterogeneous group of peoples distributed north and south of the lower Kasai River, its tributaries, and the lower Congo River as far as Kinshasa all speak Bantu languages more closely related to each other than to those of adjacent peoples. Many of these groups, particularly those at the periphery, have been influenced by adjacent peoples—the Mongo in the north and peoples of the Kwango River in the southwest.

Vansina has distinguished several clusters, each including the group giving its name to the cluster and others. The Tio cluster

Zebra, common in the savanna regions of central and southern Zaire
Courtesy Zaire National Tourism Office

A square-shaped, thatched-roof hut, typical of the Kasai-Oriental Region, provides shelter against the heavy rains.

includes the core peoples of the Tio Kingdom and several others, some of them never incorporated into the kingdom. The Boma-Sakata cluster includes the Nku and several smaller groups. The Yans-Mbun cluster includes a number of smaller entities. The Kuba cluster includes the Leele, the Njembe, and a number of groups governed by a ruling group called the Bushong, together called Kuba.

The Tio Kingdom was established along both sides of the Congo River north and south of Stanley Pool (now Pool de Malebo) at least as early as the fifteenth century and influenced the development of smaller kingdoms and chiefdoms along the lower Kasai thereafter. At the eastern end of the region, the kingdom of the Kuba, already in existence but not well developed, was reorganized in the mid-seventeenth century and exercised considerable influence in the region west of the Tshiluba-speaking peoples. Between the Tio in the west and the Kuba, most of the peoples in the region were organized into small kingdoms or chieftainships that extended beyond the level of the village or local community. The only important exception was the Leele. There were Leele chiefdoms, but the chiefs had no real significance, and the villages were essentially autonomous and often in conflict.

Local communities were governed by local chiefs in almost all cases. There were superior chiefs nearly everywhere and, in three cases at least, kings, but their powers were often limited. In the cases of kingdoms, one task of the superior chief was to collect tribute.

The Tio Kingdom was large but decentralized. One of the segments in what is now Zaire was essentially autonomous, paying tribute to the king irregularly. The other was more closely controlled, and in certain legal cases, appeals to the king from the judgments of the local chief were possible. The Kuba Kingdom was much more tightly organized. In Vansina's view, this was perhaps the most complex state organization in Zaire, with the exception of the Lunda Empire.

Peoples Between the Kwango and the Kasai

Four clusters have been distinguished among the mixture of peoples in this area. The Yaka cluster includes, among others, the Suku. The Mbala cluster also includes several groups and is perhaps the most fragmented of the lot. The Pende cluster includes the Kwese; the Lunda cluster includes the Soonde and the Chokwe. The Lunda, closely related to the peoples of western Shaba, are included here by Vansina because they are separated from their core area and have had a longtime relationship with the other peoples in the area.

Mixture and mutual influence have characterized these peoples, often in less than peaceful ways. In general, Lunda expansion led to the formation of Lunda-ruled states, a process that continued through the first half of the nineteenth century. The Chokwe, who became such a powerful presence in the core Lunda area in western Shaba in the second half of the nineteenth century, also drove north here in the same period, fragmenting local groups but also incorporating many of them. They were stopped only in 1885 by a coalition of Mbun, Njembe, and Pende, the first two being peoples of the lower Kasai.

Except for the members of the Lunda cluster, most of the peoples in the area originally spoke a dialect of Kikongo or a language related to it. Over a period beginning in the seventeenth century, a good deal of movement was set in train by the expansion of the Lunda Empire. The result was the establishment of Lunda-influenced political patterns among Kongo peoples in the area.

The Kongo Peoples

The Kongo have long occupied all of Bas-Zaïre Region. Most but not all of these peoples, together with substantial numbers in Angola and smaller numbers in Congo, were originally inhabitants of the kingdom of the Kongo encountered by the Portuguese in the late fifteenth century. For all practical purposes, that kingdom had disintegrated into a number of small chiefdoms by the early seventeenth century. The end of the kingdom's political power did not preclude the continuing spread of Kongo influence, however, and some groups may have become Kongo in culture later.

Given the size of the population and the territorial range of the Kongo, much dialectical variation in their language has developed, to the point that some dialects are barely mutually intelligible. There are similar variations in other aspects of culture. From the seventeenth century until the arrival of the Belgians, there were shifting combinations of smaller chiefdoms into larger entities under the domination of one or another chief, the power of a dominant chief often reflecting his easier access to or more effective exploitation of the slave and ivory trade of the period. The hierarchies thus established were usually ephemeral. In the end, the effective units were the clans, their larger constituent units called by anthropologist Wyatt MacGaffey houses (the units controlling land), and lineages, rather shallow units. All of these units were based on matrilineal descent. Although each unit had a head, authority was shared with persons both inside and outside the unit in a complex fashion.

Because of their early contact with Europeans, the Kongo were among the groups early and heavily influenced by Roman Catholic and Protestant missionaries and by the schools established by them. The Roman Catholics placed particular emphasis on the traditions of the Kongo as they understood them and in turn communicated these reconstructed traditions to their students. The complex interaction of myth, competition, and the ambition of some leaders of Kongo origin as the prospect of independence loomed made the Kongo the largest single group to define themselves in ethnic terms for political purposes in the late 1950s and one of the few to develop an articulate ethnic ideology (see The Rise of Militant Ethnicity: Abako, ch. 1).

The Significance of Ethnic Identification

Ethnic identity may best be understood as a construct useful to both groups and individuals. It may be built around group members' perceptions of shared descent, religion, language, origins, or other cultural features. What motivates members to create and maintain a common identity, however, is not shared culture but shared interests. Once created, ethnic groups have persisted not because of cultural conservatism but because their members share some common economic and political interests, thus creating an interest group capable of competing with other groups in the continuing struggle for power.

The construction and destruction of ethnic identities has been an ongoing process. The name *Ngala*, or *Bangala*, for example, was used by early colonial authorities to describe an ethnic group that they imagined existed and lived upriver from the capital and spoke Lingala. The name *Ngala* figured prominently on early maps. The fact that Lingala was a lingua franca and that no group speaking Lingala as a mother tongue existed did not prevent colonial authorities from ascribing group characteristics to the fictional entity; they gave *Ngala* further substance by contrasting Ngala characteristics with those of downriver peoples such as the Kongo. In the preindependence era, some of the upriver Africans briefly adopted the identity of Bangala; they found it useful as a rallying point in creating a political party. Unfortunately, the party failed to win significant electoral support. Without the prospect of winning political and economic spoils, the Bangala identity was perceived as useless and was quickly discarded.

Other ethnic group identities have proven more enduring. Zaire's two largest ethnic groups, the Kongo and the Luba, have been widely mistrusted by many other Zairians as excessively arrogant, ambitious, and inclined to nepotism. Here again, however, traits considered to be innate to the group are in fact ascribed, products of specific historical conditions. Both groups were early adapters to the influences of the West. Their numerical preponderance in Zaire's postcolonial business, church, educational, and governmental hierarchies is a product of their history of early schooling and early acquisition of the skills of literacy rather than of any timeless expression of innate characteristics of ambition and arrogance. Groups on the borders of Kongo and Luba influence have sometimes affirmed their common identity with their larger neighbor or denied it, depending on the historical advantages or disadvantages to be gained.

The significance and divisiveness of ethnic identities were highlighted during the struggle for political power at the time of independence and in the period preceding it. The politically ambitious seized on ethnic identity as the most practical basis for organizing political parties, and a nation fragmented along ethnic lines was the result. In Kasai Province (now Kasai-Occidental Region and Kasai-Oriental Region), ethnic conflict broke out between the Lulua and the Luba-Kasai. In Katanga Province (now Shaba Region), tension had long existed between the Lunda and others (such as the Tabwa from eastern Katanga), who consider themselves "authentic Katangans," and Luba-Kasai immigrants, whose material success the Lunda resented. When Katanga seceded in 1960, its Lunda president, Möise Tshombe, briefly attempted to expatriate the Luba-Kasai from Katanga back to Kasai Province; the net result was to exacerbate hostility between the two groups.

When Mobutu came to power in 1965, his first concern was the reestablishment of public order; ethnicity was widely perceived as having contributed to intra-Zairian conflicts, so Mobutu began a concerted campaign against its expression both in political parties and in government. The several hundred existing political parties, most of them organized along ethnic or regional lines, were banned. They were replaced with one national party, Mobutu's Popular Revolutionary Movement (Mouvement Populaire de la Révolution—MPR). Ethnic associations and appeals to ethnic unity were proscribed. Within government, administrative centralization led to a reduction in the number of provinces and other administrative units and the abrogation of the autonomy of such units. The staffing of government ministries and of high-level posts was consciously balanced to ensure ethnic diversity. Also, the constant rotation of both civilian and military heads of regional and subregional units prevented anyone from building an ethnic following in his or her home region.

Despite these measures, Mobutu's government has been widely perceived as having if not an ethnic, then a regional Équateurian bias. Équateur Region is sometimes knowingly referred to as

"Bethlehem" or "The Promised Land" by non-Équateurians. One major factor in this perception is the fact that Équateurians have profited from Zaire's equivalent of an educational affirmative-action program. Education is perceived as the key to social mobility, and the government's establishment of a regional quota system for university admissions (allotting set numbers of entry places by region) has effectively disadvantaged secondary students graduating from regions with numerous schools, such as Bandundu or Bas-Zaïre, relative to those with fewer schools, notably Équateur and Haut-Zaïre. Students from regions rich in schools have long been angered by the fact that lesser-qualified graduates are occupying university seats solely because they come from the north. In addition, many key posts in the security network generally have been staffed by Équateurians.

Ethnic identity has remained a potent force, and ethnic tensions have festered, exacerbated by the country's economic and social deterioration. Events in Shaba and Nord-Kivu in the early 1990s amply demonstrate this renewed tendency toward ethnic violence. Some groups have come to feel threatened by others they perceive as more successful. And, in a climate of economic collapse and increasingly fierce competition for scarce resources, they have taken action to rid themselves of the offending groups, witness the "authentic Katangans forcing Luba-Kasai out of Shaba and the resentment of indigenous peoples in Nord-Kivu of the numerous Banyarwanda. Many observers also believe, however, that the Mobutu regime has deliberately encouraged this ethnic tension in order to foster anarchy and undermine mass political mobilization against the regime (see Subsequent Political Developments, 1990–93, ch. 4).

Nevertheless, despite the persistence of ethnic tensions demonstrated by interethnic violence in the early 1990s, from the individual Zairian's standpoint, ethnicity is still but one source of identity among many, one that may or may not be expressed depending upon the advantages to be gained or lost. Class identity, for example, may well be more important than ethnic identity to a member of the politico-commercial elite in determining how he or she reacts to a given situation. Religious identity might be more significant than class or ethnic identity to clergy. And patron-client ties throughout the society may undercut or strengthen religious, ethnic, or class identities. Few contemporary analysts would attempt to predict either an individual or a group's probable course of action based on ethnic factors alone.

Indigenous Social Systems

In most cases, the boundaries of indigenous societies, defined as

Men offering to sell a cayman, Équateur Region
Women on their way to the market, Équateur Region

politically autonomous units, were narrower than ethnic boundaries established on the basis of linguistic and cultural similarity. A community was often just a cluster of villages or hamlets, and even that cluster might consist of descent groups, each of which was in some ways autonomous or potentially so (that is, it might move out and establish itself elsewhere). This autonomy was by no means absolute, however. Lineages, and sometimes villages, were exogamous and therefore relied on other groups for spouses, which in turn led to connections of political relevance between lineages. In addition, marital and other cross-cutting ties, such as trade ties or secret societies, sometimes cut across ethnic boundaries, particularly at the territorial periphery of the group.

The environmental range inhabited by Zairian communities and their varied origins made for substantial differences of detail in their patterns of subsistence and modes of sociopolitical organization. Nevertheless, the characteristic way in which most groups came to the places where they finally settled was conducive to a good deal of interpenetration of communities with different traditions and the transfer of aspects of culture from one community to another. Typically, a people entered a region not as a wave inundating or driving out its earlier inhabitants but as small bands filtering in, sometimes conquering, sometimes pushing out, and sometimes peacefully absorbing the communities already there. In a number of cases, these processes were still continuing in the early 1990s.

Communities sharing language and culture were often thinly scattered in a given area. The widespread practice of shifting cultivation meant that each village required a good deal of land, much of which was not under cultivation at any time. If the population of a village or related hamlets grew substantially, some segment of it, usually defined as a lineage, would leave to establish itself elsewhere. The establishment of colonial rule eventually put an end to such movements, however. The Belgians insisted that villages be combined and stabilized, in part to make administrative control easier, in part so that cash cropping could be encouraged.

With very few exceptions, indigenous Zairian communities had chiefs of some kind. There was, however, a good deal of variation in the scale of the entity under a single head and therefore in the extent to which any chiefdom was marked by a hierarchy of chiefs. There were also considerable differences in the secular authority of chiefs at any level.

Chieftainship was linked in principle, and often in fact, to the system of unilineal (patrilineal or matrilineal) descent groups that provided the basic sociopolitical framework of most Zairian groups.

94

The politically significant descent groups were often those localized in a single village or a cluster of related villages.

Another feature of precolonial Zairian societies was the existence
of some form of slavery, usually as a result of warfare. The precise
social and economic position of slaves varied from society to society. Rarely, if ever, was it exactly like the chattel slavery characteristic of much of the New World. In traditional Zairian societies,
slaves had some rights and could improve their position to some
extent. Nevertheless, slaves, and often their descendants, were in
a marginal position.

Of the varied sociopolitical patterns characteristic of indigenous
Zairian communities, only some elements, altered and adapted during the colonial era and since independence, remain significant in
the lives of Zairians generally and those in rural areas particularly. Broadly, the persisting units are the local communities, often
changed by the aggregation of smaller units into larger ones; the
descent groups, which bear a variable relationship to local communities; and the networks of kin connections in which each individual is involved.

In general, the range of fairly important kin is wider than that
in the West and has not appreciably narrowed, even in modern-
day urban society, in part because many urban Zairians maintain
ties with the rural areas from which they come, in part because
kin ties provide ways of coping with some of the difficulties of urban life. In some cases, obligations to kin become burdensome in
an urban context, particularly to those who have had some degree
of success and are expected to help new arrivals. Kin may be more
trustworthy than others, however, and for the ambitious person
they may provide a nucleus of dependents and followers necessary
to further success.

In a number of the more complex chiefdoms, aspects of the hierarchy have survived. Some traditional chiefs still wield considerable influence. Many do not, however. Moreover, disputes over
succession were not uncommon in the precolonial era and have
persisted into the modern period so that at any time a group may
be divided among factions supporting specific claimants to the
chiefdom.

With very few exceptions, indigenous Zairian communities distinguished their members on some scale of worthiness based on
age and sex, and such distinctions persist. In general, other things
being equal, age requires respect, although seniority does not necessarily confer access to the office of highest status in the descent group
or local community. Again in general, males have higher status than

females, despite the presence in many communities of matrilineal descent groups and matrilineally based succession and inheritance.

Zairian Social Classes

In the years since independence in 1960, Zaire has become an increasingly stratified and polarized society. One way of understanding how this process has occurred and what the social profile of the country has become is by distinguishing among the various classes that have evolved. Zaire specialist Michael G. Schatzberg's notion of class is a useful tool in conceptualizing these changes. He argues against a rigid conception of class that identifies any single individual as a member of an exclusive category such as the proletariat or the bourgeoisie. He argues instead that class identity is situationally based; an individual may be a member of one class in one interactional situation and a member of another in a different situation. Crawford Young and Thomas Turner, adopting this more fluid concept of class, and building on previous models of Zairian stratification elaborated by Georges Nzongola-Ntalaja, Jean Rymenam, and others, have distinguished the following social classes.

The External Estate

Non-African expatriate numbers fell from 110,000 before independence to a figure fluctuating between 40,000 and 60,000 thereafter, but foreigners remained a significant elite social force in Zaire. Belgian colonial officials, missionaries, and businessmen predominated in the preindependence era. Belgian colonial officials and security personnel left during the crisis at the start of the Katangan secession in 1960, and their positions were quickly Africanized. But Belgian employees of private companies left more gradually. Although they still constitute the majority of resident aliens in Zaire, if refugees are excluded, Belgian traders and settlers have been supplanted or joined over time by Greek, Levantine, Portuguese, Italian, and Indo-Pakistani family-based mercantile networks. West Africans constitute another elite expatriate group.

These family-based transnational businesses generally began in trade and moved on to acquire farms, mills, and small factories. In addition, trade manipulation (including smuggling, rigged invoices, and illicit currency transactions) is an important source of windfall profits, indulged in by Zairians and foreigners alike. Despite the expulsion of West African traders in 1971 and the temporary expropriation of Mediterranean and Asian businesses in 1973 and 1974, many family-owned transnational businesses have remained. In 1980, for example, fully half of Kisangani's locally owned businesses were in the hands of resident Greeks and Asians.

Most significant as a reference group for Zairian elites are the several thousand foreign personnel of various nationalities who serve in the foreign-aid missions, public-sector agencies, and the education system. They are much more socially fragmented than their colonial-era predecessors, in that Belgians, French, Americans, and Japanese have created separate social milieus, each with their own schools, clubs, and religious institutions. Yet their common cosmopolitan life-style, frequent travel, automobiles, and expensive household consumer goods effectively define Zairian elites' standards and aspirations for the "good life."

Western missionaries are a case apart. Although diminished in number and influence, they continue to work toward the institutionalization of African churches. Their progressive Africanization of church hierarchies, modest consumption standards relative to other expatriates, willingness to work in rural areas, and, most important, their provision of high-quality health care and education have earned them a high status throughout much of the country.

The Politico-Commercial Class

This class has ruled Zaire since independence. Two key features of this "national bourgeoisie," as Nzongola calls it, have been its dependence upon the state for its social status and its use of political power to amass economic power. By looking at the shifting popular terms of reference for the group over time, its salient features can be sketched.

The origins of this class lie in the colonial-era group called the *évolués* (sing., *évolué*—see Glossary). The *évolués* were drawn from the ranks of colonial clerks, teachers, and nurses. They sought recognition as a group set apart from the African masses, one which embraced and emulated European patterns of culture and behavior. Whereas *évolués* were intermediaries between the Belgians and the Congolese masses, not all intermediaries were *évolués*. Clergy, noncommissioned officers (NCOs), and chiefs were intermediaries who did not have *évolué* status. Clergy in particular had a distinctive status, being the only Africans in colonial society who were considered on a plane of approximate social equality with Europeans.

With the growth of nationalism in the late 1950s, the term *évolué* was gradually displaced and rejected in favor of the new status term, *intellectuel* (intellectual). An *intellectuel* was generally someone who had some secondary education and a white-collar job. This class was well positioned to take advantage of the flight of Belgian civil servants and army officers following independence in 1960. Although there was only a modest difference between the income opportunities of colonial-era *évolués* and other Congolese, the opportunities available to the new elite were substantial. Clerks and NCOs moved up into the vacated positions above them, and Congolese who shot up into the senior executive ranks of the civil service or into national and provincial ministerial offices enjoyed huge increases in income. In the nation's first cabinet, nineteen of the twenty-three ministers were former clerks.

This new elite quickly invested in those commercial sectors where the state's regulatory position could be converted into competitive advantage, including the acquisition of urban land titles, supplying the state, constructing rental housing, and selling licenses for the right to import goods. In addition, corruption served as a source of capital for the new politico-commercial class; by 1971 theft of state funds was estimated by one analyst at 60 percent of the national budget.

The new class profited spectacularly from the government's 1973 Zairianization (see Glossary) decree in which all foreign-owned plantations and many commercial firms were turned over to nationals (see Zairianization, Radicalization, and Retrocession, ch. 1; Zairianization, ch. 3). The term used to describe a politically connected individual who was given ownership of a foreign business was *acquéreur* (literally, acquirer). First used as an administrative term, *acquéreur* rapidly became transformed in public usage to a synonym for a member of the ruling circle; it further degenerated into an epithet shouted out by children whenever a Mercedes drove by. In Young's words, ''In the metamorphosis from *évolué* to *acquéreur*, social respect was transformed into class conflict.''

Because few members of the politico-commercial class own productive resources unrelated to political influence or protection, they remain dependent and insecure. Turnover in the upper echelon of the regime is rapid, so economic security for its members has been precarious. This elite has consequently preferred either to invest in short-term, high-return enterprises like the import-export trade, urban property, or taxis, or to stash its funds abroad for safekeeping.

The New Commercial Class

In addition to the economically predatory politico-commercial class, a new economic class has been developing. This class is unconnected to the political authorities, is relatively uneducated, and is not made up of *acquéreurs*. It has grown in regional centers such as Kisangani, far from the capital, where the state presence and state provision of public services are weakest. Amassing capital through trade and other successful commercial activities, this class has became strong enough in some areas to replace the state as a provider of infrastructure, such as airstrips, electrical generators, and road maintenance.

Other High-Status Groups

Ranking military officers, Zairian university staff, and clergy all enjoy high social status in Zaire but have developed quite different profiles. Officers have received rewards from the president for their loyalty and have been given wide leeway to develop lucrative outside businesses. They are, however, in much the same position as members of the politico-commercial class in that they are frequently promoted and demoted at the president's whim and have little security of tenure. Staff at the main Kinshasa campus of the National University of Zaire (Université Nationale du Zaïre— UNAZA) have tended to be absorbed into the politico-commercial class; this is particularly the case with those faculty in fields such as economics, commerce, and law. They have served as appointees in high government posts or have found lucrative consultancy opportunities. Kinshasa campus staff not in these fields and university staff outside the capital have had an increasingly marginalized economic position but have nevertheless retained considerable social prestige. In general, the clergy have retained much of the status and security they enjoyed before independence. For example, in the transition from single-party rule beginning in 1990, Monsignor Laurent Monsengwo Pasinya, archbishop of Kisangani, played a major role, reflecting the continuing prestige of the Roman Catholic clergy.

The Subbourgeoisie

Underneath the politico-commercial class and the other elite groups, yet above the working class, is the subbourgeoisie. This group includes the nation's teachers and clerks, military NCOs and junior officers, and low-level bureaucrats or local government officials. Although the early members of the politico-commercial class came from the subbourgeoisie, the waves of university graduates that filled the upper echelons of government from 1965 onward effectively blocked this class from any hope of upward mobility. Totally dependent on the state, yet marked by a deteriorating income and status, this was a highly disgruntled group in the early 1990s.

The subbourgeoisie provides a clear example of what Schatzberg means by situational class membership. Relative to those above them in the class hierarchy, teachers, clerks, NCOs and chiefs have felt "out of the loop," without power or influence. Their perceptions of powerlessness are well justified. With the exception of some university-educated secondary school teachers, who might be posted outside their home areas, chances of geographical or professional mobility are nil. While totally dependent on the state as a source of livelihood, their salaries have fallen woefully behind inflation. They frequently wait months to receive their salaries and, even then, their superiors might appropriate much of what is disbursed.

Nonetheless, from the perspective of those people below them, namely workers, peasants, and Zairians in the informal sector, these salaried members of the subbourgeoisie are part of the privileged, exploiting class. Many low-level state functionaries require bribes before exercising their services. Teachers may demand money to pass a student, government clerks may request a bribe in order to get funds disbursed or a certificate or license delivered. And state security personnel may demand a donation in order to let travelers pass an impromptu roadblock or escape an infraction of the law, whether real or imagined. Even for those state employees who retain a sense of professionalism, the need to feed their families when salaries go unpaid has proved a powerful inducement to abuse of official position. As a consequence, a member of the subbourgeoisie may be viewed as a member of the victimized lower class or of the victimizing upper class, depending upon the onlooker.

Historically, the position of the subbourgeoisie has been most precarious in times of trouble. During the 1964 rural insurgencies, for example, the subbourgeoisie lacked the ability of elite personnel to flee and consequently bore the brunt of popular anger against the establishment; tens of thousands of teachers, clerks, and low-level government personnel were killed in many rebel-held areas. Fear of such popular anger, together with the habits and mindsets of their professional roles, have kept the subbourgeoisie generally compliant in their role as, in Young's words, "the indispensable capillaries of the power system."

The Working Class

This class includes employees of public and parastatal (see Glossary) entities, large private companies, small companies, rural plantations, and lumbering enterprises. The public-sector employees have been the least content, principally because many are not covered by civil service status and have known repeated layoffs, delays in pay, and insecure work conditions. Turnover in the work force of large corporations, however, including the large parastatal General Quarries and Mines (Générale des Carrières et des

100

Mines—Gécamines), has tended to be low. Consistently paid salaries, company stores, and company medical services have been key elements in retaining the long-term loyalty of such employees. Turnover also appears to be rather low in rural enterprises, where isolation has resulted in localized recruitment patterns and little contact with other workers.

Workers have shown a sense of class consciousness in launching episodic strikes beginning as early as 1941, when at least sixty were killed at Élisabethville (now Lubumbashi). Unions, however, have been generally weak, and the postcolonial state has generally controlled similar episodes by coupling the offer of limited concessions with the jailing or intimidation of strike leaders. Whereas workers have shared a clearly articulated sense of who "they" are—namely, *acquéreurs,* politicians, *abacost* (see Glossary) wearers, Mercedes owners, and regime courtiers—"we" has been a less clear-cut category and has tended to be defined by place of work, city, and ethnicity. Still, the general consciousness of inequality and of social polarization has remained acute; fueling it has been the dramatic decline in workers' incomes (see Gross Domestic Product, ch. 3).

The Informal Sector

This category has grown substantially in the years since independence, particularly in the cities. It consists of people who lack regular wage employment and who engage in a wide variety of economic activities. Typical occupations include tailoring, shoe repairs, housing construction, taxi and bus services, soft-drink vending, masonry work, petty retailing, artisanal crafts, prostitution, and petty criminality. In border cities, the latter category includes smugglers, who have sometimes grown wealthy from their illicit activity. Participation may be transitional or permanent. School leavers have been typical transitional members as they may engage in such activities on a part-time subsistence basis while searching for permanent employment. Older persons, women, and individuals lacking educational qualifications for wage employment have tended to remain in this sector permanently. Although poverty grips most people in this sector, individuals have occasionally prospered. More importantly, the size, ingenuity, and redistributive capacity of this group have served as buffers to individual hardship during periods of economic calamity.

Peasants

The peasantry is the class that has probably lost the most since independence. Although the Belgian colonial state laid an onerous burden of labor and taxation on its rural subjects, it did provide some medical and educational services and built a substantial transportation network. All of these services have deteriorated. Resources, whether they are budget appropriations, consumer goods, gasoline, or medicines, have been targeted first to the urban population, with only the remainder going to the hinterland. Rural government hospitals and dispensaries have continued to exist, but have rarely had medical supplies. Rural schools have increased in quantity but, outside of selected schools run by church networks, have greatly decreased in quality. And the road network has so deteriorated that in many areas crops cannot be transported to market and have been left to rot at collection depots.

The decrease in state services has not meant a corresponding decrease in state exactions, however. State economic policies have kept the price of foodstuffs and cash crops alike at low levels, disadvantaging rural producers and favoring urban populations and middlemen or state marketing organs. Production quotas for peasants have continued to be enforced, including those for export crops such as cotton. Coercion is applied not only in the form of hectarage quotas for specified crops but also through direct taxation. Each adult household head must pay a tax, and, prior to 1990 at least, party dues were levied on top of that. Census-takers passing through a village charged fees both for adding names to the roster in case of births and for deleting names from the roster in case of deaths.

Fines have been another form of taxation on rural producers. Fines may be levied for failure to perform unpaid labor for state projects, for digging an improper latrine in contravention of sanitary regulations, or for failing to plant the required hectarage. On top of these charges are the many illegal extortions imposed by government agents. Local police, army units, or party youth groups have long set up impromptu roadblocks where identity cards, official party cards, or other documents can be demanded, declared out of order, and retrieved only after payment of a "fine." Or a market-bound villager's bundle of game meat might be declared to belong to an endangered species protected by law, justifying confiscation on the spot. Young has speculated that "as much as 50 percent of real and potential village income is extracted by the state or its representatives."

Polarization and Prospects for Conflict

Given the polarization of Zairian society since 1960 into an upper class dominated by the external estate and the politico-commercial elite and a lower-class group of subbourgeoisie, workers, members of the informal sector, and peasants, open conflict

*Women
and children,
Équateur Region*

would seem inevitable. At least three major reasons why this has not occurred may be cited.

One is the power of the myth of educational mobility (see Education, this ch.). A link between education and upward mobility is widely believed to exist, which has given parents hope that however bad their own current conditions, through education their children might advance and prosper. Parents have made painful financial sacrifices in order to get their children into and through secondary school.

The myth obscures the fact that schools vary widely in quality and that only some urban and church-run schools offer the quality of instruction needed to pass the national state secondary school examinations. In addition, many parents in the politico-commercial class send their children abroad to be educated in Europe and elsewhere, giving their offspring an advantage unavailable to the children of other classes. Nevertheless, despite the progressive closure of avenues of advancement through education, the myth of its availability has been a significant factor in dampening social unrest.

A second factor is the availability of outside force to back the state in case of rebellion or invasion. The external estate depends on the government as a guarantor of the order needed to conduct its economic activities and to protect its luxurious lifestyle; thus, it has tacitly backed the status quo. The state in turn depends on the external estate in order to operate the mining industry; that industry has long furnished it with the bulk of its revenues. Both the external estate and the government are closely linked with a group of Western states, most importantly Belgium, France, and the United States. Whenever the external estate or key productive installations, such as Zaire's copper or cobalt mines, were threatened, foreign powers intervened militarily. The knowledge that their rulers might rely on outside military aid has had a restraining effect on those in the lower classes who might otherwise have contemplated active opposition to the state.

A final factor in the failure of the people to revolt in response to their pauperization is their own strength in creating alternatives to the formal market economy. The informal sector has shown remarkable resilience and has provided a means of subsistence where the formal economy has failed. The weakness of the state in its attempts to regulate or control these parallel markets has, paradoxically, helped to ensure their survival. For people who would starve if limited in their activity to the formal market, the parallel markets of the informal sector offer a chance for survival.

Strategies of Survival

Zairians have not revolted in the face of their progressive pauperization. Instead, faced with a steady decline in income and a rise in exactions from authorities on their declining income base, they have responded in three ways: by adapting, by resisting, and by fleeing. These strategies cut across class distinctions, although the specific actions taken might be shaped by class.

One key to understanding popular adaptive strategies and their underlying ideologies may be found in the terms of reference and address, idioms, and phrases used in everyday life. Paralleling the official ideologies of authenticity (see Glossary) and Mobutism (see Glossary) have been those methods created by the Zairian people in their efforts to cope with an economy in decline. Phrases heard in daily conversation embody the strategies used to negotiate an increasingly difficult economic climate.

Coping and Hustling

A simple translation of the French term *se débrouiller* (verb; noun form, *débrouillardise*) might be "to fend for oneself," or "to cope," but that literal translation would need to be elaborated with the connotations of hustle, know-how, and the ability to get by or to get what you want. It may consist of knowing how to get a ride on one of the rare commercial trucks that still ply the deteriorating roads of the interior and that furnish what is often the only passenger service available. It may involve knowing which official to bribe in order to get one's salary released or knowing which kinship connection to tap in order to get a sought-after secondary school slot opened for one's child or cousin after enrollment is formally closed. Or *débrouillardise* may be demonstrated by the ability to locate on the black market drugs needed by a hospitalized family member or by paying a hospital or dispensary nurse to "acquire" the needed medications from institutional stocks. The term may also be adapted to refer to the entire unofficial economy.

The popular admonition that "you need to know how to cope/hustle" (*il faut savoir comment se débrouiller*) implicitly contradicts official party and state slogans such as "*servir, oui, se servir, non*" (serve yes, serve oneself, no). The popular phrase embodies an ideology of aggressive individualism that contradicts the state-promoted ideology of selfless public service.

Theft and Bribery

The widely used Lingala phrase, *yiba moke,* meaning "steal just a little," did not originate in popular conversation but in the text of a speech by President Mobutu in 1977. He was speaking out against runaway corruption and advised his countrymen that they should "steal just a little" or, perhaps, "steal wisely" and that they should invest the proceeds inside the country rather than stowing it abroad. Intended as a moderating counsel, Mobutu's words have come to epitomize the scale of corruption under his rule, corruption so commonplace as to command public presidential acquiescence so long as its practice remained "moderate." Some analysts, notably David Gould, have identified this massive corruption as the essential grease that has served to lubricate the machinery of state and without which it might cease to function.

Corruption is extremely widespread. A survey of government personnel in Lubumbashi in 1982 documented the variety of means by which state employees supplemented their irregular and inadequate salaries. These means included embezzlement (including direct payroll theft, often through the padding of payrolls with fictitious names), payoffs, forgeries of official signatures and seals, sale of false documents of certification, illegal taxation, second jobs, and foodstuff production and sale. Other analysts have added to the above false bills and profit-margin cheating on the allowed rate of profit for business; import, export, and excise stamp fraud; sale of merchandise quotas; postal and judicial fraud; and extortion at military barricades.

Bribery, too, is commonplace. A rich vocabulary for bribes is one index of its ubiquity. Anthropologist Janet MacGaffey has cited as examples in Lingala, *madesu ya bana* (beans for the children) and *tia ngai mbeli* (stab me); in Swahili, *kuposa koo* (refresh the throat) and *kulowanish a ndebu* (moisten the beard); and in French, *comprendre, s'arranger,* and *coopérer* (to understand, to come to terms, and to cooperate), which may be used by a speaker to indicate that a bribe is appropriate. Sometimes a gesture may be used, such as stroking under the chin, to signal that a bribe is expected. Although analysts debate whether the term bribery is an appropriate characterization of these exchanges, the scale of the phenomenon and the bottom-to-top direction of the flow of resources has not been contested.

The sense that public and commercial coffers are prizes to be won may be found in conversational phrases and in popular music. Adults knowingly speak of the *avantages de la caisse* (the advantages of the cashbox) in discussing a chief's economic position. Children in the early and mid-1970s would frequently shout out to passing expatriates a phrase from a popular song *mondele, donnez-moi la caisse* (white man, give me the cashbox), showing not only an appreciation of the continuing economic power of the first estate but also the sense of treasury as trophy. This sense extends to the upper reaches of society; university students in Kisangani would at times exonerate those responsible for thefts of public funds with the phrase *s'il y a l'anarchie, profitez-en,* (if there's anarchy, profit from it).

Patron-Client Relations

Patron is a term of address that means, crudely, "boss" or "patron." Patron-client relations are marked by unequal status, reciprocity, and personal contact, and their use is common throughout Zaire. Individuals may circumvent the power of state officials by locating someone in the bureaucracy to whom they are related by ties of ethnicity, locality, kinship, religious affiliation, or class. In appealing to such ties in order to get a permit issued, a court case resolved, or a child admitted to school, for example, bonds are forged that may be used by the patron or the client in future matters. Such bonds may undercut or reinforce other bonds of class, regional, or ethnic solidarity, depending on the situation.

Such bonds and the need for them subvert official ideology as well as official structures and procedures. Under the state and party ideology of authenticity, all citizens were equal and the appropriate term of address among all Zairians was *citoyen* (fem., *citoyenne*), or citizen. The term was mandated for public use in order to do away with the perceived hierarchical distinctions of *monsieur* and *madame.* Not only does use of the term *patron* undercut this aim by creating new hierarchies, but Zairians often reversed the egalitarian intent of the term *citoyen* itself in their use of it. The term was often reserved for addressing members of new and old elites, the politico-commercial class, and the external estate; a foreigner might find himself or herself addressed as *citoyen,* while a Zairian worker or farmer might not.

Resistance

Under Mobutu, resistance through public or institutional channels of expression generally has met with state repression and/or co-optation. Political resisters are often bought off with the offer of high-salaried posts. In the past if this failed, leaders might be imprisoned or sentenced to internal exile in their home villages.

Strikes by workers have occurred intermittently but have not been effective tools for social or economic change. Typical is the 1980 secondary school teachers' strike against low pay and overcrowded classrooms in Kisangani. Strikers were threatened with dismissal, and strike leaders were repeatedly summoned to appear in the offices of the secret police. Threats against strike leaders' lives were made, and the strike was eventually broken. When an institution's personnel have gone on strike or had the temerity to hold public protest marches, as university students have done periodically since the late 1960s, the state has responded with force.

The hopelessness of public protest has given rise to alternative forms of resistance. Farmers' resistance to compulsory cotton cultivation quotas has been well documented. Faced with low producer prices and dishonest state marketing boards, farmers sabotaged cotton production by diverting fertilizer intended for cotton production to their own food crops, by failing to space plants appropriately, and by refusing to replant their fields as instructed. Farmers then redirected their energies to the cultivation of more profitable food crops such as corn, cassava, and peanuts. No more cotton hectarage was planted than was required to escape fines and imprisonment.

A similar form of resistance has been practiced in the area of palm oil production. Low wages for palm oil plantation workers and low prices for palm nuts purchased from petty producers resulted in workers deserting plantations in areas such as Bunia, near Lake Albert. Their preferred course of action was to abandon commercial crop production in order to concentrate on producing food crops.

Resistance has also taken other forms. Illicit mining of gold in the Kivu regions and Haut-Zaïre occurs on both an individual and group basis. Mukdrya Vwakyanakazi has documented the formation of villages of illicit gold miners in Kivu, villages that have their own authority structure independent of the government. In Haut-Zaïre, people engaged in illicit mining activities protect themselves and their operations with private militias against government soldiers and officials, or, elsewhere, local officials are paid off for protection against interference. Similar arrangements have been reported for illicit diamond mining.

Smuggling across Zaire's porous borders is another means of resisting pauperization. A large-scale illicit trade flourishes in all commodities that can be sold for foreign currencies, among them gold, coffee, ivory, diamonds, cobalt, tea, cotton, and palm oil.

Finally, resistance is expressed linguistically, in the labels used to deflate state institutions and ideologies and to create an alternative folk consciousness. In this vein, the national army's proud slogan of being *toujours en avant* (always out front) is transformed into *toujours en arrière* (always behind). The national airline, called Air Zaïre, has become known as "Air Peut-être" (Air Maybe) and the national highway authority, the Office des Routes, is called in popular parlance the Office des Trous (Department of Holes).

Such resistance began long before the economic crises of the late 1980s and early 1990s. When Mobutu officially changed the names of the nation, the Congo River (name change not recognized by the United States), and the national currency to Zaire, and referred to them as Les Trois Z—*Notre Pays, Notre Fleuve, Notre Monnaie* (The Three Zs—Our Country, Our River, Our Money) in 1967, the *radio trottoir* (literally, sidewalk radio; meaning public grapevine) quickly recharacterized the president's program as Les Trois M—*Mwasi, Moyibi, Masanga* (The Three Ms—Women, Thieves, Booze). Or when students in Bandundu were required in the name of the state doctrine of authenticity to replace their European first names with African ones in 1971, first names such as Mambo Ve (Doesn't Matter) suddenly appeared on teachers' class rosters.

Flight

Another strategy for survival is flight, which for the politico-commercial class might mean sending family and fortune abroad when conditions appear threatening. For undercompensated workers, flight might mean movement from a low-wage job in plantation agriculture to self-employment elsewhere as an independent farmer, miner, or petty merchant. For undercompensated farmers, it might mean migration to the cities; part of the impetus behind urban migration is the heavier levies on people in rural areas (where they are within the government's reach) than on the urban population. And for some groups, flight into deep forest and the establishment of villages entirely independent of the state has been a solution.

The Status of Women

Women in Zaire in the 1990s have not attained a position of full equality with men. Although the Mobutu regime has paid lip service to the important role of women in society and although women enjoy some legal rights (e.g., the right to own property and the right to participate in the economic and political sectors), custom and legal constraints still limit their opportunities.

The inferiority of women was embedded in the indigenous social system and reemphasized in the colonial era. The colonial-era status of African women in urban areas was low. Adult women were legitimate urban dwellers if they were wives, widows, or elderly. Otherwise they were presumed to be *femmes libres* (free women) and were taxed as income-earning prostitutes, whether they were or not. From 1939 to 1943, over 30 percent of adult Congolese women in Stanleyville (now Kisangani) were so registered. The taxes they paid constituted the second largest source of tax revenue for Stanleyville.

Opportunities for wage labor jobs and professional positions remained rare even after independence. For example, in Kisangani there were no women in law, medicine, or government in 1979, nineteen years after independence. Moreover, educational opportunities for girls remained constricted compared with those for boys.

By the 1990s, women had made strides in the professional world, and a growing number of women now work in the professions, government service, the military, and the universities. But they remain underrepresented in the formal work force, especially in higher-level jobs, and generally earn less than their male counterparts in the same jobs.

In addition, certain laws clearly state that women are legally subservient to men. A married woman must have her husband's permission to open a bank account, accept a job, obtain a commercial license, or rent or sell real estate. Article 45 of the civil code specifies that the husband has rights to his wife's goods, even if their marriage contract states that each spouse separately owns his or her own goods.

Adapting to this situation, urban women have exploited commercial opportunities in the informal economy, outside of men's control. They generally conduct business without bank accounts, without accounting records, and without reporting all of their commerce. Anthropologist Janet MacGaffey's study of enterprises in Kisangani showed that 28 percent of the city's large business owners not dependent on political connections were women; these women specialized in long-distance distribution and retail and semi-wholesale trade. About 21 percent of the retail stores in the commercial and administrative zone of the city belonged to women, and women dominated the market trade.

Rural women find fewer such strategies available. Saddled with the bulk of agricultural work, firewood gathering, water hauling, and child care, they have generally seen an increase in their labor burdens as the economy has deteriorated. In Zaire's eastern highlands, conditions have grown particularly severe. The state-promoted expansion of cash-crop hectarage for export, particularly of coffee and quinine, has reduced the amount and quality of land available for peasant household food-crop production. Plantations owned by the politico-commercial and new commercial elites have increasingly expanded onto communal lands, displacing existing food crops with cash crops. And within peasant households, men's control of the allocation of household land for export and food crops has led to greater use of land for export crops and the diminution of women's access to land and food crops.

Even when male producers turn to cultivating food crops, the

110

household does not necessarily profit nutritionally. Food needed for household consumption is frequently sold for cash, cash needed to pay for daily necessities, clothes, school fees, taxes, and so on. Higher-priced and nutritionally superior food crops such as sorghum are frequently sold by producers who eat only their cheaper, less nutritious food crops such as cassava. Widespread malnutrition among children has resulted.

Among groups where women have more power, the situation is less severe. Among the Lemba, for example, women not only have more say in determining what is grown but also in what is consumed. In a country where the most widespread pattern is for the men to be served the best food first, with the remainder going to women and children, Lemba women traditionally set aside choice food items and sauces for their own and their children's consumption before feeding the men their food. Their nutritional status and that of their children is correspondingly better.

Rural women have arguably borne the brunt of state exactions. In some cases, women have banded together to resist the rising tolls and taxes imposed on them. Political scientist Katharine Newbury studied a group of Tembo women growers of cassava and peanuts west of Lac Kivu who successfully protested against the imposition of excessive collectivity taxes and market taxes levied on them when they went to market. The local chief was hostile. But a sympathetic local Catholic church, which provided a forum for meetings and assistance in letter writing, was helpful, as was the ethnic homogeneity of the group. Although they could not nominate a woman for election to the local council, they did succeed in voting for males friendly to their position. The newly elected councillors hastened to suspend the taxes and the tolls.

Not all women's organizations have been equally successful. In Kisangani the Association of Women Merchants (Association des Femmes Commerçantes—Afco) failed to advance the interests of the assembled women merchants. The group instead turned into a vehicle for class interests, namely those of the middle-class president. MacGaffey clearly saw the case as one of the triumph of class solidarity over gender solidarity.

A continuing challenge for women has been the limited integration of women's experience and perspectives into the development initiatives of Western development agencies. As Brooke Schoepf has documented, little effort has been made to create agricultural extension networks for women, who have continued to contribute the overwhelming bulk of agricultural labor. In addition, project production goals rarely have taken into account the effect of the withdrawal of women's time from current food production and household work to meet the goals of the new programs. Development in such a context often has meant a step backward rather than a step forward from the perspective of the women being "developed."

Religion

The majority of Zairians belong to one Christian church or another. Although statistics are imprecise, roughly 46 to 48 percent are Roman Catholics; 24 to 28 percent, Protestants; and as many as 16.5 percent may belong to the indigenous Kimbanguist Church. Islam counts only a small number of adherents in Zaire, perhaps 1 percent of the population, principally clustered in the former Maniema Subregion of Kivu (now Maniema Region) and in pockets in eastern Zaire from Kisangani south to Shaba. Most of the remaining population practices traditional African religions.

A clear delineation of religious affiliation into these membership categories can give a misleading picture of Zairian reality. The number of persons who can be categorized as belonging exclusively to one group or another is limited. Overlapping affiliations are more common. As with class identity or with ethnic identity, an individual Zairian's religious identity may be situational. Different spiritual traditions, agents, and communities may be sought out for assistance, depending on the situation at hand. For example, Christian students in Christian schools may employ sorcery with the objective of improving their individual exam scores or of helping their school's soccer team win in competition against their opponents. Sophisticated urbanites, faced with disease in a family member, may patronize indigenous healers and diviners. And Zairians practicing traditional African religions may also go to both established Christian clergy and breakaway Christian sects in search of spiritual assistance. In the search for spiritual resources, Zairians have frequently displayed a marked openness and pragmatism.

The Roman Catholic Church

The impact of the Roman Catholic Church in Zaire is difficult to overestimate. Schatzberg has called it "Zaire's only truly national institution apart from the state." Besides involving over 40 percent of the population in its religious services, its schools have educated over 60 percent of the nation's primary school students and more than 40 percent of its secondary students. The church owns and manages an extensive network of hospitals, schools, and clinics, as well as many diocesan economic enterprises, including farms, ranches, stores, and artisans' shops.

The church's penetration of the country at large is a product

High-school students,
Bas-Zaïre Region

Parents with a newborn on the
way to have the baby baptized,
Bandundu Region

of the colonial era (see The Apparatus of Control, ch. 1). The Belgian colonial state authorized and subsidized the predominantly Belgian Roman Catholic missions to establish schools and hospitals throughout the colony; the church's function from the perspective of the state was to accomplish Belgium's ''civilizing mission'' by creating a healthy, literate, and disciplined work force, one that was obedient to the governing authorities. From the perspective of the church, evangelization was the primary goal, and the number of converts baptized was the measure of its success. Although different in emphasis, church and state goals were sufficiently complementary that the state and church were perceived by the population as sharing the same purpose. As Joseph Cardinal Malula, who was for many years the head of the church in Zaire, put it, ''For our people, the Church was the State, and the State was the Church.'' When independence came in 1960, the bill for church collaboration came due; Roman Catholic personnel were the frequent subjects of attacks by angry Congolese throughout the country, while Protestant missionaries and Kimbanguist personnel were, outside of Bas-Zaïre Region, largely spared.

The church's reversal of its role in relation to the state since independence has been striking. Formerly a reliable ally, it has increasingly become the state's most severe institutional critic (see Interest Groups, ch. 4). Overt conflict first erupted in 1971 when the state, as part of its efforts to centralize and extend its authority, nationalized the country's three universities, including the Catholic church's Lovanium University outside Kinshasa. State attempts to implant sections of the official party's youth movement, the Youth of the Popular Revolutionary Movement (Jeunesse du Mouvement Populaire de la Révolution—JMPR), in Catholic seminaries were strongly resisted. The conflict intensified in 1972 when, as part of the authenticity campaign, all Zairians were ordered to drop their Christian baptismal names and adopt African ones. Cardinal Malula protested the decision and told his bishops to ignore it. The regime retaliated by forcing the cardinal into exile for three months and by seizing his residence and converting it into JMPR headquarters. In addition, the state banned all religious publications and youth groups.

Following a brief thaw in 1973 and early 1974, during which the cardinal was permitted to return from exile, relations between church and state continued to deteriorate. The state declared that Christmas would no longer be a Zairian holiday, banned religious instruction from the schools, and ordered crucifixes and pictures of the pope removed from schools, hospitals, and public buildings; the removed items were replaced by pictures of President Mobutu.

The president was characterized by the regime as a new messiah, and the state took over direct control of the nation's schools. Courses in Mobutism supplanted courses in religious instruction. Students in the former church schools found themselves participating in daily rallies led by JMPR members, during which they were obliged to chant "*Mobutu awa, Mobutu kuna, Mobutu partout*" (Mobutu here, Mobutu there, Mobutu everywhere).

The tables turned in late 1975 as the effects of Zairianization and the fall in copper prices resulted in a progressively worsening economy. As living standards fell, more and more state officials exploited their positions to steal from the citizenry. Roman Catholic clergy issued public denunciations of these exactions. Increasingly pointed pastoral letters denouncing state corruption were published by all of Zaire's bishops in 1977 and 1978.

Meanwhile, although privately furious at such criticism, Mobutu was preoccupied with the deteriorating economy and the invasions of Shaba Region (see External Threats to Regime Stability, ch. 1; Shaba I, ch. 5; Shaba II, ch. 5). In addition, the state's lack of managerial skills and resources had rendered its takeover of the education system a disaster. Faced with these realities, the president asked religious institutions to resume responsibility for church schools, which, by 1976, they had done. Courses on religion were once again integrated into the curriculum.

Tensions remained high throughout the 1980s and into the 1990s. The bishops' episcopal letter of June 1981, for example, castigated the regime for corruption, brutality, mismanagement, and lack of respect for human dignity. An angry Mobutu retaliated by warning the church hierarchy to stay out of politics; he also stationed JMPR militants in all places of worship to monitor priestly homilies. Coincidentally, attacks and attempted attacks were launched during the following months by unknown parties against several highly placed Catholic clerics; Cardinal Malula's home, for example, was attacked and his night watchman killed. The cardinal advised Zairians before the 1984 presidential elections to consult their consciences before casting their ballots; his act was denounced by the government as religious zealotry.

Tensions would have been still greater but for divisions within the church and for the ambiguity of the church's role relative to the state. Conflict within the church exists between the lower clergy, who are in day-to-day contact with the population, and the higher clergy; the former argued for a more radical critique of the regime, while the latter prevailed in arguing for a more limited, moral criticism. Many bishops wished to protect the church's institutional position and to avoid the retaliation that a more militant attack on the state could well provoke.

Too sharp a structural critique could also expose vulnerabilities in the church's position. High church officials enjoyed many of the economic and social privileges of other prominent Zairians, privileges that could easily be called into question. In addition, the church continued to depend on grants from foreign sources; as of 1976, none of Zaire's forty-seven dioceses was financially self-sufficient, a situation of dependency that appeared little changed by the early 1990s. The dependence of the largely Africanized church leadership on substantial numbers of expatriate priests, nuns, and brothers at lower and middle staff levels was another weakness. Finally, while church officials generally sided with the populace against the government in labor disputes, tax revolts, and individual cases of injustice, they sometimes made common cause with the regime; in its management role in Catholic schools, for example, the church found itself siding with the government against striking underpaid teachers in the early 1980s.

Protestant Churches

Protestant missionaries have been active since 1878 when the first Protestant mission was founded among the Kongo. Early relations with the state were not warm. During the existence of the Congo Free State (1885–1908), some Protestant missionaries witnessed and publicized state and charter company abuses against the population during rubber- and ivory-gathering operations. That evidence helped lead to the international outcry that forced King Léopold II to cede control of the Congo Free State to the Belgian state (see The Léopoldian Legacy, ch. 1). Situated outside the governing colonial trinity of state, Roman Catholic Church, and companies, Protestant missions did not enjoy the same degree of official confidence as that accorded their Catholic counterparts. State subsidies for hospitals and schools, for example, were (with two individual exceptions) reserved exclusively for Catholic institutions until after World War II.

The colonial state divided up the colony into spiritual franchises, giving each approved mission group its own territory. At independence in 1960, some forty-six Protestant missionary groups were at work, the majority of them North American, British, or Scandinavian in origin. The missions established a committee to maintain contact and minimize competition among them. This body evolved into a union called the Church of Christ in the Congo, now the Church of Christ in Zaire. The Church of Christ developed rules that permitted members of one evangelical congregation to move to and be accepted by another. It also established institutions that served common needs, such as bookstores and missionary guest houses.

Since independence, church leadership and control have been widely and successfully Africanized, though not without conflict. Most mission property has been transferred to autonomous Zairian churches, and many foreign missionaries now work directly under the supervision of a Zairian-run church. The new indigenous leadership has succeeded in expanding its churches in Africa's largest francophone Protestant community.

Protestant churches are valued, as are their Catholic counterparts, not only for the medical and educational services they provide, but also for serving as islands of integrity in a sea of corruption. Explicit recognition of this role came in 1983 when Mobutu sent emissaries to Europe and the United States to encourage increased involvement by foreign mission boards in Zairian institution-building; a conference in Kinshasa with local and international Protestant officials followed. Not only was a renewed church involvement sought with struggling institutions, such as the formerly Protestant university in Kisangani (nationalized in 1971), but churches were asked if they would be willing to station representatives within the major government ministries in order to discourage and/or report acts of corruption by state officials. Sensing the threat of co-optation, the Protestants respectfully declined.

State solicitation of Protestant action was logical. The state sought a counterweight to its critics in the powerful Roman Catholic Church. Protestant churches, and particularly the Church of Christ leadership, have been consistently supportive of Mobutu, making them an attractive potential partner. And the Church of Christ served the state in areas where state-church interests coincided. Both church and state looked askance at the formation of new uncontrolled religious movements and splinter groups. The government's requirement that religious groups register with the state and post a Z100,000 (for value of the zaire—see Glossary) deposit in a bank in order to be legally recognized helped limit their development; so too did the lingering effects of the colonial franchise system. When, for example, a charismatic preacher of the officially recognized but noncharismatic Church of Christ of the Ubangi (Église du Christ de l'Oubangi) broke away in 1988 to ally his own congregation with a charismatic but officially recognized church community in distant Kivu, the Church of Christ in Zaire stepped in to adjudicate. The governing body prevented the Kivu church from accepting the rebellious preacher and his congregation, leaving him with no outside allies or resources and effectively localizing his potential impact.

117

The Kimbanguist Church

The Kimbanguist Church, an indigenous Zairian religion, emerged from the charismatic ministry of Simon Kimbangu in the early 1920s. Kimbangu was already a member of the English Baptist Mission Church when he reportedly first received his visions and divine call to preach the word and heal the sick. Touring the lower Congo, he gained a large following drawn both from members of Protestant churches and adherents of indigenous religious practice. He preached a doctrine that was in many ways more strict than that of the Protestantism from which it evolved. Healing by the laying on of hands; strict observance of the law of Moses; the destruction of fetishes; the repudiation of sorcery, magic, charms, and witches; and the prohibition of polygyny were all part of his original message.

Unfortunately, the extent of his success caused increasing alarm among both church and state authorities. Numerous preachers and sages appeared, many of them professing to be his followers. Some of these preachers and possibly some of Kimbangu's own disciples introduced anti-European elements in their teachings. And European interests were affected when African personnel abandoned their posts for long periods in order to follow Kimbangu and participate in his services.

In June 1921, the government judged the movement out of control, banned the sect, exiled members to remote rural areas, and arrested Kimbangu, only to have the prophet ''miraculously'' escape; the escape further amplified his popular mystique. In September he voluntarily surrendered to the authorities and was sentenced to death for hostility against the state; the sentence was later commuted to life imprisonment, and Kimbangu died in prison in 1950. His movement, however, did not die with him. It flourished and spread ''in exile'' in the form of clandestine meetings, often held in remote areas by widely scattered groups of congregants. In 1959, on the eve of independence, the state despaired of stamping out Kimbanguism and afforded it legal recognition.

The legalized church, known as the Church of Jesus Christ on Earth by the Prophet Simon Kimbangu (Église de Jésus-Christ sur Terre par le Prophète Simon Kimbangu—EJCSK), has since succeeded in becoming one of the only three Christian groups recognized by the state, the other two being the Roman Catholic Church and the Church of Christ in Zaire. The Kimbanguist Church has been a member of the World Council of Churches since 1969. Estimates of its membership vary depending on the source. The church claims 5 million members; yet its own internal figures indicate no more than 300,000 practicing members. Individual congregations are scattered throughout much of the country, but the greatest concentrations have always been in Bas-Zaïre; some villages there have long been totally Kimbanguist.

Since being legalized, the Kimbanguists have bent over backward to curry favor with the state. The church's head, Simon Kimbangu's son, regularly exchanges public praise with Mobutu and has become one of the state's main ideological supports. Structurally, the church organization has been changed to parallel the administrative division of the state into regions, subregions, zones, and collectivities. The Kimbanguist Church deliberately rotates its officials outside their areas of origin in order to depoliticize ethnicity and centralize power, a policy taken directly from the state. An insistence on absolute obedience to the leader and a ban on doctrinal disputes also are shared by both institutions. In many ways, the Kimbanguist Church and the Roman Catholic Church have exchanged places in their relationship with the state; the former outlaw has become a close ally and the former ally an outspoken critic.

Other African Christian Movements

Africanized variants of traditional Christianity can be found throughout the continent. In spite of state prohibitions, new churches outside the three officially recognized in Zaire have sprung up and, so long as they remain small and nonthreatening, have usually been left alone by authorities. Some have been founded by figures known as prophets, individuals who respond to situations of popular dissatisfaction with existing spiritual agents and organizations by creating new religious movements. New movements often recombine familiar elements with new ones, a synthesis effected sometimes with exclusively indigenous elements and sometimes with a mixture of Christian and indigenous elements.

Jamaa

The Jamaa movement (*jamaa* means family in Kiswahili), like other Christian sects in Africa, has taken root under the umbrella of an existing church, in this case the Roman Catholic one. Jamaa is actually a European-African hybrid in that it was initially founded by a Flemish Franciscan priest, Placide Tempels, in 1953. Tempels helped to form small groups of African Catholics who met regularly with one another and with Tempels and his associates. Drawing from both African roots and Franciscan tradition, the movement emphasizes the importance of an emotional encounter with God and fellow believers and strives to draw out in group meetings the "vital force" Tempels believed to be characteristic of Bantu belief and practice.

Although accepted by the Roman Catholic Church (members continue to participate in parish activities and do not withdraw from the institutional church), the church hierarchy has periodically questioned the degree to which Jamaa deviates from Catholic belief and practice. The church has never denounced the Jamaa movement, but the hierarchy has grown steadily more wary of it.

Kitawala

A much more radical product of the synthesis of African and Christian elements is the Kitawala movement, which appeared in Katanga Province (now Shaba Region) during the 1920s. Born of the black American missionary activity in South Africa of the Watch Tower Bible and Tract Society (Jehovah's Witnesses), the movement converted miners who then spread the movement northward from their South African base into the Katangan copper belt.

Watch Tower missionaries preached racial equality, equal pay for equal work, the imminent arrival of God's kingdom, and the impending struggle for the restitution of Africa to Africans. Although anticolonial in ideology, the movement had no concrete strategy of revolution, which, however, did not prevent the state from cracking down on it. As with Kimbanguism, the state attempted to repress Kitawala by relegating its members to isolated rural regions. Ironically, this strategy once again simply served to speed the spread of the movement as exiled adherents converted their rural neighbors.

Over time the movement became more Africanized and more radical, slowly transforming itself from a branch of the worldwide Watch Tower Church into what has been termed a form of peasant political consciousness. Theological messages varied from place to place, but a common core of beliefs included the struggle against sorcery, the purification of society, and the existence of a black God. Kitawala denounced all forms of authority as the work of Satan, including taxes, forced labor, and most other coercive elements of colonial rule. The movement's anticolonial message was so strong that the worldwide Watch Tower movement formally renounced it.

Colonial bannings failed to eradicate the movement, however. And the independent state that succeeded colonial authority, black African though it be, has been no more successful in converting the Kitawalists from their apolitical, antiauthoritarian stance. Kitawalists continue to resist saluting the flag, participating in party-mandated public works (Salongo), and paying taxes. At times they have resisted state pressure violently, as in Shaba in 1979 when the appearance of army units in their midst provoked an attack by Kitawalists on the state's administrative offices and the killing of two soldiers. The state retaliated with a vicious repression. More frequently, Kitawalists withdraw when state pressure becomes excessive. Entire communities have moved into deep forest in areas such as Équateur Region in order to escape any contact with civil authorities.

Traditional African Religions

The wide variety of African indigenous beliefs and practices makes generalizations difficult, but some commonalities may nonetheless be noted. In general, Zairians believe themselves to be subject to a number of unseen agents and forces. Most indigenous communities recognize a higher being, and many attribute to him the role of creator; otherwise, he has few specific characteristics beyond that of ultimate cause.

Far more significant are ancestors, who are believed to continue to play a part in community life long after their death. In general, the living are required to speak respectfully of ancestors and to observe certain rites of respect so that the dead will look favorably on their descendants' activities. Africans do not engage in ancestor "worship"; rather, the living address and relate to their deceased elders in much the same way that they relate to their living ones. Often the terms of address and the gifts given to placate a dead elder are identical to those accorded a living one.

Nature spirits live in particular places, such as rivers, rocks, trees, or pools, or in natural forces such as wind and lightning. A typical practice involving a nature spirit in much of northern Zaire is the commonplace tossing of a red item (palm nut, cloth, matches, etc.) in a river before crossing it, particularly in places where the water is rough or turbulent. Thus placated, the spirit will refrain from stirring up the waters or overturning the boat.

Nature spirits play a minor role in negotiating everyday life compared with that played by witches and sorcerers. Witches are individuals who possess an internal organ giving them extraordinary power, generally malevolent power. The organ and its powers are hereditary. Witches can bring death and illness to crops, animals, and people, and their actions can be voluntary or involuntary. A witch might dream an angry dream about a friend or relative, for example, and awake to find that person struck ill or dead by the agency of that dream. Sorcerers are the possessors of nonhereditary powers that can be bought or acquired. A sorcerer might be consulted and paid to provide a medicine or object that strengthens

121

the client in the hunt (or, in contemporary life, in taking an exam) or that brings misfortune on an enemy.

In the event of illness, or of crop failure, or of misfortune in some other sphere of life, the stricken party may consult a diviner in order to identify the agent responsible for his or her affliction. The diviner is a specialist skilled in identifying the social tensions present in the community of the afflicted, and, for a fee, will identify the agent responsible for the individual's misfortune. By obtaining details of the afflicted person's life and social situation, the diviner will diagnose the misfortune by citing the agency of angry ancestors, nature spirits, sorcerers, or witches. Different ethnic groups add or subtract from the set of agents of affliction, but these are the most common. Once a diagnosis has been made, the diviner will then prescribe the appropriate cure. Diviners' powers are beneficent and their role highly valued.

From an outsider's perspective, the most striking aspect of indigenous belief and practice is its determinism; accidents are virtually unheard of, and there is always a cause behind any misfortune. In many indigenous societies, for example, a death is always followed by an inquest at which the cause of death and the identity of the killer are determined. Measures are then taken against the alleged miscreant, even when someone dies of disease in bed at an advanced age.

Education

Statistically, education would appear to be one of the healthiest institutions in contemporary Zaire. Though precise numbers vary among sources, the overall growth trend has been unmistakable. The number of illiterates over fifteen years of age, both absolute and as a percentage of population, has continued to decrease, from 68.7 percent in 1962 to 38.8 percent in 1985. By 1992 the rate of illiteracy was estimated at just 28 percent (16 percent for males over age fifteen and 39 percent for females). Numbers of schools, teachers, and pupils have grown (see table 8, Appendix). According to UN estimates, however, enrollment ratios (the percentage of the school-age population enrolled in school) remain relatively low—79 percent for primary school in 1990 (89 percent for males and 67 percent for females), up from 70 percent in 1965; and 23 percent for secondary school (16 percent for females). Moreover, only 56 percent of primary school-aged children reach the fourth grade.

In higher education, the nation boasts three universities, a network of teacher training, technical, and agricultural institutes; and several university-affiliated research institutes—this in a country that began its independent existence in 1960 with a total of thirty

Congolese university graduates among its population of more than 16 million.

Quantitative growth, unfortunately, has served to mask a pervasive and accelerating decline in quality at all levels. The causes of this decline may be found in shifting and inconsistent state policies, in church-state conflicts, in problems within the schools, and in the economic impoverishment suffered by the country as a whole.

Despite the deficiencies of the education system, most Zairians share a faith in the value of education and a belief that their children might have, through schooling, a better future. This hope has been cited as one of the major factors behind the citizenry's disinclination to political activism in the face of a pervasive and continuing decline in living standards. Some analysts, however, have noted a progressive narrowing of access to the education system. For example, Schatzberg has argued that the perceived openness of the system to all children is a myth. Access to education has increasingly been denied to those who are not part of the state bureaucracy and its class.

Policy Changes

The state's initial goal was to rectify the severe imbalance between primary schooling, where the colonial state had excelled, and secondary and university schooling, where it had done almost nothing. At independence the nation had one of the highest literacy rates on the continent and fully 70 percent of the primary school-age population enrolled in school. (However, over 70 percent of these schools offered only two grades, and dropout rates were among the highest in colonial Africa.) At the secondary level, however, the enrollment total of 28,951 students was a mere 2 percent of the primary school enrollment. The colonial bias toward creation of a minimally educated populace was clear.

The new government responded by rapidly expanding education at all levels, with special emphasis on increasing the number of postprimary institutions. Whereas the state established some primary and secondary schools under its own direction, it generally preferred to continue the existing pattern of subsidizing Catholic missions to carry out state educational goals. (Protestant and Kimbanguist schools were also subsidized; the former had received few funds under the colonial state, and the latter had received none.) The general pattern was for the state to set curriculum, to pay staff salaries, and to provide some educational materials. Recruitment of teachers and staff and management of the schools themselves were left to the churches.

Primary schools taught grades one through six, and secondary schools were responsible for grades seven though twelve. Secondary schools were subdivided into the *cycle d'orientation* (junior high) and *cycle long* (senior high). Diplomas were awarded not for simply finishing classes with passing grades, but for passing a rigorous nationwide examination administered by the state, the *examen d'état*.

By the mid-1980s, higher education had expanded into more than twenty postsecondary institutions providing university-level education. The four campuses of the National University of Zaire (Université Nationale du Zaïre—UNAZA) led the six that grant university degrees. UNAZA consists of the University of Kinshasa (Université de Kinshasa; originally Lovanium University, the Catholic university, founded in 1954), the University of Kisangani (Université de Kisangani; originally the Free University of the Congo, or Université Libre du Congo—ULC, the Protestant university, founded in 1963), the University of Lubumbashi (Université de Lubumbashi, formerly the state-run Université Officielle du Congo—UOC, founded in 1964), and the University of Kananga (Université de Kananga, created in 1985). The two teacher-training centers, the National Teaching Institute-Kinshasa (Institut Pédagogique National-Kinshasa) and the National Teaching Institute-Bukavu (Institut Pédagogique National—Bukavu) also award university-level degrees. These institutions offer undergraduate programs lasting four to five years leading to a *license* (the rough equivalent of a B.A. or B.S. degree). The other institutions offer a three-year course of study leading to a *graduat* diploma (the rough equivalent of an A.A. degree).

With Mobutu's accession to power, the drive to nationalize and centralize Zairian institutions, including the education system, eventually eclipsed all other educational policy issues. Universities, all privately run, were the first target. Students there had repeatedly displayed their independence, resisting Mobutu's attempt at establishing on-campus chapters of his party's youth organization, the JMPR, as well as striking and demonstrating against particular state policies. Student opposition was neutralized for a long time by the army's shooting of a large number of demonstrators in 1969, by closing the universities, and by drafting the entire student body into the army for one year.

The autonomy of the universities themselves was formally ended in August 1971 by their nationalization and reorganization as three separate campuses under one body, UNAZA. Administration was centralized in Kinshasa. The takeover of the universities and implantation of JMPR chapters on each campus have not succeeded in permanently stilling dissent. Periodic closings of campuses are decreed by the state when student activism appears threatening. When such measures fail to work, force is used. In May 1990, troops of the Special Presidential Division (Division Spéciale Présidentielle—DSP) flew by night from Kinshasa to Lubumbashi, where they surrounded student dormitories and beat, robbed, and killed up to 100 unarmed students before returning under cover of darkness to the capital (see Subsequent Political Developments, 1990-93; Opposition since 1990, ch. 4).

Primary and secondary schools (mostly church-owned and church-operated) were nationalized in their turn in 1974. While officially intended to implement the state ideology of authenticity, the action was also motivated by the desire to wrest control of the schools from the powerful Roman Catholic Church (see Religion, this ch.). Several years later, the government, faced with other more pressing crises, reversed course and formally asked the churches to resume their former role in school administration. The churches accepted. Staffs and faculties were quickly rebuilt, but the damage done to many schools' physical facilities while under state management, including the stripping of desks, chairs, books, doors, and windows, was so extensive that some schools were permanently abandoned.

Institutional Problems

The quality and status of teachers have long been problems. A 1976 World Bank (see Glossary) report notes that students who complete teacher training prefer to use the credential to seek positions outside their profession. Teachers' salaries are insufficient to live on and are paid irregularly. Popular music reflects the declining esteem in which teachers are held, referring to them as ''two shirts,'' two shirts being all the clothes a teacher can afford.

Schools are often seriously understaffed. One government response has been to require university students to teach as recompense for the cost of their state-subsidized schooling. Unfortunately, large numbers of these teachers-by-decree regularly fail to report to their assigned institutions.

When teachers have organized to protest their salaries and working conditions, they have met with repression. Demoralized and underpaid, many teachers resorted to corruption to make ends meet, accepting and sometimes demanding gifts from their students as the price of advancement from one year to the next. A 1988 poll published in the periodical *Zaïre-Afrique* showed that fully 80 percent of the teachers polled approved of students giving gifts to teachers. There was no significant difference in responses between educators teaching in religious schools and educators teaching in secular ones. Such systemic corruption has systemic causes; in effect, the state's unwillingness and inability to pay teachers a living wage has forced educators to seek income elsewhere in order to survive, whether by moonlighting or through less honorable means.

Students face considerable difficulties within the system. Education is not free, and school fees represent a significant percentage of household budgets; often schooling is cut short for lack of funds. Boys are routinely given priority over girls in household allocations of school fees. Students in rural areas can be required to provide free labor for their schools and teachers, repairing classrooms and teachers' homes, or working for a period each day in a teacher's garden. Gifts are frequently required for academic advancement. Female students often face sexual demands from teachers and staff at the postprimary levels. And successful students, namely those who succeed in passing the state exams at the end of secondary school studies, face the hurdle of a regional "affirmative action admissions policy" for university entry, one that favors applicants from historically underrepresented areas at the expense of those from historically better-schooled regions. In fact, the regional quota system also has created tension and dissatisfaction within regions. Disadvantaged groups regard the quotas as giving those who are ahead in education an unfair proportion of the region's slots at the university.

In the early 1990s, the state-run education system, like all state-funded social services, had deteriorated further. Most state-run schools are reported to have been closed. Nevertheless, at least some children (whose parents could find the means) continue to seek and find education through private schools at all levels (including several private universities reported to exist or be in the making in 1992) that have sprung up to fill the gap—another manifestation of Zaire's informal economic and social systems. The elite continue to send their children abroad to be educated, primarily in Western Europe.

Health and Medical Services

Zairian health statistics are similar to those of other countries in Central Africa. Life expectancy at birth in 1992 was estimated at fifty-two years for males and fifty-six years for females. While unimpressive by United States standards, the statistics on life expectancy have improved markedly, a real achievement given the challenges to public health the country faces.

Incidence of Disease

Infectious and parasitic diseases are a major health threat,

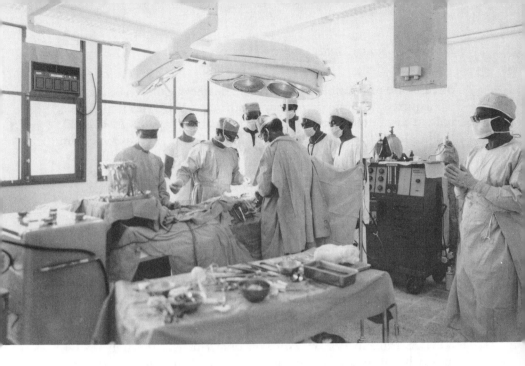

Operating room at a Gécamines hospital in Lubumbashi
Courtesy Gécamines

accounting for at least 50 percent of all deaths in Zaire. (The United States rate, by comparison, is 1.5 percent.) Malaria, trypanosomiasis (sleeping sickness), onchocerciasis (river blindness), and schistosomiasis are all endemic. Malaria, long a significant cause of illness and death, is increasingly menacing because of its growing resistance to antimalarial drugs. Cases of trypanosomiasis are increasing, primarily because of a reduction in the number of mobile teams engaged in controlling the spread of the vector, the tsetse fly. Diseases such as measles, diarrheal diseases, tetanus, diphtheria, pertussis, poliomyelitis, tuberculosis, and leprosy are preventable or curable given available technology; unfortunately, only 30 to 40 percent of the population has access to such technology and services. The UN has estimated the immunization rate in the early 1990s to be only 38 percent for measles and 35 percent for diphtheria, pertussis, and tetanus. In addition, a majority of the population is infected with intestinal worms, including ascaris, hookworms, and ankylostomes; the effect of these parasites is to further weaken a population already suffering from widespread malnutrition.

The disease burden has fallen particularly heavily on children under the age of five. They constitute roughly 20 percent of the population and account for 80 percent of all deaths. Malaria is the primary killer among infants, while measles, malaria, and diarrheal diseases are responsible for the bulk of deaths of children under five.

Acquired immune deficiency syndrome (AIDS) and other sexually transmitted diseases have been spreading rapidly. As of 1990, the number of reported cases in Zaire totaled 11,732, a 60 percent increase over 1989. In urban areas, the AIDS epidemic is the most threatening public-health problem facing the nation. Seropositivity statistics (the proportion of a population whose blood serum tests positive for the AIDS virus) in Kinshasa for the general population in 1987 were 6 to 8 percent; among prostitutes the figure was as high as 30 percent. The scanty data from rural areas show a lower incidence, but the samples are too small to be statistically significant.

AIDS is regarded as a potentially even greater public-health hazard in the face of the virtual collapse of the state-run health care system. By most accounts, in 1993 the majority of blood banks had been closed, and blood screenings were rare.

AIDS transmission in Zaire occurs primarily through sexual, mostly heterosexual, intercourse (80 percent); infected blood transfusions and contaminated skin-piercing instruments account for 15 percent of cases, and transmission from infected mothers to their offspring for 5 percent. The significance of heterosexual intercourse in the spread of the disease is documented in the ratio of afflicted men to afflicted women; in Zaire it is 1:1.4, while in the United States it is 13:1.

Initial public reaction to the early warnings sounded by the medical authorities tended to be skeptical. In a play on the French acronym for AIDS, SIDA (*syndrome immunité déficient acquis*), Kinshasa street slang labeled the new disease the *"syndrome inventé pour décourager les amoureux,"* or, crudely translated, "syndrome invented to discourage lovers." But as increasing numbers of well-known musicians and other public figures have contracted the disease and died, public attitudes have grown more sober. Public health authorities have attempted to promote safe-sex education in their health education programs. In addition, the United States Agency for International Development (AID) funded AIDS research programs and health education programs through Project SIDA, and the government used a US$500,000 grant from the World Health Organization, together with money from other international agencies, to establish a national AIDS control program. Thus far, however, success in slowing the spread of the epidemic remains elusive, and rates of prophylactic use remain low.

Health Care System

In a regional context, the health care system established to meet these challenges appears impressive, at least on paper, although the UN estimates that only 50 percent of the population had access to health care in the early 1990s (see table 9, Appendix). The ratio of physicians to population in the early 1990s was claimed to be approximately one per 14,000, markedly higher than in neighboring countries such as Rwanda (one to 35,000) or Burundi (one to 45,000), for example. The ratio of nurses to population was estimated as approximately one to 1,900, spectacularly higher than the sub-Saharan African average of one to 45,000. Average population per hospital bed was approximately 700, a better rate than neighboring Burundi's 850, for example.

In theory, the nation is divided into health zones, each covering a population of 100,000 to 150,000 and containing on average one referral hospital, between one and three reference health centers, and fifteen to twenty-five standard health centers. Each standard health center is staffed with at least one certified nurse and provides basic preventive and simple curative services to the five to ten villages in its area. Serious medical cases are referred upward to the health zone's reference health centers and referral hospital.

The health care system is considerably less impressive in practice, however. The relatively high physician- and paramedic-to-population ratio masks the fact that the quality of medical education has seriously deteriorated. Moreover, salaries of medical personnel are too low to permit staff the luxury of full-time attention to their professional duties. Virtually all people employed in the public sector must seek outside income in order to survive. It is not uncommon for state hospital nurses, for example, to demand private payment from a hospitalized patient or the patient's family before changing a dressing, or before administering a medication prescribed by the patient's physician. In fact, according to Janet MacGaffey, doctors, nurses, and other medical personnel routinely require payment of a personal fee before they will care for a patient. Even emergency cases are not admitted to a hospital until payment has been made.

The large number of health centers and health zones cited in statistics is similarly misleading. Many government health centers are dysfunctional, completely lacking in medications or in basic medical equipment and personnel. In the early 1990s, the public health system had deteriorated further as a result of civil and political unrest and severe economic disruptions. Indeed, the government's health services have in essence collapsed. What health care Zairians find comes more often from private sources. The elite continue to seek quality health care abroad.

Zaire: A Country Study

Religious organizations, notably the Roman Catholic, Protestant, and Kimbanguist churches, and international relief organizations provide the bulk of health care in Zaire, particularly in rural areas, as happened in the preindependence era as well. The Catholic medical service network is the largest and involves primary responsibility for some ninety health zones. The Protestant network participates in the development of fifty health zones; as the implementing agent of an AID-supported rural health project, it plans to develop fifty more health zones over a seven-year period. Kimbanguist medical work centers on the rehabilitation of two urban hospitals and on management of 180 health centers scattered all over the country. Private enterprises also manage large health care facilities where they provide high-quality care. The large parastatal General Quarries and Mines (Générale des Carrières et des Mines—Gécamines), for example, owns seven hospitals and six clinics with about 2,264 beds.

Sanitation and Nutrition

According to UN estimates, only 14 percent of the population has access to safe water (52 percent urban and 20 percent rural). Potable water is provided to approximately half the population in urban areas through private connections or through public standpipes. The remaining 50 percent get their water from wells and surface water of varying quality. Roughly 30 percent of the urban population has access to a sewerage system, 10 percent use septic tanks, and 60 percent use latrines. There is no garbage collection system. In rural areas, water quality varies widely. Only about 10 percent of the rural population has access to communal standpipes. About 20 percent of the population uses pit latrines.

Malnutrition is widespread in Zaire. Measures of children's standard weight-for-age show at least 25 percent of the country's children to be undernourished. Protein-calorie malnutrition and anemia are widespread. Iodine-deficiency disorders resulting in the growth of goiters and in cretinism are commonly seen in Équateur and in Haut-Zaïre.

The major cause of malnutrition is poverty. Gross domestic product (GDP—see Glossary) per capita has been decreasing in the 1980s and early 1990s, and Zaire's per capita GDP places Zaire among the poorest and least-developed countries in the world. Local markets are reported to have abundant supplies of food, but most of the population cannot afford to buy it. For example, average earnings in the capital of Kinshasa are not enough to buy the minimum basket of essential foods. Deficiencies in food production and diet are additional causes of malnutrition. Food and Agriculture

130

Organization of the United Nations (FAO) statistics show national average calorie production per inhabitant as less than the minimum daily consumption requirements. The balance is made up by importing food. Dependency on cassava as a staple further degrades the diet. Cassava contains few nutrients, and the cyanide it contains is not always properly leached out in the process of food preparation.

Family Planning

Family planning began late and was accepted slowly in Zaire. In 1972 the Mobutu regime officially expressed interest in limiting births to "desirable" ones and thus promoted family planning for reasons of health and as a human right. In 1973 a presidential decree created an official clearinghouse committee for family-planning information. It was not until 1978, however, that the state established a nongovernment organization dedicated to family planning, namely, the Zairian Association for Family Well-Being (Association Zaïroise pour le Bien-Être Familial—AZBEF). It was formed in order to acquire technical and financial aid from the International Planned Parenthood Federation. Evaluation teams sent in 1981 were unable to evaluate the impact of the early programs because of the lack of data and the small numbers of acceptors.

Not until the launching of an AID-funded program in 1982—the Project for Planned Birth Services (Projet des Services des Naissances Désirables—PSND)—did family-planning efforts begin in earnest. Problems in coordinating PSND efforts with AZBEF led to the establishment of three systems working in parallel, PSND, AZBEF, and Rural Health (Santé Rurale—Sanru), a rural family health care project with a family-planning component.

PSND statistics have been the most complete. PSND selected fourteen urban areas with a target population of about 800,000 women and aimed to increase contraceptive use from 1 percent to 12 percent by 1986. Early returns were disappointing, with only 1.6 percent usage reported by a mid-term evaluation mission in 1985. Later trends were more encouraging, including a 1984–87 quadrupling of family-planning acceptors (see table 10, Appendix).

In rural areas, AZBEF family-planning units and Sanru have been active, although the numbers of personnel are insufficient to reach the bulk of the population. To supplement their efforts, AID has funded efforts to make contraceptives available through community-based distribution projects. A Tulane University program distributed birth-control pills, condoms, and contraceptive foams in Bas-Zaïre in a pilot project; the effort demonstrated that such distribution is less effective than making supplies available in health facilities. Companies such as Gécamines that operate health care facilities receive aid from PSND to promote family planning among company workers and their families. Most significant are commercial marketing projects. Forty pharmacies in three zones of Kinshasa spread information on contraceptive methods and products and sell attractively packaged and well-priced contraceptives, which are quite popular. Recent efforts in social marketing organized by Family Health International have had promising results in their test areas, although the collapse of the economy in the early 1990s has compromised any precise evaluation of their overall effectiveness.

Barriers to acceptance of family planning remain, however. As long as child mortality remains high, both men and women will continue to value large families. Demand for family-planning services remains low. In fact, the availability of such services has been almost unknown by the community, even in the immediate neighborhood of family-planning units. Although occasional radio, television, and press programs have been generated, and T-shirts, posters, and brochures bearing family-planning messages have been distributed, follow-up has been lacking and evaluation of family-planning informational campaigns has not been done. Given the relative lack of success in promoting family planning and birth control, Zaire faces a continued high rate of population growth, which will exacerbate deteriorating social and economic conditions.

*   *   *

Periodicals provide the best source of current social and cultural information on Zaire, although many of the best are either in French or unavailable in many libraries. Still, the curious reader can find many good and widely available books on Zaire in English. Crawford Young and Thomas Turner's *The Rise and Decline of the Zairian State* provides a good overview of the country's institutional history and development since independence. The extraordinary scope of state corruption is painstakingly documented as it pertains to Équateur Region by Michael G. Schatzberg in *Politics and Class in Zaire* and in *The Dialectics of Oppression in Zaire;* David J. Gould's *Bureaucratic Corruption and Underdevelopment in the Third World: The Case of Zaire* does the same on a national scale.

Zairians' strategies of adaptation to their ongoing impoverishment have been well documented in several more recent works. Edited anthologies such as Georges Nzongola-Ntalaja's *The Crisis in Zaire: Myths and Realities* and Janet MacGaffey's *The Real Economy of Zaire* both contain accounts of the dynamic informal economy and the varying survival strategies used by different ethnic groups, classes, regions, and genders. The literature on women's roles in adaptation is particularly well developed in books such as Jane L. Parpart and Kathleen A. Staudt's *Women and the State in Africa.* Articles by Catharine Newbury and Brooke G. Schoepf in this volume as well as in the volume edited by Janet MacGaffey provide insights into the ways African women have confronted state oppression by forming local alliances and by creatively exploiting the potential of the informal economy.

Students of Zairian ethnography interested in an overview would do well to start with Jan Vansina's recent *Paths in the Rainforests;* its bibliography contains references to more specialized studies and ethnic groups that the reader could subsequently consult. People interested in Zairian religions would profit from reading any of Wyatt MacGaffey's several books on the Kongo people, the most recent of which are *Religion and Society in Central Africa* and *Astonishment and Power.*

Finally, for those interested in health care, the complexities of its provision are detailed in *The Social Basis of Health and Healing in Africa,* edited by Steven Feierman and John M. Janzen. The volume includes discussions of indigenous concepts of disease and modes of diagnosis and therapy, elements not always considered in public health delivery planning. (For further information and complete citations, see Bibliography.)

Chapter 3. The Economy

Traditional wooden mask

INDEPENDENT ZAIRE HAS NEVER lived up to its enormous economic potential. The political turmoil that followed independence from Belgium in 1960 irrevocably disrupted the economy. Even after political and civil order was restored by Mobutu Sese Seko in the mid-1960s, efforts at economic revival consistently fell short. Indeed, the government's misguided and overambitious economic policies, first of Zairianization and nationalization of foreign-owned enterprises and then of large-scale industrialization, undertaken on the basis of the country's mineral wealth and at the expense of the agricultural sector, brought economic disaster in their wake. The regime resorted to heavy foreign borrowing to fund economic development and grandiose industrial projects. When the prices of commodities (especially copper), on which Zaire was heavily dependent, dropped drastically in the mid-1970s, export earnings and government revenues dropped sharply, and Zaire faced a grave economic and financial crisis. Thereafter, the country, urged on by Western donors and by the World Bank (see Glossary) and the International Monetary Fund (IMF—see Glossary), attempted a series of economic reforms and structural adjustments. But ultimately all efforts at reform or significant change were undercut by the patrimonialism (see Glossary) and rampant corruption that characterized the regime.

In the early 1990s, as the regime of President Mobutu appeared on the verge of collapse, the economic situation was desperate. The country remained heavily indebted and impoverished, despite its vast mineral wealth and early economic promise. A large proportion of its population lived outside of the formal economy, eking out a marginal existence through subsistence agriculture and informal trade or barter. The standard of living for most of the population was low and continued to decline as inflation skyrocketed.

By most accounts, the export-oriented Zairian economy has been in a free-fall for a number of years, suffering the effects of monumental, institutional corruption, neglect, and mismanagement. But the economic crisis was worsened by the rampant looting and rioting by unpaid troops in late 1991 and again in early 1993, which in turn led to the mass exodus of the foreign technicians who had kept the economy going—in particular copper production and the maintenance of economic infrastructure.

By the end of 1992 and throughout 1993, Zaire's economy was described as being in ruins, the formal economy having virtually ceased to function. The banking system had in essence collapsed because of the rampant hyperinflation and drastic fall in the value of the currency. Most banks were closed; those that were open had no reserves, so only cash transactions were possible. Shoppers reportedly circulated in Kinshasa with sackfuls of virtually useless paper currency. The central bank, which had in the past served as Mobutu's personal piggy bank, was for all practical purposes bankrupt. The tax collection system was defunct, and few if any customs revenues were collected. Most foreign aid had been cut off, and copper production, long the mainstay of the economy and the main source of government revenues, had dropped off significantly. The government was able to pay its bills only by printing new currency. But even that avenue was being closed off as foreign printing companies rebelled at printing money without being paid.

The effects of the economic chaos on Zairian society were enormous. Unemployment and poverty were widespread. According to press reports, the public-service sector was no longer operational. The economic infrastructure had virtually broken down as well. The telephone, electric power, and transportation systems were all a shambles. By some estimates, as little as 10 percent of the road network in existence at independence was still functioning. Road and rail links between major cities were being overgrown by the jungle.

Background and Overview of the Economy
Early Economic Activity

In the precolonial era, economic activity in most communities in Zaire was largely subsistence in nature, characterized by a varying combination of shifting cultivation, hunting, fishing, and collecting. The agricultural technology of most groups was comparatively simple. Livestock was limited to chickens and sometimes a few goats or sheep. In most communities—particularly those in and on the fringes of the forest—the men valued hunting far above agriculture and devoted not only time but much ritual activity to it. This pattern was consistent with the division of labor: at best men played a small part in cultivation, usually that of cutting and burning forest or bush before planting. The high esteem of hunting persisted even where the declining availability of game made it economically less important.

Along the Congo River and its many tributaries, thriving riverine economies developed. The men of some groups devoted themselves wholly to fishing and the women to pottery, exchanging these items for food and other goods produced by their neighbors. These fishermen were also active traders along the navigable waters.

Other groups devoted themselves entirely to hunting and collecting. Occasionally these groups lived in villages with settled agricultural communities. More often they lived in physically separated hamlets but in symbiosis with specific cultivating communities, exchanging the products of the hunt for bananas and other crops.

Various groups in precolonial Zaire also played a substantial role in the trade of such commodities as ivory, rubber, copper, and slaves. To meet the demand for such goods, sustained caravan trade involving Arab and mixed Arab-African traders occurred throughout the interior of Central Africa, including territory in what is now Zaire. Although never great traders themselves, the Lunda apparently profited handsomely from controlling and supervising the caravan trade of others. And both the Kazembe Kingdom and later the Luba Empire prospered as a result of their control of the ivory trade (see Early Historical Perspectives, ch. 1).

From Colonial Times to Independence

After the 1884–85 Conference of Berlin gave undisputed sovereignty of the region of modern Zaire to Léopold II, king of Belgium, the first order of business was to structure the area's economy to suit Belgian needs. The goal was to make an economically viable and self-sustaining entity out of the Congo Free State, as Zaire was then known (see The Colonial State, ch. 1). In 1908 the Belgian parliament voted to remove the region from direct control of the king, make it a colony, and rename it the Belgian Congo. The Belgian government wanted to avoid subsidizing the administration of the new colony while at the same time reaping whatever profits might eventually be generated by the country. Therefore, the colony itself was to be responsible for financing its administration and security.

Although exploitation of the country's mineral and agricultural wealth was substantial during the colonial period, economic development bore little direct relationship to the needs of the indigenous population. The production of cash crops for export was stressed at the expense of the production of food crops. Moreover, monetary benefits accrued almost entirely to non-Congolese, the foreign shareholders of the industrial and agricultural companies that constituted the modern sector, and the colonial state, which had holdings in many of the companies.

The colonial government's major aim was to encourage foreign investment in the Belgian Congo to develop agricultural commodities for export, to exploit the country's mineral resources for the same purpose, and to establish a transportation infrastructure to facilitate the export of goods. The colonial state concerned itself very little with such basic social needs as health care or education, which were provided by religious missions and to some extent by the large concessionaire companies. Policies designed to promote state economic objectives emphasized measures to ensure adequate supplies of labor at low wages. Among such measures were the use of forced recruitment and restrictions on the establishment of foreign commercial trading activities, which would have encouraged the farm population to produce surpluses for sale rather than take low-paying work on plantations and in mines. Colonial authorities obtained through coercion the indigenous labor necessary to perform public works and private investment projects. A decree of 1917, for example, required African peasants to devote sixty days a year to agricultural work, and mandated penal sanctions for disobedience.

By offering exceedingly generous terms, the Belgian government induced major foreign financial groups to invest in its colony. The colonial state itself laid claim to a significant share in the ownership of corporations in the extractive and transportation sectors. In 1906 the General Holding Company of Belgium (Société Générale de Belgique—SGB), a powerful Belgian trust, formed the Upper Katanga Mining Union (Union Minière du Haut-Katanga— UMHK), the International Forest and Mining Company (Société Internationale Forestière et Minière—Forminière), and the Bas-Congo to Katanga Railroad Company (Compagnie du Chemin de Fer du Bas-Congo au Katanga—BCK). A majority shareholder in the UMHK and Forminère, the colonial state could potentially have run both companies. State capitalism did not extend to active involvement in company affairs, however; the colonial administration merely collected its dividends.

SGB was given mineral rights to already-prospected ore deposits in Katanga Province (now Shaba Region) and a ninety-nine-year monopoly on any mineral deposits it could identify within a six-year period on a tract of 140 million hectares. BCK was given mineral rights to 21 million hectares in the area along the two main rail lines from Matadi to Léopoldville (now Kinshasa) and from Port Francqui (now Ilebo) to the mining centers in Katanga and also was permitted to run the railroad with indigenous labor provided by the colonial state. By the 1920s, the rich mineral base was being exploited, and SGB had consolidated its control over the three companies that dominated the colony's economy.

After World War II, government recognition of growing social discontent among the African population led to support for wage increases and to promoting the development of an indigenous middle class. Import-substitution (see Glossary) industries were established to meet the growing demand for consumer goods. The colonial administration encouraged corporations and missions to expand social services and to construct hospitals and educational facilities for the Congolese. These reforms, however, were largely unsuccessful; at independence the economy was still primarily export-led, that is, geared toward the export of raw materials, and expatriates held most of the managerial and technical positions.

Postindependence

The political turmoil that followed independence from Belgium in 1960 resulted in the collapse of civil administration and severe economic dislocations (see The Crisis of Decolonization, ch. 1). The rapid departure of Belgian administrators and technicians left government and industry in the hands of low-level cadres. Vital transportation facilities and trade services were disrupted. Export earnings declined. After political and civil order were restored following the rise to power of President Mobutu in 1965, the government of the Congo (as the country was then known) soon launched a comprehensive and ambitious attempt to achieve economic independence through nationalization. The largest expropriation was that of the Belgian-owned mining company, UMHK, and its transformation into General Quarries and Mines (Générale des Carrières et des Mines—Gécamines). After much wrangling with Belgian industrialists and the government, Zaire and Gécamines agreed to a reimbursement plan, which included a percentage of revenues of the new company to be paid to the former owners.

The government also promoted a series of development programs designed to transform a primarily agrarian economy into a regional industrial power. Zaire's enormous mineral wealth of copper, cobalt, gold, and diamonds was intended to serve as the engine for this transformation. The ultimate goal was ostensibly to move the economy to a stage of development comparable with that of the Western industrial powers. The new Congolese government thus expected to realize the early colonial aspirations for the country to be the breadbasket and principal industrial power of Africa.

This strategy of industrialization was to be financed through external lending and was based on projections of increases in mineral prices, production, and sales. Justified by the doctrine of economic nationalism, grandiose and ill-conceived projects based on copper and energy development and financed on terms unfavorable to Zaire were undertaken. In 1967 the IMF concluded an agreement with the Congo for monetary and economic reform. The currency was devalued to control inflation, and the Congolese franc was replaced by the zaire (for the value of the zaire—see Glossary). Within two years, the reform program, combined with political tranquility, a rise in the price of copper, and increased exports, had led to a stable currency and an increase in foreign-exchange reserves. Zaire (as the nation was called from 1971) rode high on the commodity price boom of the early 1970s along with other primary commodity-producing countries.

In retrospect, it appears that the economic and financial policies of this period were the result of a desire both to transform Zaire into an industrial power and to maintain in power, as well as enrich, what was to become the country's ruling political and economic elite. As several observers have noted, Mobutu's authoritarian paternalism gave rise to rampant corruption incompatible with economic diversification and development. Regardless of the motives for the economic decisions of the late 1960s and early 1970s, economic decline set in as grace periods expired on the enormous debt that the government had incurred from foreign governments, as well as international lending agencies, to finance its ambitious industrial development projects and as the neglect of transport and agriculture began to take its toll.

The cost of living rose rapidly, while new foreign borrowing raised the nation's external debt from US$763 million at the end of 1972 to US$3 billion by 1974. In November 1973, Mobutu announced measures to place all businesses in the hands of Zairians.

Zairianization

Economic nationalism was a common theme throughout post-independence Africa, frequently manifesting itself in the expulsion of foreign merchants and/or expropriation of foreign assets. For Zaire, economic autonomy and political independence were seen as dependent on each other. Zairianization, the expropriation plan announced in November 1973, represented both a combination of the nationalistic impulse for economic independence and personal aggrandizement for President Mobutu, who practiced a form of patrimonialism. Zairianization created a vast pool of goods and money for personal distribution to loyal family members and the political class composed mainly of government and army officials. It was the final and clearest demonstration that political power was the primary means of acquiring wealth. The entrepreneurial risk and initiative in building up business enterprises required to develop an infrastructure for economic development were thus not characteristic of the Zairian elite that came to dominate the country's economy.

Open-pit mining of copper and cobalt at the Gécamines
Musonoi Mine near Kolwezi
Steam shovel loading copper and cobalt ore to be processed
at Musonoi Mine
Courtesy Gécamines

143

Mobutu's announcement on November 30, 1973, before the National Legislative Council, the country's parliament, of his intention to seize and redistribute the nation's foreign businesses was a demonstration of his total rule over the country. The wisdom, timeliness, or practicality of the nationalization measures were not discussed, much less debated. There seems to have been no prior consultation with anyone, including the political elite.

Expropriated property consisted of commercial buildings, light industry, and agricultural holdings including a vast network of plantations, much of which was acquired by the president and held in partnership with Belgian interests. Administratively, expropriation was managed by various government ministries. Most recipients were ministers, members of the party's political bureau, and top army officers. Smaller properties were allocated to local notables. The term used to describe someone who benefited from the distribution of the spoils was *aquéreur,* or acquirer.

In practical terms, Zairianization represented a financial windfall for the country's political elite, which was to be allocated businesses, and which brushed aside any economic risks involved in such a takeover. On the level of rhetoric, on the other hand, Mobutu spoke of Zairianization as promoting radical economic nationalism, and helping the lot of the country's masses. Zairianization was to promote rural development by creating a landed gentry to induce greater investment in the countryside. Thus, the ruling elite transformed a mythology of state autonomy and economic sovereignty into a tool for its own enrichment.

Ultimately, Zairianization resulted in asset stripping, liquidation of inventory, and capital flight. In some instances, single enterprises were allocated to more than one individual. Integrated agro-industrial enterprises were broken up. Many of the new owners had neither the expertise nor the interest to manage and to maintain their newly acquired holdings. Many were unable to obtain credit and had no commercial experience. Their first impulse was frequently to dispose of liquid assets as quickly as possible and then to abandon the properties and enterprises to ruin. Throughout 1974 this lack of interest and expertise led to a devastating dislocation of the commercial infrastructure. The adverse effects were especially evident in small businesses where the new owners often simply sold the goods and then left. Shortages of food and consumer goods became common countrywide.

The final blow to Mobutu's development strategy was the collapse in the price of copper in 1974. The price paid for copper in world markets dropped from US$0.64 per kilogram to US$0.24 per kilogram between 1974 and 1975. Zaire's trade balance deteriorated further when its bill for imported oil reached US$200 million, or 20 percent of its foreign-exchange earnings. The continued sharp fall in commodity prices brought export receipts and government revenues down with a crash and produced a decline in the overall standard of living.

After only twelve months, Zairianization was acknowledged to be a failure, and enterprises that had been given to Zairians were nationalized. The economy continued to slide, however, and in December 1974, under a plan called retrocession (see Glossary), former owners were invited to return to Zaire and reclaim a proportion of their businesses. In practice, the requirement that Zairians retain a sizable stake in such businesses was largely ignored for those expatriates who did return.

Economic Decline

By early 1976, Zaire was in a grave economic and financial crisis and faced international bankruptcy. Mobutu and the unproductive political elite sought relief from the eleven members of the Paris Club (see Glossary), the World Bank, and the IMF as debt arrears mounted rapidly. However, the thorough implementation of changes and reforms required by the World Bank, the IMF, and other Western donors was perceived as a threat to the very basis of the elite's power—access to and free use of the nation's resources. If the president were to execute effectively the reforms his foreign partners demanded, the heart of his authority: complete personal discretion and the fiscal privileges and corruption that bound the system together, would be undermined. As a result, Mobutu and the political elite used their control of government institutions to sabotage economic change by manipulating their donors' economic interests against one another and by exploiting foreign anxieties about the instability that might result from a collapse of the regime.

The members of the Paris Club fitfully coordinated efforts to persuade Zaire to service debts, control expenditures, diminish corruption, and implement hard economic decisions. They attempted to draw up joint plans of action, but they sometimes worked at cross purposes as their national interests did not always coincide. Lack of coordination among the different donors and multilateral institutions was also a problem. Foreign contractors were often not entirely supportive of reform since many of them actually benefited from the economic chaos and the opportunities for personal enrichment. Pressure for reform from the West fluctuated as governments changed hands. Mobutu took skillful advantage of these differences and lapses in attention; the inability of Western governments to sustain effective coordination presented Mobutu and those close to him with opportunities to deflect the pressure to reform.

Between 1975 and 1983, Zaire experienced a relentless economic decline. Significant economic and financial imbalances including high inflation and a decline in per capita income gripped the country and turned Zaire into a beggar in the international marketplace. The nationalization measures of 1974, while short-lived, destroyed commercial distribution networks and undermined private-sector confidence.

From 1975 to 1978, the gross domestic product (GDP—see Glossary) dropped 3.5 percent annually. Annual inflation rates averaged 75 percent. In 1980 and 1981, the price of copper recovered briefly but then dropped again the following year. Prior to 1975, Zaire had shipped almost half of its Shaba Region copper exports to the Angolan Atlantic seaport of Lobito via the Benguela Railway. The closure of this rail line in 1975 because of the Angolan civil war forced Zaire to export a large share of its mineral exports via the more costly and politically embarrassing South African route.

The period from the early 1970s to the early 1980s was also marked by excessive government regulation of the economy. The central government imposed price controls on food, fuel, and other items, regulated interest rates, and overvalued the zaire. The country sustained chronic budget deficits, and the infrastructure was allowed to deteriorate further into dilapidation.

In the early 1980s, the IMF appointed Erwin Blumenthal, of the central bank of the Federal Republic of Germany (West Germany), to monitor and advise Zaire's central bank, the Bank of Zaire. Blumenthal cut off credit and foreign-exchange facilities to firms of key members of the political elite, which led to conflict with President Mobutu. Blumenthal's efforts to impose budgetary control over the president and others were delayed and circumvented.

The Zairian political elite thus blocked efforts by international lenders to control the country's financial practices. The IMF supported Zaire with four stabilization programs between 1976 and 1983, and there were as many Paris Club reschedulings and five currency devaluations. These efforts were aimed at cutting corruption, rationalizing expenditures, increasing tax revenues, limiting imports, boosting production in all sectors, improving the transportation infrastructure, eliminating debt-service arrears, making principal payments on schedule, and improving economic planning and financial management. But the custom for Zaire quickly became to make the first drawing and then to drift away from the economic reform performance criteria. The 1981 program of special drawing rights (SDRs—see Glossary) 912 million was blocked in September of that year after disbursement of only SDR175 million because of Zaire's failure to meet performance criteria, mainly budgetary deficit limits. The fate of other programs during this period was similar. In 1983, however, Zaire finally agreed on another economic reform plan.

The 1983 Reforms

Devaluation of the currency was the centerpiece of the 1983 reform. An initial 80 percent devaluation and subsequent adjustments in the value of the currency reduced substantially black-market activity, which had mushroomed when the currency was way overvalued at the official rate. The central bank and commercial banks began to meet weekly to fix a rate for the zaire on the basis of recent transactions among themselves. The supply of foreign exchange at the official rate increased markedly, and traders were readily able to purchase foreign exchange from commercial banks for the import of most necessities. Nonetheless, restrictive monetary and fiscal policies made it difficult for many firms to muster the deposit in local currency that the commercial banks required to open a letter of credit.

The government's 1983 attempts at economic liberalization were the first serious reform efforts since the economic crisis began in 1974. The government reduced its role in the decision making of state-owned industries and in the economy as a whole. Most prices were decontrolled except for petroleum products, public utilities, and transportation. Deficit and government expenditure reduction efforts were undertaken. The trade regime was liberalized, customs duties (a significant source of government income) revised, and external debt payments regularized.

Results were positive, and exporting enterprises were more free from government intervention than at any time since the seizure of UMHK in 1967. Where government chose to maintain its ownership of a company for strategic reasons, important decisions on production, investment, and marketing were increasingly taken by the company rather than by the government itself. Interest rates were deregulated, and controls on producer and retail prices were largely dismantled, though firms remained subject to a subsequent review by Zairian authorities to ensure compliance with legal profit margin limits.

In late 1983, after Zaire had undergone a year of fiscal discipline, the IMF approved a support plan of SDR114.5 million and an additional fifteen-month standby loan amount of SDR228 million, both repayable over five years. This plan was accompanied by Paris Club multilateral debt rescheduling, the fifth rescheduling of Zaire's external debt in a period of eight years. Under the agreement, loans totaling US$1.2 billion for 1983–84 were rescheduled. These actions ensured a marginally positive net transfer of resources to Zaire between 1983 and 1986. Although immediately after the devaluation inflation doubled, debt arrears continued to build, and GDP rose by only 1.3 percent, by 1984 inflation had dropped to 52 percent and GDP grew by 1.3 percent.

The 1983 reforms began to unravel in 1986. Export earnings in 1986 were indeed far below expectations because of extremely low copper and cobalt prices. The government raised civil servant salaries despite stagnant budget receipts. Over half of the budget was paid to foreign and domestic creditors. Frustrated by the slow pace of recovery, the government reestablished some controls and discontinued some reforms. Deficit spending rose dramatically, inflation accelerated, and the zaire began a rapid depreciation. Gains from the reform effort had been largely eroded by late 1986.

Much of the opposition to the reform plan was voiced by members of the political elite and organs of the sole legal political party, the Popular Revolutionary Movement (Mouvement Populaire de la Révolution—MPR). Their complaints were voiced under the guise of economic nationalism in opposition to the "economic imperialism" of the donors. They especially vilified the IMF. Their actual opposition to the 1983 reform may have stemmed less from national pride than from the fact that the previously untouchable political elite was being made to pay taxes and duties and was being denied the economic privileges and access to resources for personal enrichment to which members had grown accustomed. Economic reform and liberalization were incompatible with patrimonial economics because they restrained the government from determining who should profit from the nation's natural wealth and domestic markets.

The 1987 Plan

In May 1987, Zaire negotiated another economic reform program with the IMF, the World Bank, and its bilateral partners. Along with the usual fiscal and monetary restrictions, Zaire agreed to revise its investment code to streamline the incentive framework and to revamp the tariff structure. Mobutu also backed away from a threat to reinstitute the fixed exchange rate and agreed to sharp increases in fuel prices and taxes. The IMF in turn allowed a 20 percent public-sector wage increase as opposed to the 40 percent increase the government had originally sought.

148

This program, like past efforts, was subsequently supported by Paris Club rescheduling. The IMF agreed to a twelve-month stand-by credit of SDR116.4 million. The World Bank initiated a US$165-million loan in June 1987 to assist with structural adjustment and balance of payments. The loan was to support improvements in the management of public enterprises and public administration, agriculture, and transportation, and to provide support for the private sector. Disbursements were to occur in two drawings conditional on meeting performance criteria.

The Paris Club rescheduled US$884 million due between May 1987 and May 1988 over fifteen years with six years' grace. Monthly debt payments were expected to drop from US$15 million to US$7 million. This agreement was exceptional because the Paris Club usually set ten-year ceilings on repayment delays. Private lenders agreed to lower repayments from US$3.5 million a month to US$3 million. A Belgian bank provided a bridge loan of SDR100 million to clear Zaire's arrears to the IMF.

Soon after the 1987 program was under way, excessive deficit spending prevented Zaire from meeting the program's targets, and further credits were withheld by both the World Bank and the IMF. Continued excessive government spending through 1988 led to a decline in foreign reserves, and the black market again became active. In 1988 the zaire depreciated dramatically against both the United States dollar and the Belgian franc. The budget deficit went from 3 percent of gross national product (GNP—see Glossary) in 1986 to 12 percent in 1988. The growth in GDP from 1987 to 1989 averaged 2.5 percent a year, well below population growth, resulting in a decline in per capita income.

The 1989 Reform

In January 1989, the government once more took steps to establish economic stability. A structural adjustment program, including the commitment to contain budget deficits, narrowed the gap between the official and black-market exchange rate to 10 percent by April 1989. In May 1989, a letter of intent was signed with the IMF for a standby loan of SDR115 million, SDR90 million of which came from the structural adjustment facility approved in May 1987 but blocked after the first drawing. A net capital outflow was expected in the first year. However, the program foresaw a net inflow of resources from multilateral and bilateral donors and creditors over the life of the agreement. The World Bank released the second drawing of the US$165 million loan for essential imports, which had been approved in June 1987 but blocked pending agreement with the IMF. Important loans for the transportation and mining sectors were sanctioned while proposed energy sector and social adjustment credits were considered. This latest IMF program emphasized, as usual, a reduction in government budget deficits, the restructuring and improvement of public-sector management, further elimination of distortions in trade policies, improvement in the climate for the growth of the private sector, and improvement in the transportation sector.

The significance of this IMF agreement, as with past agreements, was the favorable impact it was expected to have on all the lenders involved. In June 1989, the Paris Club met to reschedule outstanding Zairian debt. Lenders were presented with three options: a twenty-five-year rescheduling; cancellation of 33 percent of service due over the period under consideration and repayment of all maturities with repayment of the balance at market interest rates over fourteen years with six years' grace; or rescheduling of all maturities involved at an interest rate 3.5 percent lower than the prevailing level over fourteen years with eight years' grace.

Despite the country's reform efforts, the pace of economic activity had not accelerated sufficiently in 1989 to boost living standards, which had fallen each year for more than a decade. The standard of living showed no noticeable improvement for the typical Zairian. Major new investment, foreign or domestic, remained elusive. Nonetheless, agricultural production rose in some areas, although Zaire was still importing substantial quantities of food. In addition, some new light industrial production appeared in Kinshasa, the national capital, including manufacturing of plastics, matches, and batteries, and light electronic assembly. Liberalization in the diamond market meant that official diamond exports and receipts rose substantially.

Inefficient and corruptly managed parastatal (see Glossary) companies had contributed to Zaire's troubled economic history and were a severe strain on the budget. As part of the 1989 reform, the government announced that it was taking steps to reduce the role of the public sector in the economy and to increase the efficiency of parastatals, and it produced a list of seventeen companies intended for partial or full privatization. The government's broad objective was to raise private investment funds and to make the private sector more responsible for productive activities, with the exception of essential public services such as utilities and other strategic activities. In agriculture, a program of divestiture led to the privatization of several state-owned companies, such as Coton-Zaïre and Agrifor, a forestry firm.

The adoption in 1989 of a liberalized pricing policy and the removal of foreign-exchange restrictions eased conditions for importers and entrepreneurs, which in turn led to an increase in the range and availability of a variety of consumer goods in the Kinshasa market. Most of these goods, however, were expensive imported food items, clothing, and other merchandise unaffordable to all except expatriates and the local rich. Liberalized pricing policies also meant a more adequate supply in a wider market of fuel products.

By the end of 1989, however, it was apparent that these latest reforms were unsuccessful in promoting sustained economic expansion. Indeed, Zairians experienced a massive drop in per capita income, as inflation rose and the GDP growth rate fell. The inflation rate for 1989 was 104 percent, a significant increase over the 83 percent rate recorded the previous year. GDP growth for 1989 was registered as −1.3 percent.

Economic indicators for 1990 were even more dismal. IMF credits had expired, and large public-expenditure deficits were expected in response to pay increases for government workers. The final figures for 1990 showed a GDP decline of 2.6 percent, a 90 percent rate of inflation in consumer prices, and further devaluation of the zaire against Western currencies.

By 1992 and continuing into 1993, most sectors of the economy were in a state of advanced decay. Hyperinflation was a permanent fixture. The country's currency continued to depreciate to new lows against the dollar (Z110 million = US$1 by December 1993), causing a demonetization of the economy and a breakdown of the banking system, as well as severely damaging Zaire's international competitiveness. Poverty and unemployment were widespread.

Role of Government

Parastatals

Until the economic reforms begun under IMF tutelage in 1983, the government controlled economic policy by heavy participation in and ownership of enterprises, particularly those in the mining sector. Gécamines, the giant mining company, was a wholly government-owned company. These parastatals, until the reforms of 1983, were characteristically inefficient, largely because of their use by government elites as sources of private enrichment. One of the most notorious offenders was the mineral marketing agency, the Zairian Commerce Company (Société Zaïroise de Commercialisation des Minérais—Sozacom). Prior to its dissolution in 1984, Sozacom was under constant government pressure to surrender its export receipts to the treasury rather than to Gécamines for reinvestment, and it also had a reputation for diverting a percentage of its receipts to members of the Zairian elite.

The emergence in 1972 of the parastatal state marketing offices to monopolize the purchase of major crops, including coffee and cotton, was another example of corrupt government involvement in the economy. These monopolies were typically inefficient, subject to corruption, and provided only small returns for the farmer. Of the eleven state marketing offices created from 1971 to 1974, only one, the Zairian Coffee Board, continued to operate in the early 1990s.

Although by the early 1990s the government still owned or held a majority interest in many enterprises, including the national railroad and airlines, major mining and petroleum companies, and utilities, in theory the private sector was expected to lead economic growth. World Bank and IMF lending has been predicated on privatization and reform of state enterprises, allowing them to be run by competent managers free of political pressure from the central government. But reform appears unlikely under the Mobutu regime.

Patrimonial Politics and Corruption

Mobutu's efforts to centralize state power in his hands in order to penetrate all aspects of society have been analyzed by Thomas Callaghy, who has demonstrated that in the economic realm these efforts met with catastrophic results. When Mobutu came to power, Zaire began major state expansion and consolidation. Key to this process was the notion of economic sovereignty. Furthermore, Mobutu sought to bring economic activity within his tight control and was especially concerned with mining activity in the secessionist Katanga and Kasai (present-day Kasai-Oriental and Kasai-Occidental) regions. Some have speculated that insecurity about Katangan separatism in part led Mobutu to construct the country's primary source of electricity, the Inga I and Inga II hydroelectric plants, west of Kinshasa, in order to increase the capital's control over Katanga. Mobutu sought to reverse the traditional dominance of the mining region over the rest of the nation. The nationalization of the Belgian-owned UMHK in 1967 and its transformation into the Zairian-owned parastatal Gécamines, for example, was both a political and an economic act, deliberately and carefully planned. Its primary objective was the consolidation of presidential authority and spending ability. To finance state goals, Mobutu had to acquire major new financial resources for development projects and for slush money.

The government became increasingly preoccupied throughout the 1970s with raising revenue to finance grandiose projects. The

The Inga dams barrage, Zaire's largest source of electricity, on the lower Congo River near Matadi
Courtesy Agence Zaïre Presse

practice of patrimonialism gave free rein to the enrichment of the president and his associates in government and other spheres. According to Callaghy, "the revenue needs of the state intersected the need of the regime to finance its patrimonial processes of power maintenance and the ambition of the emergent political class for a swift accumulation of wealth."

These needs and ambitions led to a continuing financial crisis. Government administration developed weak, inefficient, and infamously corrupt financial structures; the revenue collection system, in particular, was little more than an open invitation for personal enrichment by favored administrators. Mobutu, as the patron of patrons, demonstrated a voracious desire for more revenue to spend as he saw fit. Much of this spending was untraceable, according to foreign technocrats brought in to salvage the economy as its crisis deepened. The expense of this quest for power and glory, and the costs of defense, grandiose projects, and a lavish life-style as well as the corruption and largesse inherent in a patriarchal patrimonial regime also brought the Zairian state to the point of collapse in the late 1970s.

In Zaire, corruption appeared to be the norm, not just an occasional or problematic exception. Access to high office was controlled by the president (see The Presidency; The National Executive Council, ch. 4). Because no one could be sure of remaining in office for very long, the incentive was to profit as quickly and as much as possible. Access to high office was the only hope of the Zairian elite or would-be-elite to attain, or maintain, a decent standard of living. The system guaranteed that top functionaries would serve the president, the ultimate source of their livelihood, rather than the nation. But corruption in Zaire was economically dysfunctional. Corruption did not serve to grease the wheels of the economic machine by creating jobs or other forms of expansion. Unfortunately for millions of Zairians as well as for frustrated foreign donors, the system was incapable of promoting sustained development. Nonetheless, to the extent that this system had enriched the president and kept him in firm control of a disparate society, it had worked well, and Mobutu appeared unlikely to abandon it, even under the heavy internal and external pressures he faced in the early 1990s.

Investment Projects

The early 1970s saw a rash of poorly conceived industrial development projects, which were launched without sensible and comprehensive economic planning and institutional support. Moreover, Zaire displayed a penchant for massive industrial and energy projects, neglecting the rural sector and transportation, both of which were in dire need of an infusion of resources. For example, an Italian consulting firm sold the idea of a steel-producing facility in Bas-Zaïre Region to Mobutu as an import-substitution scheme. The consulting firm that developed the plant at Maluku was a subsidiary of the contracting company. The project, begun in 1972 and completed in 1975, cost the Zairian government US$250 million. There were no foreign equity investors. Because there was no serious planning to develop iron-ore deposits, the mill operated on costly imported scraps at 10 percent of capacity until it ceased operations in 1980.

The massive Inga I and Inga II hydroelectric facilities also created a severe drain on Zairian resources. The project was initially scheduled for completion in 1978 but was not finished until 1982. The load forecast used to justify the project was based on overly optimistic expectations of copper price rises, mining expansion, and rapid expansion of the economy generally. Its cost was estimated at US$2 billion in 1983 prices, financed by the United States Export-Import Bank and the governments of Italy and Sweden. But cost overruns and underestimated management costs for foreign managers turned cheap power into expensive electricity as Zaire struggled under the heavy debt burden incurred to build and maintain the project. In 1990 Inga II generated only 14 percent of its total capacity. A planned free-trade zone and a Swiss aluminum refinery near the dam had also failed to materialize.

The Zairo-Italian Society Refinery (Société Zaïro-Italienne de Raffinage—Sozir) oil refinery, in Moanda on the Atlantic coast, was another costly operation built by an Italian firm. It was constructed in 1967 before offshore crude oil production began. The refinery was designed to refine a lighter crude than was eventually produced from Zaire's coastal wells. Refining Zaire's production would result in too much heavy fuel and not enough lighter products. It was therefore more economical to export Zairian crude oil and to import most refined products and all the crude petroleum to be processed at the Sozir plant. The refinery ran at 10 percent of capacity until September 1984 when it was closed. Subsequently, in 1986 small shipments of Nigerian crude were refined, but the refinery remained essentially idle.

Structure and Dynamics of the Economy
Gross Domestic Product

Zairian and other official statistics on the composition and growth of GDP should be taken as approximations at best, in particular given the chaotic nature of the economy and society in the early 1990s. Nevertheless, some basic trends can be observed. The Zairian economy grew slowly throughout most of the 1980s (except for 1982) but declined sharply beginning in 1989. Real GDP growth in 1980 was registered as 2.4 percent. The rate increased to 2.9 percent in 1981, but dropped sharply to − 3.0 percent in 1982, a year of decline in the price of copper. Thereafter, it increased once again and sustained positive real growth rates of 1.3 percent in 1983, 2.7 percent in 1984, 2.5 percent in 1985, 2.7 percent in 1986 and 1987, and 0.5 percent in 1988. In 1989, however, the growth rate fell to 1.3 percent and continued its decline with negative growth rates of − 2.6 percent in 1990, − 7.3 percent in 1991, and − 8.0 percent in 1992.

Zaire's poor economic performance has had a severe impact on the populace's standard of living. Even in years of modest GDP growth, economic growth was outpaced by the nation's very high population growth rate, which has been estimated at over 3 percent per year. As a result, per capita GDP has often fallen, or risen only slightly, even in years of improved economic performance. In terms of per capita GDP, mineral-rich Zaire found itself among the poorest African nations.

Nevertheless, although living conditions and purchasing power for the average peasant and city dweller are indeed meager, and for many people desperately low, official estimates of per capita income indicate a much lower standard of living than has actually been the case, especially prior to 1992. Many Zairians eke out a living through subsistence agriculture and barter and informal trade in a range of goods and services that show up nowhere in official government or donor country statistics. This energetic informal economy is often described by the apocryphal article fifteen of the first postindependence constitution, ''fend for yourself'' (see The Informal Economy, this ch.).

The sectoral composition of GDP has changed substantially since independence because of a drop in the real value of mineral production and because of the chronic weakness of other sectors, such as transportation and manufacturing, which the government has neglected. According to estimates by the government's Ministry of National Economy and Industry, agriculture accounted for 22 percent of GDP in 1970, industry for 8 percent, mining and metallurgy for 22 percent, and services for 48 percent. By contrast with the rest of sub-Saharan Africa, where agriculture lost ground to other sectors, Zairian agriculture's share of GDP had risen to 32 percent by the late 1980s, with industry dropping to about 2 percent, mining and metallurgy rising to 24 percent (but then dropping to 17 percent by 1990), and services and other sectors falling to about 42 percent. The increased contribution of agriculture to the GDP despite the fall in agricultural output in staples and cash crops is a vivid indication of the overall weakness of the economy. The increased importance of the mining and metallurgy sector was caused principally by the success of the legalization of the artisanal (panning) diamond market in 1983 and a substantial increase in cobalt production. The surprisingly large service sector is generally attributed to a bloated and grossly inefficient public sector and the fact that people receiving government pensions were included in this figure.

In a regional division of GDP, it is not surprising that Shaba accounted for 30 percent of the nation's total and Kinshasa for another 20 percent. The remainder was divided fairly evenly among the other regions.

The Informal Economy

In Zaire, as in many developing nations, a great deal of economic activity takes place outside of the official economy. Such activity, variously termed the informal, parallel, underground, unrecorded, or second economy, is in many cases so extensive that

*Women selling food
at a Kinshasa market
Courtesy Sandy Beach*

*Central Market,
Kinshasa
Courtesy Zaire
National Tourism Office*

it should not be regarded as marginal or supplemental, but, rather, as the way such economies really work. In her study of the second economy (her preferred terminology) in Zaire, anthropologist Janet MacGaffey concludes that smuggling and other unofficial activities constitute the real economy of Zaire. Second-economy activities are fully institutionalized and in most respects more rational and predictable than official trade and production activities. The second economy provides access to goods and services unavailable in the official economy and compensates for the deficiencies of the official system in infrastructure and services, such as construction, transportation, distribution networks, and provision of capital.

The magnitude of the informal economy far exceeds official economic activity. In the early 1990s, Zaire's informal economy was estimated to be three times the size of the official GDP. In Zaire, as elsewhere, the size of the informal economy reflects the increasing inability of the official system to serve the needs of the populace. The informal economy has grown dramatically as economic and social conditions have deteriorated and as purchasing power has dropped. Citizens have increasingly been forced to turn to informal economic activity to survive.

The informal economy in Zaire includes a wide array of economic activities, similar only in that all are unmeasured, unrecorded, and, to varying degrees, illegal in that they are unlicensed and designed to avoid government control and taxation. They range from small-scale street vending to the production of illicit goods, to open and relatively large-scale trading and manufacturing enterprises, to cross-border smuggling, to barter arrangements such as rural-urban exchanges of food for manufactured goods, to various schemes intended to avoid the payment of taxes on legal production (e.g., concealing legal production and falsifying invoices).

Despite its significance, however, MacGaffey concludes that Zaire's bustling second economy is a mixed blessing. A cost-benefit analysis of the second economy provides a varied picture. On the plus side, the informal economy in Zaire has enabled the bulk of the populace to get by and occasionally to prosper. Profits from such activities have been invested in community services and in some instances in official economic activity, thus contributing to national prosperity. In the social realm, the informal economy has empowered women and various segments of the population not able to participate in the formal economy (see The Informal Sector; Polarization and Prospects for Conflict; Strategies of Survival; The Status of Women, ch. 2).

Nevertheless, there are also negative aspects to the second economy. Drawbacks include the inherent unfairness and unevenness of both access to the resources needed to participate in the second economy and the distribution of benefits from such participation. Those already rich and powerful and the employed tend to benefit far more than the unemployed, the urban poor, or rural producers. There are also negative effects on the official economy in that the state is deprived of both revenue and foreign exchange (for example, smuggling out food crops because of price controls in Zaire forces Zaire to use scarce foreign exchange to buy imported food), and labor shortages may also result from the proliferation of unofficial economic activity.

On balance, although the second economy is dynamic and contributes to the well-being of most of the Zairian populace, long-term economic development and national prosperity depend on reforming and energizing the formal economy, transferring to it the dynamism of the second economy. The prospects for such a radical transformation, however, appear bleak so long as the Mobutu regime remains entrenched in power.

Currency

In 1967 the Congolese franc was replaced by the zaire, a non-convertible unit with a value of US$.50 to the zaire. This exchange rate held good until March 1976 when the zaire was revalued to Z1.1 to the SDR. A succession of devaluations in 1978, 1979, 1980, and 1981 temporarily gave the zaire a realistic value, but, because the fixed link with the SDR was retained, the black market quickly took over again as the principal market for exchange. A few exporters, notably Gécamines and other government-owned companies as well as the offshore oil consortium, normally observed the official exchange rate, a policy that inevitably had an adverse impact on their cash flow because the local currency they were paid was considerably less than the real value of their foreign-exchange earnings.

The overvaluation of the zaire led to consistent shortages of hard currency at the official rate, making it difficult for local industries to import necessary inputs and spare parts. This limitation and restrictions on repatriating profits by overseas investors gave rise to a black market where the zaire sold at a fraction of its official value. For example, the parallel rate stood at five times the official rate in September 1983.

The parallel rate was the principal currency vehicle for business. Recorded diamond exports dropped sharply as smuggling offered a considerably higher profit margin than operating officially. Diamonds were sold at one point by nondiamond-producing Burundi. Coffee exporters were required to present their export documents to official channels in order to register their allocated percentage of Zaire's international coffee organization quota. However, it was common practice to ask bankers to deliver foreign-currency receipts to another customer, who would then pay the exporter zaires at the parallel rate minus a commission. Some exporters simply smuggled coffee to neighboring countries. Access to limited and grossly undervalued foreign exchange depended on political and family connections. In this way, many members of the Zairian elite gained easy access to hard currency, as opposed to those Zairians and foreigners engaged in more entrepreneurial pursuits.

Throughout the early 1990s, the Zairian government accelerated its attempts to acquire hard currency and to control foreign-exchange transactions. In October 1993, the regime required all Zairian exports to be paid for in advance in foreign currency. In addition, all incoming foreign exchange had to be "sold" to the central bank for domestic currency within forty-eight hours of receipt.

In terms of the United States dollar, the zaire has registered a dramatic decline in value since 1985, when Z50 equaled US$1, and 1986, when Z60 equaled US$1. The average annual value of the zaire per US$1 was registered as Z112 in 1987, Z187 in 1988, Z381 in 1989, and Z719 in 1990. The zaire was devalued in August 1991 in order to match the official exchange rate with the black-market rate, resulting in a new official rate of US$1 = Z15,300. But in 1992 the rate plummeted to US$1 = Z114,291 and continued to deteriorate. The official rate was Z1,990,000 = US$1 by December 1992 (the average annual rate for 1992 was Z645,549 = US$1).

In January 1993, the regime attempted to introduce a new Z5 million note. But opposition forces denounced the move as inflationary and encouraged merchants to refuse to accept the note. When many of them did so, soldiers who had been paid in the notes went on a rampage, and extensive rioting and looting occurred. By March 1993, the exchange rate was Z2,529,000 = US$1.

In October 1993, the regime again attempted to resolve its chronic liquidity crisis by announcing the introduction of a new zaire (nouveau zaire—NZ), each supposed to be worth 3 million of the old zaire and set at an official rate of three new zaires to the United States dollar; the old currency was to be withdrawn from circulation. The change had not been implemented by the end of 1993. The result of the announcement alone has, however, been a drastic plunge in the exchange rate in the black market and another surge in prices. The zaire traded against the United States dollar at a seemingly ridiculous rate of 8 million to one in October 1993;

by December the rate was a patently absurd Z110 million to the dollar and still rising. Once again some rioting and looting occurred when opposition forces promoted a boycott of the new currency.

Inflation

Zaire often financed its large budget deficits by borrowing from the domestic banking sector. This process in turn led to excessive growth in the money supply and rapid inflation. The black market, persistent government overspending, and a lack of control of the money supply led to high rates of inflation, rising to 77 percent in 1983 according to the central bank. A key objective of the stabilization program of 1983 was to control the growth of the money supply and inflation by gradually instituting measures designed to restrict credit expansion. During the 1983–86 period, these measures resulted in a sharp decrease in domestic liquidity and a lower inflation rate—52 percent in 1984, 24 percent in 1985, and 47 percent in 1986. Commercial bank deposit rates increased. Pressure on the exchange rate diminished.

In 1987 and 1988, however, after the 1983 plan unraveled, the rate of inflation soared to 90 percent and 83 percent, respectively, as the money supply exploded. The zaire dropped dramatically against the dollar and against the pound sterling. In January 1989, the government tried again to contain the budget deficit and to limit monetary financing of the deficit. By April 1989, domestic liquidity had declined, real interest rates were positive, and inflation was briefly lowered. As was the case with previous reforms, however, the economic gains from this plan were short-lived, and the inflation rate for 1989 rose to 104 percent. In 1990 inflation was conservatively reported by the IMF to have dropped to 81 percent. (Other sources reported a 296 percent rate in 1990.) But the rate rose dramatically to 2,154 percent in 1991 (3,524 percent according to other sources). By 1992 and continuing throughout 1993, the economy had deteriorated to such an extent that, although no reliable figures had been produced by the government, inflation was wildly estimated at rates ranging between 3,500 and 23,000 percent. Some sources cited an average rate of 4,129.2 percent in 1992.

In late 1993, analysts noted that the rate of inflation, although still very high and rising, had not accelerated as much as expected despite the drastic decline in the value of the zaire. They attributed this situation to the severe reduction in imports and the virtual demonetization of the economy. Some believed that the average annual inflation rate for 1993 would prove to be in the neighborhood of 275 percent rather than the 7,000 percent to 10,000 percent originally predicted.

Budget

The government has regularly overspent since independence, largely because of enormous and costly development projects. Financial administration has been marked by poor budgetary control, accompanied by widespread mismanagement and corruption. Money for the ambitious plans to make Zaire a regional industrial power was provided by foreign governments and commercial banks, anxious to channel the country's enormous potential petrodollar surpluses into assets.

The budget was drafted by the financial ministries and promulgated by the National Legislative Council. Accountability was lacking, however, and much of Zaire's government spending was untraceable until reform efforts began in the mid-1980s. World Bank and IMF technical experts who tried to audit Zairian government expenditures were only partially successful. Budgets in the early 1980s distributed 50 percent of outlays to political institutions and government, 23 percent to the military, 3 percent to health, and 3 percent to education. Agriculture was not a high budgetary priority.

The budget for fiscal year (FY—see Glossary) 1987, drafted under IMF tutelage, estimated revenues at Z100 billion. Current revenue accounted for Z82.3 billion, and counterpart funds (contributions from external sources) accounted for Z17.7 billion. The main sources of current revenue were: customs and duties, Z28.3 billion; direct and indirect taxes, Z25.9 billion; Gécamines, Z15.3 billion; and oil revenue, Z7 billion.

Expenditures for FY 1987 were Z106 billion. Of that amount, Z88.3 billion went to current expenditures, with costs broken down into administration, Z26.5 billion; external debt service, Z26.5 billion; personnel, Z16.8 billion; capital, Z13.2 billion; and internal debt service, Z5.3 billion. The defense ministry was the largest item under administrative costs, receiving Z5.2 billion or 50 percent of all ministry expenses. The IMF permitted Zaire to run a Z6 billion deficit in FY 1987. The investment budget stood at Z13.2 billion, compared with planned investment expenditures of Z167 billion in the 1986–90 period.

The public finance deficit widened to over Z60 billion in FY 1988, when revenue stood at Z134.4 billion and expenditures at Z195.1 billion. First-quarter revenues in FY 1989 exceeded expenditures by 9.5 percent, creating a small budget surplus. But the situation greatly deteriorated in FY 1990 when consistent and credible economic policy was made impossible by a prolonged political crisis, resulting in several revisions of the fiscal year's draft budget (see

Political Reform in the 1990s, ch. 4). The initial draft budget providing for expenditures of Z584,300 million and revenue of Z554,300 million was revised after the government admitted that the economy was uncontrollable because of a fall in export revenues resulting from weak commodity prices, and a hyperinflation rate of an estimated 1,300 percent (other figures for the country's inflation rate were vastly higher). Following devaluation of the zaire, the revised budget approved in July 1991 estimated expenditures at Z4,600,000 million, with revenues projected at Z3,600,000 million. The budget deficit for FY 1992 was Z703,632 million, more than ten times higher than planned; the FY 1993 deficit was projected to total almost Z1,098 billion.

All reports indicate that the government is bankrupt. The tax collection system is defunct, few if any customs revenues are collected, and foreign aid (other than humanitarian assistance) has been virtually cut off. Copper production, formerly a major source of government revenue, has dropped off significantly; however, many sources believe that the Mobutu regime continues to obtain funds from the diamond trade (both legal and illicit). To pay its bills, the government has had new currency printed abroad, first in Germany and then in Britain, and flown in but increasingly has had difficulty even paying these printing bills. In late 1993, Zaire was reported to be deeply in debt to the British and German firms that printed Zairian money for the Mobutu regime.

Debt

The external debt quintupled between 1967 and 1973. Massive and rash spending and borrowing when revenues were high, rampant corruption and fiscal mismanagement, and lack of understanding and concern about the rapidly deteriorating economic situation by Mobutu, the political elite, and foreign lenders characterized the period. The debt stood at US$1.5 billion in 1973. Debt-service payments jumped 353 percent between 1967 and 1973, or in absolute terms to US$81 million. By 1976 the external debt was more than a third of total expenditure and 12 percent of GDP. In 1977 debt service amounted to 43 percent of export earnings and 49 percent of total revenues.

At the end of 1988, Zaire's debt was estimated at US$7 billion (excluding what was owed to the IMF). Unlike many other debtor nations, most of Zaire's debt was owed to bilateral government creditors; multilateral institutions accounted for only 14 percent and commercial banks for only 6 percent. Mobutu and his government regularly pointed to this fact when seeking debt forgiveness or other relief. Without debt rescheduling, Zaire would have had a 50 percent to 60 percent debt-service ratio. However, debt reschedulings reduced debt-service payments, resulting in an actual debt-service ratio of between 12 percent and 19 percent. This ratio fell to 7.3 percent in 1988 because Zaire stopped most debt-service payments to bilateral creditors in May and accumulated substantial arrears. Zaire's debt was again rescheduled in June 1989. Altogether, there had been sixteen multilateral debt reschedulings since 1975, more than for any other African nation. Zaire regularly threatened to suspend debt-service payments but invariably resumed payments in the context of renewed reform efforts and rescheduling.

The local currency cost of external debt-service payments increased substantially with the depreciation of the zaire. Payments of external debt service amounted to 11 percent of total government expenditures in 1988 and were thought likely to account for 23 percent of government expenditures in 1989.

In 1989 foreign debt was US$9.2 billion. Zaire's total foreign debt in 1990 amounted to US$10.1 billion, with the external debt-service ratio at 15.4 percent. By the year's end, all of Zaire's main bilateral and multilateral lending partners had frozen their financial aid programs as Zaire's political and economic situation deteriorated and specifically as a direct result of the killing of student demonstrators at the University of Lubumbashi in May 1990. (The World Bank did, however, continue to make disbursements to Zaire so long as Zaire kept up debt-service payments.) In 1991 Zaire's external debt stood at US$10.7 billion, including US$9.1 billion in long-term public debt. In 1992 Zaire virtually ended all payments on its foreign debt, paying only US$79 million of the more than US$3.4 billion due.

In February 1992, the IMF issued a Declaration of Noncooperation with Zaire, signaling that Zaire's arrears had made it ineligible for further borrowing. In July 1993, the World Bank froze all disbursements to Zaire because of arrears on debt-service payments to the bank. (Previously Zaire had kept up with debt-service payments to the World Bank, which had as a result not cut off financial flows to Zaire.) Moreover, it appears that so long as President Mobutu remains in power, the country's lending partners are unlikely to agree to reschedule or cancel its debts, as analysts argue that debt cancellation will encourage bad economic practices from the past.

Banking

The banking system in Zaire has traditionally been underdeveloped and largely confined to urban areas. Zaire's banking system consists of a central bank, called the Bank of Zaire (Banque du Zaïre), and seventeen commercial banks, including development or investment institutions. In addition to the traditional functions of a central bank—issuing currency, establishing monetary policy, and acting as cashier for the national government—the Bank of Zaire also has the power to control all financial institutions in Zaire and to administer the country's gold and foreign monetary reserves.

The Bank of Zaire experienced difficulties in the early 1990s because of the country's dire economic situation. Mobutu's government had survived primarily by printing new money abroad to pay its loyal troops but became deeply indebted to German and British printing firms.

Of the seventeen commercial banks, only one, the People's Bank, is publicly owned. The other sixteen commercial banks are mostly subsidiaries of Western banks, the largest being the Zairian Commercial Bank, which is associated with a Belgian industrial conglomerate. The two most important investment organizations are the Development Finance Company (Société Financière de Développement—Sofide) and the National Savings and Real Estate Fund (Caisse Nationale d'Épargne et de Crédit Immobilier—CNECI). Sofide is a joint stock company, financed by the government, the World Bank, and the private sector, and is responsible for lending money to create or modernize industry in Zaire. CNECI promotes savings from the private sector and grants loans to individuals for housing or mortgages.

As of 1993, the banking system has virtually collapsed. The central bank is bankrupt, and most other banks have closed. Despite the demise of the official banking system, however, many banking services are available through the informal sector. Visitors to Zaire have reported that Zairian women "bankers" operating in the informal economy have ample supplies of foreign currencies for exchange.

Labor

Employment statistics are considered extremely unreliable because the national agency responsible for their collection, the National Institute for Social Security, has limited resources. The latest available published figures from 1984 showed 1.1 million employed in the official economy out of an employable population of about 15 million. A breakdown of the persons employed had almost 800,000 workers in the private sector and the remaining 300,000 employed in public administration. Teaching was the largest single component in the public sector with 200,000 employees, and the mining conglomerate Gécamines was the largest single corporate employer with a work force of roughly 37,000.

Skilled industrial labor was in short supply, and often workers had to be trained by individual companies. Salaries were generally low, but employers were required to provide a variety of benefits, including medical care, family allowances, transportation, and sometimes housing and subsidized food. Termination of an employee was a difficult procedure.

Incomplete statistics make detailed analysis of employment patterns difficult, but several generalizations can nevertheless be made. A large part of the population stands outside the formal economy and ekes out a living by subsistence farming, informal trade or barter, or smuggling and other illicit activities. Women are severely underrepresented in the formal economy; by some estimates, only 4 percent of formal-sector employees are women. As a result, they have recourse in large numbers to the informal economy.

Although the population rose from 16.2 million in 1960 to 34 million in 1989 and to 39.1 million by 1992, total formal-sector employment remained about the same in the early 1990s as at independence; increases in the labor force were probably absorbed by an increase in the number of subsistence farmers. A lack of new jobs in urban areas would imply high urban unemployment for the growing populations of the cities (Kinshasa alone added 2 million inhabitants from 1960 to 1984). One estimate placed unemployment in the mid-1980s at 40 percent for Kinshasa and as high as 80 percent for other cities. Only mining towns had unemployment at lower figures.

The government encouraged foreign employers to minimize the number of expatriate employees. As an investment matured, the number of foreign workers was expected to diminish. The government controlled foreign labor through a tax on expatriate salaries and issuance of work and residence permits.

The National Union of Zairian Workers (Union Nationale des Travailleurs Zaïrois—UNTZA), the country's only official trade union until mid-1990 when independent trade unions were legalized, was in reality a branch of the MPR (see Interest Groups, ch. 4). UNTZA employed 1,000 full-time staff members and claimed to represent all Zairian workers. Disputes were settled by a government order that labor and management agree to settlements that were usually compromises between their respective demands. Union militancy was rare. UNTZA rarely, if ever, called strikes. Any work disruptions that occurred were outside the context of the union.

Mobutu's April 1990 announcement that the country would make a transition to a pluralistic, multiparty political system ended UNTZA's role as the nation's sole trade union, although it remained the most influential union in the early 1990s. Subsequently, some twelve trade unions sprang up, all officially recognized by the government, representing various political constituencies, political parties, and industrial sectors. To protest low wages, trade union pluralism led to more frequent strikes as well as other demonstrations against the government. By 1992, for example, the public-service system had virtually ceased to function. Most public employees, including hospital workers and teachers, were on strike to protest lack of payment by the bankrupt government.

Agriculture

Throughout the 1980s, nearly 65 percent of the work force was engaged in subsistence and commercial agriculture, and the sector accounted for approximately 32 percent of GDP. Because of the various economic distortions since independence, such as exchange controls, price controls, overvaluation of the currency, and the smuggling out of cash crops such as coffee, agriculture's contribution to the economy was usually undervalued in official reports.

Zaire has the potential to be a net exporter of agricultural produce, but, as in other economic sectors, the country has never lived up to its potential. Indeed, as of the 1990s, Zaire was not even self-sufficient in food production. The agricultural sector has suffered as a result of the dislocations from Zairianization, an inadequate infrastructure for the transport of agricultural produce and an inadequate banking system, both of which have also affected other sectors of the economy, and inattention from the urban elite, resulting in few rural ventures and limited funds for investment.

Small-scale subsistence farmers primarily grow four staple food crops—rice, corn, cassava, and plantains—together on small scattered plots. Women generally handle food production, transport to market, and sale. Traditional slash-and-burn clearing methods are used, and the only capital inputs are hand-held tools and seed raised on the farms. Land clearing is labor intensive and thus has limited the areas under cultivation.

The average growth rate of the food supply in Zaire fell from 4.1 percent a year in the late 1960s to 1.8 percent in the 1970s compared with an estimated population growth rate of about 2 percent in the 1960s and approximately 3 percent in the 1970s and 1980s. Rural areas continue to provide much of the food for urban areas, but food imports have been increasingly important for the swelling urban population, with considerable illicit traffic crossing the borders, such as corn brought in from Zambia and Tanzania. By many accounts, Kinshasa subsists mainly on imported food: wheat, corn, flour, and canned and dried fish.

There is much disparity between official and unofficial estimates of food imports. In 1985, for example, official estimates placed food imports at 157,000 tons, while unofficial figures were estimated at 393,000 tons. In 1986 Zaire imported 170,000 tons of wheat and 64,000 tons of flour, up from 156,000 tons and 31,000 tons, respectively, the preceding year. The 1987 bill for imported wheat was estimated at US$33 million in July 1987 prices. Wheat and flour imports were estimated to total 220,000 tons in 1990.

Zaire's agricultural potential is greatly underutilized. By some estimates, as little as 1 percent of the land is under cultivation. Compounding the problem, government expenditures on the sector are inadequate, amounting to only 1 percent to 2 percent of government outlays, most of which goes to government administration.

Under the colonial administration, coercion was frequently used to keep production up. Nonetheless, extension services and supplies for small farmers were far superior to the postindependence government's ability or efforts. Agricultural buying offices have frequently been sources of corruption and are unable to provide small shareholders with adequate fuel, spare parts, buying stations, or bonuses-in-kind, such as the salt or sugar that were sometimes provided by the colonial administration. The poor transportation network is one major obstacle to increased production. Small farmers raise crops primarily for their own subsistence because of the difficulty of transporting goods to market. Middlemen who provide transport can reap huge profits.

In the 1950s, many agribusiness enterprises, or corporate plantations, were established, especially in the Bas-Zaïre and Kivu regions. There was livestock raising and food processing, and cotton, wood, and rubber were produced and used in local manufacturing. However, full vertical integration in such areas as cotton production and textile manufacturing did not materialize.

The 1973 policy of Zairianization resulted in agricultural stagnation, as many enterprises were stripped of their assets or abandoned. In addition, price fixing, a colonial legacy used to hold down prices in order to restrain urban wages, led to some profit in the import sector but discouraged production of food crops. Adjustments in producer prices under the stabilization plans were limited; the government felt that higher food prices would cut incomes in the urban areas. Donors advised the government to direct scarce resources to maintenance of the existing road system, development

Car ferry crossing the Kasai River in Bandundu Region
Cassava truck on a dirt road in Bandundu Region

169

of a delivery system for tools and seeds, and provision of credit. They also noted that long-term investment in infrastructure development, technological research, and institution building were needed. But the Zairian government failed to act on this advice, and the stagnation of agriculture, which dated back to 1959, thus continued. In 1993 some observers predicted an impending agricultural crisis as a result of the failure to plant crops in areas such as Nord-Kivu in which ethnic violence had occurred.

National Land Law System

A national system of land law exists in Zaire. However, it is based on a legal dichotomy, and its system of land registration is reported to be highly ineffective and insecure. The Zairian land law system was established by national legislation and is based legally and in practice on the legacy of Belgian colonialism as well as the Zairian customary system of land tenure. The European principle of individual ownership of land was unknown in Zaire's indigenous system. Instead, historically, land was the property of a lineage or descent group (see Glossary). In this system, a "land chief" exercised authority over land allocation in a village, and cultivators held usufruct rights to the land, which was farmed through shifting cultivation.

This indigenous system was transformed by the colonial legacy of the Congo Free State (1885–1908) and the Belgian Congo (1908–60), during which the land law system was established to favor the exploitation of the country's natural resources by the Belgian authorities. "Vacant lands" were decreed to belong to the state, with the lands "occupied by the native population, under the authority of their chiefs" continuing to be governed by the customary laws and customs of the lineage groups. However, the notion of "vacant land" was never clearly defined, and in practice land that lay fallow was considered "vacant," even though it was meant to be used eventually by indigenous cultivators. Moreover, the state completely ignored hunting and gathering rights, which were well-defined and governed by customary law.

Another element in this system favoring the colonial authorities was the introduction of land registration, with any lands coming under the state's domain ceasing to be governed by customary law and thus eligible to be granted by the state to individuals and enterprises. It was estimated that by 1944, Europeans controlled approximately 12 million hectares of land, out of a total land area of 234 hectares in the Belgian Congo.

The colonial period's land law system remained in force following independence in 1960, at which time four broad categories of land-holding existed: state-owned lands, lands owned by individuals and companies, concessions, and lands occupied by indigenous populations covered by customary law. The newly independent state now had to resolve inherent conflicts, in particular the status of preindependence lands controlled by foreign interests as well as lands controlled by Congolese under customary law, and the applicability of the land registration system in determining the rights of nationals.

The Bakajika Law, enacted in June 1966, was the first in a series of laws designed to ensure government control of the land and its riches. It gave ownership of all wealth above and below the ground to the state, thus ensuring that the government could claim all public mineral rights. On December 31, 1971, the enactment of a constitutional amendment and promulgation of a law empowered the state to repossess all rights to the land. In July 1973, the General Property Law was enacted to organize the country's new land law system. With the enactment of the 1971 and 1973 laws, all lands now belonged to the state, with individual land rights derived from either concessions by the state or indigenous customary law. The new laws did not abrogate preexisting customary land rights, but they left unclear the future concessionary status of these lands.

Another problem confronting practical application of these early 1970s laws is the fact that very little privately owned land is registered in Zaire, causing tenure to be precarious. Lack of clear title prevents land from being offered as collateral for a loan and discourages individual farmers from making the capital investment in land improvement needed to raise output. The situation is exacerbated both by the limited government resources available to embark on a large-scale land registration and the practice by concessionaires of bribing local officials to postpone indefinitely investigations of further development activities on the concession. Political interference has also obstructed the resolution of land disputes. The theft of documents and files relating to land disputes is another common practice. The irresolution of these problems has led to an increase in the number of land disputes in Zaire.

Crops

The major food crops are cassava, corn, rice, plantains, and, to a lesser extent, bananas, beans, and peanuts. Millet, sorghum, yams, potatoes, and various fruits are also significant (see table 11, Appendix). The food most universally eaten is cassava (also known as manioc), annual production of which was estimated at 18.2 million tons in 1991. Cassava is grown throughout the country under all climatic conditions; not only do the tuber and its products form a major element of the diet, but the leaves are also eaten as a vegetable.

Corn, like cassava, is grown nationwide, but its principal culture is centered in the south. In much of Shaba Region, corn is the preferred staple; cassava is eaten chiefly during periods of corn shortage. Rice is grown mainly in the humid climate of the Congo River basin, particularly along the Congo in Équateur Region and also near Kisangani in Haut-Zaïre Region. Plantains and bananas are cultivated throughout the country but are of special importance in the northeast and east, particularly in the former Kivu Region, where in some places they are planted on about half the land devoted to agriculture and form the principal staple.

Millet and sorghum are grown exclusively in the savanna areas and are important only in the relatively dry far northern and southeastern parts of the country. A considerable part of the sorghum and millet harvests is used for making beer, a profitable activity for Zairian women in particular.

Yams and potatoes are cultivated principally in the forest zones of central Zaire, where they occasionally constitute the main staple. Peanuts are grown outside the central forest zones, and, before the turmoil of the 1960s, peanut oil was a significant export crop.

The principal cash crops have traditionally been coffee, palm oil and palm kernel oil, sugar, cocoa, rubber, and tea. All are grown on large plantations. Cotton and tobacco are produced mainly on smallholdings.

Coffee has long been Zaire's most important agricultural cash crop. Coffee is grown by both smallholders and large plantations. However, plantation owners reap proportionately much larger profits. Moreover, large exporter firms often buy coffee at low prices from small farmers. Then the exporters and the state, through the official Zairian Coffee Board, reap large profits when world prices are high, such as in 1986 when the International Coffee Organization suspended export quotas in the wake of the 1986 Brazilian freeze and failed harvest.

To circumvent state controls, low prices, and quotas, many producers have engaged in illicit trade. By some accounts, as much as 30 percent to 60 percent of the coffee crop has traditionally been smuggled out of the country each year since independence—a tendency increased by the economic crisis of the early 1990s.

Two varieties of coffee are grown: robusta, used primarily in the manufacture of instant coffee, and arabica, exported in bean form. Cultivation of robusta is widespread and accounts for approximately

Cassava plants at a government showcase farm

90 percent of the coffee grown; arabica requires the cooler temperatures of highland areas. In 1988 an estimated 99,000 tons of coffee were produced. In 1989 approximately 107,000 tons of coffee were produced, and the 1990 crop was 120,000 tons. But the coffee crop was reported to be threatened by the fungal disease, tracheomycose, and production is estimated to have dropped to 102,000 tons in 1991. In the early 1990s, coffee production and exports also suffered because of the shortage of fertilizers, credit for farmers, and low world prices.

In August 1993, Zaire and other African coffee producers joined the Association of Coffee Producing Countries (ACPC), formed by Latin American producers in July 1993. The association aimed to force a rise in coffee prices by withholding a portion of production from export. World coffee prices did rise in the last quarter of 1993.

Prior to independence, Zaire was the second largest producer of palm oil in Africa, producing as much as 400,000 tons annually. Production dropped during the 1960s as civil disturbances damaged palm plantations and farmers switched to the more lucrative coffee. Plantations also deteriorated as the decline in the price of palm oil reduced profitability. In 1988 and 1989, Zaire produced 178,000 tons annually. Subsequent production figures were unavailable in 1993.

Information on tea, cocoa, and rubber is meager. Tea is grown in the highland areas of northeastern Zaire. Although the government has made various attempts to increase its cultivation, annual production of tea in the late 1980s (about 3,000 tons) was less than two-thirds of the amount grown in 1978. The increased use of synthetic rubber also led to a decline in rubber cultivation; annual tonnage for the late 1980s, between 17,000 and 24,000 tons, was less than half the amount for 1978. In 1990 and in 1991, production was estimated at only 10,000 tons. Cocoa is grown in the more humid areas of Bas-Zaïre and Équateur regions. Cocoa production levels remained fairly constant through the 1970s and early 1980s, but generally declined in the late 1980s and early 1990s, from 6,000 tons in 1988 to 4,000 tons in 1991.

The colonial state relied on coercion—fines and prison—to force peasants to invest the labor-intensive energy needed for cotton production. The imposed system of export crop production still existed in the early 1990s, and fines were levied for noncompliance. In 1952 some 102,000 tons were produced; 180,000 tons were produced in 1959. Since that time, cotton growing has diminished steadily as farmers, where possible, have chosen to grow the more lucrative cash crop, coffee. Only 26,000 tons of cotton were produced each year from 1988 to 1991. By 1992 production reportedly had dropped to 11,000 tons.

Cotton output has been affected by farmers' difficulties with credit, supplies of seeds and insecticides, and the lack of agricultural extension programs. Cotton imports, which grew as local production fell in the early 1990s, have also discouraged local production. Zaire imports large quantities of used Western clothing and foreign-made traditional African textiles. Nearly 7,500 tons of cotton were imported from the United States for spinning in 1986.

Forestry

Zaire is the most heavily forested country in Africa, with a forest cover extending over 122 million hectares. The country has an estimated 6 percent of the world's forestland. Only a small portion of Zaire's forest area, however, had been exploited commercially by the early 1990s, primarily because of the lack of transportation infrastructure, particularly in the interior of the country.

There are three main areas of economic interest: the Mayombé Forest in western Bas-Zaïre covering 240,000 hectares, an area north of the Congo River in Équateur Region covering 21 million hectares, and the tropical rain forests in northern Bandundu Region with 101 million hectares. Bas-Zaïre, close to Kinshasa and the country's ports, has been the site of the heaviest logging in the country. Much of the Mayombé Forest was seriously depleted by logging operations in the 1960s, and some logging restrictions are now in force there. The forests in Équateur Region have been partially degraded because of slash-and-burn farming techniques. The hardwood central basin forests in Bandundu Region remain relatively untouched, although some encroachment from itinerant slash-and-burn agriculture has begun to affect the northern and southern borders.

In effect, all forestlands are owned by the Zairian state, which has granted long-term (usually twenty-five-year) logging concessions over huge areas to multinational companies. In the early 1990s, timber concessions had already been granted for 37 percent of Zaire's exploitable forest area. Eleven foreign-based companies or joint ventures accounted for 90 percent of the country's logging operations. One German subsidiary alone accounted for 40 percent of logging in Zaire.

On average, 500,000 cubic meters of timber traditionally were extracted annually, but figures were lower in the late 1980s and early 1990s. In 1988 about 416,500 cubic meters of logs were extracted; production rose to 419,000 cubic meters in 1989 and to 465,000 cubic meters in 1990 but dropped to 391,000 cubic meters in 1991. Sawn wood production was much lower, at 131,000 cubic meters in 1989, dropping to 117,000 cubic meters in 1990, and 105,000 cubic meters in 1991. Zairian production is extremely modest when compared with that of major international producers.

In the early 1990s, planning was underway for major increases in logging production—up to 5 million cubic meters by the year 2020. Production increases would be accompanied by promotion of Zairian wood products in overseas markets, particularly in Europe, the United States, and Japan. There were also plans to increase timber exports to East Africa, currently at a low level. Such an increase would depend, however, on the construction of a road network in the interior of the country.

Over the years, attempts have been made to increase growth, diversity, and development in the forestry sector, but to no avail. Zaire's timber, like most African timber, continues to be exported primarily in its cheapest raw material form—as raw logs rather than sawn wood. Moreover, production of other products such as veneer and plywood remains quite limited. As with other areas of agricultural development, ecologically sound and profitable growth in forestry depends on dramatic improvements in transportation and both private and public management capabilities, neither of which appears likely in the foreseeable future (see Environmental Trends, ch. 2).

Fishing and Livestock

Zaire has only a small coastline, but fish are abundant in all of Zaire's lakes and rivers with the exception of Lac Kivu. Nevertheless, although fish is an important source of protein in the diet, the amounts harvested are below demand and are considered to be well below the potential; imports, mostly of salted fish, are required to meet demand. Imports, primarily from South Africa and Zimbabwe, normally total about 100,000 tons per year. Marine fishing is under the control of a government organization that operates a small fleet of fishing boats off the mouth of the Congo River. The marine catch, however, is only slightly more than 1 percent of the country's total and is used almost entirely by urban centers in Bas-Zaïre and by Kinshasa. Zaire's total fish catch was 162,000 tons in 1988, about 166,000 tons in 1989, and 162,000 tons in 1990. Of these totals, only 2,000 tons were from the Atlantic each year; the remainder came from inland waters. Actual annual production compares very unfavorably with estimated production potential of 330,000 tons per year.

Most of the traditional livestock herding is found in the higher eastern sections of the country, where the tsetse fly, which transmits sleeping sickness, is less of a problem. Commercial herds also are raised in the highland areas of Shaba and Kasai-Occidental regions. Estimates in 1991 showed 1.6 million head of cattle, 910,000 head of sheep, more than 3 million goats, and 830,000 pigs. There were an estimated 19 million chickens in 1987. Sheep and goats are raised by villagers in all parts of the country. Sheep, of a small domestic variety that produces little wool, are raised for their meat and skins; goats are kept for milk and meat. Hogs are generally raised near urban centers. Most villages have flocks of chickens and ducks, and, in the mid-1970s, the government established a model farm outside Kinshasa to supply large quantities of eggs and fowl to the capital. Yet as of the early 1990s, Zaire was still not self-sufficient in animal products and imported sizeable quantities of meat and dairy items—in particular those for which the elite had acquired a taste.

Mining

Mining has been the cornerstone of Zaire's wealth since colonial times. In the late 1980s, Zaire was the world's largest producer of cobalt, second or third largest producer of industrial diamonds, and fifth largest producer of copper. Mining, mineral processing, and petroleum extraction accounted for 17 percent of the GDP in 1990 (down from 24 percent in 1987), and mineral exports, principally copper, cobalt, diamonds, and gold, provided nearly 75 percent of all export earnings. The mining industry, primarily the giant Gécamines, also provided a significant percentage of ordinary government revenues, although the company failed to reinvest profits, resulting in worn-out equipment. In addition, to enrich itself the presidency repeatedly diverted the firm's funds. Throughout the early 1990s, the deterioration of Gécamines was both a symbol and a result of the country's economic chaos. Most skilled expatriates working for the company fled following military looting in 1991 and further unrest in 1992. Since then Gécamines's facilities have been systematically gutted, and the company is now bankrupt.

Mining is centered in the southeastern and eastern parts of the country with the exception of petroleum, which is found in the far west in Bas-Zaïre Region, and diamonds, mined in Kasai-Oriental and Kasai-Occidental regions (see fig. 10). Shaba Region has the greatest concentration of minerals, with copper, cobalt, and zinc mined in a narrow crescent known as the copper-cobalt zone, stretching roughly from Kolwezi to Lubumbashi. Shaba Region also contains most of Zaire's known deposits of coal and manganese. A broad belt in eastern Zaire from northern Shaba to eastern Haut-Zaïre Region contains deposits of tin and gold with lesser amounts of tungsten-bearing wolframite, niobium, and tantalum.

Copper and Zinc

Zaire has traditionally been the world's fifth largest copper producer after Chile, the United States, Canada, and Zambia, accounting for about 8 percent of world copper production. Most copper (90 percent) is mined by the giant parastatal Gécamines in Shaba Region. Shaba's ores are rich in copper—from 4 percent to 6 percent, or twice the Zambian average concentration. Some mines produce ore with copper content as high as 15 percent. In comparison, United States producers have been working ores with less than 1 percent copper. Mining officials estimated in the late 1980s that known reserves would last for another forty years at a production rate of approximately 500,000 tons annually, about 6 percent of world production.

Copper production began to fall in 1988, however. Competition from substitute materials as well as from lower-cost copper producers elsewhere in the world (such as Chile), strikes, and technical problems, including a cave-in in September 1990, all contributed to the downturn. In the early 1990s, copper mining, although once the mainstay of the economy, had virtually collapsed following years of neglect by Gécamines and as a result of the

Figure 10. Mineral Resources, 1993

prevailing economic chaos. Actual production of copper ore was 465,000 tons in 1988, declining to 440,600 tons in 1989, then 355,500 tons in 1990. Production was 291,500 tons in 1991, and 146,000 tons in 1992. Estimates for 1993 indicated a very low production figure of 80,000 tons.

About 80 percent of Zaire's copper has traditionally been sold to Western Europe. A substantial share of the country's production is shipped to Belgium for final processing by a subsidiary of the General Holding Company of Belgium (Société Générale de Belgique—SGB).

Another copper-mining company, Industrial and Mining Development Company (Société de Développement Industriel et Minier de Zaïre—Sodimiza) was founded in 1969 and was owned briefly by Japanese interests before being taken over by the Zairian government. The Canadian firm Philip Barrat Kaiser held a management contract until April 1987 when the government decided to merge Sodimiza with Gécamines. Sodimiza had produced between 6 percent and 10 percent of Zaire's annual copper output.

Zinc is produced as a byproduct of copper from a single mine near Lubumbashi. Copper output from this mine has steadily decreased. Because zinc reserves there are substantial, the mine is expected to produce primarily zinc by the mid-1990s. Zinc production totaled 64,000 tons in 1985 but had fallen to 38,200 tons by 1990. Production in 1992 was estimated to be only 18,350 tons.

Cobalt

Zaire has traditionally been the world's largest producer and exporter of cobalt, accounting for about half of all production. Cobalt production in Zaire is entirely a byproduct of copper mining by Gécamines. The company produced 9,429 tons of cobalt in 1989 and 10,033 tons in 1990, but production fell to 8,800 tons in 1991 and to 6,600 tons in 1992. Production in 1993 was projected to fall to about 3,500 tons. World cobalt prices are extremely volatile, and true to form they fluctuated dramatically in the 1980s and early 1990s. The market price rose temporarily in early 1992, but because of its reduced production, Zaire was not able to capitalize on this favorable situation.

Manganese

Manganese is found at two locations in western Shaba Region, but only one, near Kisenge, has been exploited. The government-owned Kisenge Mining Company ceased production of manganese shortly after the Benguela Railway to the Angolan port of Lobito was closed in 1975. Sporadic sales since 1975 have been from huge stockpiles accrued before the railroad closed. Production in 1968 amounted to over 300,000 tons. Foreign businesses, usually backed by supplier credits and requiring substantial down payments, offered a number of proposals to restart manganese production, including building a battery factory. Nothing had come of these plans by the early 1990s, although there was hope for renewed production once the Benguela Railway reopened.

Tin and Related Minerals

Deposits of cassiterite, the chief source of tin, are found in a broad zone extending from northern Shaba Region through Sud-Kivu and Nord-Kivu to Haut-Zaïre Region. Associated with the cassiterite are commercially exploitable amounts of ores of tungsten, niobium, and tantalum. The Kivu Mining and Industrial Company (Société Minière et Industrielle du Kivu—Sominki) has responsibility for tin mining in Nord-Kivu and Sud-Kivu regions, and the Zaire Tin Company (Compagnie Zaïrétain—Zaïrétain) carries out open-pit operations in Shaba Region. In 1993 there were reports that Sominki had ceased production of tin ore.

Known deposits are large. In the mid-1940s, Zaire was the world's second largest producer after Bolivia, but thereafter production decreased steadily. Mining of cassiterite (and associated ores) continued to slacken through the early 1990s because of weak prices and expensive and time-consuming transport from the remote locations where it is mined. Production was estimated at 1,943 tons in 1988, dropping to 1,642 tons in 1989, and 1,600 tons in 1990.

Gold

Gold is found in minable quantities in various locations in eastern Zaire. Three companies have been involved in gold production: the Kilo-Moto Gold Mine Board (Office des Mines d'Or de Kilo-Moto—Okimo), which has the main gold mine, Sominki, and Gécamines. In addition, artisanal gold mining, legalized in 1983, has long been substantial. Official gold receipts dropped in the early 1990s because of smuggling and looting from industrial production sites, as well as extensive smuggling of artisanal production into neighboring countries. The Okimo and Sominki mines are located in isolated areas, where smuggling and looting are relatively easy and transport and resupply difficult. Artisanal producers have consistently chosen to smuggle out their production rather than accept the lower prices paid by the official purchasing counters (*comptoirs*).

Together the Okimo and Sominki mines accounted for nearly half of official gold exports, or about 900 kilograms out of the more than 2,000 kilograms that were officially exported in 1988. Of the 1988 total, Okimo produced about 260 kilograms of gold; Sominki produced approximately 625 kilograms; and individual artisanal producers accounted for 1,212 kilograms (Gécamines's production was negligible). In 1988 Okimo awarded contracts worth US$14 million to a Brazilian firm and the United States subsidiary of a British firm for rehabilitation of two potentially highly productive mines. These contracts were expected to result in increased output in the 1990s, but in fact production continued to drop as the economy deteriorated. Production was estimated at only 225 kilograms in 1990.

Diamonds

In 1992 Zaire was the world's third largest producer of industrial diamonds after Australia, which became the largest producer in 1986, and Botswana, which surpassed Zaire in 1992 because of Zaire's reduced production. In 1984 and 1985, Zaire accounted for nearly 30 percent of world production, dropping to about 26 percent in 1986 as new Australian mine production came on stream. Diamond production occurs in the Kasai-Occidental and Kasai-Oriental regions, mostly around the regional capital of Kasai-Oriental, Mbuji-Mayi, near Tshikapa, and in Lodja, about 300 kilometers north of Mbuji-Mayi. In 1993 there were also reports that diamond deposits had been discovered in Équateur Region, in Haut-Zaïre Region, and in southern Bandundu Region along the Angolan border. Diamond ore in Zaire yields about 6 carats per cubic meter. Although Zaire mines both gem quality and industrial diamonds, 90 percent of production is of industrial quality.

Bakwanga Mining Company (Société Minière de Bakwanga—Miba), the state-owned mining concession in Kasai-Oriental Region, produces much of the country's total export in diamonds, from alluvial deposits near Mbuji-Mayi and from kimberlite deposits. The Miba concession covers 62,000 square kilometers. Miba's production is marketed by a subsidiary of the South African company DeBeers, with whom the government has negotiated a guaranteed price per carat. Thousands of individuals also mine for gold, many of them illegally mining the huge Miba concession, whose perimeters are difficult to patrol.

Because of their value on the international market, diamonds have long been smuggled extensively in Zaire. Diamond smuggling spread quickly in the early 1960s. By the late 1970s, the amount of diamonds smuggled was believed to equal nearly 70 percent of official production (5.5 million carats smuggled; official production was almost 8.1 million carats). Smuggling decreased following the legalization of artisanal diamond mining in 1983 and the establishment of official, licensed purchasing counters to buy and market artisanal production; official production increased correspondingly. But by 1987 there were already indications that smuggling was once again on the increase, and it soared in the troubled early 1990s.

In the first eleven months of 1991, Miba exported an estimated 9.6 million carats. The artisanal purchasing counters accounted for an additional 7.2 million carats. Actual output was much higher than the official combined total of 16.8 million carats, as a result of extensive large-scale smuggling. Reportedly, many of the smuggled diamonds originate from the artisanal counters, aided by high-level government collusion.

The figures for 1991 diamond exports were lower than the 18 million carats produced in 1990 because of the country's chaotic situation, including factors such as looting and flight out of the country by diamond traders. Zairian diamond production in 1992 was estimated at just 15 million carats. Despite its decline, the diamond industry remains vital to the Zairian economy—and to the Mobutu regime—because it is widely regarded as the country's last remaining source of hard currency. A large portion of Miba's official revenues—US$46.3 million in 1991—are believed to go directly to Mobutu's coffers. Moreover, diamond dealers pay Zaire's central bank 1.5 percent of their official total exports, estimated at US$185 million in 1991. Illicit trade in the 1990s was estimated to be as much as twice the officially recorded transactions, but it was not known how much Mobutu profited from the unregistered diamond trade.

Industry

The manufacturing sector accounted for an estimated 1 percent of GDP in 1987, and 1.7 percent in 1988, down from 9 percent in 1981. The sector is concentrated in Kinshasa and the mining area of Shaba Region and consists largely of consumer goods, such as food processing, textile manufacturing, beer, cigarettes, metalworking and woodworking, and vehicle assembly. Manufacturing as a whole is hindered by many problems, including chronic mismanagement, lack of foreign exchange as well as long-term investment capital (especially the reluctance of foreigners to invest because of past nationalization schemes), a lack of spare parts, an inadequate transportation system, limited access to international markets, and a small domestic market that largely consists of consumers with little expendable income. Liberalization of economic policies in the late 1980s, however, resulted in an increase in production in some fields, most notably textiles, plastics, tobacco, and breweries.

The policy of import substitution begun between 1969 and 1972 was largely abandoned during the 1980s. The two most important enterprises established under the import-substitution policy were a General Motors vehicle assembly plant and a Continental Grains wheat mill, which was dependent on imported wheat. Goodyear also built a US$16 million tire plant in 1972. Promised rubber plantation investments never materialized.

By 1987 both General Motors and Goodyear had sold their enterprises to local businessmen, who were rumored to be backed

Room where copper is electrolyzed at the Gécamines Luilu refinery near Kolwezi
Flow racks for the electrolyzed copper, Gécamines Shituru refinery near Likasi
Courtesy Gécamines

by high government officials. General Motors and Goodyear had had chronic difficulties competing with cheap imports, which were frequently smuggled into the country or brought in exempt from import duties. Additionally, the proportion of raw materials imported for manufacturing was high. Moreover, companies suffered tremendous production difficulties when the foreign-exchange crisis of the mid-1970s hit.

Throughout the 1980s, most Zairian factories operated at just 30 percent of installed capacity. By most accounts, manufacturing in the formal economy had virtually ceased by 1992 in the wake of general economic chaos and several waves of military-led looting and rioting in Kinshasa. Factories, stripped bare, were forced to close, leaving thousands in the capital out of work. Shops and restaurants also closed.

Traditionally, numerous Zairian entrepreneurs have operated small- (three to four employees) and medium-sized businesses in the informal sector in Kinshasa. Such activities have continued, producing a wide range of products—e.g., furniture, clothes, crafts, food, and even vehicle chassis. Most such enterprises are unlicensed, but they fill a critical need in supplying the populace with otherwise unavailable or unaffordable goods.

Energy

The government has a broad involvement in the energy sector. It holds part ownership in all energy enterprises, including the National Electric Company (Société Nationale d'Électricité—Snel), it sets price controls, and it reviews all investments in the sector. The Ministry of National Economy and Industry had authority over pricing for electricity and oil products but eventually lifted price controls in 1983. The government also holds minority shares in the fuel-product distribution companies: Mobil, Fina, and Shell.

Exploitation of major resources at times has been poorly adapted to meeting the country's overall energy needs. The government has tended to concentrate primarily on petroleum resources and electric power and to neglect the potential of the country's abundant biomass. The lack of sector-wide planning and coordination, a weak energy infrastructure, ill-defined pricing policies, and institutional deficiencies have constrained efficient development and utilization of energy resources.

Various government energy entities execute their duties in isolation, and responsibility is divided among the numerous and diverse agencies, with none having access to information required to define sector policies or the capacity to implement them. This decentralization and the absence of an effective coordinating agent

Gécamines Lubumbashi copper smelter
Concentrators for copper and cobalt at Gécamines Kamoto mills near Kolwezi
Courtesy Gécamines

185

have hindered the formulation of a cohesive sector strategy. In response to this disorder, a National Energy Commission within the Department of Land Management, Mines, and Energy was created in 1985. The French provided and funded an adviser to the commission, but its effectiveness remained in doubt.

Petroleum and Other Fuels

In 1956 exploration began of the Atlantic coastal basin, the most accessible of Zaire's petroleum reserves. Offshore oil production began in 1975, while onshore production started in 1979. Chevron-Gulf led a consortium controlling offshore production, while a Belgian concern had the onshore concession. In June 1992, the Zairian government seized the assets of United States and European oil companies operating in Zaire in order to relieve fuel shortages. The Zairian government, avoiding use of the word *nationalization,* promised compensation and insisted that the measure was temporary.

Until the late 1980s, Zaire's petroleum reserves were small by world standards but larger than those of many countries in sub-Saharan Africa. In the early 1990s, oil reserves were estimated at 140 million barrels. It seems likely that these reserves will be exhausted unless continuing exploration near the borders with Uganda and Tanzania is successful.

Because domestic production is a heavy crude best suited for fuel oil, all of it is exported for refining. Production was 10.7 million barrels in 1988, down from previous years, 9.9 million barrels in 1989, some 10.9 million barrels in 1990, and 9.9 million barrels in 1991. Gas-injection techniques are used in the oldest onshore fields to increase petroleum production.

Petroleum consumption since the late 1970s has remained fairly constant; limited availability of foreign exchange is the main constraint on increased purchases. Indeed, as reserves of foreign exchange began to dwindle in the 1990s, Zaire suffered an acute gasoline shortage. Shortages also were due to riots and looting. In addition, Zaire's poor road and rail network restricts supply to outlying areas (see Transportation and Telecommunications, this ch.). In June 1985, PetroZaïre, the national petroleum company, lost its import monopoly for fuel and other finished petroleum products, and at the same time the government removed price controls. Supply and distribution improved gradually.

Zaire imports all of the petroleum that it refines because its sole refinery, located in Moanda on the Atlantic coast, is not designed to handle the heavy crude produced domestically. The government has been unable to secure financial backing to overhaul the plant so that it can refine heavy Zairian crude. As a result, the refinery is forced to operate solely on small quantities of crude oil imported from Nigeria. The refinery has an installed capacity of 750,000 tons per year, but in 1986 processed under 90,000 tons.

Domestic coal sources are all of low grade. Located in central and northeast Shaba Region, coal is used entirely by a cement plant at Kalemie. Production was estimated at 123,000 tons in 1988; it increased to 125,000 tons in 1989 and 126,000 tons in 1990. Higher grade coal and coke needed for the metallurgical industry are imported.

Fuelwood and charcoal are by far the most heavily consumed energy sources in Zaire, used primarily for household cooking. But there is no organized supply of fuelwood in urban areas, and population growth in urban areas, such as Kinshasa, has contributed to deforestation. The price of charcoal has risen because it has to be trucked in to urban centers from ever greater distances. The steady price increases have constrained growth in small-scale industries that use wood, such as fish smoking, and have put pressure on household budgets. Moreover, the use of wood exceeds regrowth of forests, and reforestation efforts have been slow.

Electricity

Electricity production is concentrated in Bas-Zaïre and Shaba regions, and about 95 percent of all electricity is sold in Kinshasa and Shaba. An estimated 73 percent of Snel's sales are made in Shaba, 57 percent of the total to the mining parastatal Gécamines. In early 1992, Snel experienced considerable losses following the destruction and looting in the country. It also lacked spare parts. By late 1992, the electrical system was nearing breakdown.

Home consumption of electricity and public lighting account for only a small percentage of electricity produced; most electricity consumption is closely tied to the copper market. Demand stagnated during the slump from 1974 through 1979, recovered slightly in 1980, and then dropped again in 1982 and 1983 before recovering and reaching a record high of 5,455 gigawatt-hours in 1986. Demand again declined in the early 1990s.

Zaire has tremendous hydroelectric potential (estimated at 100,000 megawatts), accounting for half of the hydroelectric potential of the entire African continent. Installed capacity was estimated at 2,486 megawatts in 1987. Hydropower, in fact, accounts for 95 percent of all electricity produced in the country, the rest coming from small thermal units.

The largest hydroelectric site is on the lower part of the Congo River, forty kilometers upstream from its mouth, where the river drops 300 meters to sea level. One hundred meters of this drop is located in a twelve-kilometer stretch at the site of the Inga dams barrage. Sketchy colonial plans to tap this source of power were postponed because of the political uncertainty at the end of the colonial period and the dearth of customers for the immense quantities of electric power to be produced.

Inga I, a dam and generating facility built on this site in 1972, has a generating capacity of 300 megawatts. The adjacent Inga II dam has a generating capacity of 1,000 megawatts. In 1986 the two produced 3,100 gigawatt-hours of electricity.

The high-voltage transmission line from the dams to the Shaba mining region was the longest direct current line in the world at the time of its construction. It stretches 1,725 kilometers from the Inga I and Inga II dams in Bas-Zaïre to Kolwezi, the northernmost mining center in the Shaba copper-cobalt mining area. The project was chosen over competing ideas for power delivery to Shaba, including the construction of a new dam in Shaba itself. The high-voltage transmission line was intended to transmit about 1,200 megawatts of power to Shaba. However, it is grossly underutilized, with installed capacity at only about 560 megawatts and actual transmission to Shaba at about 200 megawatts. By late 1992, observers feared that the vital Inga-Shaba power line could not long remain operational. Its upkeep has been problematic since the departure in late 1991, following widespread rioting and looting, of the foreign technicians and mechanics (mostly Belgians and Italians) who provided most of its maintenance.

In the late 1980s, the Zairian state again demonstrated its fascination with hydroelectric schemes. A small hydroelectric power station was opened at Mobayi-Mbongo near Mobutu's birthplace in a remote section of Équateur Region near the border with the Central African Republic.

In July 1992, Zaire and Egypt reached agreement on the construction of a high-tension electric line from the Inga dams to Egypt, to transmit 600 megawatts of electricity to Egypt. Observers believe this plan is unlikely to be realized, however. The Inga power stations do supply some power to neighboring Congo, and the potential certainly exists for Zaire to export electricity to other neighbors should its economic situation ever be normalized.

Transportation and Telecommunications

Zaire's severely dilapidated transportation infrastructure is perhaps the major constraint on the country's economic development. The country's large size and the physical limitations imposed by its topography are major factors in the underdevelopment of the transportation system, but poor management by inefficient parastatals and corruption are primarily responsible for the sector's daunting deficiencies. During colonial times, the transportation system was well developed to transport food products from Kivu and minerals from Shaba (then Katanga Province) to the Atlantic Coast for export. The transportation infrastructure has been neglected since independence, however.

Roads traditionally played a secondary role in the Zairian transportation network, behind railroads and waterways. A network of approximately 145,000 kilometers of roads exists in Zaire, although the country's vast interior is virtually devoid of roads (see fig. 11). Only 2,500 kilometers are paved, originally including the 350-kilometer Kinshasa-Matadi link, which is nearly thirty years old and was not built for the heavy loads it carries. By 1992 there were reports that only about forty kilometers of the Kinshasa-Matadi road were still paved. The road from Kikwit to Kinshasa and the links among the mineral centers of Lubumbashi, Kolwezi, and Likasi in Shaba also are paved. In the early 1990s, the entire road network had slipped into a state of serious disrepair; a journey of 150 kilometers could take up to twenty-four hours.

The situation has obvious implications for the movement of both passengers and in particular freight, 80 percent of which reportedly moved by private road transport in 1988. This vital service is, however, in jeopardy in the early 1990s. Trucks, spare parts, and fuel are in short supply, and the condition of most roads (especially secondary and rural roads) ranges from appalling to unusable. Local residents and entrepreneurs, religious groups, and some large companies have attempted to maintain some roads but with limited success nationwide.

Official passenger transport services in Kinshasa are also inadequate, but unofficial, mostly unlicensed suppliers have been able to fill much of the gap. Deploying an armada of pickup trucks, covered trucks, and taxibuses, they provide half the city's public transportation, offering better service at a lower cost to the city's workers and residents.

Zaire has 5,138 kilometers of railroad in three discontinuous lines. A 366-kilometer standard-gauge (1.067 meter) line links Kinshasa with Zaire's main port of Matadi. Over 1,100 kilometers of narrow-gauge (1 meter and 0.6 meter) rail connect towns in northeast Zaire. The bulk of the system, however, consists of a network of standard-gauge lines in southeast Zaire used primarily to export minerals. International connections exist with Angola's Benguela Railway (not operating in the early 1990s), with the Zambian

189

Figure 11. Transportation System, 1993

and South African rail systems, and with Tanzania's rail lines via a ferry across Lake Tanganyika.

The Zairian National Railroad Company (Société Nationale de Chemins de Fer Zaïrois—SNCZ) is headquartered in Lubumbashi, the regional capital of Shaba. Since 1974 SNCZ has been a state-owned company, responsible for the operation and maintenance of the rail line between Lubumbashi and Ilebo on the Kasai River. The National Transport Board of Zaire (Office National des Transports au Zaïre—Onatra) manages the Matadi-Kinshasa line as well as transport on the Congo River.

The railroads, too, are in desperate need of repair. Train transport is slow, cumbersome, and unreliable. Little attention has been paid the railroads since independence. The railroads are suffering from a lack of working locomotives and rolling stock as well as deteriorating railbeds. In the late 1980s, SNCZ undertook a US$75 million rehabilitation effort financed by the World Bank, the African Development Bank, and the governments of Belgium, France, and West Germany. By 1989 the project was at the half-way point in terms of committed funding. It sought to refurbish 263 kilometers of the Kinshasa-Matadi and Lubumbashi-Ilebo links. Track beds were rebuilt and new rail and cross ties installed. The plan called for the overhaul of twenty diesel locomotives and thirty-eight electric locomotives as well as for the purchase of new rolling stock and material to manufacture rail cars locally. Most of the project had been set for completion in the early 1990s, but little if any progress was expected in light of the prevailing economic chaos.

The rail and river transportation network between the copper-mining region of Shaba and the country's principal port of Matadi is called the National Route (Voie Nationale). This network is Zaire's lifeline, a 2,665-kilometer combination of railroad between Lubumbashi and Ilebo, river transport from Ilebo to Kinshasa, and rail once again between Kinshasa and the port of Matadi. (Because of rapids below Kinshasa, the river is not navigable between Kinshasa and Matadi.) It is the only route between the mining region and the ocean entirely within Zaire. This route became even more crucial after the 1,400-kilometer Benguela Railway linking Shaba to the sea via the Angolan port of Lobito was closed in 1975 because of the Angolan civil war. (In 1991 plans were underway to reopen this rail line following an agreement between Portugal and Belgium, but no further progress had been made by 1993.) Zaire once sent almost half of its exports via the Benguela Railway. Mineral shipments traveling via the National Route to Matadi can take as long as two months and average about forty-five days. Moreover, because the load on the route is limited, Zaire has been forced to rely heavily on South African rail lines for between 33 percent and 40 percent of its mineral exports.

Inland waterways have traditionally been an important mode of internal transportation, but in the early 1990s, river transport was limited because the marking of navigable channels had been neglected, and barges were both old and in short supply.

The Congo River is the most significant of the country's rivers, and both passenger and freight ships ply the navigable section between Kinshasa and Kisangani. In late 1993, however, there were reports that riverboats had ceased operating between Kisangani and Kinshasa because of lack of fuel and spare parts.

Ports are limited because Zaire, nearly landlocked, has only a tiny coastline of just forty kilometers. Matadi on the lower Congo

River is Zaire's principal port and handles 90 percent of the country's nonmineral exports. Efficient cargo and passenger transportation at the Atlantic port of Boma, at Matadi, and between Ilebo on the Kasai River and Kinshasa are constrained by lack of equipment, the need for better charting and maintenance along the two rivers, and the fact that Matadi is a relatively shallow port and thus not accessible by large vessels. Donor countries have attempted to improve service at the ports of Kinshasa and Matadi, and a new deep-water port at Banana on the Atlantic also was at one time under consideration but has been abandoned given the economic situation prevailing in the early 1990s.

The cut-off of aid to Zaire and the deterioration of the economy in the early 1990s have halted economic development efforts, and shipping, like other forms of transport, is in serious disarray. According to one report, Zaire's maritime company has been forced to sell off all its boats.

Large distances between urban centers and a lack of modern ground transportation make air transport of particular importance, although domestic air services deteriorated substantially in the 1980s and 1990s. The number of airlines serving Zaire had increased significantly in the 1980s, and included the formation of at least two private Zairian airlines that competed with the state-owned national carrier, Air Zaïre. Both the number of destinations served within Zaire and the international links grew substantially in the wake of liberalization measures begun in 1983. Several European carriers as well as Air Zaïre and a private airline, Scibe Airlift, linked Kinshasa to places in Europe and the rest of Africa. But by 1992 most foreign airlines no longer landed at Kinshasa's airport, which was badly damaged by looting in late 1991. (Some flights resumed in late 1992.) People wishing to enter Zaire by air often land in Brazzaville in Congo and take a ferry across the Congo River to Zaire.

Air Zaïre has been under the management of the French airline, Air Transport Union (Union de Transports Aériens—UTA) since the fall of 1986, but became virtually bankrupt as a result of the country's economic crisis in the 1990s. Air Zaïre once operated four jets, but one was repossessed by Belgium and another by Israel for nonpayment of debts. Mobutu reportedly commandeered the other two to bring in newly printed bank notes from the printer in Germany.

The Postal and Telecommunications Board provides overseas telephone and domestic and overseas mail service. In 1984 the country had only 30,300 telephones, almost all of them in the capital. A new satellite ground station was installed at Matadi in 1985, which

Ferry
on the
Congo River,
Équateur Region

Maréchal Mobutu
Bridge over
the Congo River
near Matadi
Courtesy Agence
Zaïre Presse

greatly improved the quality of international calls. Calling Brussels from Kinshasa, in fact, was reportedly far easier than making a connection to a city in the interior. An American company, in partnership with local business interests, established a cellular telephone system for Kinshasa in June 1991. In 1990 there were reported to be 32,000 telephones in Zaire, but by 1992 the telephone system as a whole was reported to be dysfunctional.

Broadcast facilities increased throughout the 1980s, and residents of most larger towns can now receive radio and television programming. Fourteen cities have television stations. There were an estimated 40,000 television sets and 3.7 million radio receivers in Zaire in 1990. The capital has one medium-wave amplitude-modulation (AM) radio station and one frequency-modulation (FM) station with programming in French; there are two other AM and two FM stations in other cities. Five shortwave stations transmit programming in French, Kiswahili, Lingala, and several other languages to listeners in more remote areas. All radio stations are government owned and part of the Voice of Zaire (Voix du Zaïre) network.

The state of telecommunications in the early 1990s was reported to be deplorable. The only reliable national radio network is said to be that of the Roman Catholic Church.

Foreign Economic Relations
Trade and Balance of Payments

Total exports for 1991 were estimated at US$1.5 billion (see table 12, Appendix). Six products—copper, cobalt, crude petroleum, diamonds, coffee, and gold generally accounted for over three-fourths of export earnings (see table 13, Appendix). Total imports in 1991 were estimated at nearly US$1.2 billion, with the largest single import, US$362 million, being goods for Gécamines (see table 14, Appendix). Luxury goods for expatriates and the Zairian elite also constitute a substantial portion of imports.

The trade balance was positive throughout the late 1980s, but by 1991 had dropped sharply because of decreases in world market prices for many of Zaire's commodity exports (copper, coffee, diamonds, crude oil, and cobalt), drops in production, and rises in import prices. The current account balance (which includes goods and services) was consistently negative, however, because of the massive increase in external debt-servicing requirements. Trade surpluses were more than swallowed up by outflows on the services account. Inflows on services could not make up the deficit, resulting in a negative current account balance and, generally, in

Spanish fishing boat at Zaire's main port of Matadi on the Congo River
Courtesy Agence Zaïre Presse
Shallow-draft dugout on Lac Tumba, Équateur Region

a negative overall balance of payments as well because net capital transfers were also insufficient to cover the deficit. Ironically, Zaire's current account showed great improvement (by more than 75 percent) in 1992, largely because of a dramatic 52 percent decline in imports, which outweighed the 35 percent drop in exports.

Belgium, the United States, and other West European countries are the destinations of most of Zaire's exports (see table 15, Appendix). However, since 1989 South Africa has also been an increasingly important trading partner. Zaire reportedly exchanges coffee, wood, and minerals for South African food, agricultural machinery, and spare parts. Official figures on trade with South Africa are sketchy, but there is an abundance of South African food products available in Kinshasa, including large quantities of fresh produce.

The economic problems confronting developing countries that rely predominantly on extractive product exports have been well documented. In Zaire agricultural exports declined steadily from nearly half the value of all exports in 1958 to 11.6 percent in 1986. Coffee was the primary agricultural export commodity, contributing 7 percent of export revenues in 1988, while cotton was no longer being exported in the early 1990s but was produced mainly for domestic consumption. Copper and cobalt alone accounted for nearly half of all export earnings in 1987 and 1988. Three of the four largest companies in Zaire (Gécamines, Gulf, and Miba) accounted for 70 percent of export earnings and were mineral or petroleum companies. Mineral prices fluctuated dramatically throughout the decade. Even for cobalt, where Zaire and Zambia had a near monopoly, the two countries had difficulty maintaining a price floor.

Theft, looting, and smuggling also are widespread in the Zairian economy. Cross-border smuggling and unlicensed trade have been widespread since independence but have expanded markedly in the troubled 1990s. Although both activities deprive the government of revenues, they do provide consumers with goods that are otherwise unavailable or unattainable because of the lack of foreign exchange and hard currency needed for official imports. Traders smuggle out primary products such as gold, diamonds, cobalt, coffee, and ivory in order to barter for or obtain the hard currency to purchase consumer goods such as vehicles, spare parts, fuel, electrical appliances, construction materials, pharmaceuticals, and foodstuffs.

Foreign Aid

In 1990 Zaire received an estimated US$711.1 million in development assistance. This sum represented a decline from US$805 million in foreign aid from bilateral donors in 1987. France, Germany, and Italy accounted for much of the foreign aid in 1990, with France (US$180 million) replacing Belgium as Zaire's primary development partner. Belgium's importance to Zaire as a source of aid and trade declined in the late 1980s and early 1990s, as relations between the two countries broke down over the issue of human rights abuses in Zaire. As Zaire's economic situation deteriorated in the early 1990s, foreign donors and creditors provided assistance primarily in the form of food aid. Most other bilateral and multilateral aid was terminated in 1990–91 and is unlikely to resume until Mobutu leaves the scene and democratization takes hold in Zaire. However, China reportedly has become more active in Zaire since the cutoff of aid from the West. More than 1,000 Chinese technicians are reported to be working in Zaire on agricultural and forestry projects.

In late 1992, in an attempt to tackle Zaire's economic crisis and court foreign donors, the government of Prime Minister Étienne Tshisekedi wa Mulumba announced its commitment to economic liberalization (including privatization of some parastatals) and stabilization. To that end, it initiated several measures, such as the imposition of import quotas and tightened controls of the money supply. In addition, the administration declared its intention of curbing government spending, controlling inflation, and ending corruption, in particular illegal disbursements and the arbitrary allocation of credit. International organizations and various foreign governments expressed interest in resuming aid but remained cautious, unconvinced that a credible stabilization program was possible in Zaire. Belgium and France provided additional humanitarian assistance, but continued to insist that a full resumption of aid depends on democratic change in Zaire (in particular, concrete evidence that the prime minister's government actually controls finances and the military) and an IMF-World Bank sponsorship of the government's economic program.

Foreign Investment

In the early 1970s, direct foreign investment ranged from US$50 million to US$100 million annually before dropping with the onset of Zairianization. To entice foreign investors to return to Zaire after the economic decline brought on by nationalization, in 1981 the government created a free-trade zone in Bas-Zaïre under the direct authority of the president. Zaire hoped to attract power-intensive export-oriented industries with the offer of relatively inexpensive power and tax incentives. But although there had been many proposals to establish industries in the free-trade zone, at the end of the 1980s there had been no firm commitments.

Zaire and the United States signed a bilateral investment treaty in 1984. The treaty was, in part, aimed at supporting Zaire's economic reform efforts. The treaty proved to be more symbolic than practical. Little new United States private investment ensued, despite promotion by the Overseas Private Investment Corporation (OPIC), which led a small investment mission to Zaire in 1986. Zaire also had bilateral investment agreements with France, Belgium, Switzerland, West Germany, Canada, Denmark, and the Netherlands. Most foreign investment, albeit a significantly smaller share than at independence, was still Belgian.

The new investment code promulgated in April 1986 was an important step toward restoring investor confidence and mobilizing foreign capital. It incorporated various existing tax benefits and introduced new ones. Further advantages were offered to investors depending on the location of the enterprise, number of jobs generated, type of activity, training and promotion of local staff, export orientation, and value added to local resources. Most of the benefits were available for five years, but some ranged from one to ten years and even longer for mining ventures, which were also exempted from taxes on reinvested profits. Repatriation of profits and earnings was guaranteed for foreign investors. Despite the code's enticements, Zaire experienced only a marginal increase in foreign direct investment. Moreover, not all projects approved under the investment code were actually started.

Despite increasing incentives, foreign investment was slow and fitful. The transportation system was still in a state of gross disrepair, although rehabilitation efforts had been under way for some time. Communication was also difficult, and the population's purchasing power remained low. In addition to the daunting physical and logistical difficulties of doing business in Zaire, new investors, especially nontraditional ones such as United States business interests, were discouraged by Zaire's reputation for unbridled corruption. It was thought in many circles that these irregularities were among the reasons that the United States business community had largely ceded Zaire to Belgium and other European countries as their sphere of economic influence.

Prospects for Growth

Zaire's ability to achieve long-term economic development and growth depends in large measure on the willingness of the government to resolve decisively the conflict between authoritarian patrimonialism and democracy. Patrimonialism has led inexorably to widespread corruption, economic mismanagement and miscalculation, and chronic borrowing.

Resolution of this conflict is considered vital to removing Zaire's primary economic constraints: a heavy external debt burden, which has grown as a result of repeated reschedulings at market interest rates; dependence on primary commodity exports—copper, coffee, cobalt, and diamonds—that have poor market price prospects and are in any case subject to severe price fluctuations; an outdated and deteriorating transportation and communication infrastructure; and a badly neglected rural sector. In order to resolve its chronic economic problems and move toward sustained growth, Zaire would need to generate confidence in its institutions and to mobilize and invest substantial additional resources, both domestic and foreign. Observers increasingly believe that such changes will not be possible so long as the Mobutu regime remains in power. Thus, political change is the key to economic development.

* * *

The writings of Thomas M. Callaghy, Thomas E. Turner, and Crawford Young continue to provide the most insightful analyses of the Zairian state. For analysis focused more directly on the economy, see David Gould's *Bureaucratic Corruption and Underdevelopment in the Third World: The Case of Zaire; Zaire: The Political Economy of Underdevelopment,* edited by Guy Gran; and Gregory Kronsten's *Zaire to the 1990s: Will Retrenchment Work?.* Janet MacGaffey's *The Real Economy of Zaire* provides an insightful analysis of Zaire's vibrant unofficial economy. The Economist Intelligence Unit's quarterly *Country Report: Zaire, Rwanda, Burundi* and annual *Country Profile: Zaire, Rwanda, Burundi* are the best sources for current economic and political trends and up-to-date statistical information. The annual *Africa South of the Sahara* also provides information on current economic developments in Zaire, as well as a statistical survey.

Data on various sectors of the economy are provided in specialized publications such as the United States Department of the Interior, Bureau of Mines, *Mineral Perspectives: Zaire;* Jean-Claude Willame's *L'Épopée d'Inga;* and the *International Petroleum Encyclopedia.* (For further information and complete citations, see Bibliography.)

Chapter 4. Government and Politics

Celebrants below a billboard of the flaming torch in the national flag,
20th of May Stadium, Kinshasa

SINCE 1965, JOSEPH-DÉSIRÉ MOBUTU, or Mobutu Sese Seko as he has called himself since 1971, has thoroughly dominated the political life of Zaire, a fact reflected in the title that he awarded himself, "Father of the Nation." Mobutu presides over a political system that has the formal trappings of a republic but is in reality the personal fiefdom of the president, who uses the national treasury as his personal checkbook and disburses both rewards and punishments at will. Corruption, nepotism, and cronyism, as well as maladministration and inefficiency, are pervasive and widespread in the Zairian political system.

From 1967 until 1990, the primary instrument of Mobutu's control of the government was the country's sole legal political party, the Popular Revolutionary Movement (Mouvement Populaire de la Révolution—MPR), a Mobutu creation. In theory, the party was a separate entity intended to parallel the state apparatus and to guide and control it. But in reality the party had virtually no independent existence from the state, so the state and party were effectively fused.

On April 24, 1990, Mobutu radically transformed the political environment by announcing the establishment of a competitive multiparty system. But his move, generally regarded as a calculated attempt to quell domestic and international pressures for change rather than a sincere commitment to reform, unleashed volatile forces that threatened to topple the regime, although Mobutu did everything in his power to retain his hold on the government. Independent political parties were permitted to register, with the Union for Democracy and Social Progress (Union pour la Démocratie et le Progrès Social—UDPS) emerging as the main opposition party.

In mid-1991 Mobutu finally convened a long-promised national conference, ostensibly designed to oversee the drafting of a new constitution and to manage the transition to a democratic, multiparty political system. But inevitably conflicts arose between a conference determined to assert its sovereign powers and a president equally determined not to cede control of the government, and the conference was very much an on-again-off-again institution throughout 1991 and most of 1992.

In August 1992, the conference passed a Transitional Act to serve as a provisional constitution. The Transitional Act established a parliamentary system with a figurehead president, a High Council of the Republic (Haut Conseil de la République—HCR) to serve as a provisional legislature; and a first state commissioner (prime minister) to serve as head of government. Under the terms of the Transitional Act, Étienne Tshisekedi wa Mulumba, head of the UDPS, was duly elected to head the transitional government. But the new administration, although recognized by the United States and other Western powers, has never been able to govern because of Mobutu's continued control of key military and security forces, which he has used to obstruct the functioning of the transitional government, to intimidate the opposition, to incite ethnic violence, and to promote instability throughout the country. In early 1993, Mobutu went further in repudiating the authority of the transitional government by appointing a rival administration under a different prime minister, Faustin Birindwa. Since that time, a political stalemate has prevailed in Zaire, with two parallel governments vying for international acceptance and political control over a country in crisis, its economy and social system in total disarray.

Postindependence Political Development

Establishment of a Personalistic Regime

After the bedlam of the First Republic, 1960–65, the preceding colonial regime seemed to offer an alternative model of order and discipline (see the First Republic, 1960–65, ch. 1). Thus, as he moved to depoliticize the legislative and administrative structures of the First Republic, Mobutu consciously restored structures of the colonial era. Mobutu and his associates attempted to establish a nation based solely on the colonial state, but without the colonial trinity, which also included the Roman Catholic Church and colonial companies (see The Apparatus of Control, ch. 1). In essence, Mobutu attempted to develop a political religion to replace the imported Christian faith, and a single party, the MPR, was to be the "church" of that religion.

Mobutu and his associates consolidated their control of the country's security apparatus by eliminating professionally autonomous military units, gradually suppressing rival ethnic and regional secessionist rebellions, establishing an effective state security agency, and maintaining linkages with external backers, who provided extensive training and equipment. To achieve greater national independence, Mobuto's regime diversified relations with external patrons (France, China, Israel, the United States, Belgium, and the conservative Arab states) and expropriated colonial enterprises. The Congo (Zaire was formally called the Republic of the Congo from independence to August 1, 1964, when it became the Democratic Republic of the Congo, which name was used until

October 27, 1971.) solicited a multitude of new links to Western multinational corporations and banks. The revenue needs of the state were to be met by sharp increases in fiscal impositions on the colonial corporate structure, which had been very lightly taxed, by perpetuation of the taxes imposed on the peasant majority, and by drawing in major new resources from abroad through loans, aid, and investments as well as by mortgaging the country's rich natural resource base.

What began as a collegial alliance of the Binza Group (a group of Mobutu supporters named for the prosperous suburb where its members lived); the top military command; some former supporters of Patrice Lumumba, who was the Congo's first prime minister; and young, often radical university graduates, gradually became an assemblage of courtiers doing the bidding of the presidential monarch (see The Second Republic, 1965–90: The Rebirth of *Bula Matari,* ch. 1). Mobutu carried out this transformation by suborning former colleagues and adversaries, thereby sapping the autonomous power bases of influential First Republic officials. Systematic rotation of high office was practiced, and a pool of vacant positions was sustained through the continuous pensioning of former collaborators into lucrative business opportunities. Access to high rank in all state agencies depended upon presidential favor. The sanction for not cooperating in this new elite was exile or imprisonment on trumped up or real charges of corruption, nepotism, or subversion.

The term *presidential monarch* became increasingly appropriate as applied to Mobutu. Mobutu's retinue was reported to consist of some 600 courtiers, and members of his family were treated as royalty. His son, Mobutu Nyiwa, was trained to succeed him, occupying a series of ministerial posts. President Mobutu increasingly spent more and more time at the several palaces he had built in his ancestral village, Gbadolite, which was transformed into a modern town, endowed with an international airport, satellite television antennas, street lights, and other amenities that most Congolese centers lacked. The president often met with his cabinet at Gbadolite, and he received foreign dignitaries there.

In 1973, espousing what Mobutu claimed to be Zairian nationalism, the regime embarked on a quest for economic and cultural emancipation in a sweeping program known as Zairianization (see Glossary). In the economic sphere, however, Zairianization resulted in an ill-advised and costly nationalization and confiscation program, highlighted by the personal aggrandizement of President Mobutu's ruling political and commercial class. Zairianization also advocated cultural pride and autonomy and aimed at rejecting and eliminating foreign cultural influences. Christian names of individuals and colonial place-names were dropped in favor of "authentic" Zairian names (see Zairianization, Radicalization, and Retrocession, ch. 1; Zairianization, ch. 3).

By 1974 the official ideology had metamorphosed into Mobutism (see Glossary), in which the acts and sayings of the leader were glorified. The state was personalized, and state and party were fused together. But Mobutism soon degenerated into a parody of Maoism. To "Founder-President" were added ever more extravagant praise-names: "Guide of the Revolution," "Helmsman" (borrowed from Mao Zedong), "Mulopwe" (emperor, or even god-king), and finally "Messiah." Important places in the president's political career were designated as pilgrimage sites. At this point, the ideology of the regime had become so overblown that many Zairians and most foreign observers found it impossible to take seriously. But as Zaire specialist Michael G. Schatzberg points out, the paternalistic strand of Mobutu's ideology corresponds to a "deeply rooted ideological and symbolic moral matrix undergirding both Zairian state and society." As he explains, "legitimate governance, in Zaire and in much of Africa, is based on the tacit normative idea that government stands in the same relationship to its citizens that a father does to his children." Yet this same moral matrix also provides the basis for opposition. When African political leaders violate the implied cultural norms and underlying premises of political "fatherhood," "legitimacy erodes, tensions mount, and instability, repression, or both, ensue."

A number of the themes in the Mobutist ideology—the yearning for cultural and economic autonomy and for strong, paternalistic leadership—resonated with deeply held opinions on the part of Zairians, among both the elite and the people in general. At the same time, however, it is difficult to avoid the conclusion that this ideology served to justify the domination of the political system by a self-serving ruling class that lived off the profits to be extracted from Zaire's interface with the world economy.

The Party-State as a System of Rule

The initial orientation of the Mobutu regime was antipolitical and antiparty. The announcement of the November 25, 1965, coup began by contrasting the performance of the armed services, alleged to be "satisfactory," with the "complete failure" of the previous political leaders, who had "shut themselves up in a sterile struggle to gain power without any consideration for the well-being of the citizens of this country." Although the proclamation made no explicit mention of political parties, there were signs of danger

206

for the existing parties in the message Mobutu sent to the joint session of the legislature on the afternoon after the coup. The message reiterated that the new government (whose members represented areas of the country, not parties) would serve for only five years, and that a *régime d'exception* (in essence a state of emergency) would be imposed throughout the country. Political activities by parties were suspended. The parties themselves were not dissolved, however, and several of them issued communiqués in support of the coup.

One reason for taking no action against the political parties during the early weeks of the regime was that Mobutu still needed their support. The first government after the coup, headed by Colonel Léonard Mulamba as prime minister, relied to a considerable extent upon the politicians of the 1960–65 era. But that reliance was nowhere acknowledged in Mobutu's public pronouncements. On the contrary, his continuing verbal assaults on the politicians presaged his attempts both to reduce their participation in his government and to create a personal instrument of power.

Mobutu claimed to depoliticize the nation by abolishing conventional political parties but then formed his own sole party, the MPR. Unlike the sweeping measures of later years, instituted almost overnight on the basis of little apparent preparation, the creation of the MPR was an incremental process, occurring over a period of about sixteen months. The first step was the creation of the Corps of Volunteers of the Republic (Corps des Volontaires de la République—CVR).

The Mobutu coup had taken place in the context of intense activity on the part of the political "youth movements" in the capital. Two days earlier, the League of Young Vigilantes (Ligue des Jeunes Vigilants) had organized a militant demonstration of 200 people at the Belgian embassy in Kinshasa. According to its statutes, the purpose of the league was "to fight resolutely and firmly against the forces which destroy national consciousness and the sense of responsibility, to assure the education and the *encadrement* of the people in order to build a truly free Congo, rid of the fear of imperialism, of the exploitation of man by man, [and] of obscurantism, [and] oriented toward the route of progress of the popular masses." The CVR, and later the MPR, would echo the diffuse radicalism of this pronouncement. Mobutu seems to have viewed such groups both as a threat to be harnessed and as potentially valuable allies in the struggle against the old politicians.

The formation of the CVR was announced to the public on January 9, 1966. A serious attempt was made to co-opt the leadership of the General Union of Congolese Students (Union Générale des

Étudiants Congolais—UGEC), the most articulate and radical of
the youth organizations. Both UGEC president N'Kanza Dolomin-
gu and former UGEC secretary for international affairs Kamanda wa Kamanda figured on the initial list of CVR leaders, but both
declined to participate. Subsequent events suggest that either the
ideological gap was too great to be bridged, as in the case of
N'Kanza, who was imprisoned, or that such elements had to be
co-opted on the highest level, e.g., in the case of Kamanda, who
was named secretary general of the presidency in December 1966,
after the prime ministership had been abolished in October and
Mobutu became head of government (see The Presidency, this ch.).

The CVR established branches throughout the capital and in
at least some of the provinces. At its first national seminar (in Kinshasa in December 1966), the group declared its ideology to be "nationalism." "Economic independence" and "nationalization of the
education system" were set as major objectives.

The CVR referred to itself as a vanguard movement rather than
a party, and its contradictory statements regarding parties doubtless reflected the fact that Mobutu's own opinion on the subject
was evolving. In fact, Mobutu faced a dilemma. The term *politician* had become virtually synonymous with *thief* or *traitor*. At the
same time, particular parties and politicians retained substantial
credit with their respective constituencies. The May 1967 Manifesto
of N'Sele, charter of the MPR, affirmed that the government administration would have to be reorganized and new personnel
brought in. It would have to be "detribalized" and "depoliticized."
Little was said as to how this would be accomplished. Administrative personnel were upgraded, but no major reorganization took
place. Rather than being "depoliticized," the administration was
merged with the MPR.

At first the MPR was given a separate structure on all levels below that of the president. Then, following a series of disputes between government and party officials on the same level, e.g.,
regional commissioner and regional president of the MPR, the duality was eliminated. At the beginning of 1972, the regional commissioner became head of the MPR on the regional level, the
collectivity chief, head of the party in the local collectivity, and so on.

Under such a system, "politics" (competition for rewards and
for control over distribution of rewards) still existed, but in the hands
of the administrators. There were party committees at each level
of the administrative structure. In a typical rural zone, the MPR
committee comprised the zone commissioner and his two assistant
commissioners, the director of the Youth of the Popular Revolutionary Movement (Jeunesse du Mouvement Populaire de la

View of Kinshasa,
with Pool de Malebo
on the Congo River
in the background
Courtesy Zaire
National Tourism Office

Modern buildings on the
outskirts of Kinshasa
Courtesy Zaire
National Tourism Office

Révolution—JMPR), the commander of the gendarmerie, the secretary of the National Union of Zairian Workers (Union Nationale des Travailleurs Zaïrois—UNTZA), and the chiefs of the collectivities that made up the zone.

Paradoxically, the fact that the party was everywhere undermined its significance; everyone was included in it (all Zairians were considered to be members by birth; the MPR was regarded as the "nation politically organized"). The only distinguishable MPR institutions were the Political Bureau and (later) the Central Committee and the JMPR, or party youth wing.

Suffrage was universal and compulsory at age eighteen, but the system offered no real political choice. All electoral choice or competition supposedly took place within the MPR. All presidential elections (1970, 1977, and 1984) were essentially plebiscites, with Mobutu as the only candidate.

Parliament was restored in 1970, but it had a very limited ability to influence the policy-making process. Nor were individual members of parliament able to play a linkage role between their constituents and the center to any significant extent. Under the system instituted in 1970, the population was asked to approve a single list of candidates for people's commissioners, or members of the legislature. The single-party list was put to the electorate, which had no choice but to vote yes or no (by casting a green or red ballot).

In 1977, under pressure from the United States, the International Monetary Fund (IMF—see Glossary), and other outside forces, Mobutu began to pay lip service to the notion of democracy for Zaire. Multiple candidacies were permitted, but within the MPR framework. The result was that the National Legislative Council served as a lightning rod for the population's resentment of its treatment by the regime. In 1982, for example, 310 members of parliament (one per 100,000 persons) were elected from among 1,409 candidates presented by the MPR. But only sixty out of 310 members were reelected.

The move toward multipartyism and democratization initiated in 1990 did, indeed, result in the formation and, ultimately, legal recognition of numerous political parties and coalitions (see Political Reform in the 1990s; Opposition since 1990, this ch.). The logical consequence would be free multiparty elections, and initially hopes ran high for a transition leading up to the presidential and legislative elections due in early December 1991. But those elections did not take place, and Mobutu made very clear his intention to stay in power beyond his constitutional mandate. Thus, in the early 1990s, free electoral choice remained an unfulfilled dream in Zaire.

Political Reform in the 1990s

Proclamation of the Third Republic

On April 24, 1990, President Mobutu Sese Seko announced to the citizens of Zaire that the country was entering a new era. Henceforth, that date would rank as a milestone, along with June 30, 1960 (independence day) and November 24, 1965 (inauguration of the Second Republic). The new era was to be one of multiparty government, replacing the single-party system that had been in place for twenty-three years.

This major reform, which would usher in the Third Republic, was presented as the product of Mobutu's personal initiative. In an exercise in direct democracy or "popular consultation," he had gone to the people and sought their views on the functioning of political institutions. Mobutu claimed that 5,310 of the 6,128 memoranda received, or 87 percent, proposed retaining the single-party status of the MPR, with some administrative and organizational changes, such as reductions in the number and size of party agencies and the recruitment of new staff. Only 13 percent of respondents called for a multiparty system. But, he said, after much reflection he had decided to go beyond the wishes expressed by the majority of the Zairian people. Thus, he had opted to experiment with political pluralism, establishing a system of three political parties, including the MPR. Each citizen would be free to adhere to the political formation of his choice. Mobutu cautioned, however, that the new multiparty system would have to avoid the errors of the past, namely allowing multipartyism to become synonymous with multitribalism.

Mobutu claimed that the Zairian people had demanded that he continue to preside over the destiny of the country in a broad sense. He would serve as chief of state and as such would ostensibly be above both the political parties and government organs, functioning as the final arbiter or last resort. Because he would be above the parties, Mobutu indicated that he was resigning that very day as head of the MPR, permitting that party to choose for itself a new leader to carry out the changes necessary to its new role. (Nevertheless, following his 1990 resignation, Mobutu accepted the leadership of the MPR once again on April 21, 1991.)

All these changes would require a transitional period of twelve months. According to Mobutu, the deliberative bodies, from the national legislature down to the collectivity councils, had been judged satisfactory by respondents and would remain in place until the next elections. However, the National Executive Council (also called the Council of Ministers), or cabinet, was considered to have resigned. A caretaker prime minister would be named, and this person would put together a transition team.

When Mobutu announced the transition to the Third Republic, he also dealt with several superficial but highly charged aspects of the aftermath of authenticity (see Glossary). Zaire's political vocabulary would be changed, and Zairians would be free to return to the more universal forms of address. Moreover, while the *abacost* (see Glossary) would remain the national dress and his personal choice, Zairians would be free to choose to wear a suit and tie. The ambiguities of the measures of 1990 were illustrated by the fact that members of the transitional government, sworn in two weeks later, all were dressed in the *abacost* or its feminine equivalent.

The whole exercise—the three-month "popular consultation" and the speech that summarized the results—was vintage Mobutu. In a masterful ploy, he cut the ground from beneath the feet of those opposition groups—the UDPS at home as well as some of the groups operating from exile—whose demands centered on political reform. He exempted himself and the directly elected deliberative bodies from the condemnation expressed by the people via their memoranda. He placed the burden for dealing with Zaire's enormous social and economic problems on the back of the new cabinet, which he would not head. At no time did he assume responsibility for the country's problems, nor did he acknowledge that his great initiative was really largely a reaction to external events and pressures. He made no mention of the fact that democratization has been a major demand of Western creditors, and that many other African states either had opted for multiparty systems or appeared to be about to do so, partly in response to the same international pressures.

Mobutu's apparent jettisoning of the party-state, ushering in the Third Republic, was a surprise move, the implications and implementation of which were far from clear. It remained to be seen how much Mobutu's personalistic regime would really change. In fact, within ten days Mobutu was already backpedaling.

Subsequent Political Developments, 1990–93

In a press conference following his April 24, 1990, speech to the country's assembled politicians, Mobutu suggested that the three authorized political parties might consist of the long-banned UDPS as well as two wings of the MPR, which he labeled "moderates" and "hard-liners." Nevertheless, despite Mobutu's attempt to constrict the political space he appeared to open up, his speech set off the inevitable multiplication of efforts to publicize existing organizations and to found new ones. The best-structured opposition movement, the UDPS, was the first to react. But on April 29, a demonstration by supporters of its most popular leader, Étienne Tshisekedi, released from house arrest on the day of Mobutu's speech, was violently suppressed. The UDPS claimed five people were killed, although the government denied this. Tshisekedi wound up in the hospital, early in May, after being attacked at his home by men apparently belonging to a government security service.

Joseph Ileo Nsongo Amba (formerly known as Joseph Ileo), in 1960 a political adversary of Prime Minister Patrice Lumumba and since 1967 a frequent member of the MPR Political Bureau and Central Committee, responded to Mobutu's announcement of the multiparty system by founding the Democratic and Social Christian Party (Parti Démocrate et Social Chrétien—PDSC). On April 29, Christophe Gbenye, a leader of the 1965 rural rebellions, announced that he had filed a request for recognition of the Congolese National Movement-Lumumba (Mouvement National Congolais-Lumumba—MNC-Lumumba).

Then on May 3, 1990, Mobutu made another speech. Political parties other than the MPR did not legally exist, he told the legislature, and were not yet authorized to hold marches or public meetings. (Thus, the UDPS meeting had been illegal.) Mobutu's twenty-three-minute speech was designed to overcome what he called "ambiguities and misunderstandings" following his announcement ten days earlier of an end to the political monopoly of the MPR. Until the authorities decided which three political parties were to be authorized—and Mobutu did not indicate when the choice would be made—politicians could meet privately to discuss organizational questions.

Most observers believed that Mobutu's espousal of political reform was in part an attempt to appease domestic calls for change, in the wake of events elsewhere in Africa and in Eastern Europe. The fall of Romanian dictator Nicolae Ceauşescu, with whom Mobutu identified, apparently made an impact on Mobutu. In addition, Mobutu undoubtedly felt it wise at least to appear to bow to Western pressure for political reform. It soon became evident, however, that Mobutu had unleashed volatile forces that he could contain only with difficulty, if at all, in the long run. Indeed, Mobutu proceeded to embark on a checkered course of half-hearted moves toward democratization, interspersed with attempts to undercut real reform and periodically interrupted by brutal crackdowns on dissent.

One of the most notorious of the crackdowns occurred in May 1990, when security forces were widely believed to have deliberately

massacred numerous protesting students at the University of Lubumbashi. The government claimed that only one student was
killed, but international human rights groups and other credible
observers estimated the death toll to be between thirty and 100.
The incident and Mobutu's refusal to allow an international inquiry
into it ultimately resulted in the suspension of aid by Belgium, the
European Community (EC), Canada, and the United States.

Faced with strong international censure and growing opposition
demands for a national conference to write a new constitution, organize new elections, and lead a transition to a democratic form
of government, Mobutu did lift the ceiling on the number of political parties in October 1990, and legislation passed in December
1990 finally opened the door for the formal registration of political
parties. He also declared that all registered parties would have access to the media.

By the spring of 1991, numerous political parties existed legally, and the regime announced that some fifty-eight had accepted
invitations to an upcoming constitutional conference, the date of
which had not been set, despite the rapid approach of December
4, 1991, the date on which Mobutu's constitutional mandate would
expire. Among the parties refusing to cooperate with Mobutu were
the principal opposition groups, namely, the UDPS, which demanded Mobutu's resignation; Ileo's PDSC; and the Union of Federalists and Independent Republicans (Union des Fédéralistes et des
Républicains Indépendants—UFERI) led by Jean Nguza Karl-i-
Bond.

At the same time, Mobutu asked the prime minister of the first
transitional government, Lunda Bululu, to resign in March 1991
and appointed a new prime minister, Professor Mulumba Lukoji.
Most ministerial appointees were from Kasai-Oriental, Kasai-
Occidental, and Shaba regions in an obvious attempt to undercut
support for the UDPS and UFERI, respectively, which drew their
strongest support from those regions. Further undermining public confidence in Mobutu's commitment to reform were a brutal
March 1991 attack on peaceful Christian demonstrators in Kinshasa, in which, according to human rights groups, thirty-five people were killed and dozens wounded; and an April attempt by police
to break up a political meeting in Mbuji-Mayi. Over forty individuals were believed to have been killed and nearly thirty seriously
wounded in the ensuing ransacking and looting by protesters.

The long-awaited national conference on political reform, ulti-
mately known as the Sovereign National Conference (Conférence
Nationale Souveraine—CNS), finally convened in August 1991.
It encompassed over 2,800 political, religious, and civic leaders,

representing some 225 political groups, whose declared goal was to draft a new constitution as a prelude to new elections. The conference was suspended by Mobutu on August 15 after opposition groups boycotted it on August 13, claiming that the government was overrepresented at the conference, had infiltrated opposition delegations (it was also alleged that the government had distributed money to some opposition delegates to sway their votes), and was preventing certain groups from attending the conference. The conference was further delayed because of the September 23–24 mutiny by some 3,000 paratroopers in Kinshasa, who were protesting low wages and lack of pay. The demonstration soon turned into a violent rampage, with hundreds of civilians joining the soldiers in looting businesses and homes. Other cities and southern Shaba Region also experienced disturbances. France and Belgium sent several hundred troops to restore order and protect foreign nationals in Kinshasa, and the United States supplied transport airplanes. But the evacuation of some 10,000 foreign residents and the virtual abandonment of numerous foreign-run businesses had a major impact on the economy. Indeed, according to most observers the economy virtually came to a standstill.

The political aftermath of the rampage was an agreement on September 29, 1991, by Mobutu and the opposition to form a transitional coalition government and a promise by Mobutu to reconvene the conference. Under the accord, UDPS leader Tshisekedi was named by Mobutu as prime minister in early October 1991, and Mobutu agreed that the cabinet would contain five Mobutu loyalists and six opposition leaders. However, Tshisekedi was fired after only one week in office in a dispute over the apportionment of ministerial portfolios. After the major opposition coalition, the Sacred Union (Union Sacrée), refused to choose a new prime minister, Mobutu named Bernardin Mungul-Diaka, a leader of a small opposition party, prime minister. Tshisekedi's firing spurred violent demonstrations and riots, including attacks on one of Mobutu's villas in Kinshasa and on the new prime minister's home. Following the unrest, France joined other Western nations that had already cut off economic aid to Zaire. In addition, civil servants resumed a long-standing strike that had been lifted in the wake of what had appeared to be positive political developments.

In late November 1991, Mobutu formed another transitional government, this time under Nguza. Nguza was a Tshisekedi rival in the Sacred Union, which he subsequently left, after other members termed his nomination a "betrayal." Now out of the Sacred Union, UFERI, headed by Nguza, organized another political coalition within the CNS, the Alliance of Patriotic Forces. This alliance of some thirty parties espoused a commitment to political change but rejected what it termed "extremist" stands.

The new government under Nguza included ten ministers from the opposition, although not from the Sacred Union's UDPS and PDSC, which boycotted the new government and called for a general strike against it. The progovernment MPR, which had not participated in the two previous transitional governments, was included, and in fact pro-Mobutu forces controlled eight posts, including the "reserved" domains of defense, interior and security, and external relations.

The long-term future of the CNS remained uncertain, and prospects for its success were dim so long as Mobutu clung to power. In any case, while the CNS was mired down in regime-opposition conflict, Mobutu's mandate quietly expired on December 4, 1991, and he made it clear that he would stay in power until new elections were held, although no firm date for such elections had been announced.

The CNS had reconvened on November 15, 1991, with a plenary session. However, disagreements over procedures for appointing a new prime minister delayed its formal resumption until December 11. At its session on December 12, Monsignor Laurent Monsengwo Pasinya, archbishop of Kisangani and president of the Episcopal Conference of Zaire, was elected president of the CNS. Monsengwo's election and his support by all of the opposition parties was a blow for Mobutu's camp, whose candidate for the conference's presidency was soundly defeated. In another blow to the Mobutu forces, the conference also elected Ileo, a leading member of the Sacred Union (and leader of the PDSC), as its vice president.

Following government attempts to pack the conference with Mobutu loyalists and to limit its powers, Prime Minister Nguza called for a suspension of the CNS on January 6, 1992, but it reconvened on January 14 to decide on issues of geopolitical representation. At the same time, pro-Mobutu delegates at the conference suspended their participation, charging that Tshisekedi's supporters from Kasai were overrepresented. On January 19, the government once again suspended the conference, with the prime minister stating that the conference proceedings were "likely to create a political crisis in the country." The suspension of the CNS was criticized by the international community.

Following a declaration by the Sacred Union that it would embark on a "concrete, logical action program" if the conference were not resumed by April 2, as well as pressure by Belgium, France, and the United States, the government announced on March 28 that the conference would meet on April 6. When it met, a majority of the more than 2,800 delegates voted to declare that the conference had sovereign powers not only to draw up a new constitution but also to legislate for a multiparty system. This represented a direct challenge to President Mobutu, who responded that ''some decisions made (by the conference) constitute an act of attempting to go beyond bounds.'' When conference delegates voted on May 6 for an act empowering them to make constitutionally binding decisions, Mobutu reacted by characterizing the step a ''civilian coup d'état.'' To Mobutu the conference's role was limited to devising a draft constitution.

In August 1992, the CNS passed a Transitional Act to serve as a provisional constitution and, under its terms, created a transitional government to govern for two years. According to the Transitional Act, the government would consist of four institutions: a figurehead president ''who reigns but does not govern'' as head of state; a High Council of the Republic (Haut Conseil de la République—HCR) to serve as a provisional legislature and to oversee new elections; a first state commissioner (prime minister) elected by the CNS as head of government with full executive powers; and an independent judiciary encompassing the courts of law. At the same time, Mobutu and the CNS agreed to abide by the principles established in the Comprehensive Political Agreement (Compromis Politique Global). The Comprehensive Political Agreement includes ten principles, the most significant being that no institution or organ of the transition should use its constitutional powers to prevent any other institution from functioning. In essence, all parties agreed to share power and to abide by the constitutional provisions embodied in the Transitional Act. In January 1993, the official status of the Transitional Act was strengthened further when the Supreme Court of Justice, acting as the Constitutional Court, declared the Transitional Act to be the country's only binding constitution.

As part of its August 1992 deliberations, the CNS, symbolizing its desire for change from the Mobutu regime, also proposed that Zaire resume its old name, the Republic of the Congo, and reinstitute the former national flag and anthem. Under pressure from Mobutu, however, the conference backed down, announcing that the country would keep its name, flag, and anthem until the proposed changes could be submitted to the electorate in a referendum.

Tshisekedi was duly elected transitional first state commissioner by the CNS on August 15, 1992. On August 30, he appointed a transitional government of ''national union'' including various opponents of Mobutu—but no Mobutu supporters. On December 6,

217

1992, the CNS dissolved itself and was succeeded by the 453-member HCR, to be headed by CNS head Archbishop Monsengwo. As the supreme interim legislative authority, the HCR was authorized to formulate and adopt a new constitution and to organize legislative and presidential elections. But Mobutu refused to accept the authority of the HCR or the legitimacy of any constitution it might formulate. Instead, in October 1992, he had reconvened the former legislature, which had been abolished, and entrusted it with drafting a rival new constitution more to his liking.

The transitional government has never been able to govern effectively because of its inability to limit Mobutu's powers except on paper. Mobutu clearly violated the terms of both the Transitional Act and the Comprehensive Political Agreement, impeding the work of the other institutions from the very start. Using troops loyal to him, Mobutu seized control of state radio and television facilities, denied HCR members and cabinet ministers access to their government offices, and took control of the central bank. Moreover, Mobutu pursued a deliberate strategy of promoting anarchy and inciting ethnic violence in order to discredit the prodemocracy movement and undermine the ability of the populace to organize against him.

Mobutu and Tshisekedi have been at loggerheads since Tshisekedi's election as transitional prime minister. But the situation deteriorated further in 1993. In mid-January 1993, the HCR declared Mobutu to be guilty of treason because of his mismanagement of state affairs and threatened to impeach him unless he recognized the legitimacy of the transitional government. Opposition forces organized a general strike to force the president's resignation. In the ensuing disturbances, five people were killed and many others injured. Then, later that month, Mobutu insisted on introducing a new currency note of Z5 million (for value of the zaire—see Glossary), which Tshisekedi denounced as inflationary and urged merchants to reject. When many did so, troops who had been paid in the currency went on a rampage of looting and violence during which sixty-five people were killed, including the French ambassador to Zaire.

In the aftermath of the violence, Mobutu attempted to reassert his political authority by convening a special "conclave" of political forces in early March 1993 to chart the nation's future, including devising a new constitution. The HCR and the Sacred Union declined to participate in any such deliberations, which clearly were intended to undermine the existing transitional government. Mobutu also "dismissed" the Tshisekedi government, although according to the Transitional Act he did not have the power to do

218

so. At his urging, the conclave then named Faustin Birindwa as prime minister of a so-called government of national salvation.

Since that time, Zaire has had two parallel, rival governments vying for domestic and international acceptance. The Birindwa government has not received international recognition, although delegations sent by that government have been accepted by several United Nations (UN) specialized agencies. But the Tshisekedi government, although legal and recognized internationally, lacks the power or resources to govern. The result of this situation is government stalemate, which has worked to Mobutu's advantage. Mobutu has continued to use his control of key military units to obstruct the functioning of the transitional government, to intimidate critical opposition leaders and newspapers, to promote anarchy and chaos, and to incite ethnic violence. Tshisekedi's frustration with the impotence of his own government in the face of the country's economic and social deterioration became so great that he requested UN intervention to restore order. In July 1993, the secretary general of the UN appointed a special envoy to Zaire, but no further international action had been taken by the end of the year.

Mobutu's ability to obstruct the democratization process has also been aided by the divisiveness of his opposition. The Sacred Union has had its defectors, including six former members who joined the Birindwa government and were immediately expelled from the Sacred Union. Tshisekedi's UDPS also has its differences with other parties in the coalition, such as Ileo's PDSC and the Unified Lumumbist Party led by Antoine Gizenga. Moreover, Tshisekedi has increasingly been under fire even within the transitional government and his own party for being too authoritarian. But Tshisekedi remains very popular, particularly in Kinshasa, with people who see him as the only opposition politician who has consistently opposed Mobutu.

At international urging, negotiations aimed at resolving Zaire's political stalemate continued throughout 1993 between representatives of the Mobutu-appointed conclave and the Sacred Union. Mobutu critics believed that he was merely using the negotiations to attempt to regain credibility in the eyes of the West. Nevertheless, some progress was made. In October 1993, the two sides reportedly reached agreement on a transitional constitution, a joint transitional parliament, and an electoral schedule (presidential and legislative elections to be held in December 1994). No details were available on the transitional constitution, but it is believed to represent a compromise between the approaches favored by the two sides. (Mobutu supporters favored a presidential or semi-presidential system while the opposition favored a parliamentary system.) The mere fact that agreement was reached on some previously thorny issues was interpreted as a positive sign. But most observers regarded any implementation of the agreement as highly problematic. First and foremost, no agreement could be reached on a prime minister acceptable to both sides, and neither Tshisekedi nor Birindwa was prepared to resign. Moreover, Mobutu himself remained a major stumbling block. The opposition refused to accept his continuation in a position of authority, and he clearly still had no intention of stepping down. Thus, at the end of 1993, Zaire's political impasse was still far from resolution.

Structure of Government

Under Mobutu, the government of Zaire has generally been described as a republic with strong presidential authority. Indeed, on paper at least Zaire possesses most of the conventional organs of a modern republic: separate executive, legislative, and judicial branches. However, mere enumeration of the organs of government conveys little about how they function. It is more useful to conceive of Zaire under Mobutu as being governed according to a system that has been variously described as patrimonialism (see Glossary) or as a presidential monarchy, in which the president exercises near-absolute power.

Zaire's constitutional situation has been murky since Mobutu's proclamation of the Third Republic and ostensible authorization of a multiparty system in 1990. The 1974 constitution (amended in 1978) is the last permanent constitution. The Mobutu-appointed government of national salvation headed by Birindwa was based on that constitution. Opposition forces, however, looked to the Transitional Act, which was passed by the CNS as a provisional constitution in August 1992 and subsequently upheld by the Supreme Court as the country's only legitimate constitution. The transitional government headed by Tshisekedi was elected by the CNS on the basis of that document, which, broadly, established a parliamentary system with a figurehead president.

Throughout 1992 and 1993, both camps continued to formulate rival draft constitutions. In October 1993, agreement reportedly was reached on a new constitution acceptable to both sides, but no details were available, and the agreement has not been implemented. At year's end, the constitutional standoff persisted, but because Mobutu controlled the state's treasury and military apparatus, the old political system clearly prevailed.

The Presidency

Mobutu deserves the label *presidential monarch* not simply because

Official presidential residence, Kinshasa
Courtesy Zaire National Tourism Office

of style, such as his use of the capitalized, plural pronoun *We*, but also because under Mobutu the Zairian state has been dominated by the institution of the presidency, which controls a huge share of public expenditure. The "reforms" announced in 1990, according to which the president would be "above politics," only reinforced the long-term trend toward an ever more powerful executive office of the president.

It should be stressed that the overdevelopment of the presidency occurred entirely under Mobutu. The Fundamental Law (Loi Fondamentale), or provisional constitution, of 1960 was based on the Belgian constitution. Power was vested in the parliament. Like a European constitutional monarch, the president had very limited powers, although his role in a constitutional crisis could be substantial. The 1964 constitution—known as the Constitution of Luluabourg (Luluabourg is now Kananga)—provided for an executive presidency that coexisted with cabinet government, under the prime minister. When Mobutu seized power in 1965, he initially continued this arrangement, serving as president while Colonel Léonard Mulamba was prime minister, heading a nonparty cabinet, formally called the National Executive Council.

The first step in building a more powerful presidency came in October 1966, when Mobutu dismissed the popular Mulamba.

221

Rather than name a new prime minister, he absorbed the functions of that position into those of the president.

The constitution of 1967 formalized the primacy of the presidency. Under its provisions, the role of the ministers was simply to execute the decisions and policies of the president. During 1977–79 and again in the late 1980s, Mobutu named prime ministers, but they were little more than vice chairmen of the cabinet, outranked by the president, who was also a member.

At the same time, Mobutu was increasing the capabilities of the office of the president. In November 1966, he created the General Secretariat of the Presidency. The secretariat comprised three general directorates (*directions générales*): economic, commercial, and cultural affairs; juridical and administrative affairs; and mines and energy. Some of the leading political figures of the Second Republic first emerged as members of the secretariat.

In October 1967, this small secretariat was transformed into the Bureau of the Presidency of the Republic and given responsibility for "a permanent mission of studies and of conceptualization, of technical coordination and of liaison between the public institutions and their organs." It comprised a director and four "colleges of counsellors," the fourth one being charged with "social and cultural problems." The new body, composed entirely of university graduates, gave Mobutu a higher level of expertise than that available through the cabinet. Perhaps more importantly, it gave him a means of co-opting young men, often of radical views, who might otherwise have found their careers blocked by the "old" independence-era politicians. Playing off these two groups against one another proved an effective divide-and-rule tactic.

The capabilities of the presidency were further enhanced by the creation of military services directly attached to the presidency. The *maison militaire*, or personal military staff of the president, and the Special Presidential Brigade—later, Special Presidential Division (Division Spéciale Présidentielle—DSP)—were loyal to the president, even more so than the armed forces in general.

The next major change in the position of the president came with the 1974 constitution, drafted by the presidency and approved by the MPR Political Bureau and the rubber-stamp legislature, formally known as the National Legislative Council, by acclamation. According to Article 28 of this constitution, Zaire was to have "a single institution, the MPR, incarnated by its President." Article 30 provided that the "President of the MPR is ex officio President of the Republic, and holds the plenitude of power to exercise. He presides over the Political Bureau, the Council of Ministers, the Legislature, and the Judicial Council." The president was to be elected by direct popular vote to a seven-year term and could serve an unlimited number of terms.

The Transitional Act of August 1992 created a parliamentary system. Mobutu, as president, was to remain head of state but was intended to serve as a figurehead with ceremonial rather than real executive powers. Mobutu refused to accept the validity of the new document, however, and continued to wield power as before, using control of the military, media, central bank, and state enterprises to his advantage. It remains to be seen what the role of the president will be in the new transitional constitution on which both pro-Mobutu and anti-Mobutu forces reportedly agreed in late 1993. It seems clear, however, that Mobutu would never voluntarily step aside and allow himself to be shunted off to a strictly ceremonial role.

The National Executive Council

In Mobutu's Zaire, there is a parliament and a Council of Ministers, or cabinet, also known as the National Executive Council, but any formal resemblance to Western parliamentary democracy is misleading. Zaire's National Executive Council is responsible not to the parliament but rather to the president. According to the constitution of 1967, the president, as chief of the executive branch, named and revoked the ministers and determined their respective powers. The ministers were responsible only to the president. In their departments, they did not carry out their own policy, but rather the program established and the decisions taken by the president of the republic. The constitution of 1974, which established the MPR as "the sole institution" of the republic, left the role of the National Executive Council essentially unchanged. It gave the president of the MPR the right to name and dismiss the members of the National Executive Council as well as to fix the council's program of action and supervise policy implementation. Mobutu's control of the cabinet was so firm that in 1980 he had abolished ministerial interpellations by establishing the Central Committee as the new decision-making body within the MPR, which action also weakened the country's parliament.

Nevertheless, the post of minister, and particularly that of prime minister, remained important despite the changes made in the cabinet's constitutional makeup. In part, the notion of ministers retained prestige from the European model, and ministerial posts were eagerly sought for that reason. Moreover, ministerial posts were major rewards for service to the patrimonial ruler, as well as providing the incumbent with opportunities for self-enrichment. Zaire's disastrous economic and social situation resulted in part

223

from this system, which guaranteed that top functionaries served the president rather than the nation.

The cabinet was subjected to frequent reshuffles, opening up some posts and assuring that those clients kept on were fully aware that they could go the next time. In a typical cabinet, all regions of the country were represented, although Mobutu's home region of Équateur was overrepresented. Often a political exile was "recuperated" and given a ministerial post. Few military personnel served as ministers. Mobutu personally retained control of the defense portfolio, and usually veterans' affairs as well, until the formation of the transitional government in May 1990. The president's control of the National Executive Council and his attempt to use it to appease and undercut the opposition were clearly evident in the formation of a succession of transitional and coalition governments following the May 1990 announcement of political pluralism.

Since March 1993, Zaire has had two cabinets. One is headed by Tshisekedi, elected by the CNS under the terms of the Transitional Act. This transitional government, the so-called government of national union, was reconfigured and broadened in September 1993; it consists of Tshisekedi as first state commissioner, or prime minister, and thirty-two state commissioners heading the various government ministries. The rival, Mobutu-appointed government, the so-called government of national salvation, is headed by Birindwa as prime minister, with three deputy prime ministers, and twenty-five other ministers. The United States government (and other Western powers) have not recognized the Birindwa government. Yet the Tshisekedi government cannot truly govern because of the ability of Mobutu to obstruct its operations, including using troops to prevent the prime minister and his cabinet ministers from occupying government offices. Tshisekedi has been forced to operate from his home.

The Legislature

The Zairian government has, since independence, included a legislative branch of government, but its powers have been steadily eroded by the presidency. The Fundamental Law, in effect from 1960 to 1964, created a bicameral legislature, which had substantial powers in that it both elected the president, who served as head of state, and chose the prime minister and cabinet ministers. But the document did not adequately define the division of power between the executive and legislative branches and thus contributed significantly to the breakdown of public order shortly after independence. The 1964 constitution retained the bicameral parliament and gave it both legislative responsibilities and the power to approve the president's appointment or dismissal of the prime minister. But after Mobutu's coup in 1965, the president increasingly assumed legislative powers. The 1967 constitution replaced the bicameral parliament with the unicameral National Assembly, which had little formal or real power because of the power given the president to rule by executive order, which carried the force of law.

According to the provisions of the 1974 constitution, the National Legislative Council (Conseil National Législatif—CNL; the new name for the former National Assembly, adopted in July 1972) remained one of the five organs of government. But it was subordinate to the party, the supreme institution of the state; the president, who was automatically president of all five organs of government; and the president's appointed ministers. The constitution provided for only limited legislative powers, in that members of the CNL, elected to five-year terms, had the right to initiate laws "concurrently" with the president.

In reality, the CNL operated within very narrow boundaries. Real legislative power was wielded by the Central Committee of the MPR, while the CNL was relegated to the subordinate position of approving party initiatives. The CNL did, however, serve as a lightning rod for the population's resentment of its treatment by the regime, particularly after 1977, when multiple candidatures for legislative seats were allowed for the first time (although all still ran under the banner of the MPR). In the September 1982 legislative elections, for example, only sixty out of 310 members of parliament were reelected.

The high point of legislative independence had come earlier, in the late 1970s. Early in 1977, the CNL had rejected the budget submitted to it by the president and denounced excessive presidential spending. Moreover, the new CNL elected that year used questioning of ministers as a mechanism for raising policy issues.

In 1979 a group of deputies from Kasai-Oriental defied presidential pressure and affixed their signatures to a report charging that the army had been responsible for the massacre of approximately 300 diamond miners at Katekalay in Kasai-Oriental. In November 1980, these dissident deputies, who became known as the Thirteen (their actual number fluctuated from episode to episode), published a fifty-one-page open letter to President Mobutu, providing a comprehensive critique of Mobutu's autocracy. The Thirteen were careful to include in their number parliamentarians from various regions, to forestall the charge of tribalism. Writing in legal brief style, the authors of the letter dissociated themselves from any advocacy of violence, invoking the constitution itself as protection for the expression of their views. Following their formation in 1982 of a second party, the UDPS, the Thirteen were imprisoned, then released under amnesty in May 1983, with several later placed under house arrest or exiled. Despite the formation of such opposition groups, the banishment of some members was a constant reminder to other deputies that no organized opposition would be tolerated by Mobutu, however peaceful their methods or aims.

The Transitional Act passed in August 1992 created the HCR to serve as a legislature, as well as to amend and adopt a new constitution and oversee new legislative and presidential elections. In December 1992, the CNS dissolved itself and was succeeded by the HCR under the terms of the Transitional Act. The 453-member HCR, headed by Archbishop Mongsengwo, was, however, never accepted as valid by Mobutu. To prove his point, in October 1992 he reconvened the old legislature, or CNL, which had been dissolved by the CNS. Mobutu established the CNL as a rival to the HCR and charged the former with formulating a new draft constitution.

The political agreement on a new transitional constitution reportedly reached by pro-Mobutu and anti-Mobutu forces in October 1993 created a new 780-member legislature, to which the government will be responsible. Encompassing both the HCR and the CNL, the new body is to be called the High Council of the Republic (Haut Conseil de la République—HCR)-Parliament of the Transition (Parlement de la Transition—PT), or HCR–PT. At the end of 1993, however, no action had been taken to implement the agreement.

The Judiciary and the Courts

The judicial system is organized hierarchically, in accordance with the country's administrative and political structure. At the apex is the Supreme Court of Justice in Kinshasa. Under it, in descending order, are three courts of appeal in Kinshasa, Lubumbashi, and Kisangani, whose jurisdiction includes several regions each; a regional tribunal in each of the ten regions and Kinshasa; and numerous urban and rural subregional tribunals (courts of the peace) with original jurisdiction over most offenses. In a formal sense, the judicial system seems to resemble its European model, but in fact non-Western customary law and other forms of local practice have been added to the colonial heritage.

Mobutu inherited the Belgian colonial judicial system, with only a few modifications dating from the First Republic. The findings at each judicial level were subject to review at the next higher level. But because the administration recognized the authority of African customary law at the lowest level, a dual legal system developed, one applying customary law for almost all Congolese, the other applying written law for Europeans. In 1958, two years before independence, a decree attempted to reform the legal system, removing the distinctions in the treatment of Europeans and Africans.

After independence the mass departure of Belgian magistrates meant that the judicial system almost ceased to function above the level of the territory (zone, in present-day nomenclature). The United Nations sponsored a program of recruitment under which magistrates were engaged from Greece, Haiti, Egypt, Syria, and Lebanon. These foreign judges slowly were replaced by locals. A 1973 decree specified that all magistrates were obligated to hold a *licence* (undergraduate degree) or doctorate in law. All magistrates typically began their careers in government administration and served provisionally for a year, after which they might be appointed to a court by the president.

Under the Fundamental Law as well as under the 1964 and 1967 constitutions, judicial power was theoretically independent of the executive and legislative powers, although judges were appointed by the president. Magistrates were supposed to remain totally aloof from all political activity.

However, the independent judiciary became an anomaly once the MPR had been declared the supreme institution of the nation. The constitution of 1974 eliminated the inconsistency. The Council of the Judiciary, comprising all courts and tribunals, was made one of five organs of government. Mobutu was its president. Although in theory magistrates were to remain independent and free in the execution of their judicial powers, they were obligated to be active party members and to interpret the law in the spirit of the party. As with other government officials, the degree of their devotion to the party was continually monitored. Thus, the MPR became the source of all legality. The president of the republic could not interpret the law, but justice was carried out in his name and under his authority.

The Mobutu regime claimed that the 1974 reforms were consistent with the principle of administrative justice as it had been practiced under the Colonial Charter, where the law was stated and executed in the name of the king, and also with the African traditional concept of a chief who is also a judge. The latter assertion is an example of a tendency, very common in Mobutu's Zaire, to justify current practice by sweeping statements regarding African

227

tradition. In fact, in many precolonial societies of Zaire, elders who were not political chiefs heard disputes and decided the outcome.

The result of this reform was the politicization of the judiciary. Nevertheless, despite this limitation to their authority, and their theoretical integration into the MPR, many magistrates continued to defend the concept of their autonomy. As Michael Schatzberg has put it, they inhabited ''a pocket of resistance internal to the state.''

The 1990 reforms were intended to reinstate the judiciary's constitutional independence. Moreover, the Transitional Act of August 1992 made the courts of law one of the four independent institutions of government. The Supreme Court gave evidence of this independence when in January 1993, in its capacity as the nation's Constitutional Court, it declared the Transitional Act to be Zaire's only binding constitution. Nevertheless, the judicial system as a whole has not been revamped because of Mobutu's continued ability to obstruct the implementation of the Transitional Act and the functioning of the transitional government. In addition, there were reports in 1992 and 1993 that Mobutu had used loyal military forces to intimidate the judiciary, along with opposition leaders and the media.

Legal dualism persisted at the local level. Early in the Mobutu years, the Ordinance of July 10, 1968, had supposedly erased the last traces of racial discrimination, had incorporated ''custom'' into the national law, and put an end to the dichotomy of judicial institutions. Moreover, under the 1968 ordinance, customary courts were to be replaced by courts of the peace, meaning that professional magistrates would replace local notables as judges.

Legislation in 1978 provided that there should be one or more courts of the peace in each zone, urban or rural. But even in the early 1990s, many areas of Zaire did not have a local court, apparently because of the inability of the government to recruit people with legal training who were willing to work in the countryside, far from urban amenities. Much of the population remained at the mercy of customary justice, as administered by the chiefs and their courts.

Local Government

Internally, Zaire is a unitary state, whose power is projected downward to the local level. In such a centralized system, local government enjoys little autonomy.

The local government of Mobutu's Zaire, like the colonial administration that served as its model, has as its major function the control of the population: counting the people, controlling their movements, issuing identity cards, and taxing them to pay for the operations of the local administrative units that carry out these tasks. Although the labels attached to the administrative units and to the administrators who hold them have changed, the structures themselves are very similar. In many ways, the texture of the relationship between the citizen and the state apparatus resembles that of the Belgian era.

At the same time, there are great differences between the Mobutu administration and its colonial predecessor in the related areas of efficiency and honesty. Few would dispute the effectiveness or probity of the colonial administration, within its own terms of reference. By contrast, the Mobutu administration is widely regarded as corrupt and inefficient. Indeed, political scientist Michael Schatzberg has shown that the administration has long constituted a powerful mechanism for pumping resources out of the impoverished rural population.

The territorial administration was the crucial armature of the colonial state. A thorough penetration of the subject society was basic to the colonial project, and the loss of control in some territories in 1959 was a mortal blow to colonial self-confidence.

Territorial control was no less central to the policy calculus of the independent state that became Zaire. The loss of effective provincial administration, and the fragmentation of administrative authority through a multiplicity of factionalized provincial jurisdictions and local rebellions, were defining characteristics of the First Republic. During the 1964–65 rebellions, the vestiges of state power even remotely responsive to Kinshasa were eliminated over large areas of the republic. Reestablishing the authority of the state, by restoring the ascendancy of its central territorial administration, was a first priority for the Mobutu regime.

Initially, it appeared that this goal was being met. The unified hierarchical grid of the centralized state was restored, at least in form. But new self-destructive tendencies became apparent by the 1970s; the credibility of the state was at issue as its inability to perform basic services became manifest, and corruption pervaded its apparatus.

Under the Belgians, the entire colony was divided into nesting subdivisions. Each province was divided into districts and each district into territories, all units on a given level being juridically equivalent. There were about 125 territories and twenty-five districts; totals varied as a result of the frequent redrawing of boundaries in a vain attempt to obtain the perfect match between administration and society. The province, the district, and the territory all were headed by Belgians. The territory was the most crucial echelon, as it represented the point at which the European administration exercised its control upon African intermediaries, the so-called chiefs.

The local colonial administration functioned without substantial oversight or control from outside bodies. There were consultative provincial councils appointed by the government, but until the last few years of the colonial era they represented only European interests (see The Colonial State, ch. 1). At the very end of the colonial period, elected communal councils in urban areas and appointed rural councils were authorized. The former continued to function in the major cities until the end of the 1960s (the last elected organs from the First Republic to survive). Rural councils never really took shape.

In the First Republic, the province was a political unit, with an elected assembly and ministers theoretically responsible to the assembly. However, such elected bodies were never created at the working level where the state had its interface with the intermediaries it had created, the chiefs.

The symmetry and formalism of the Belgian system, its density (almost unparalleled in Africa), and its relative freedom from legislative oversight, all were powerful influences on contemporary Zaire. The Second Republic attempted not only to reconstitute this system, but to extend its application to the cities and to the local level in the countryside.

In February 1966, three months after his seizure of power, Mobutu signalled his intention to bring the provinces to heel by reunification and depoliticization. By the end of the year, the twenty-one so-called *provincettes* had been reduced to eight provinces (renamed regions in 1972), plus the capital, Kinshasa, meaning that colonial provincial boundaries had been almost completely restored. The exceptions were the division of the former Kasai Province into Kasai-Oriental and Kasai-Occidental and the division of the former Léopoldville Province into Bas-Zaïre and Bandundu (see fig. 4). The provinces, once quasi-federal political units with their own governments, were reduced to administrative subdivisions of the unitary state. Their chief officers were named by the president, they were rotated frequently, and they generally were assigned outside their home areas.

The heads of the various administrative subdivisions all had essentially the same role—representing the central state. The similarity in role was symbolized by the adoption of uniform terminology: the regions, subregions, zones, and collectivities (as the colonial provinces, districts, and territories were known from 1972 on) all were headed by commissioners (*commissaires*). However, the weight of the colonial legacy was reflected in a decision in 1982 to revive the prestigious title of *gouverneur* (governor), in place of regional commissioner (*commissaire de région*).

Although the governors clearly were dependent upon the president, problems of control did not disappear. At first the governors were kept on a short leash by the simple expedient of shifting them very often. Despite the frequent changes, some governors briefly succeeded in building up personal political machines. To prevent this process, and generally to keep an eye on the regional administration, Mobutu added a parallel control organ of state inspectors. The state inspectorate seems not to have served its purpose; it was abolished in 1971. By the late 1970s, Mobutu also had abandoned the practice of constant reshuffling; instead, governors were named to three-year terms.

Although in theory the Mobutist state was highly centralized, in practice local administrators enjoyed a degree of autonomy. They were charged with implementing within their regions the decisions taken by the president, and an administrative memorandum stipulated that the word "decisions," which appears in the constitution, must be understood in a very broad sense. Mobutu frequently made such decisions, and governors often had nothing more to go on than a radio broadcast, telephonic instructions, or a vaguely worded telegram. Thus, they had considerable discretion as to how decisions should be implemented. There were risks at the same time; if their interpretations were subsequently to incur presidential displeasure, they could lose their jobs.

Since 1977 the Mobutu regime supposedly has been committed to a policy of decentralization, beginning with urban areas. In fact, there seem to be two contradictory tendencies: toward decentralization and democratization, under pressure from external aid donors, and toward tighter administrative controls. Also in 1977, a plan was announced for sweeping reorganization of rural areas, so that no zone would contain more than 200,000 people and no subregion would comprise more than three zones. New subregions were created in parts of Bas-Zaïre, Équateur, Kasai-Oriental, and Shaba. But full implementation of this plan would have meant a huge expense, and it was never completed.

Reorganization moves reflected both the administrative rationale and political considerations, particularly in Mobutu's home region of Équateur. Mobutu's transformation of his home village of Gbadolite into a city, and the development of the small town of Gemena, also in northwest Équateur, into an important center as a result of his activities and those of his relatives and associates, led to the creation of new subregions around them. Had greater importance been attached to "administrative rationality," then surely the reorganization of Équateur Region would have been completed. Indeed, plans had been prepared for all the remaining "unorganized" regions and portions thereof, but the deteriorating politico-economic situation led to their indefinite postponement.

This wave of reform affected only the number and scope of the administrative units, not their relationship to the center. Not until 1984, when Mobutu accepted suggestions from external aid donors that he carry out political "liberalization," were the regions given legislative assemblies and a degree of politico-administrative autonomy.

In May 1988, Mobutu proposed improving the functioning of the regional structures and redrawing their boundaries, so as "to bring the administrator closer to the administered." The experiment was to begin with the division of Kivu Region into three new regions, Nord-Kivu, Sud-Kivu, and Maniema; the reorganization was not implemented immediately, but seemed to be in effect by the early 1990s. Zaire thus was divided into ten regions plus the city of Kinshasa.

Political Dynamics

Managing the Military

Mobutu's regime emerged from a coup but is not a military regime because it has never given priority to the interests of the military. Since 1965 Mobutu has continued to manage the armed forces by the same methods he used, as chief of staff, to rebuild them after 1960, i.e., by tying individual units and officers to him. Rather than a traditional pyramidal organization, the Zairian security forces resemble a wheel with Mobutu at the hub. Time and again, when existing units have proven to be unreliable, he has created new units trained by foreigners (see Armed Forces Missions and Organization, ch. 5).

In addition, Mobutu has been careful both to keep the military under his personal control and to minimize military participation in the civilian government. He has usually been the only military man in the cabinet, filling the role of minister of defense and veterans' affairs.

The reforms announced in April 1990 ostensibly included depoliticization of the armed forces, presumably to include elimination of the official MPR presence within the military, which had annoyed many of the officers. But in a broader sense, of course, the military services remain political in that they are under the control of President Mobutu. As one part of that control, Mobutu's cronies and relatives head key military units.

Nevertheless, despite the military's role as the backbone of the regime, it is also a potential Achilles' heel. Military coup attempts were reported in 1975, 1978, and 1984. For several years, there were no further reports of coup attempts. Then in August 1987, the Voice of Zaire (La Voix du Zaïre) announced that a large cache of arms and ammunition brought illegally into the country had been discovered in a military camp in Kinshasa. Each of the alleged coup attempts was followed by a major purge of high military officers. These purges, as well as Mobutu's general organizational policy, made it clear that political reliability would be given higher priority than military effectiveness.

The events of September 1991, in which unpaid paratroopers mutinied and engaged in a frenzy of looting throughout Kinshasa cast into doubt the morale and loyalty of the military. Such doubts were reinforced by the periodic bouts of looting that occurred throughout 1992 and 1993, as well as an exchange of fire between paratroopers and the Civil Guard in June 1992, prompting fears that many armed forces elements were beyond any control.

Nevertheless, Mobutu has shrewdly retained the loyalty of his most important military units, the DSP in particular. In the early 1990s, the beleaguered Mobutu reportedly continued to receive bags of newly printed currency flown in from abroad, which he disbursed to key military personnel.

Opposition to the Regime prior to 1990

As the Zairian political scientist Ilunga Kabongo has observed, the origin of the Mobutu regime, together with subsequent foreign aid, had the effect of generating "a myth of the foreign element in Zairian politics." Whereas foreign, and especially American, scholars have tended to underplay foreign influence as secondary to local forces in shaping Zairian events, "it is overemphasized by many a Zairian scholar, the political elite as well as the commoners, to a point where most Zairians think that any change in their condition will have to come from outside decisive influence." This interpretation explained the futility felt by Zairian opposition groups, whose activities consisted mainly of lobbying Western powers in order to persuade the latter to remove Mobutu. One could extend Ilunga's argument to cover groups that relied on violence to overthrow Mobutu, most of which have depended on foreign support. The People's Revolutionary Party (Parti Révolutionnaire du Peuple—PRP) may be an exception to this rule. Certainly the aura of foreign influence, or foreign protection, as well as lobbying by international human rights organizations, conditioned the eventual emergence of successful opposition movements, notably the UDPS, which was able to survive within Zaire and to demonstrate that, like the government, it too had support from the United States.

Armed Opposition

The best-known of the groups committed to armed struggle probably is the Front for the National Liberation of the Congo (Front pour la Libération Nationale du Congo—FLNC), whose armed forces invaded Zaire's Shaba Region in 1977 and 1978, from bases in Angola (see Shaba I; Shaba II, ch. 5). The FLNC was led by Nathaniel Mbumba, a former police officer. On the basis of its activities on Zairian soil and its declarations, the FLNC had no discernible program other than to overthrow Mobutu. Despite recruiting largely from Lunda and other ethnic communities of southwestern Shaba Region, there was no sign of Shaba separatism in its pronouncements or actions. The FLNC continued to exist in the early 1990s, but it had expelled Mbumba in 1987; neither the party nor its one-time leader played a major role in the transitional period after May 1990.

Some observers noted the FLNC's failure to coordinate its activities with the other major armed opposition group, the PRP. Headed by Laurent Kabila, a leader of the Lumumbist insurrection of 1964–65, the PRP maintained a "liberated zone" in the Fizi area of southeastern Kivu (in present-day Sud-Kivu). This zone had been out of government control since 1964. PRP forces in the area apparently existed in symbiosis with the government forces sent to exterminate them. Assignment to that theater of operations reportedly was popular with Zairian military officers, who profited from smuggling gold, ivory, and other commodities out of the PRP zone.

In contrast to the FLNC, the PRP had a well-defined program for social revolution. According to one publication, it foresaw regrouping peasants in *cités agricoles,* which would be organized as agricultural cooperatives, and equipped with a dispensary, maternity clinic, nursery school, playing fields, movie theater, market, and branch of the savings bank. It was unclear how this socialist paradise in rural Zaire would be financed.

The PRP was briefly in the headlines in 1975, when its guerrillas kidnapped four foreigners (three American, one Dutch) at a Tanzanian wildlife research station. In 1984 and again in 1985, the PRP captured the town of Moba (eastern Shaba, on Lake Tanganyika) before being expelled each time by the Zairian army. The government claimed that 1,500 PRP fighters surrendered in 1986, but in the early 1990s, the PRP apparently held its small pocket of rural territory.

Another Lumumbist group, the Congolese Liberation Party (Parti de Libération Congolaise—PLC), attacked small army and police posts and government transport around Beni, between Lake Edward and Lake Albert, Kisangani, and Kwilu in 1987. At the end of the 1980s, the PLC apparently still had a small guerrilla force in the Ruwenzori Mountains, along the Ugandan border. Abandoned by their leader, Marandura Kibingo, some of the PLC fighters reportedly were hiding their guns and descending to western Uganda to grow food. In the meantime, Marandura was said to be living in Dar es Salaam on money supplied by Libya to the PLC.

The Congolese National Movement-Lumumba (Mouvement National Congolais-Lumumba—MNC-Lumumba) was involved over the years in small-scale, low-visibility border incursions from the east, which did not pose a serious threat to regime stability. In 1984, however, the MNC-Lumumba claimed responsibility for bomb blasts at the Voice of Zaire and the central post office in Kinshasa, in which one person was killed. Zaire placed the blame for the incidents on Libya, but the Belgian government expelled MNC-Lumumba secretary general François-Eméry Lumumba Tolenga (son of Patrice Lumumba), saying it "would not permit acts of terrorism to be organized from Belgian territory." The 1984 blasts remained isolated incidents of urban terrorism.

In the turbulent mid-1990s, a revival of armed opposition appeared possible. In Luanda, Angola, a group calling itself the Congolese National Army (Armée Nationale Congolaise—ANC) announced its intention of beginning an armed struggle in Zaire. The ANC presented itself as the military wing of the "radical opposition," and said that its main objective was "to restore legitimacy and democracy" to the "ex-Zaire" or "future Democratic Republic of the Congo." It claimed that it had fighters based in Uganda, Tanzania, Zambia, and Angola.

Fragmented Exile Movements

For the most part, groups in exile, including the Lumumbists, remained fragmented and unable to pose much of a threat to Mobutu. Their weakness is exemplified by the meeting held in Switzerland in 1987. Thirteen Zairian opposition movements took part and agreed to establish a government in exile, the sole aim of which was "to overthrow the Zairian dictator by any means." But no sooner had the composition of the government in exile been announced than the supposed "president of the Constituent Assembly" denied his participation and appealed to exiles "to return to the country to take part in the immense task of national reconstruction.''

An earlier attempt to unite the exiled opposition was the Council for the Liberation of the Congo (CLC), set up by former Lumumbist politician Bernardin Mungul-Diaka. Mungul-Diaka had been a minister under Mobutu, then fled the country in 1980, and surfaced in Brussels as head of the CLC. This council supposedly brought together five organizations, including the FLNC, the PRP, and the Progressive Congolese Students, all of which identified the country by its former name, rejecting ''Zaire'' as a creation of Mobutu. It was clear that the FLNC and PRP existed; it was less clear that the CLC would be able to coordinate their activities, or indeed to survive the return of Mungul-Diaka from exile. Equally ephemeral were the Congolese Front for the Restoration of Democracy, created in 1982 by Nguza Karl-i-Bond, and the African Socialist Force (Force Socialiste Africaine—FSA), formed by Cléophas Kamitatu in 1977. Such opposition groups competed with one another for aid from foreign supporters and were vulnerable to the co-optation of their leaders by Mobutu. They were important in that they managed to publicize abuses of the Mobutu regime but posed little threat to its endurance.

The UDPS

Alone among pre-1990 Zairian opposition groups, the UDPS began as a dissident faction within the legislature. In November 1980, thirteen members of parliament signed an ''open letter to the president of the republic,'' a ten-point document cataloging corruption and abuse of power in the regime, and calling for legalization of a second political party. The thirteen signatories were arrested and stripped of their parliamentary seats.

In July 1982, some of the Thirteen—as the ex-deputies were known; but the exact number involved was unclear—were sentenced to fifteen years in prison for aggravated treason. In 1983 Mobutu lifted the prison sentences of six members of the group, but banished them to their home villages. The Thirteen became an opposition party in 1982 or merged with an existing clandestine party, under the rubric of the UDPS. Frédéric Kibassa Maliba, a former minister under Mobutu, was the party's first head.

The UDPS stood out among opposition groups as being distinctly moderate. The party identified itself as ''the Party of Peace and Justice for all'' and committed itself to achieving democracy in Zaire through nonviolent means. It aimed at establishing a multiparty political system with free elections, freedom of the press and association, and a free-market economy.

The UDPS suffered from several handicaps. It was seen as a party dominated by Luba-Kasai. In fact, of the original thirteen deputies who signed the open letter in November 1980, about half were from the Luba or related groups from Kasai-Oriental or Kasai-Occidental, while others represented other regions of the southern half of the country. The most prominent members, including Tshisekedi, were Luba-Kasai. When the UDPS emerged as a party, new members were brought in from other regions. Nonetheless, the government had some success in painting the UDPS as an ethnic movement.

A second handicap, which contributed to frequent incoherence in the message of the UDPS, was the split between leaders in the country and in exile. This division was at the same time a strength of the UDPS. Its survival, when so many other opposition groups disappeared, was linked to its double status as a group within and outside Zaire. Particularly helpful was the willingness of Tshisekedi and others to attempt to work within the country. Also important was the early success of the UDPS in attracting the support of several United States congressmen.

On June 24, 1987, Mobutu announced that the last leaders of the UDPS had rejoined the MPR. "Apart from a few dozen noisy supporters, prudently based outside the country—notably in Brussels and Paris—and true militants isolated in Kinshasa—the UDPS had no impact in this too vast country of Zaire," the Paris weekly *Jeune Afrique* commented. It was too soon to write off the UDPS, however. Tshisekedi explained that permission had been granted to allow the group to continue as a "tendency" within the MPR. In January 1988, he attempted to address a public meeting in Kinshasa. Police beat and arrested hundreds of participants, including Tshisekedi himself.

In February 1989, when thousands of students took to the streets of Kinshasa to protest IMF-inspired austerity measures, including a hike in tuition fees, and inadequate and expensive transportation, security forces arrested Tshisekedi's wife, apparently to pressure the UDPS leader into confessing that he had instigated the demonstrations. In the meantime, Mobutu, perhaps attempting to subvert the opposition, named former UDPS president Kibassa to the low-ranking post of minister of sports.

Opposition since 1990

As noted previously, Mobutu's April 1990 announcement of political pluralism emphasized that three political parties would be permitted. Soon thereafter, however, he opted instead for "integral multipartyism," apparently seeing more scope for his habitual divide-and-rule tactics than in a three-party arrangement. Numerous parties formed and ultimately received legal recognition in 1990, but most were small and not major contenders in elections. By late 1991, the number of registered political parties was placed at 230.

The major opposition parties are the UDPS, led by Tshisekedi; the PDSC, led by Ileo; and UFERI, led by Nguza. Other noteworthy opposition political parties are the Common National Front (Front Commun National or Front Commun des Nationalistes—FCN) of Kamanda wa Kamanda; the African Socialist Party (Parti Socialiste Africain—PSA), led by Jibi Ngoyi; the Unified Lumumbist Party, led by Antoine Gizenga; and the Rally of Liberal Democrats (Rassemblement des Démocrats Libéraux—RDL), led by Mwamba Mulanda and generally allied with UFERI.

By late 1991, several opposition parties had formed a coalition, the Sacred Union (Union Sacrée). Among the participants, in addition to UFERI, were the UDPS and the PDSC, which led the so-called radical wing of the coalition, as well as the Lumumbist Unified Party. The radical wing refused to participate in the newly formed government of Nguza. Nguza and UFERI then left the Sacred Union and organized another political coalition within the CNS, the Alliance of Patriotic Forces, encompassing some thirty opposition parties, ten civic associations, and various individuals united in opposition to the Mobutu regime, but rejecting "extremist" stands. Adolphe Kishwe-Maya, president of a UFERI faction, headed the Alliance's coordination bureau. Pro-Mobutu forces, led by the MPR, which reportedly changed its name to Popular Movement for the Revival (Mouvement Populaire pour le Renouveau), worked together in the United Democratic Forces (Forces Démocratiques Unies—FDU) coalition.

In June 1993, six defectors from the Sacred Union, claiming that the Sacred Union had become too extremist, formed their own coalition, which they called the Restored Sacred Union (Union Sacrée Rénovée). The six had joined the Birindwa government, and as such could no longer be regarded as ardent opponents of the Mobutu regime, so their role in the anti-Mobutu, prodemocracy movement is suspect. The same can be said of Nguza's UFERI and Alliance of Patriotic Forces, given Nguza's position as first deputy prime minister in charge of defense in the Birindwa government. In fact, some observers see Nguza's acceptance of the ministerial post as evidence that he has been co-opted by Mobutu.

In early September 1993, Tshisekedi formed another coalition to organize opposition to a Mobutu plan for a constitutional referendum to be held in October 1993 and followed by elections in December. The new group is called the Democratic Forces of the

Animateurs, *cheerleaders for the MPR, after a rally in Équateur Region*

Congo-Kinshasa (Forces Démocratiques de Congo-Kinshasa). Its relationship to the Sacred Union is unclear, but presumably close.

The Sacred Union, still the principal component of the anti-Mobutu campaign, reportedly has been beset by divisiveness. In addition, Tshisekedi has been criticized both within the transitional government and within the UDPS for being too authoritarian and failing to hold a party conference. Such disunity within the opposition has continued to undermine its effectiveness and to play to Mobutu's advantage in the early 1990s.

Interest Groups

Political scientists frequently characterize Zaire and other African states as "corporatist," manifesting a system in which interest groups are officially sanctioned and noncompetitive. Although corporatism has not been a dominant theme in official Zairian discourse, it is present, notably in the oft-repeated phrase, "toutes les forces vives" (all the vital forces). When a new policy is to be launched, "toutes les forces vives" of the nation or of the region, as appropriate, are called together—representatives of the employers, employees, churches, and other pertinent groups.

In 1991, as Zaire initiated a national conference on the model of those held in Benin, Congo, and other French-speaking African states, a new expression arose to refer to interest groups: civil society (*la société civile*), a sociological expression that originated in the writings of nineteenth-century German philosopher Georg Wilhelm Friedrich Hegel.

Organized Labor

The case for corporatism was strongest in the area of labor relations until 1991, when independent trade union organizations were officially recognized. The political pluralism of the First Republic had given labor unions freedom to maneuver among the various interest groups and parties. Trade unions performed an opposition role but were by no means united over what that role ought to be. Some were reformist, others more radical.

In 1967 the Mobutu government forced the unification of the country's fractious trade unions into a single organization, the National Union of Zairian Workers (Union Nationale des Travailleurs Zaïrois—UNTZA). Then the government brought UNTZA under its control, making clear that UNTZA was to be an instrument of support for the regime. Officially UNTZA was a specialized branch of the MPR, carrying out some syndicalist functions, such as negotiating contracts with various firms, but operating under the supervision of the MPR secretariat.

Resolutions of the 1978 UNTZA congress reveal a balance between political concerns and purely syndicalist ones. There was a motion of support for Mobutu. By contrast, several specific resolutions dealt with the interests of workers, such as control of consumer prices, equitable distribution of revenues and goods, and representation of workers on the administrative councils of public enterprises. It is revealing, however, that all the resolutions were drafted in the MPR secretariat in the expectation that they would be adopted by UNTZA without significant debate.

Having a captive trade union federation did not spare the regime from labor strikes. What it meant was that any strike was a "wildcat" strike and had no official leaders with whom to negotiate.

The clearest evidence that structural conflicts between the trade unions and the regime were being papered over came early in 1990, when Mobutu called for a national dialogue. Memoranda prepared by various groups were not supposed to be released to the public, but *Jeune Afrique* claimed to have learned that the Kinshasa office of UNTZA was the author of a memo calling for the resignation of Mobutu.

Following Mobutu's April 24, 1990, announcement of the end of the one-party state, UNTZA lost its monopoly position and with it the right to the "check-off" or withholding of union dues at source. UNTZA remains the strongest trade union federation but has to contend with eleven other officially recognized unions, some of which represent Christian, liberal, or social democratic tendencies while others have grouped employees in particular trades or sectors. In the new, competitive environment—amid a deteriorating socioeconomic situation—strikes are even more common. Indeed, teachers, medical personnel, and other public-service personnel are frequently on strike because of low or nonexistent pay, and the lack of public services resulting from the strikes has further contributed to the deterioration of the economy and society.

Religious Groups

The Roman Catholic Church

Until the inauguration of multipartyism in 1990, the most persistent and most effective opposition to the Mobutu regime came from the Roman Catholic Church. Mobutu's ambitions for state expansion necessarily implied conflict with organized religion, and the main adversary of the expansionist regime was the Roman Catholic Church, which claims 46 to 48 percent of the population as active members. The Catholic network of schools, clinics, and other social services was as large as that of the state, and more efficiently run. The role of the church thus was pervasive, and its moral authority made it an uncomfortable competitor for the comprehensive allegiance that Mobutu sought.

Initially, the church had welcomed the new regime and supported the consolidation of its authority. The founding of the MPR led to the first tensions, and in 1969 a conference of bishops privately noted "dictatorial tendencies" in the regime. The following year, Joseph Cardinal Malula, the head of the church in Zaire, publicly expressed fears regarding the regime's intentions during a mass celebrating the tenth anniversary of independence.

In 1971 the regime struck at the symbol of the Catholic education system, absorbing Lovanium University (along with the Protestants' fledgling university) into the new National University of Zaire. Even more offensive to the church was the announcement that branches of the JMPR (party youth organization) had to be established in the seminaries. After weeks of tension and closure of the seminaries, in April 1972 the bishops accepted JMPR cells on the condition that their party links pass through the church hierarchy.

Another battle took place over the concept of authenticity, which the Catholic hierarchy began to see as a threat to Christianity. The regime's stress on "mental decolonization" and "cultural disalienation" could be read as a veiled attack on Christianity as an import from the West, as could the appeal to the values of traditional African culture as an alternative to indiscriminate Westernization.

Authenticity also included the banning of Christian names, a measure that particularly offended the church. The Zairian bishops briefly resisted the measure, then acquiesced. The church's opposition earned Cardinal Malula attacks as a "renegade of the revolution"; he was evicted from the residence the regime had built for him and forced to leave the country for three months.

Late in 1972, the regime banned all religious publications and dissolved church-sponsored youth movements. Indoctrination of Zairian youth should be an exclusive function of the party, it was argued. The zenith of this campaign came at the end of 1974 when the religious school network was nationalized, public celebration of Christmas was banned, and the display of religious artifacts was limited to the interior of churches.

Soon thereafter, the regime began to concede tacitly that it had gone too far. The school networks eventually were returned to church management when the state proved unable to operate them effectively.

By 1976, the Catholic church had reemerged as the strongest critic of the existing sociopolitical order. Following the abandonment of the education "reforms" and of Zairianization of the economy, and the fiasco of intervention in Angola, a mood of profound demoralization settled over the country, and the church expressed the prevailing mood in a pastoral letter. Outraged, Mobutu summoned the Catholic bishops and demanded that they disavow the letter; they flatly refused.

Since that time, church-state relations have been on a see-saw. Mobutu welcomed the visits of Pope John Paul II, in May 1980 and August 1985, perhaps because they lent a reflected glory to his regime. But at other times, relations have been very bad indeed. In 1982, for example, *Le Monde* reported that Cardinal Malula and three bishops had been subjected to violent intimidation by the authorities.

The death of Cardinal Malula in 1989 removed the most prominent opponent of Mobutism. But when Mobutu called for a national dialogue, early in 1990, the Catholic bishops produced a memorandum that was sweeping in its condemnation of Mobutu's autocratic system of rule.

Monsignor Etsou, bishop of Mbandaka, was named archbishop of Kinshasa in 1990, then raised to the rank of cardinal, succeeding Malula in both posts. These decisions doubtless were motivated by the needs of the church; however, "Mobutu's bishop" appeared to have been chosen by the church over other potential successors. This impression was strengthened, early in 1991, when Etsou cancelled a proreform march in Kinshasa, and he ordered priests to keep out of politics.

Yet other currents in the church clearly still oppose Mobutu and have been in the forefront of democratization efforts. Monsignor Laurent Monsengwo Pasinya, archbishop of Kisangani, was elected president of the CNS in April 1992 and, as head of the HCR, has continued to lead negotiations aimed at political reform. Moreover, in December 1993, Zaire's Catholic bishops once again issued a public condemnation of the Mobutu regime, accusing Mobutu of using state terrorism, ethnic cleansing, and economic sabotage to destabilize the country and maintain control of the state apparatus.

The Protestants

Zaire's Protestant leaders were less resistant than the Catholics to the excesses of Mobutu's Second Republic. The Protestant churches, claiming about 24 to 28 percent of the population as communicants, acquiesced to the 1971 government-imposed merger of the various Protestant groups (analogous to the unification of the trade union movement, discussed above). The result was the Church of Christ in Zaire (Église du Christ au Zaïre—ECZ), an umbrella organization. Some Protestants welcomed this action because it gave them equal standing with the Catholics. Conservative Protestant churches and missions refused to join, only to be faced by a government law recognizing the ECZ as the only legal framework for Protestant activity in the country. Sixty-two Protestant denominations were recognized as "communities" within the ECZ. Numerically, the most important were the Baptists, the Congregationalists, the Methodists, and the Presbyterians.

Leaders of the ECZ seem to have decided that the Mobutu regime's authenticity campaign offered them an historic opportunity. Unlike the Catholics, they embraced authenticity and its leader, Mobutu. The clash between Cardinal Malula and President Mobutu, culminating in the nationalization of Lovanium University and the exile of the cardinal, seemed to compensate for the advantages Catholicism had enjoyed under Belgian colonialism. Even though they lost their own newly established university, the Free University of the Congo (Université Libre du Congo—ULC), the Protestants apparently considered that what was bad news for the Catholics necessarily was good news for them.

The Protestants remained committed to the regime until after Mobutu's announcement of a process of popular consultation.

243

Then, in February 1990, the ECZ's Executive committee for Kasai-Oriental Region submitted a memorandum in which it criticized the constitutional structure of the Second Republic, denounced the failures or abuses of the functioning of the various institutions, and proposed a series of changes. The memorandum was particularly direct in criticizing the ''excessiveness of the powers held in the hands of only one man,'' i.e., the president. What is interesting in light of subsequent events, however, is that this memorandum did not demand the replacement of the regime and made no mention of multipartyism.

A month later, the head of the ECZ submitted a memorandum to Mobutu, on behalf of the entire ECZ. The memorandum recommended that the president assume the role of ''guarantor of national unity and sovereignty, making the government responsible before the people (the parliament) for the acts it commits.'' The ECZ called for a multiparty system with a minimum of two and a maximum of three parties, affirmed that only Mobutu could guide the country through the transition to multipartyism, and promised its prayers for the success of the president's efforts.

The proposals of the Protestants were curiously similar to those made by Mobutu in his speech of April 24, notably the limitation of three parties and the placing of the president above the parties. Some observers concluded that the ECZ had been influential in shaping Mobutu's ideas, but of course it is equally possible that leaders of the ECZ were well enough informed as to what the president planned to say, three weeks later, that they were able to tailor their document to correspond to the president's plans.

Following the massacre of students on the campus of the University of Lubumbashi in May 1990, the national executive committee of the ECZ met at Goma in Nord-Kivu, where Mobutu himself was passing a considerable period of time. The committee reportedly recommended that the ECZ abstain from commenting on the Lubumbashi affair. This position was opposed by the regional leaders from Kasai-Oriental and especially by those from Shaba (of which Lubumbashi is the capital). Under the pressure of these delegations in particular, the ECZ issued a pastoral letter that went farther than any of its earlier statements in condemning the chaotic state of affairs. As to what should be done, the ECZ called for ''a general amnesty'' that would make it possible for all political tendencies to participate in a national conference.

Other Religions

The points of view of the Kimbanguist Church and of the much smaller Muslim community are similar to that of the Protestants, i.e., recognition by the Second Republic was welcome in that it gave the organizations far more status than they had previously enjoyed. As the political scene opened up in 1990, the Kimbanguists and Muslims were even slower than the Protestants to oppose the regime to which they owed so much.

Students

Students of the universities and other institutes of higher education have been politically active and influential since independence. At first, their political clout derived from their elite status (university training virtually guaranteed access to the elite). In subsequent years, with the expansion of university education, the number of students increased rapidly, outstripping employment opportunities.

Until 1968 there was a student union at each of the country's three universities and a national union, representing the three campuses as well as students overseas. By far the most influential organizations were the General Union of Congolese Students (Union Générale des Étudiants Congolais—UGEC) and the General Association of Lovanium Students (Association Générale des Étudiants de Lovanium—AGEL). The UGEC, whose leadership advocated ''scientific socialism,'' was ambivalent regarding Mobutu. It originally supported him out of dislike for Moïse Tshombe and because of Mobutu's symbolically important gestures, such as the nationalization of the Upper Katanga Mining Union (Union Minière du Haut Katanga—UMHK) and the naming of Patrice Lumumba as ''National Hero.'' Some UGEC leaders in fact joined the presidential staff. However, many student activists viewed the outcome of the UMHK conflict as a surrender, in that Mobutu ultimately was forced to reimburse many of the original owners, and found the Mobutu government too closely tied to the United States.

In 1968 UGEC was banned from Congolese universities by government order, and the youth wing of the MPR became the only officially recognized student organization. However, the student JMPR sections were allowed a degree of freedom not available in all party structures, in that they elected their officers. These elections generally pitted candidates of ethno-regional coalitions against each other, a key question being which blocks would align themselves with the favored students of Équateur, Mobutu's home region.

Over the years, student discontent continued to be expressed in manifestos, strikes, and demonstrations. There was a serious outbreak on June 4, 1969, which led to a clash between Lovanium students and security forces in which about thirty students were killed; it was commemorated in 1971 and 1977 by protest marches.

As the Second Republic drew to an end, students again were in the forefront of opposition to the regime. In February 1989, thousands of students took to the streets of Kinshasa, in reaction to the imposition of IMF-sponsored austerity measures including elimination of student bus services and 80 percent hikes in tuition fees. The government attempted, unsuccessfully, to blame the unrest on the illegal opposition party, the UDPS.

On April 6, 1990, university and high school students demonstrated on Kinshasa's Avenue de la Victoire and set several vehicles on fire. Far from calming the students, Mobutu's April 24 speech stirred them up even further. On May 7, a group of university students stopped a bus carrying several members of parliament, abused them, and cut the hair of some of them. Further demonstrations occurred in Kinshasa the following day, especially on campus. On May 9, the government announced a series of measures to deal with the wave of student unrest: expulsion of all students guilty of vandalism, introduction of legal sanctions against the same students, and organization of elections at all institutions of higher learning to choose student representatives.

Two days later, students at the University of Lubumbashi took violent action against alleged government spies in their midst. In response, security forces surrounded the campus and killed a large number of students (up to 100 according to some reports) after separating and sparing those from Équateur. This incident and the refusal of the government to allow an inquiry into it resulted in the cutoff of most international aid to Zaire.

Ethnic Groups

According to Mobutu's diagnosis, "tribalism," or ethnic politics, was one of the First Republic's major ills. The Manifesto of N'Sele and other major statements of "authentic Zairian nationalism" declared overt promotion of ethnic identity to be illegal. Steps taken against tribalism included suppression of institutional arenas in which ethnicity could be mobilized, apparent exclusion of overt ethnic patronage within the state, and prohibition of the articulation of ethnic ideologies. The first step included dismantling electoral assemblies and political assemblies, which was accomplished during the Second Republic regime's first year. The bewildering assortment of political parties—more than 200 of them had taken part in the 1965 balloting—was swept away by the stroke of a pen. They were replaced by a single party, the MPR, "the nation politically organized." The twenty-one *provincettes* were recombined, ultimately becoming eight regions (plus Kinshasa), which became mere administrative subdivisions of the recentralized state.

First Republic politicians had sustained their clientele through the open use of the resources of the state for patronage. Particular ministries had become ethnic fiefdoms, both at the central and provincial levels. Local administrators were named at the provincial level, with ethnic criteria frequently paramount. Most of these practices were swept away by the new regime's total centralization of power. The state remained a vast patrimonial domain, but the distribution of benefits was above all a presidential prerogative. Functionaries in the command hierarchy of the territorial administration were posted outside of their ethnic zones as a matter of principle. Ministers were frequently rotated, inhibiting the entrenchment of particular ethnic groups in given departments.

Ethnic associations were banned early in the Second Republic. But it is clear that they continued to exist, as was made evident on each national holiday when they were among the groups sending messages of congratulations to President Mobutu. Moreover, Mobutu was widely regarded as favoring his own ethnic group and region.

Political liberalization, following Mobutu's speech of April 1990, did not extend to recognition of ethnic political parties. Those groups denied recognition included a revived version of the Kongo ethnic party, Alliance of the Kongo People (Alliance des Bakongo—Abako) and a new party, Anamongo, which would have represented the Mongo of Équateur, Tetela-Kusu of Kasai-Oriental and Maniema, and related groups.

Nevertheless, ethnic rivalries and tensions continued to fester. Interethnic fighting in Shaba between adherents of Nguza and UFERI—primarily Lunda, the dominant ethnic group in Shaba—and Tshisekedi and UDPS supporters—primarily Luba-Kasai—erupted in August 1992 and continued sporadically thereafter. The specter of secession also arose anew, as Shaba expressed its opposition to the Tshisekedi government. The region's governor, Gabriel Kyungu wa Kumwanza, a disciple of Nguza, went so far as to recommend the expulsion of Luba-Kasai living in Shaba, and Nguza bitterly denounced the CNS (whose investigative commission had recommended that he be indicted for his role in the Shaba ethnic violence) and refused to rule out the eventual secession of the region.

Throughout 1993 violence continued in Shaba, and indigenous ethnic groups in Nord-Kivu also initiated attacks on people originally from Rwanda and Burundi, collectively known in Zaire as the Banyarwanda (see The Significance of Ethnic Identification, ch. 2). In both instances of ethnic tension, there is a history of enmity and resentment. But most observers believe that the recent violence is less historical than the result of deliberate government manipulation designed to divert popular resentment of the Mobutu regime.

In Nord-Kivu, government and security officials condoned and even instigated the attacks. In Shaba local government officials also played a major role in inciting ethnic violence. In fact, Kyungu launched a campaign known as "Katanga for the Katangese." Under its auspices, vigilante youth brigades, calling the Luba-Kasai "insects" and "foreigners" who were to blame for the misery of the true Katangan people, began attacking the homes and businesses of Luba-Kasai, in effect systematically expelling them from Shaba.

In several public appearances in late 1993, Kyungu, with the apparent approval of Nguza, reiterated calls for Shaban autonomy, threatening to pursue it immediately if Tshisekedi were to be "forced on" the nation as prime minister in a political settlement. He also repeated demands for Luba-Kasai to leave Shaba.

Observers note that Kyungu and Nguza have used both the autonomy drive and the ethnic cleansing campaign to promote their own political agenda and the interests of UFERI, to the detriment of Tshisekedi and the UDPS. Some observers also see their actions as an indication that Nguza and Kyungu, both formerly Mobutu opponents but now both part of the Birindwa government, Nguza as first deputy prime minister in charge of defense and Kyungu as governor of Shaba, have been bribed or co-opted by Mobutu. Mobutu can thus be seen as using them to reinforce his position as the only one who can hold Zaire together. Indeed, few would argue that mineral-rich Shaba is vital to Zaire's future.

Other Interest Groups

Other important interest groups include the Zairian League for Human Rights, founded in the late 1980s, and professional associations such as the Medical Association and Bar Association, which existed for decades but only acquired political significance in the freer political environment. By contrast, the National Association of Enterprises of Zaire (Association Nationale des Entreprises du Zaïre—ANEZA) has remained in the hands of close associates of Mobutu and apparently has little independent political weight.

The Media

Control of the mass media has long been a central element of Mobutu's domination of Zairian political life. Indeed, control of television and radio in particular has been critical to Mobutu's ability to survive and retain power in the early 1990s. In order to assert his authority and undercut the viability of the Tshisekedi government, Mobutu deployed military forces loyal to him to seize control of state radio and television broadcast facilities in Kinshasa, surrounding the buildings with tanks and troops. Throughout 1992 and 1993, the military also systematically attacked the offices of newspapers critical of Mobutu.

During the 1980s, "restructuring" of the press reduced the number of newspapers being issued. In the early 1990s, there were three dailies: *L'analyste, Elima,* and *Salongo,* all of Kinshasa. The Lubumbashi and Kisangani papers, formerly dailies, had become weeklies after financial problems.

In the aftermath of Mobutu's speech of April 24, 1990, the situation of the press changed dramatically. While *Salongo* retained its pro-MPR position, *Elima* became sharply critical of the regime. Although *Elima*'s editor-publisher spent some time in jail early in 1991, there can be little doubt that his courage opened the field to an independent press. A number of other papers and news magazines appeared, mainly weeklies, and vied with one another in criticizing the government. Because more than half of the population does not speak French, there are periodicals appearing in African languages as well as in French.

The only domestic news agency is the regime-controlled Agence Zaïre-Presse (AZAP). Some foreign agencies, including Agence France-Presse, Xinhau, and Reuters, also have bureaus in Kinshasa.

The regime also practices censorship of foreign media, e.g., by forbidding sale of the issue of *Jeune Afrique,* in March 1990, which carried the text of the memorandum of the Catholic bishops on reforms needed in Zaire. Mobutu virtually conceded that this ban had been ineffective, however, by referring in his April 24 speech to having taken into account "even" the bishops' memorandum.

It should be noted that newspapers and magazines serve mainly educated Zairians. The electronic media reach many more among Zaire's population of some 39.1 million. The government-owned radio network, the Voice of Zaire (La Voix du Zaïre), and regional stations could be received on approximately 3.7 million radio receivers, as of 1990. The government-operated, commercial station Zaïre Télévision broadcast from Kinshasa, and service was relayed by satellite to the cities of the interior. In 1990 there were approximately 40,000 televisions in Zaire.

Throughout the Mobutu regime, the content of radio and television news broadcasts has been tightly controlled. Television news follows the official order of protocol, meaning that all news of

249

President Mobutu, however routine, comes before any news of the prime minister, which in turn precedes any news of other ministers. At the height of the cult of personality in the late 1970s and early 1980s, each television news broadcast began with the president's face appearing, godlike, in a bank of clouds.

However, the events of 1989–90, when political change swept the communist states of Eastern Europe and reform occurred in many of Africa's party-states, made it clear that the efforts of the Zairian regime to control the flow of information to the public were ineffective. When Mobutu told Zairians that *perestroika* was not needed in their country, and people in Kinshasa made jokes about "Mobutu Sesesescu," it was clear how capable the Zairians were of following international news. The role of Brazzaville television and radio, easily picked up in Kinshasa, and of various foreign shortwave radio stations, also heard elsewhere in Zaire, seems to be crucial in this respect.

Foreign Policy

Relations with the West

Zairian political scientist Georges Nzongola-Ntalaja argues that "the United States eventually replaced Belgium as the major arbiter of Zaire's destiny, but continues to deal with Zairian affairs within a multilateral strategy of imperialism in which Belgium and France are its key partners." For Crawford Young, in contrast, Mobutu's survival has been due in large measure to his success in multiplying external patrons. These two views, only partly contradictory, illuminate two aspects of the foreign relations of Mobutu's Zaire, which is both dependent and uncontrollable.

The Mobutu regime has long enjoyed, and is perceived as depending on, the support of Western powers: first Belgium, then France, and then also the United States. Because of its size, mineral wealth, and strategic location, Zaire was able to capitalize on Cold War tensions to garner support from the West. In the interest of maintaining stability in Central Africa and in exchange for his support for their foreign policy goals in Angola, Western powers rewarded Mobutu with substantial economic and military assistance and for the most part maintained silence in the face of growing evidence of the abuses of his regime. In the early 1990s, however, with Zaire facing severe internal turmoil, and with the ending of the Cold War superpower rivalry in Africa between the United States and the former Soviet Union, the country's main Western allies, reversing earlier positions, have put pressure on

Mobutu to improve his human rights record and to institute multiparty democracy.

Relations with Belgium

Belgo-Zairian relations have been on a roller coaster throughout the Mobutu years, in part because of disputes involving the substantial Belgian commercial and industrial holdings in the country. Also contributing to the tumultuous relationship are the numbers of Zairian students who continue to congregate in Belgium and the persistent symbols of the former colonial relationship, which remain highly charged for both Zairians and Belgians. The coup of November 1965 was interpreted by some observers as having been actively supported by Belgian military officers in Mobutu's entourage. Others noted that the coup was a loss for Belgium in that it prevented the return to power of Moïse Tshombe, the most reliable defender of Belgian interests in the ex-colony.

In any case, Belgo-Congolese relations were cordial until Mobutu raised the question of revising the Convention of February 6, 1965, which supposedly settled the *contentieux belgo-congolais,* i.e., the bundle of disputes concerning assets and debts of the former colony. Belgium rejected the demand to revise the convention but agreed to reopen negotiations, because it had some unsatisfied demands of its own. When bilateral negotiations failed to produce substantive results, the Congo acted unilaterally on July 13, 1966, breaking off the negotiations, freezing the assets of certain Belgian organizations, and seizing a number of their properties in Kinshasa.

Relations with the Belgian-controlled mining company UMHK also deteriorated in early 1966. On June 7, the government ruled that the headquarters of all enterprises operating in the country must be transferred to the Congo and promulgated a law, called the Bakajika Law, which in effect cancelled concessions granted before independence. All titleholders wishing to continue in the country were given thirty days in which to introduce a request for renewal of title.

Discussions with the Belgian government and UMHK continued until December 1966, when the Congo decided to break off the talks. On December 23, when UMHK announced its refusal to transfer its headquarters to Kinshasa, the government suspended copper exports and blocked the transfer of the mining company's funds. On January 2, 1967, Kinshasa authorities announced formation of the state-owned company, General Quarries and Mines (Générale des Carrières et des Mines—Gécamines) to replace UMHK. In February 1967, Gécamines signed a technical cooperation agreement with a sister company of the former UMHK, and copper exports were resumed. Although the matter of indemnities for UMHK properties remained in suspense, the accord marked a turning point in relations.

Belgium subsequently took a number of steps to ensure closer relations with the former colony. In early June 1968, President Mobutu and his family were received as houseguests of the Belgian king and queen, the first such visit by statesmen from the new nation since 1960. The two governments signed a convention for scientific and technical cooperation on August 23, 1968, and the minister of state for foreign affairs and foreign trade announced the release of certain Belgian funds that had been blocked in the Congo since 1960. During a return visit by King Baudouin and Queen Fabiola in June 1970, a treaty of friendship was signed.

In the early 1970s, the relationship periodically soured over various issues. But starting in 1976 both sides made efforts to move closer. A new cooperation agreement was signed in March, and Zaire promised to compensate Belgians who had lost assets under the Zairianization policy. Zaire later allowed foreigners whose property had been expropriated to recover 60 percent of their assets, leading to a Belgian renewal of interest in investment. Improved relations notwithstanding, Mobutu complained that students and exiles hostile to the regime were allowed to publish and be active in Belgium.

During the second Shaba invasion in 1978, Belgium sent paratroopers, as did the French, to rescue the stranded Europeans at Kolwezi. Planning to negotiate with the FLNC rebels, the Belgians proceeded cautiously, landing their forces at Kamina, more than 200 kilometers away. Their hand was forced, however, when the French preceded them by landing directly at Kolwezi and counterattacking. Fearing the extension of French influence in their former domain, the Belgians promoted the formation of a joint African defense force to repel future attacks by Zairian dissidents.

Despite such support, by 1989 Zaire apparently was closer to a total break with its former colonial ruler than at any time since the crisis at independence. In November 1988, Belgium had offered to postpone for ten years the due dates of state-to-state loans and to make new arrangements concerning Zaire's guaranteed commercial debt to Belgium. However, this relatively liberal stance toward Zaire was criticized in the Belgian parliament and especially in the press, where Mobutu was depicted as an autocrat who had led his country into economic ruin. In response, Zaire renounced all measures of reduction of its debt undertaken by Belgium. All Zairians with property in Belgium were to dispose of it or transfer it out of Belgian territory. By the end of the academic year, every Zairian studying in Belgium would have to leave.

Zaire then escalated the conflict by terminating the treaties governing Belgian aid to Zaire, calling for an inventory of all specific aid agreements and termination of all those that did not contribute to the development of Zaire, and reopening the *contentieux belgo-congolais*. Belgium replied that the *contentieux* had been definitively settled and that it was suspending cooperation with Zaire, although pending aid projects would be completed.

The Francophone Summit held in Dakar in late May 1989 provided Zaire with considerable debt relief and also brought its dispute with Belgium nearer to resolution. The highlight of the meeting was French president François Mitterrand's announcement of the cancellation of US$2.6 billion of debts from thirty-five African states. Attracting less attention, but of more direct importance to Zaire, which accounted for 80 percent of the US$500 million of guaranteed debt owed to Belgian banks by developing countries, were the debt relief plans announced by Belgium's premier, Wilfried Martens, at the summit.

Suddenly, in July, the crisis was over, and Belgo-Zairian relations were back to "normal." During a ceremony in Rabat on July 26, President Mobutu and Premier Martens signed an agreement that formally ended the dispute between the two countries. The accord wrote off nearly US$277.7 million in commercial and government debt and rescheduled the remaining commercial debt of US$296.7 million. Relations between Belgium and its former colony were cordial once more. They stayed that way for about a year, then worsened again over the killings at the University of Lubumbashi in May 1990, in the aftermath of which Belgium cut off all but humanitarian aid. Mobutu retaliated by expelling 700 Belgian technicians and closing all but one Belgian consular office in Zaire. In October 1991, Belgium dispatched troops to Zaire to help restore order and protect foreign nationals following a mutiny and rampage by paratroopers in Kinshasa in September 1991. But Belgium increasingly began to voice criticism of the Mobutu regime's human rights abuses and lack of democratization. Moreover, there was a growing consensus among most Belgian politicians in favor of the departure of President Mobutu from office.

In late 1992, Belgium, along with France and the United States, expressed official support for the Tshisekedi government, despite fears that its power was more apparent than real. Belgium also showed some cautious interest in resuming aid to Zaire if democratization continued and if Zaire received IMF and World Bank backing for its economic program. But no such resumption appeared likely at the end of 1993.

In response to another wave of violence in Zaire in early 1993, Belgium again sent troops to Zaire to evacuate its nationals. However, Mobutu refused to permit the Belgian forces to enter Zaire, forcing them to remain in Brazzaville. In the aftermath of the violence, in February 1993, Belgium joined France and the United States in voicing continued support for the Tshisekedi government and democratic forces in Zaire. The three nations demanded that Mobutu live up to his agreement and transfer power to the Tshisekedi government. They subsequently refused to recognize the rival Birindwa government appointed by Mobutu in March 1993. Nevertheless, Belgium, France, and the United States have stopped short of taking stronger action to oust Mobutu, such as confiscating his assets abroad—a measure advocated by the European Parliament in early 1993—or imposing economic sanctions on the regime. In July 1993, Belgium did send a pointed diplomatic message to Mobutu by not including him among those invited to attend the funeral of King Baudoin I, with whom Mobutu had enjoyed a good relationship prior to 1990.

Relations with France

In recent years, Zaire has taken pride in its standing as the second most populous French-speaking country, after France itself, and has developed its relations with France as an alternative to the thornier relationship with Belgium. During the First Republic, France and its former colonies tended to side with conservatives and federalists in the former Belgian colony, against Patrice Lumumba and the radical, unitarist forces. In December 1963, after the Katangan secession had been defeated, France signed a treaty of cultural and technical cooperation with Zaire.

Links with France were strengthened after Mobutu's coup of 1965. His first major initiative in African regional policy was the creation of a Union of the States of Central Africa (Union des États d'Afrique Centrale—UEAC), which initially linked Zaire to the two least advantaged states of former French Equatorial Africa, namely Chad and the Central African Republic, but aimed to form a pole of attraction for other states. The French apparently took seriously the threat the new organization posed to the Customs Union of Central African States (Union Douanière des États de l'Afrique Centrale—UDEAC) and launched a diplomatic counterattack. French emissaries prevailed upon the Central African Republic to withdraw from the UEAC, which then limped along for several years as a partnership of Chad and Zaire, which lack a common border.

Under France's President Charles de Gaulle, who had been interested in the continent for many years, African affairs became part of the "reserved domain" of the president. This quasi-constitutional arrangement continued under de Gaulle's successors and led to the development of personal diplomacy, including state visits, working visits, and so-called "personal visits," a style of diplomacy that Mobutu found very congenial.

At the beginning of 1971, French finance minister Valéry Giscard d'Estaing visited Zaire, where he met with Mobutu. This visit initiated a personal relationship between Mobutu and Giscard d'Estaing, which continued and developed after the latter became president. Starting in 1973, France became an important military partner of Zaire. Mobutu ordered Mirage jet fighters, Puma helicopters, and other items from France, and the following year the two countries signed an accord on "technical military cooperation" (see Foreign Influences, ch. 5).

The election of Giscard d'Estaing, in May 1974, as successor to President Georges Pompidou, led to a reaffirmation of France's African role. Giscard d'Estaing visited Kinshasa a year later and received a triumphal welcome from over 1 million Zairians. Observers noted that Giscard d'Estaing was being warmly welcomed in part because Mobutu was distancing himself somewhat from Belgium and from the United States. Speaking to the leadership of the MPR, the French president called for a meeting of copper producers and consumers. Zaire reportedly agreed to grant a French company new prospecting rights for copper in Zaire, in exchange for which France would accord Zaire a moratorium on repayment of debts. And France announced it would equip Zaire with an ultra-modern satellite telecommunications system. The radio and television installations of the Voice of Zaire, the largest in Africa, built by French companies with French government aid, opened in 1976. Since then, France has continued to devote a major portion of its aid to Zaire to the communications sector.

When the FLNC invaded Shaba Region in 1977 and the Belgians and Americans hesitated to assist Mobutu, France stepped in. The French government reportedly responded to Mobutu's call for help by asking King Hassan II of Morocco to supply troops, so that the conflict would appear to be settled "among Africans." Obviously, however, France's role in transporting the Moroccans to Zaire was crucial. During the second Shaba invasion in 1978, France upstaged Belgium, sending its Foreign Legion paratroopers straight to Kolwezi while the Belgians landed at Kamina. Thereafter, France trained and advised two Zairian airborne brigades. Again in 1989, France upstaged Belgium, when President François

Mitterrand announced at the Francophone Summit that his country was writing off debt totalling US$2.6 billion owed by thirty-five of the world's poorest countries, including Zaire. The subsequent Belgian announcement that much of Zaire's debt would be written off or rescheduled appeared anticlimactic.

France was slower than Belgium or the United States to condemn the Mobutu regime or to cut off support. It did not, for example, cut off aid following the killing of students at Lubumbashi in May 1990—a step taken by Belgium, the EC, Canada, and the United States. France and Belgium both sent troops to restore order and protect foreign nationals in the aftermath of a mutiny and violence by unpaid paratroopers in Kinshasa in September 1991. Then, as events unfolded in Zaire, France, too, cut off economic aid to Zaire in October 1991. In addition, the French government, together with Belgium and the United States, in 1992 put pressure on President Mobutu's government to proceed with the national conference and to hold multiparty legislative elections that year.

In August 1992, France warmly endorsed the Tshisekedi government, exhibiting far fewer reservations on its viability than Belgium and the United States. The prospect of renewed French aid to Zaire also was addressed.

But 1993 immediately introduced new tensions into relations between France and Zaire. During rioting by Zairian military personnel that began in January 1993, the French ambassador to Zaire was killed, apparently in an act of random violence. French troops were sent to Zaire to evacuate French nationals. In the aftermath of the violence, France joined Belgium and the United States in demanding that Mobutu live up to his agreement and transfer power to the Tshisekedi government. Like Belgium and the United States, France also has steadfastly refused to recognize the Mobutu-appointed Birindwa government. But all three Western nations have stopped short of taking stronger action against Mobutu. Indeed, France, even more than Belgium or the United States, is regarded as unwilling to impose economic sanctions on the Mobutu regime or to confiscate Mobutu's assets, believing that any strong actions against Mobutu could harm French interests in Zaire.

Taking advantage of the West's indecision and lack of resolve, Mobutu enjoyed some diplomatic successes in 1993, particularly at the October 1993 Francophone Summit in Mauritius. According to some reports, Mobutu definitely made his presence felt. Far from being treated as a pariah, he stood next to Mitterrand at the official ceremonies. Moreover, Mitterrand received him at a meeting along with leaders of Rwanda, Burundi, and Congo. The official

French line was that Mitterrand had agreed to the meeting only to encourage Mobutu to put off elections in order to allow the opposition more time to organize. But some observers saw the meeting as an indication of a French softening toward Mobutu. Earlier in the year, French permission for Mobutu to enter France in order to receive dental treatment was similarly viewed. But in that instance the public outcry was so great that France was forced to back down and denied Mobutu a visa for any subsequent visits to France.

In September 1993, a new French ambassador arrived in Kinshasa. The appointment made France one of the few Western nations to maintain normal diplomatic relations with Zaire. Most other countries had reduced representation to the chargé d'affaires level.

Later in 1993, there were reports that France had tired of Tshisekedi's "intransigence" and no longer supported him as prime minister. There seems to be some evidence that French support for the Tshisekedi government is not unequivocal. Indeed, French statements appeared to offer general support for transitional political forces rather than specific support for Tshisekedi.

Relations with the United States

By most accounts, the United States was involved in both the death of Lumumba and the coup of 1965, which brought Mobutu to power, although the extent of this involvement is not certain. In any case, because of his longstanding relations with the American intelligence community, Mobutu was very aware of United States backing both as a resource and as a handicap.

Zaire generally received firm American support in the late 1960s and found American influence helpful in various economic and political disputes. The promulgation of a generous investment code in 1969 and a moderate political stance lured extensive foreign, including American, investment, and a substantial program of United States aid was continued. Mobutu returned from a visit to the United States in 1970 with pledges of substantial new investment. Relations continued to be warm until the Zairianization decree of November 30, 1973, which led to the transfer of a large number of foreign-owned enterprises, including facilities owned by international oil companies, into Zairian hands. Thereafter, relations were chilly.

But in 1975, the United States and Zaire found themselves supporting the same faction in the Angolan civil war (see Regional Relations, this ch.). The United States, apparently deciding that it needed a stable Zaire for political and economic reasons and sensing the potential for Zaire to support United States strategic interests in sub-Saharan Africa, promoted the relationship with Zaire.

Secretary of State Henry Kissinger's first official trip to Africa in April 1976 included a long visit to Kinshasa.

The Carter administration, which had declared its number-one foreign policy objective to be the promotion of human rights, posed a problem for the Mobutu regime, with its poor human rights record. For the first time, criticism of Mobutu by members of Congress and by voluntary agencies was met with some sympathy by the United States president. However, the skeptical attitude toward the Zairian government was partially reversed by Shaba I and Shaba II. On the occasion of the second invasion in 1978, President Jimmy Carter supported Mobutu's accusations of Cuban and Soviet involvement, even though no hard evidence was presented. But the United States refused to become involved militarily and sent only nonlethal military supplies, such as medical and transportation equipment. In 1980 the House of Representatives (concerned over human rights violations and the misuse of United States aid) voted to end all military assistance to Zaire; but the Senate reinstated the funds, reacting to pressure from Carter and American business interests in Zaire.

The election of the more conservative Ronald Reagan as United States president was well received in Zaire, and in fact United States concerns about Mobutu's human rights record became muted. Moreover, Mobutu again was seen as providing useful services to the United States in its struggle against the Soviet Union and Soviet allies such as Libya and Angola. The domestic context in the United States had changed, however, in that an increasing number of American groups had become opposed to administration policy toward Zaire.

As United States-Zaire relations became more visible in Washington, Mobutu countered by becoming more active in promoting a positive image of himself and his country. Two Washington lobbying firms with ties to the Reagan administration received hefty contracts from Mobutu.

Nevertheless, in November 1990, Congress cut military and economic aid (except for some humanitarian aid) to Zaire, crystallizing the longstanding division between Congress and the executive branch and between liberals and conservatives on Zaire policy. As it adjourned, Congress denied the Bush administration's request for US$4 million in military aid and stipulated that US$40 million in economic aid be funneled through humanitarian agencies not affiliated with the Zairian government. Its decision was based on human rights violations—the September 1990 Lubumbashi massacre in particular—and accusations that Mobutu's vast wealth was largely stolen from the Zairian people.

Mobutu meets with President George Bush at the White House, June 1989.
Courtesy The White House (David Valdez)

By 1992 the United States-Zaire relationship had reached a turning point. The end of the Cold War had diminished the strategic significance of Zaire to the United States, and events in Zaire since 1990 had made it clear that Mobutu's days in power were numbered. In 1991–92, the United States, together with Belgium and France, attempted to promote peaceful political change in Zaire, by pressuring Mobutu to oversee the transition to democratic government and to depart voluntarily. The Zairian opposition, however, still perceived this approach as a continued ''propping up'' of the Mobutu regime and called for an unequivocal United States rejection of Mobutu, which was not forthcoming.

In October 1992, the United States joined Belgium and France in extending official support to the Tshisekedi government. The United States also reiterated its support for the national conference and its hope that the conference would lead ultimately to fair and free elections.

Since that time, the United States has continued to support the legitimacy of the Tshisekedi government and to insist that the Mobutu government live up to its promise to turn over real power to that government. It has consistently denounced Mobutu's obstruction of the transition process and has refused to recognize the rival Birindwa government. Moreover, the Clinton administration has taken several concrete steps to show its displeasure with the

Mobutu regime. At the end of 1993, the United States still had not replaced its ambassador to Zaire, who was reassigned in March 1993. The United States also refused to allow Zaire's central bank governor into the United States to attend a World Bank-IMF meeting and has made it clear that Mobutu is not welcome in the United States. Nevertheless, the United States has stopped short of taking or even advocating harsher measures against the regime, such as the imposition of economic sanctions or the confiscation of Mobutu's assets abroad. As such, in the view of some observers the United States has put only very limited pressure on Mobutu to step down. Many see this policy as an indication that the United States still regards Mobutu as a stabilizing factor, a viewpoint that would explain United States acceptance of Mobutu as part of the transition process in Zaire. The United States-brokered political accord that accompanied the Transitional Act permitted President Mobutu to remain as titular head of state and thus a legitimate institution of government, albeit with limited powers. One unintended effect of this arrangement has been to confer some legitimacy on Mobutu and thus allow him to obstruct the transition process and the functioning of the legitimate government under Tshisekedi.

Throughout 1993 the United States continued to urge the various political forces in Zaire to continue negotiating, apparently believing that ongoing negotiations will eventually lead to a power-sharing compromise. It appears increasingly likely that the United States would accept a so-called ''neutral administration'' replacing both the Mobutu-appointed government and the Tshisekedi government.

Relations with the Communist World

Mobutu's Zaire had cooler relations with the Soviet Union than with most other major states, the coolness being a remnant of the First Republic, when the Soviet Union attempted to assist Lumumba in his efforts to reconquer secessionist Kasai and Katanga in July–September 1960. Mobutu expelled Soviet and Czechoslovak diplomats and personnel when he first seized power on September 14. Nikita S. Khrushchev then tried unsuccessfully to use the ouster of Lumumba as the catalyst for a Soviet-Afro-Asian voting bloc in the UN and an assault on the position of the UN's secretary general, Dag Hammarskjöld. After this double defeat, the Soviet Union was left in a marginal position, with little influence in Zaire (see The Crisis of Decolonization, ch. 1).

The wave of Lumumbist ''second independence'' rebellions that swept the country in 1963–65 seemed to offer an opportunity for an expanded Soviet role. In January 1964, as Chinese-trained

Lumumbist Pierre Mulele began his insurgency in Kwilu, all personnel of the Soviet embassy were expelled from Zaire, on the grounds of complicity (probably fictitious) with the rebellion. In fact, Soviet support for the insurgents was largely rhetorical. The Soviet Union eventually began to supply significant aid to the secessionists, overland from Sudan. But after several truckloads of arms had been stolen by rebels in southern Sudan and turned against the Sudanese government, Khartoum cut off the route to Zaire. During 1965 most communist aid to the rebellions came from China and Cuba (uncoordinated with the Soviet Union).

The Soviet Union initially reacted very negatively to Mobutu's 1965 coup, denouncing the "American grip on the country." However, the nationalization of UMHK and the reorientation of the new regime's African policy led to more positive assessments by Soviet spokesmen.

In 1967 negotiations between Zaire and the Soviet Union led to the reestablishment of normal relations between the two countries, and a new Soviet ambassador presented his credentials early in 1968. Formal ties with the Soviet Union were useful, as Mobutu, still closely linked to the United States, attempted to present an image of nonalignment. However, the chief utility of a Soviet presence was still to provide a visible scapegoat; Soviet diplomats were expelled in 1970 and 1971, on the grounds that they had fomented unrest among university students and carried out other "subversive activities."

When Mobutu developed ambitions for a leadership role in Africa and the Third World, he turned first to China rather than the Soviet Union, as a symbol of his nonalignment. In a sense, this move foreclosed the possibility of warmer ties to the Soviets, given the level of animosity between the communist superpowers. There are indications that a state visit to Moscow was in the planning stages late in 1974 but failed to materialize when the Soviet Union declined to provide the extravagant ceremonials to which Mobutu was becoming accustomed. Instead, the Zairian leader made a sudden visit to the Democratic People's Republic of Korea (North Korea) and China at the time originally announced for the visit to the Soviet Union.

The Portuguese coup of 1974 and the struggle for control of Angola placed Zaire and the Soviet Union in conflict once again. Not anticipating heavy Soviet and Cuban backing for the Popular Movement for the Liberation of Angola (Movimento Popular de Libertação de Angola—MPLA), Mobutu took the fateful decision to commit Zairian army units to Angola, backing the National Front for the Liberation of Angola (Frente Nacional de Libertação de

Angola—FNLA) of Holden Roberto. Zairian forces probably were operating in Angola as early as March 1975. In November 1975, the Zairian-FNLA column was almost in sight of Luanda—where an FNLA government would have been installed—when it encountered Cuban troops. The Cubans inflicted a crushing defeat on the men of Mobutu and Holden, who fled back into Zaire, and the MPLA governed Angola alone.

The fact that the Soviet Union and Zaire had backed opposite sides in the Angolan civil war had a decisive impact on Zaire's foreign policy for the next decade or more. Mobutu's claim to African leadership was foreclosed, as most African governments sided with the MPLA regime. Economic and military needs pushed Mobutu back into the arms of the United States and its allies, and Mobutu took a pro-American stance on such matters as Israel's position in international organizations.

In 1977 and 1978, Zaire was invaded by a few thousand men of the FLNC (see External Threats to Regime Stability, ch. 1). These men had come from Angola, where they had been based since the early 1970s, and perhaps had undergone Cuban training there. It has been alleged that the German Democratic Republic (East Germany) was assigned the job of destabilizing Zaire, on behalf of the Soviet Union, and that the FLNC was the chosen instrument. Both in 1977 and 1978, Mobutu chose to blame the invasions on the Soviet Union and Cuba, but no evidence supporting Soviet or Cuban involvement ever came to light.

Since the Shaba invasions, there has been little significant shift in Zaire-Soviet relations. In 1986 Mobutu made an effort to "play the Soviet card," i.e., to promote the idea of closer relations with the Soviets as a ploy in his much more important struggle to maintain or augment the flow of aid and investment from the West. In sum, the Soviet Union, before it broke up into independent republics, remained of symbolic importance to Zaire and occasionally served either as a scapegoat for difficulties that were entirely or mainly domestic or as a threat to the relationship between Zaire and its Western partners.

Relations with China were cold at first because of Chinese aid to Mulele and other rebels, and Mobutu opposed seating China at the United Nations. By 1972, however, he began to view China as an important counterweight to the Soviet Union. Zaire recognized China along with North Korea and East Germany in November 1972, and in the following year Mobutu paid a state visit to Beijing from which he returned with promises of US$100 million in economic aid. The friendship with China deepened when the two countries found themselves supporting enemies of the MPLA in the Angolan civil war. During a second state visit to Beijing in 1974, Mobutu and Chairman Mao Zedong discussed further aid to the FNLA. Mobutu appeared to have been so impressed by what he saw in China and in North Korea that his rhetoric became noticeably more radical. He instituted the takeover of schools by the party and began advocating the establishment of agricultural cooperatives.

After the defeat of the FNLA, China became more circumspect in its dealings with Zaire, but Mobutu continued to emphasize his ties to China as a counterpart to his close relations to the United States and South Africa in the eyes of the world. During the second Shaba invasion, China sided firmly with Mobutu, accusing the Soviet Union and Cuba of destabilizing Central Africa by their interference. In 1983 Zaire received partial relief from its massive debt burden, as Premier Zhao Ziyang, during his eleven-nation African tour, announced that China was cancelling Kinshasa's US$100 million debt. The money borrowed would be reinvested in joint Chinese-Zairian projects. In the late 1980s, China provided Zaire with some military equipment and training. Following the cutoff of Western aid to Zaire in 1991, China is reported to have become more active in Zaire. An estimated 1,000 Chinese technicians reportedly were working on agricultural and forestry projects in Zaire in the early 1990s.

Because of the alleged support by Cuba and East Germany of the Shaba invasion, Zaire suspended relations with those countries in the spring of 1977. Relations with Cuba were restored in 1979, in order to facilitate Zairian participation in the nonaligned summit held in Havana in September of that year. Relations with North Korea cooled after the country recognized the MPLA regime, and North Korean military instructors left Zaire in the spring of 1977.

Romania remained one of Zaire's closest foreign partners until the fall and execution of Nicolae Ceauşescu in 1989. Part of the attraction doubtless was the independence of the Ceauşescu regime vis-à-vis Soviet hegemony. Mobutu seems also to have admired the cult of personality surrounding his Balkan counterpart. Relations were not just state-to-state but also party-to-party between the MPR and the Romanian Communist Party. The fall of Ceauşescu, vividly presented on Kinshasa television, reportedly made a strong impression upon Mobutu, whose announcement of democratization followed shortly thereafter. Popular humor in the capital speculated upon the future of "Mobutu Sesesescu."

Regional Relations

Any African state must be concerned about relations with its neighbors, since national borders usually divide ethnic groups, and neighboring states often shelter opposition parties. Zaire's immediate environment poses a particular challenge in that Zaire borders on nine other states.

Following the coup of 1965, one of Mobutu's early objectives was to transform Zaire's position in regional politics. He dispatched a former Lumumbist to Ghana to explain and justify the coup. Kwame Nkrumah (shortly before he himself was overthrown) indicated that he was prepared to accept and support the Mobutu regime, if it would commit itself to nonalignment and support a pro-African policy.

A series of gestures during 1966–67 reinforced the nationalist image of the regime. Zaire broke relations with Portugal and declared Lumumba a "national hero." The Bakajika Law and the UMHK struggle conveyed a sense of assertion of Zairian economic rights. These moves helped to set the stage for the Mobutu regime's acceptance into the African family of nations, symbolized by the acceptance by the Organization of African Unity (OAU) of Mobutu's invitation to meet at Kinshasa in 1967. This acceptance in turn guaranteed that the fragmented remnants of the rebellious forces would be denied sanctuary.

By 1968 Zairian ambitions began to expand, the abortive creation of the UEAC forming the first major initiative. Mobutu assumed an active role in African diplomacy. He served as a member of the multinational OAU team designed to bring about an end to the Nigerian civil war (1967–70) and then offered his services to reconcile Nigeria with the four African states that had recognized the secessionist state of Biafra. He proposed his services to ease the tense relations between Tanzania and Uganda in 1971. Mobutu also mediated disputes between Burundi and Tanzania, created by border violations by Burundi forces assaulting Hutu refugees in Tanzanian territory. In 1973 he spent no fewer than 150 days outside Zaire, visiting twenty-six countries, including fourteen in Africa.

Mobutu's active regional diplomacy was based on intimate personal relationships with other heads of state. Regular "tripartite" consultations were held with the leaders of Rwanda and Burundi. The Zaire-Rwanda-Burundi relationship was formalized in 1976 as the Economic Community of the Great Lakes Countries (Communauté Économique des Pays des Grands Lacs—CEPGL). In 1972–75 there were also frequent triangular summits with the leaders of Tanzania and Zambia, largely devoted to southern African problems. Mobutu gave strong backing to Ugandan president Idi Amin Dada in his quest for African recognition and opposed the transfer of the 1971 OAU summit from Kampala.

In the early years of the Second Republic, the only neighboring state with which relations were periodically troubled was Congo. Kinshasa did not easily forgive Brazzaville's role in harboring rebel headquarters and training camps. Amicable relations had barely been resumed when they were poisoned again by the summary execution in Zaire of former rebel leader Pierre Mulele, who left Brazzaville under an amnesty guarantee. A new crisis broke out in 1972 when Zaire provided sanctuary and some arms for a small group of Congolese rebels who were largely eliminated by early 1973. Through the entire period, the fact that Zaire supported the FNLA while Congo supported the MPLA in Angola was a source of tension. Despite all these irritants, Mobutu developed a close personal relationship with Congo's Marien Ngouabi, which was maintained with his successors.

Involvement in the Angolan Civil War

The Angola crisis, set off by the Portuguese coup of 1974, was a turning point in Zairian foreign policy. The prospect of imminent independence for Angola represented both a threat and an opportunity from Mobutu's perspective. Since 1960 Zaire had had close ties to the FNLA, whose ethnic base was among the Kongo of the area bordering Zaire. Many of the FNLA leaders, including Holden Roberto, had lived in Kinshasa most of their lives. Roberto had quasi-kinship ties with Mobutu through his second wife, who originated in the same village as Mobutu's then-spouse (though she was not Mama Mobutu's sister, as the press often asserted). The FNLA was allowed to run military camps on Zairian territory.

By contrast, Zaire's relations with the Marxist-oriented MPLA had been consistently hostile. Since 1963 the MPLA's main external headquarters had been in Congo. The MPLA guerrilla effort was seriously handicapped by Mobutu's denial of transit rights from its Congo bases into the main part of Angola.

These relationships had developed in the context of the Cold War. The FNLA had received sporadic United States support, which resumed after the Portuguese coup. The Soviet Union had supported the MPLA, although the relationship was in abeyance in April 1974. Zaire's close relations with China, beginning in 1973, and China's anti-Soviet orientation, led to a substantial Chinese military and diplomatic commitment to the FNLA.

The dominant African diplomatic position was that only a coalition among the three major liberation movements—MPLA, FNLA, and National Union for the Total Independence of Angola (União Nacional para a Independência Total de Angola—UNITA)—

could bring a peaceful transition to Angolan independence. While formally supporting the consensus, Zairian diplomacy really aimed at excluding the MPLA from a share of power, thus ensuring a friendly Angolan regime.

In 1974, when Mobutu's strategy took form, he held what looked like considerable advantages. The FNLA, with 2,000 guerrillas inside Angola and 10,000 to 12,000 in the Zairian camps, had the largest military force. The new Chinese alliance could be used to rapidly augment FNLA armaments, and by mid-year a large flow of Chinese equipment to the FNLA camps was under way. The MPLA was divided, and one of its factions might be (and was) wooed away. Although Zambia and Tanzania could not be expected to support the FNLA, they might be attracted to some combination including UNITA and an MPLA faction. The lethal competition between UNITA and MPLA forces in eastern Angola seemed to offer a possible Zaire-FNLA-UNITA alliance. The United States had a long-standing antipathy to the MPLA and could be counted upon to mount an effort to block its bid for power. South Africa also was disposed to assure a flow of military supplies to UNITA and the FNLA to prevent an MPLA victory. Finally, Zaire had a long common border with Angola and a large army that it could employ on the side of the FNLA.

Most of the supposed advantages proved illusory. The FNLA and Zairian forces were ineffective in the decisive phases of the war. The Soviet Union, unwilling to see an easy American and Chinese victory, began armed deliveries at an accelerating rate from early 1975. The unforeseen Cuban military intervention began with advisers in the summer of 1975, but involved combat troops in the crucial months of November and December 1975. Meanwhile, the exposure of CIA involvement and especially the full-scale invasion by South African military units in October 1975 led to OAU backing for the MPLA. By mid-1975, the Chinese apparently concluded the risks were too high and pulled out.

Diplomatically as well as militarily, Zaire's defeat could hardly have been more complete. The MPLA was in power in Angola, buttressed by a strong Soviet-Cuban presence, which had been legitimated in African eyes by United States and South African intervention. Zaire again was a pariah state in tropical Africa. The residual costs of the Angolan adventure were illustrated when Zaire was rebuffed in its attempt to join the Southern African Development Coordination Conference (SADCC), formed in 1980 after Zimbabwe's independence in order to reduce regional dependency on South Africa. Subsequently, Zaire's bid to join the

Preferential Trade Area (PTA) for Central and Southern Africa was blocked by Angola.

In 1983 Zaire became a charter member of an alternative economic union, the Economic Community of the States of Central Africa (Communauté Économique des États de l'Afrique Centrale—CEEAC), which brought together the five members of the UDEAC (Cameroon, Chad, Central African Republic, Congo, and Gabon), the three members of the CEPGL (Burundi, Rwanda, and Zaire), and two mini-states, Equatorial Guinea and Sao Tome and Principe. Angola sent a minister to the founding meeting but declared itself unable to join because of the civil war. As late as its sixth summit (in Kigali, Rwanda, in January 1990), the CEEAC had little to show in the way of concrete accomplishments. The conference authorized the free circulation of certain categories of citizens (mainly researchers, students, and residents of border areas) within the CEEAC community, approved measures aimed at strengthening cooperation between airlines, and gave priority to improving the roads linking Burundi and Rwanda to the Congo River port of Kisangani.

In contrast to the snub by the SADCC, a slow recovery of Zaire's reputation was reflected in its election to the UN Security Council in 1981 and again in 1989, with support from the African caucus. Zaire's troops were part of an OAU peacekeeping force in Chad in 1981–82 (and returned, at Chadian invitation, in 1983). Zaire sent 3,000 troops to Chad in July 1983 to support the French-backed government of Hissein Habré. The two countries signed a military cooperation agreement in July 1985.

Relations with Angola since the War

Relations between Mobutu's Zaire and the MPLA government in Angola have ranged from formally correct to openly hostile. An initial move toward normalization, in 1976–77, was set back by the two invasions of Shaba Region by the FLNC from bases in Angola. After the collapse of the FNLA, Zaire had been supporting Jonas Savimbi's UNITA, also supported by South Africa, against the MPLA government. Starting in 1985, the air base at Kamina in southeastern Zaire served as a transit point for American aid to UNITA fighters. In May 1986, Zambia charged that the United States was covertly supplying weapons to UNITA via Zaire, but Mobutu denied these allegations, and in July 1986, he visited Angola and declared his support for the MPLA government.

In April 1987, Zaire, Angola, and Zambia signed a declaration of intent to restore cross-border traffic on the Benguela Railway, providing an outlet to the Atlantic that is crucial to the copper industries of both Zambia and Zaire. The railroad's international functions had been effectively shut down since 1975 by UNITA operations. UNITA reportedly agreed to the resumption of traffic on condition that the railroad not be used to move arms or troops. However, continuing insecurity made it difficult to rehabilitate the rail line.

By 1988 international efforts to end the impasse over Namibian independence had led to linkage of South African withdrawal from Namibia to a phased Cuban withdrawal from Angola. But no agreement had been reached to end the fighting within Angola itself. When Mobutu went to Zambia in August to attend a conference, he found himself in an informal summit of southern African leaders, including those of Zimbabwe, Tanzania, Mozambique, and Uganda. Apparently it was put to Mobutu that his continued logistical support for UNITA was retarding progress toward Namibian independence. That same month, the chairman of the OAU called together the heads of state of Angola, Congo, Gabon, and Zaire to find a solution to the Angolan problem.

Over the next nine months, a series of meetings, bilateral as well as regional, took place, often at the level of heads of state. In the course of these meetings, Mobutu improved his relations with Angola's president, José Eduardo dos Santos, and distanced himself somewhat from UNITA. Early in May 1989, the heads of Angola, Congo, Gabon, Mozambique, Sao Tome and Principe, Zaire, Zambia, and Zimbabwe met in Luanda and announced their commitment "to end the interference in Angola's internal affairs" and "guarantee security and stability" on Angola's frontiers. They were to meet again in August.

Suddenly, however, came the Gbadolite Summit of June 22, at the time a triumph for Mobutu. The Angolan peace process seemed to have slowed, with the Luanda government still refusing to negotiate with Savimbi in person. Some days before June 22, Mobutu began inviting African heads of state to Gbadolite; eventually, seventeen of them took part. Dos Santos and UNITA's Jonas Savimbi shook hands at Gbadolite, and a declaration was signed endorsing a cease-fire and integration of UNITA leaders into the Luanda government. With the successful Gbadolite meeting behind him—and with his difficulties with Belgium and the IMF resolved at least temporarily—Mobutu flew to Washington, where he was the first African head of state to be received at the White House by President George Bush. Soon thereafter, the agreement collapsed, when it became apparent that Mobutu had misrepresented the positions of the Angolan rivals. It took another year of negotiations, this time mediated by Portugal, before UNITA and the

MPLA government were able to reach an agreement on ending their struggle of nearly two decades.

Relations with Other Neighbors

During the 1980s, the closest threats to Zaire seemed to lie to the east, because relations with Zambia and Tanzania had sunk to the lowest point since the first years of the Mobutu regime, and Burundi and Sudan seemed open to anti-Mobutu activity as well. The "rebel" attacks on Moba, on the Zairian shore of Lake Tanganyika, in 1984 and 1985 led to harsh Zairian criticism of Tanzania, Rwanda, and Burundi, which were alleged to have permitted, if not encouraged, the attacks.

Relations with Zambia were at least as bad, with several shooting incidents taking place along the frontier. In August 1984, long-standing tensions heated up when Zaire rounded up Zambians (mostly in Shaba) and announced they would be deported, in reaction to Zambia's expulsion of immigrants from Zaire and West Africa in July. Mobutu revoked the expulsion orders on August 25 and ordered government officials to release all detained Zambians, but reportedly hundreds had already fled across the border. Lusaka radio alleged that Zairian officials had tricked the Zambians by calling them to stadiums on the pretext of disseminating important information from Lusaka; they then were detained, and many were beaten.

The strains in the Zambia-Zaire relationship are linked to Zaire's position in the global economy. Smuggling from Zambia into the isolated Shaba Region of Zaire has long caused considerable tension between the two countries. In 1983 Zambia stationed troops on the border to stem the flow of contraband. Since then there reportedly have been occasional border incidents involving exchanges of gunfire between Zairian and Zambian soldiers. Late in 1984, Zaire announced creation of a Civil Guard to patrol the frontier so that such incidents would not lead directly to confrontations between the two armies. The smuggling problem remained, and in 1988 the two countries introduced strict visa controls in an attempt to deal with it. In 1989 Zaire and Zambia signed an agreement defining their common border. In early November 1991, rail traffic between Zaire's Shaba Region and Zambia resumed, following an incident reportedly provoked by Zairian troops deployed along the border.

Relations with Congo and Uganda also continued to cause problems. In 1989 Congo expelled a large number of Zairians whose status was "irregular," and Zaire responded in kind. It was thought unlikely that Congo would close the border, however, since it was so dependent upon goods imported (or smuggled) from Zaire. In the early 1990s, Congo undertook an operation designed to deport 15,000 illegal Zairian immigrants. In February 1993, a breach in relations between Zaire and Congo occurred following a ferry accident on the Congo River that resulted in the deaths of nearly 150 Zairians being deported from Congo.

Historically, Ugandan-Zairian relations have been complicated by border problems, including cross-border smuggling and disputes over fishing rights in the lakes along the border. Border incidents caused by Zairian rebel groups operating from bases in Uganda increased the strain between the two countries, as did an appearance in Zaire by former Ugandan president Idi Amin Dada in January 1989. He apparently intended to return to Uganda with an estimated 500 armed supporters who were to meet him in northeastern Zaire. Uganda requested the former president's extradition, intending to try Amin for atrocities committed during his eight-year reign. Kinshasa rejected this request because there was no extradition treaty between Uganda and Zaire. Instead, the Mobutu regime detained Amin in Kinshasa and expelled him from the country nine days later. Thereafter, relations between Kampala and Kinshasa were cool, leading to the mutual expulsion of ambassadors. On September 8, 1989, however, the two countries restored full diplomatic ties.

Throughout 1990 Ugandan and Zairian officials worked to stabilize their common border, but the failure of these meetings to achieve any progress has prompted Zaire to close the borders periodically. The border between the two countries appears likely to remain unstable for the foreseeable future.

Unrest in Zaire arising out of economic deterioration and a stalemate over political reform also contributed to the security crisis in southwestern Uganda in 1992 and 1993. Ugandan officials claimed that more than 20,000 Zairian refugees had entered Uganda, seeking refuge from marauding Zairian troops and antigovernment rebel banditry. By contrast, Zaire served as a refuge to thousands of Burundians fleeing ethnic violence in their country in 1993.

Zaire has fostered close relations with Rwanda. In October 1990, when Rwanda was invaded by Uganda-based forces of the Rwandan Patriotic Front, Belgium, France, and Zaire intervened militarily to protect the lives of foreigners and to back the Rwandan government. In February 1991, Mobutu was mandated by a regional meeting of presidents and the secretary general of the OAU to initiate a dialogue leading to a cease-fire agreement between the Rwandan government and the rebels. Representatives of the OAU, along with officials from Rwanda, Burundi, Tanzania, and Zaire, met several times in 1991 and 1992 and urged the warring parties to observe the cease-fire agreed to in March 1991, but fighting continued.

Relations with North Africa

During the 1980s, Mobutu's most bitter rival was undoubtedly Libya's Colonel Muammar Qadhafi. Speaking in Burundi in May 1985, the Libyan leader called on the Zairian population to "physically eliminate" Mobutu. On June 9, Zairian authorities announced they had dismantled a "pro-Libyan terrorist network" operating in the country and arrested four people carrying passports issued by unidentified neighboring states. Zaire's information minister said two of the four suspects were "closely linked" with bombings in March 1984, at the Voice of Zaire and the central post office in Kinshasa. The other two suspects allegedly were among twelve "Zairian terrorists trained in Libya" who had been identified by local authorities.

Libya urged the OAU, the African states, and all African nationalist forces and organizations "to adopt a serious position regarding the Mobutu regime which, it is now confirmed, is a hireling regime that conspires directly with the two racist regimes in South Africa and occupied Palestine against the security, safety, and stability of our African continent." In fact, Zaire had taken a leading role among sub-Saharan African states in breaking relations with Israel in 1973, but once Egypt and Israel had signed a peace agreement and Israel had withdrawn from the Sinai and thus from Africa, Mobutu renewed his relations with the Jewish state (in May 1982). Israel, anxious to secure a bridgehead in Africa, became a significant supplier of foreign aid to Zaire, including training and directing the Special Presidential Brigade (later the Special Presidential Division), which guards the president. Mobutu also maintained commercial ties with South Africa at least as early as 1989, although diplomatic relations were not established until September 1993.

In 1975, when Zaire intervened on the side of the FNLA, Libya favored the victorious MPLA. In Chad Mobutu favored Hissein Habré (who also was backed by Egypt and Sudan) against former President Goukouni Oueddei (backed by Libya). Zaire's contingent was small and played an inconsequential role compared to that of France, but had Zaire not intervened, the French would have appeared to be the lone bakers of Habré. Nevertheless, the Mobutu regime was acting in its own interest, because a Libyan-dominated Chad would menace both Sudan and the Central African Republic, states contiguous with Zaire. In June 1992, Zaire and Libya discussed normalizing relations between the two countries.

Mobutu was a close ally of the Sudanese regime of Jaafar an Nimeiri, which Libya opposed. The overthrow of Nimeiri, and his replacement by a regime more friendly to Libya, apparently represented a further threat to Mobutu. By 1990, however, he was on good enough terms both with the Arab-dominated government in Khartoum and John Garang's Sudanese People's Liberation Army to be able to undertake mediation between the two.

On a continental level, Mobutu took the lead in articulating the dissatisfaction of moderate sub-Saharan African states with the OAU. In July 1984, he called on those states to break away from the OAU and form a new regional organization. Although negative reactions led him to soften his position, claiming that the proposed new group would not conflict with the OAU (just as North African states can belong to the OAU and the Arab League), Mobutu continued to promote the idea for several years, even though it was anathema not only to the North Africans but also to "progressives" south of the Sahara. There is no evidence that Mobutu was promoting the split between North Africa and sub-Saharan Africa because of his ties to Israel and/or South Africa, but such a split was in the perceived interest of the latter countries.

In contrast to the apparently anti-Arab initiative of promoting a sub-Saharan African organization, Mobutu has maintained close relations with Egypt and especially with Morocco. The latter sent troops to Shaba in 1977 to suppress the FLNC invasion, and Mobutu apparently paid back this assistance by supporting Morocco's claim to the Western Sahara. In fact, Zaire boycotted the OAU from 1984 to 1986 in protest over its admission of the Saharan Arab Democratic Republic. Mobutu visited both Egypt and Morocco in April 1992 in an apparent attempt to improve ties with Arab states in the face of deteriorating relations with the West.

* * *

The best sources on politics and government in Zaire continue to be the various works of Thomas M. Callaghy, Michael G. Schatzberg, Thomas E. Turner, and Crawford Young. Of particular note are Callaghy's *The State-Society Struggle: Zaire in Comparative Perspective* and *Culture and Politics in Zaire;* Schatzberg's *The Dialectics of Oppression in Zaire, Politics and Class in Zaire,* and *Mobutu or Chaos? The United States and Zaire, 1960–1990;* and Young and Turner's *The Rise and Decline of the Zairian State.*

The Zairian human rights record, as well as its legal system, have been investigated in Makau wa Mutua and Peter Rosenblum's *Zaire: Repression As Policy—A Human Rights Report,* published by the Lawyers' Committee for Human Rights, as well as in specialized reports by Amnesty International and the United States Department of State's annual *Country Reports on Human Rights Practices.*

Up-to-date information about Zaire can be found in the annual editions of *Africa South of the Sahara;* the Economist Intelligence Unit's quarterly *Country Report: Zaire, Rwanda, Burundi* and annual *Country Profile: Zaire, Rwanda, Burundi;* issues of *Current History;* and print and broadcast articles reproduced in the Foreign Broadcast Information Service (FBIS), *Daily Report: Sub-Saharan Africa.* (For further information and complete citations, see Bibliography.)

Kuba wooden cup

THE ZAIRIAN ARMED FORCES (Forces Armées Zaïroises— FAZ) are responsible for Zaire's national security. The FAZ consists of an army, navy, air force, and gendarmerie. Zaire also has a Civil Guard that is technically not part of the FAZ, although it does play an integral security role. The army is the most important branch; the other forces are either small (navy and air force) or marginal factors in the area of national defense (gendarmerie and Civil Guard). The FAZ totalled approximately 49,100 in 1993: the army consisted of 25,000 personnel; the navy, 1,300 (including 600 marines); the air force, 1,800; and the gendarmerie, 21,000. The Civil Guard had an estimated strength of 10,000 personnel in the early 1990s.

The stated mission of both the army and the gendarmerie is to secure Zaire against external threats, but in practice these forces mainly fulfill an internal security role and serve to bolster the rule of President Mobutu Sese Seko. During the chaotic and anarchic period of the early 1990s, this role has degenerated into occasional looting and violence against the population by armed forces elements that have not been paid. In view of the role of parts of the military (and the security services) in lootings and various mutinies in the early 1990s, it is unclear what de facto or de jure chain of command exists within the FAZ. Observers speculate, however, that Mobutu has shrewdly retained the loyalty of key units by paying them regularly. Continued loyalty on the part of at least some military and security forces is apparent from their role in suppressing political dissent and thus bolstering the Mobutu regime.

Lack of coherence in the armed forces and security services, of which there is a confusing array, is not new. For example, since the dissolution of the national police force in 1972, the National Gendarmerie has functioned as a de facto police force, and its ability to perform its paramilitary role is virtually nonexistent. The Civil Guard was formed to function as a national police force in order to permit the gendarmerie to resume its stated mission as the country's first line of defense. The interaction between these two organizations has, however, never been fully defined. As a result, Zaire in essence has two competing police organizations with overlapping responsibilities.

The FAZ's lack of coherence has at times degenerated into chaos. This situation did not start at independence but was rooted in the history of the Belgian colonial armed forces, the Force Publique.

The Zairian military's lack of discipline was first displayed shortly after independence when the Force Publique mutinied against its Belgian officers. Despite the removal of the Belgian officers, and the renaming of the force as the Congolese National Army (Armée Nationale Congolaise—ANC), the disintegration of the armed forces continued.

Throughout the first five years of independence, the armed forces fragmented into several competing power centers, working for various ethnic political leaders as well as their own interests. A combination of ineffective national leadership and a chaotic political and social environment limited the ANC's ability to operate in a professional manner. As a result, the ANC was a national armed force in name only. It was not only incapable of protecting the country, but at times even threatened its existence. Only the performance of the United Nations (UN) forces in ending the 1960–63 secession of Katanga Province (now Shaba Region) kept Zaire intact.

A succession of governments proved unable to restore calm to the country until Joseph-Désiré Mobutu (subsequently Mobutu Sese Seko) seized power in a bloodless coup d'état in November 1965. From 1965 until 1970, Mobutu consolidated and expanded his power by pacifying the countryside, eliminating political and military rivals, and consolidating coercive power in his hands. Although Mobutu used the military to gain power, he did not establish a military dictatorship; instead, he relegated the armed forces to a secondary supporting role.

Throughout the early 1970s, Mobutu continued to build up his military with significant United States and Belgian assistance. Despite this effort, the armed forces, known as the FAZ from late 1971, were not much improved when Mobutu decided to commit them to support the National Front for the Liberation of Angola (Frente Nacional de Libertação de Angola—FNLA) in 1975 during the Angolan civil war. Mobutu hoped to prevent the Soviet-backed Popular Movement for the Liberation of Angola (Movimento Popular de Libertação de Angola—MPLA) from gaining power. Despite initial advances, the Zairian force was routed by Cuban and MPLA forces. Mobutu's bold adventure with a demonstrably weak force would prove disastrous eighteen months later, when a Zairian dissident group, the Front for the National Liberation of the Congo (Front pour la Libération Nationale du Congo—FLNC), backed by the now victorious MPLA, invaded Zaire in the first of two incursions of Zaire's mineral-rich Shaba Region. These invasions, in 1977 and 1978, highlighted the political and military weakness of the Mobutu regime, and only foreign intervention kept the Zairian state intact.

Zaire responded to this demonstrated lack of capability during the Shaba crises by an extensive reorganization of the military. This process, however, improved neither the discipline nor the performance of the FAZ. For example, in November 1984, the FAZ was unable to prevent a small armed band from the People's Revolutionary Party (Parti Révolutionnaire du Peuple—PRP) from taking the town of Moba on the shore of Lake Tanganyika. Although the town was retaken two days later, this action demonstrated that some portions of the country still escaped government control. Moba was again occupied by PRP partisans in June 1985, but government forces quickly retook the town. Reprisals against civilians in Moba after these incidents, particularly in 1984, were condemned by Amnesty International and served as further examples of the FAZ's lack of discipline.

Once again, Mobutu responded to the FAZ's poor performance by reforming and reorganizing the military. He forced many senior officers to resign, established the post of inspector general, and created a Civil Guard. Despite these changes, low and irregular pay, corruption, and poor morale continued to plague the armed forces and undermine their capabilities. The widespread political, economic, and social disintegration that characterized Zaire in the early 1990s further undermined military coherence and capabilities. As a result, the status of the FAZ in the early 1990s is uncertain.

National Security Environment

Through the mid-1980s, Mobutu had characterized Zaire as surrounded by a ''red belt'' of radical states supported by the Soviet Union and Libya. Except for Angola, however, these countries lack either the motivation or the militarily means to threaten Zaire seriously. In the early 1990s, Zaire's relations with even its most hostile neighbors had improved. As a consequence, Zaire does not face any serious external threats, although border flare-ups, cross-border smuggling, refugees, and mutual support of insurgent groups have caused strains between Zaire and many of its neighbors (see fig. 1; Regional Relations, ch. 4). Militarily, the most serious strains have occurred in Zaire's relations with Uganda, Tanzania, Zambia, and Angola.

Relations with Uganda at times have approached open conflict. Uganda's instability since the 1971 rise to power of Idi Amin Dada concerns Zaire, particularly because the border region between the two countries is remote and mountainous, and neither side exercises effective control over the area. A considerable amount of smuggling also occurs along the border, often resulting in violence. In response to this violence, Zaire announced in June 1988 that it would set up a naval unit on the Zairian side of Lake Edward to reinforce security and to stop smuggling and piracy. Despite the intent to keep this force on the Zairian side of the border, observers feared that Uganda might regard the measure as provocative.

Another contentious issue between the two countries is their perceived mutual support of insurgent groups. Zaire's alleged ties to Amin concerned successive Ugandan administrations. In January 1989, the Zairian government rejected an attempt by the former Ugandan president to establish residence in Zaire. Amin was expelled from Zaire, bound for Saudi Arabia, although Uganda had earlier requested his extradition to Kampala. Zaire's conflict with Uganda also concerned the activity of the Zairian insurgent group, the Congolese Liberation Party (Parti de Libération Congolaise— PLC), which operated primarily out of bases in the Ruwenzori Mountains along the Zaire-Uganda border. The organization began insurgent attacks in 1985, and during the next three years attacked several small towns along the Zairian side of the border. Although the PLC was unable to take and hold any terrain, it demonstrated Zaire's inability to control the area effectively, and the PLC's rout of small FAZ detachments highlighted the military's deficiencies.

Zaire's relations with Tanzania have been similarly strained because of Kinshasa's belief that Tanzania supported and harbored Zairian insurgents, specifically the PRP. This organization caused extreme embarrassment to the Zairian government in 1984 and again in 1985 when it captured the Zairian town of Moba along the shores of Lake Tanganyika. Although in both instances Zairian government forces were able to recapture the town a few days later, their demonstrated lack of control in integral parts of Zairian territory and the poor performance of the Zairian troops who fled before the PRP were sore points for Kinshasa. Nevertheless, although the Zairian government accused Tanzania of active complicity in these attacks, observers believed it unlikely that Dar es Salaam did more than provide safe haven for the PRP.

Much of the distrust centered on the poor relations between Mobutu and Tanzania's former president, Julius Nyerere. Mobutu opposed Nyerere's socialist orientation, and Nyerere considered Mobutu a puppet of the United States. However, Mobutu's relations with Nyerere's successor, Ali Hassan Mwinyi, seem much better, particularly because the latter stated that he would not permit insurgents to use his country as a springboard for attacks against a neighboring country. Observers believe that this remark, along with Tanzanian support for President Mobutu's efforts to mediate national reconciliation in Angola, might presage greater cooperation between the two countries.

Relations with Zambia have also been tense because of the extensive smuggling activity along the border. Also, the FLNC's use of Zambian territory during its 1978 invasion of Zaire's Shaba Region proved an irritant to bilateral relations, as did a century-old border dispute over the area between Lake Tanganyika and Lake Mweru.

In the late 1980s, however, relations between the two countries improved. Although smuggling continued to be an irritant, Zaire and Zambia settled their border dispute on September 18, 1989. In addition, Zambian support for Mobutu's efforts to mediate an end to the Angolan civil war contributed to improved relations.

Angola has presented the gravest potential threat to Zaire's national security. This threat has its roots in the support each country gave to the other's insurgent groups. Zaire supported the Angolan insurgent group, the FNLA, against the communist-backed MPLA, and after the FNLA's demise, Kinshasa transferred its support to the National Union for the Total Independence of Angola (União Nacional para a Independência Total de Angola—UNITA). Angola, on the other hand, supported the FLNC and its invasions of Zaire's Shaba Region in 1977 and 1978. Although relations improved periodically during the late 1970s and early 1980s, Zairian support for UNITA, particularly the alleged use of Kamina's military base in Shaba Region as a transit point for supplies from the United States, kept relations somewhat tense.

Zaire's concern was based on the size and strength of Angola's armed forces. Angola had the largest military (more than 100,000 personnel) of all of Zaire's neighbors. Its services were also the best equipped, possessing large quantities of sophisticated Soviet weapons. Moreover, because of the experience gained in its long-running civil war against UNITA, the Angolan military's capability easily surpassed that of the FAZ. This imbalance, along with the long land border between the two countries, made Luanda loom large in Kinshasa's national security concerns.

Several factors, however, limited the Angolan government's ability to threaten Zaire. The ongoing UNITA insurgency forced Luanda to orient its military toward this internal threat. Furthermore, past Western support for Kinshasa, especially during the Shaba crises, had not gone unnoticed in Luanda. There were also close military ties between Zaire and the United States. Reportedly, the United States had supplied weapons through Zaire to UNITA in the late 1980s.

Relations between Angola and Zaire started to improve somewhat in late 1988 when negotiations began over repatriation of refugees to their respective countries. Although the repatriations stalled because of mutual suspicions, negotiations resumed, and on September 27, 1989, the first refugees returned home. Approximately 310,000 displaced Angolans remained in Zaire in 1992.

Also during this period, President Mobutu arranged for a summit of African leaders to discuss Angolan national reconciliation. The summit, which took place in Gbadolite, Zaire, on June 22, 1989, led to a temporary cease-fire in the Angolan civil war and also called for subsequent negotiations on national reconciliation. Known as the Gbadolite Declaration, this agreement both necessitated and resulted in improved negotiations between Kinshasa and Luanda. Although the Gbadolite Declaration agreement was short-lived, the 1991 cease-fire agreement between Luanda and UNITA and resultant attempts to form a new broad-based Angolan government were expected to reduce potential conflict between Angola and Zaire.

As for relations with other African states, Zaire's support for Western initiatives and conservative regimes in Africa has had mixed consequences. Actions such as training Chadian soldiers at the Zairian Commando Training Center and sending troops to Chad to support United States and French policy in that country helped Zaire secure Western economic and military assistance, but they also earned Mobutu the enmity of many African leaders. Particularly important in this regard was Zaire's support for the UNITA insurgency in Angola.

Evolution of the Armed Forces

The Colonial Period

The FAZ traces its lineage back to the late nineteenth-century creation of the Force Publique in the area then known as the Congo Free State (see The Colonial State, ch. 1). In October 1885, King Léopold II of Belgium directed the organization of a government for the Congo Free State and charged the Ministry of Interior to create necessary police and military forces. In 1886 Belgium sent Captain Léon Roget to the Congo Free State with a small group of European officers and noncommissioned officers (NCOs) to organize a military force, although the Force Publique was not formally constituted until 1888.

From its inception, the Force Publique was an ethnically mixed African army although officered by Europeans. It was both a defense force, for counterinsurgency operations, and a gendarmerie. The repressive measures employed by the Belgian colonial authorities to attain the quiescence of the local African population ultimately produced relative stability in the Congo Free State. There were, however, a number of mutinies, and during the early 1890s, battles were fought against Arab invaders who had entered the country from the east looking for slaves and ivory and had established control over much of the eastern part of present-day Zaire. By 1894, however, the Belgian colonial administration had eliminated Arab control of this region.

Some of the worst tendencies of the present-day FAZ are traceable to the early organization and practices of the Belgian colonial force. Particularly evident during the colonial period prior to World War II was the extensive autonomy of territorial administrators, who operated virtually independent fiefdoms. These administrators often used the military to gain their own ends, diverting soldiers to various nonmilitary activities and treating local military units as private armies. Although this practice contravened colonial policy, the state proved unable to control its own coercive instruments. The practice of scattering military personnel among numerous small garrisons in the hinterland compounded the problem. The soldiers at isolated posts received little military training and were at times no more than undisciplined armed bands. A shortage of officers and the practice of diverting them from military to administrative duties further aggravated this situation, because the Force Publique was inadequately supervised.

The organization of the Force Publique remained unchanged throughout the period of the Congo Free State (1885–1908) and the pre-World War I Belgian Congo (as Zaire was called from 1908 to 1960). By the beginning of World War I, the Force Publique was not a coherent, well-organized army but more of a police force designed to aid civilian authorities in occupying the territory. As a result, the force initially assumed a defensive posture against German forces in German East Africa (later Tanganyika) and was virtually incapable of offensive action during the first eighteen months of the war. In fact, in most of the country the highest echelon of command in the Force Publique was the company; beyond that there was no semblance of military command. Specialized units such as artillery or engineering did not exist. Only in Katanga were there battalion-size units with an autonomous command structure.

These organizational problems continued to plague the Force Publique throughout the war, hindering effective operations. Belgian colonial forces in East Africa, however, did enjoy limited tactical success as part of a half-hearted cooperation with the British against the hopelessly outnumbered German East Africa Force known as the Shutztruppe. Ironically, one reason for the force's success may have been its reputation for cannibalism. Historian Charles Miller notes that many Africans in German areas believed that the Belgians economized on pay and food by serving their porters to the troops when the loads they carried had been used. Nevertheless, although the Force Publique's reputation for cannibalism may have been of peripheral concern to German forces, Belgian success in East Africa resulted mostly from the greater numbers of Allied forces, not from superior tactical skills.

The problems experienced in World War I led the Belgian administration to reorganize the army along lines that would better fulfill the dual missions of external defense and internal security. A commission convened to study this matter recommended that units of the force be organized for army or police duties. The colonial administration eventually adopted this recommendation and established the Garrison Troops (Troupes Campées) as a general military force oriented against external threats and the Territorial Service Troops (Troupes en Service Territorial) to handle police and gendarme duties, both under the commandant of the Force Publique. Troops performing police duties would rotate periodically with soldiers garrisoned in military units.

This reorganization did little to improve professional competence during the interwar years and in fact laid the base for many of the problems that continued to plague the FAZ in the 1990s. The Territorial Service Troops, which became known for their lack of discipline, were particularly derelict. In 1929 even the commandant of the Force Publique noted that the Territorial Service Troops were poorly trained and of little value. In 1933 the commandant commented again that command of the Territorial Service Troops was "more often a fiction than a reality" and that they were incapable of conducting "serious operations of whatever scope, or even coping with local riots." These problems continued throughout the interwar period and even (though to a lesser extent) through World War II and forced the local administrators to use the Garrison Troops to provide internal security. This diversion, however, proved destructive to the troops' cohesion, training, and discipline. The colonial government attempted to rectify these problems on numerous occasions, with little effect. A 1946 commission to study the reorganization of the Force Publique actually found itself facing the same concerns that had plagued the force prior to World War I.

Despite these internal difficulties, the Force Publique performed adequately during both world wars when employed outside the boundaries of the colony. As early as 1914, a detachment was deployed to the Cameroons to join French forces in operations against German forces there.

The Force Publique again mobilized in 1940, when Belgium was overrun by Germany. In early 1941, Congolese troops deployed to Italian East Africa (present-day Ethiopia) to help eliminate the last Italian centers of resistance, and in the next year, other Congolese troops joined forces with the West African Frontier Force in British colonial Nigeria. Later, Congolese soldiers went to Egypt where they guarded supply dumps and prisoner-of-war camps. During both wars, Allied leaders commended the actions of these representatives of the Force Publique.

During the early postwar period, Belgium, like other colonial powers, failed to recognize the strengthened desire of the Congolese elites to have a hand in shaping their own political destiny, especially following the successful deployment of Congolese soldiers among Allied units in World War II. Even in the late 1950s, the Belgian authorities had no intention of granting independence to the Belgian Congo in the near future. As a result, the composition and organization of the Force Publique remained unchanged (except that the Territorial Service Troops were known as the gendarmerie from 1959) from the end of World War II until independence. The Force Publique remained officered by Belgians, and only in the late 1950s did the colonial administration take steps to institute a military education system to prepare Congolese for commissioned service. In 1958 Belgium accepted only twenty-three Congolese for enrollment in the military secondary school. At this rate, it would have taken generations to completely Africanize the military. This approach was based on the premise that Europeans would continue to staff key institutions, such as the military, for a prolonged period after independence.

At independence in 1960, none of the top military leaders were African. Moreover, Belgium's attitude toward the Congo (or, more formally, Republic of the Congo and then Democratic Republic of the Congo), as Zaire was known from 1960 to 1971, was little different than it had been throughout the colonial period. An excellent example of this posture occurred a few days after independence. When Lieutenant General Émile Janssens, Belgian commander of the Force Publique, heard grumbling by the Congolese soldiers and NCOs who saw little chance to advance in an army still controlled by expatriates, he called a meeting of the Léopoldville (now Kinshasa) garrison on July 5, 1960, to remind them of their oaths of loyalty and obedience. In addition, he wrote on a blackboard, "After independence equals before independence." The indignation aroused in the Congolese soldiers by this comment led to a mutiny by the end of the day. At a meeting that evening, the mutineers called for Janssens's removal and the immediate Africanization of the officer corps. This mutiny set off political turmoil that embroiled the newly independent republic for the next several years (see The Crisis of Decolonization, ch. 1).

The Congolese National Army

The mutiny quickly spread throughout the country; soon the Force Publique was in full-scale revolt. Prime Minister Patrice Lumumba promised a one-grade promotion for all army personnel, but this action failed to mollify the mutineers. As reports circulated concerning ugly incidents perpetrated by mutinous black soldiers against European residents, panic gripped the white population, and several thousand fled the country. Brussels put its military on alert and decided that it must act unilaterally. Early on the morning of July 10—the tenth day of independence—Belgian troops intervened in Élisabethville (now Lubumbashi), where they quickly brought the situation under control, but disorder spread to other parts of the country. Belgian paratroopers dropped into several key areas to restore order. Although temporarily effective, the greatest impact of this intervention was to convince the newly independent country that Belgium was trying to reassert its colonial control.

Within days Lumumba removed the more than 1,000 European officers from the command structure, although a few remained as advisers, and replaced them with Congolese NCOs. These new officers were chosen mainly on the basis of seniority, but some were elected. Lumumba appointed two political followers with prior military experience to head the army. Victor Lundula was promoted to major general and named commander of the army to replace General Janssens, and Mobutu was promoted to colonel and made chief of staff. Lumumba also changed the name of the Force Publique to the Congolese National Army (Armée Nationale Congolaise—ANC). But within two weeks of independence, the newly named army had degenerated, in many cases, into armed gangs of renegades whose loyalties were to local strongmen, ethnic groups, or regions rather than to the national government.

This process was aggravated further when eleven days after independence, Katanga, the country's richest province, seceded. Although Belgium declined to grant diplomatic recognition to the new state, it did supply military assistance and may have seconded officers and NCOs to Katanga's military force, the Katangan Gendarmerie (Gendarmerie Katangaise). In addition, other Belgian functionaries remained at their posts, and the European sector in general lent crucial support to the rebels. Soon after, the southeastern portion of the diamond-producing province of Kasai, corresponding to the southern portion of what is now the Kasai-Oriental Region, also seceded. As a result, by August 1960 the new state had lost the two areas that had produced over half its revenues and foreign exchange and faced the threat of permanent disintegration.

Because of the general breakdown of law and order and to prevent the complete overthrow of authority, President Joseph Kasavubu and Lumumba appealed for United States, United Nations (UN), and Soviet assistance in July 1960. An uneasy international accord arranged that the UN would provide assistance, and within three months the UN had established a force in the country that numbered 20,000 at its peak. Once the UN force was present, the Congo in effect had several armies competing for power: the UN force, two secessionist forces, and the ANC. Furthermore, the splintered loyalties of the ANC meant that there were a variety of other competing military organizations as well.

The armed forces became as much a threat to state authority as an instrument of it. The various units were, at best, uncertain weapons in the hands of various contenders for power. In the capital and the surrounding area, Mobutu, rather than the central government, commanded the loyalty of ANC personnel. The ANC troops in Kasai supported the secessionist movement led by Albert Kalonji. Lumumba, dismissed by the president in September, later fled toward the northeastern Congo, but was captured en route and subsequently killed by Katangans. The February 1961 announcement of his death sparked an uprising in the northeast Congo and particularly in the Stanleyville (now Kisangani) area where the ANC and General Lundula backed Antoine Gizenga, who claimed to represent the only legitimate government of the republic (see fig. 5; The Center No Longer Holds, ch. 1). In Katanga, Moïse Tshombe had his own force of Belgian-advised gendarmes. Since these forces were concerned primarily with maintaining the positions of their patrons, the UN provided the main element of security in the country. Furthermore, in this competition, the capacity to pay troops was instrumental to any semblance of control. Here Mobutu had a major advantage, primarily because he had access to the disorganized national treasury.

The central government defeated the Kasai secession—as well as the northeastern regime led by Gizenga, which sought national power—relatively quickly, but the larger insurgency in Katanga proved more difficult. It was not until January 1963 that UN forces were able to end the Katanga secession. Peace was, however, short-lived. A wave of rebellions broke out again in various parts of the republic in late 1963. Soon after the departure of UN forces in June 1964, these rebellions controlled roughly one-third of the country (see fig. 6; Rural Insurgencies: The "Second Independence," ch. 1).

The most interesting of these rebellions was the Kwilu uprising in the area around Kikwit, led by Pierre Mulele. Mulele is credited with organizing the first large-scale peasant insurrection in an independent African state, espousing a combination of Marxism and Maoism heavily imbued with magico-religious overtones. The Kwilu revolt continued until December 1965, and the threat of Mulele to the central government did not end until his execution in October 1968.

To help deal with the insurgencies, former Katangan secessionist leader Moïse Tshombe was brought back as national prime minister in mid-1964. Tshombe mobilized his Katangan gendarmes, recalling them from exile in Angola, recruited white mercenaries, and obtained aid from Belgium and the United States to turn back the insurgents. Although the latter received Chinese and Soviet assistance and also, for several months in 1965, help from a Cuban contingent under Ernesto "Che" Guevara, government forces eventually gained the upper hand. Nevertheless, several months passed before the government could reestablish a tenuous authority in many affected areas.

The defeat of these rebellions took a great toll on both the government and the military. The army had performed poorly and was clearly unable to maintain order without external reinforcement. After defeating the insurgents, the army took out its humiliation on those it suspected of aiding them. These episodes combined to implant in the populace an indelible fear of disorder and insecurity and a deeply ingrained suspicion and distrust of the military, which continued in the early 1990s.

During 1965 the political situation deteriorated. General Mobutu had become commander in chief of the ANC, and, as the individual controlling the largest number of loyal troops, he staged a bloodless coup d'état on November 24, 1965, becoming president of the country (see Mobutu's Second Coming, ch. 1).

The Military under Mobutu

Mobutu did not initially establish a military dictatorship; the ANC continued in its role as the government's armed force rather than becoming the government. Mobutu stated that he had seized power in order to end the chaos and anarchy that had existed since the country had gained independence. He sought also to extract the country from its perennial government stalemate, largely caused by a power struggle between President Kasavubu and Prime

Marshal Mobutu Sese Seko, president of Zaire and
supreme commander of the FAZ
Courtesy Agence Zaïre Presse

Minister Tshombe, as well as to eliminate Kasavubu's threat to
get rid of the white mercenaries at a time when they were needed
to crush the Lumumbist rebellions. He also initiated efforts to encourage foreign assistance to reequip and train the ANC along
modern lines. Belgian and United States involvement in these objectives became particularly important. Meanwhile, the ANC, aided
by white mercenaries, continued to fight against insurgents around
Kikwit and in Kivu.

Another threat to national security occurred in July 1966 when
former Katangan gendarmes, who had joined the ANC during
Tshombe's comeback, mutinied and took over the city of Stanleyville (see Toward Political Reconstruction, ch. 1). The rebels
managed to hold out for two months, but the ANC, spearheaded
by white mercenaries, finally retook the city. Again the next year,
the ANC found itself fighting against a combined force of Katangans and mercenaries who had captured Bukavu, near the Rwandan border. The rebels held off a much larger ANC force for more
than three months before United States air logistic support forced
the insurgents to negotiate for safe passage out of the country.

While relying on the military to stay in power, Mobutu based
his legitimacy on the country's only legal political party, the Popular

Revolutionary Movement (Mouvement Populaire de la Révolution—MPR), which he created in 1967 (see The Party-State as a System of Rule; Managing the Military, ch. 4). Thus, despite his rank as field marshal, Mobutu rarely appeared in uniform. To safeguard his authoritarian rule, he staffed a high proportion of the top echelons of the military with people of his own ethnic group, while at the same time shuffling high-ranking personnel to weaken the army's professional independence or the emergence of any elements within the military that might threaten his rule. At the same time, he obtained foreign support to improve the capabilities of his military forces, particularly in counterinsurgency. Mobutu and his supporters maintained their hold over the defense ministry, which meant control of the army and the security forces.

Over the years, Mobutu took a number of steps to improve the military's capability. In 1969 he established the National Security Council to provide coordination over external and internal security responsibilities. During the same period, he created military schools to train young Congolese at home rather than having them sent off to Belgium or another foreign country. By 1969 this effort had succeeded to the point that recruits from other African countries were trained in the Congo (see Military Schools, this ch.).

Despite this progress, the military still relied heavily on foreign aid programs to train its soldiers during the early 1970s. Americans, Belgians, and Israelis provided assistance with various aspects of military training and invited Zaire (as the country was called from October 1971) to send officers and NCOs to train in their countries. By expanding and diversifying the sources of military assistance, Mobutu hoped to reduce Zaire's reliance on any one source of aid. This process would give him greater flexibility and could also provide more assistance as the various donors competed for access. The wide variety of sources of military education assistance, however, did have negative consequences. First, it produced a kaleidoscope of military education that at times made it difficult for officers in the same unit to interact effectively. It also created pockets of competing pressure groups that believed that their source of training was superior to the others. For example, until the mid-1980s, officers trained in Belgium and, to a lesser extent, France, had an advantage over United States-trained officers when it came to promotions and high-level assignments.

Creation of the Zairian Armed Forces

In the late 1960s and early 1970s, Mobutu inaugurated his authenticity (see Glossary) campaign, which was intended to reject European values and develop a Zairian identity (see The Quest for Legitimacy, ch. 1). As part of this initiative, Mobutu changed the name of the country to Zaire, dropped his Christian name and ordered his countrymen to do the same, and changed the name of the military to the Zairian Armed Forces (Forces Armées Zaïroises—FAZ).

During the mid-1970s, the FAZ experienced extensive turmoil. The army was shaken in mid-1975 when several generals, colonels, and lower-ranking officers were arrested and accused of plotting to overthrow the government. In August forty-one alleged plotters, including nine civilians, were tried in secret by a military court that handed down death sentences to three generals and four other army officers. One of the generals, Fallu Sumbu, was considered one of the brightest young officers in the military. Again in 1978, the government executed eight officers and five civilians alleged to have plotted against Mobutu. Although it is uncertain whether or not these plots ever existed, according to Zaire specialist Thomas Turner, what is certain, ''is that the purges reflected both generational and ethnoregional cleavages. Those eliminated in 1975 were mainly Tetela and others from Kasai-Oriental and Kivu regions, while those eliminated in 1978 were mainly Luba from Kasai-Oriental.'' These purges also had a significant negative impact on a military whose performance was characterized by gross incompetence during this period. In an interesting sidenote that reflects the sometimes bizarre policies of the Mobutu regime, a decree issued following the coup forbade marriage between officers and foreign women and ordered officers already married to foreigners to give up either their wives or their commissions.

Involvement in Angola

Despite the deficiencies of the FAZ, during the early 1970s Mobutu was viewed as a major player in Africa, and the Zairian military was considered to have improved. As a result, Mobutu sought to acquire the image of power broker by involving himself in the Angolan civil war. Anxious to prevent the victory of the Soviet- and Cuban-backed MPLA, Mobutu sent several battalions of the Zairian army into Angola to support anti-MPLA forces. These units advanced south toward Luanda with FNLA elements and also entered Cabinda with forces of the Front for the Liberation of the Enclave of Cabinda (Frente para a Libertação do Enclavo de Cabinda—FLEC). During October 1975, FAZ/FNLA forces advanced in the direction of Luanda, encountering gradually stiffening resistance from MPLA units defending the city. MPLA forces received assistance from Zairian exiles and Cuban units. This combined force routed the Zairian/FNLA soldiers and counterattacked, sending them fleeing toward the Zairian border. As the FAZ retreated, it disintegrated into disorganized bands looting the countryside. According to historian Crawford Young, the result for Mobutu could hardly have been worse: "humiliating defeat for the army; the entrenchment of his enemies in Luanda; and the exposure of Zaire as a junior partner" to the United States and South Africa.

Shaba I

Mobutu's ill-considered involvement in Angola returned to haunt him in March 1977 when the Front for the National Liberation of the Congo (Front pour la Libération Nationale du Congo—FLNC) invaded Zaire's Shaba Region. Included in the invading force was a small remnant of the Katangan gendarmes. When Kasavubu recalled Tshombe from exile in 1964, elements of this force had been incorporated into the ANC to help fight the insurrections simmering throughout the country. After Tshombe disappeared from the political scene, the Katangan contingent mutinied in 1966 and again in 1967. When these uprisings failed, most of the contingent left for Angola under Nathaniel Mbumba's leadership. During the late 1960s, the former gendarmes began to congregate in Angola along Zaire's southern border, and during the late 1960s and early 1970s, they fought for the Portuguese against Angolan nationalist movements. After the Portuguese departed in 1975, the MPLA enlisted the rebel Zairians in their cause and, with Cuban assistance, continued to arm and train them. It was the remnants of this force, augmented by other Zairian dissidents from Shaba and elsewhere, and still led by Mbumba, which invaded Shaba in 1977.

The invaders launched a three-pronged attack on March 8, 1977. Within weeks the FLNC had captured several towns and controlled the railroad to a point thirty kilometers from the copper-mining town of Kolwezi. Shortly after the invasion began, the dissidents made it clear that they were not merely a reincarnation of the earlier Katangan secessionist movement but instead aimed to take over the entire country and depose Mobutu. After their initial success, the rebels stalled on their way to Kolwezi; nevertheless, Mobutu's position seemed dire. This rapid advance and the threat to Kolwezi forced Mobutu to appeal for international assistance.

Belgium, France, and the United States responded to Mobutu's request by immediately airlifting military supplies to Zaire. Other African states also supported Zaire during this crisis, and Egypt and Morocco joined Belgium, France, and the United States by providing assistance. Egypt provided fifty pilots and technicians. The pilots flew the French-built Mirage jets of the Zairian air force throughout the conflict. Morocco provided 1,500 combat troops. French aircraft airlifted these soldiers to Kolwezi on April 9, and on April 14, a combined Zairian and Moroccan force counter-attacked. This reinforcement immediately improved the FAZ's morale, and by the end of May the joint force had regained control of Shaba. In addition to the recapture of Shaba, the Moroccan presence had the added benefit of permitting Mobutu to keep his elite airborne units in Kinshasa, ready to respond to a crisis elsewhere in the country.

The invading force had expected a general uprising in support of its operation; however, because of the fragmentation of Zairian opposition groups, as well as the FLNC's distinctive ethnic base (Lunda and Ndembu), this uprising did not materialize. The FLNC was prevented from consolidating its gains and became susceptible to the Zairian-Moroccan counterattack. Nevertheless, during what came to be known as the Eighty-Day War, the FLNC suffered no serious defeats, its troop strength had not diminished significantly, and its capability to conduct insurgent operations remained intact. The FLNC withdrew to Angola, and possibly to Zambia, and began to regroup for another attack. Thus, although to a limited extent the crushing of Shaba I might be regarded as a model of international cooperation, the victorious forces failed to complete the job. Probably more significant, however, was Zaire's failure to follow up its military success with political and economic reforms to ensure long-term stability. Government reprisals after Shaba I drove 50,000 to 70,000 refugees to Angola. Also, Zaire's continued support for Angolan dissident groups ensured continued Angolan government support for the FLNC.

The poor performance of Zaire's military during Shaba I gave evidence of chronic weaknesses. One problem was that some of the Zairian soldiers in the area had not received pay for extended periods. Senior officers often kept the money intended for the soldiers, typifying a generally disreputable and inept senior leadership in the FAZ. As a result, many soldiers simply deserted rather than fight. Others stayed with their units but were ineffective.

During the months following the Shaba invasion, Mobutu sought solutions to the military problems that had contributed to the army's dismal performance. He implemented sweeping reforms of the command structure, including wholesale firings of high-ranking officers. He merged the military general staff with his own presidential staff and appointed himself chief of staff again, in addition to the positions of minister of defense and supreme commander that he already held. He redeployed his forces throughout the country instead of keeping them close to Kinshasa, as had previously been the case. The Kamanyola Division, at the time considered the army's best unit and referred to as the president's own, was assigned permanently to Shaba. In addition to these changes, the army's strength was reduced by 25 percent, presumably to eliminate disloyal and ineffective elements. Also, Zaire's allies provided a large influx of military equipment, and Belgian, French, and American advisers assisted in rebuilding and retraining the force.

Shaba II

In contrast to the first Shaba invasion, where the FLNC had launched an outright invasion of Zairian territory, Shaba II started with an infiltration of Zaire. Then during early May 1978, ten FLNC battalions entered Shaba through northern Zambia, a sparsely populated area inhabited by the same ethnic groups (Lunda and Ndembu) that made up the FLNC. A small element headed toward Mutshatsha, about 100 kilometers west of Kolwezi, to block the path of Zairian reinforcements that might attempt to move into the area. During the night of May 11–12, the remainder of the force moved to Kolwezi, where it linked up with the rebels who had infiltrated the town during the previous six months. Although the FAZ had picked up many intelligence indicators pointing to an invasion, the town of Kolwezi was lightly defended.

The FLNC struck at dawn on May 13 and took Kolwezi by 10 A.M.; FLNC forces also captured Mutshatsha. Unlike the previous year, the insurgents did not disperse their force. The FLNC invasion of 1978 differed from Shaba I in another important respect. In 1977 the insurgents had done little physical damage. Although their forces had occupied nearly a third of Shaba, they had stopped short of the strategically important Kolwezi, not interfering with mining operations or endangering Europeans. In 1978 the rebels aimed directly at Kolwezi. By immediately striking this economically vital area, and by threatening Europeans, the FLNC provoked a much different international response than in 1977. This attack was a bold maneuver and might have succeeded were it not for the arrival within a week of 700 French and 1,700 Belgian soldiers, supported logistically by the United States Air Force.

The FAZ performed little better than it had done the previous year. Indeed, as Zaire specialist Thomas Callaghy notes, Mobutu's harsh suppression of an attempted military coup in February 1978 (in which he dismissed, imprisoned, or executed 250 officers, including many foreign-trained officers) "clearly had a detrimental effect on military performance during Shaba II, in which Zairian troops performed only marginally better than during Shaba I." Units of the Kamanyola Division collapsed immediately. Many took refuge in the European residential area, where most of the expatriate casualties were later suffered. Many Zairian troops removed their uniforms and took part in the general mayhem that occurred. In fact, most of the senior and mid-ranking officers had vanished prior to the attack, leaving junior officers and NCOs to lead the defense of the area. The small Kolwezi defense force (about 300 strong) was quickly overrun. The airport also fell to the insurgents in the initial onslaught, so Kolwezi was effectively under enemy control. In the attack on the airport, two helicopters and four Aermachi counterinsurgency jets belonging to the Zairian air force were destroyed on the ground, and two other Aermachis were damaged. Thus, Zaire was unable to use even the relatively limited amount of modern combat equipment that would have given the FAZ a significant tactical advantage over the FLNC.

Shortly after taking Kolwezi, the invaders' discipline broke down, which led to widespread drunkenness, looting, pillaging, and murder. Although initial reports reaching the outside concerning the slaughter of Europeans turned out to be somewhat exaggerated, the white community was undoubtedly under assault, and many local Zairians were also murdered.

The FLNC was unable to retain control of Kolwezi's airport, however. On May 17, Zairian regular units reinforced by a paratroop company and supported by air strikes counterattacked, forcing the rebels to withdraw. The FLNC claimed that white soldiers also participated, but this claim is dubious. Although the airborne unit was trained and advised by the French, French policy precluded the deployment of advisers in combat, and Paris denied that members of the French advisory mission participated.

Determining the number of rebels involved in Shaba II is difficult. Some sources have offered a figure of 4,000, although they differ on the percentage of this force that infiltrated prior to the commencement of hostilities. However, probably no more than 500 seasoned FLNC troops took part in the actual attack, with the balance consisting of infiltrators and other personnel recruited locally.

On May 19, a 700-member battalion of the French Foreign Legion parachuted into Kolwezi under orders to rescue the hostages held by the FLNC and to prepare to evacuate all whites from the war zone. The Belgians sent a paratroop regiment to Kamina (more than 200 kilometers north of Kolwezi) and proceeded by road to Kolwezi with orders to use their weapons only if fired on first by the rebels. The Belgian commander reportedly had disarmed his men (by taking away their bullets) to avoid the possibility that they would fire on the Legionnaires, who were committing atrocities.

This action led to strained relations between the Belgian forces and the Legionnaires, which continued in the early 1990s. The United States sent eighteen C-141 transports to fly logistics missions for both the French and Belgian forces.

FLNC resistance evaporated quickly as the Legionnaires swept through the city streets in a house-to-house search for rebel troops, and the French encountered little organized resistance as they cleared the town. Most of the opposition they met came from Zairian deserters, armed looters, and FLNC irregulars. The bulk of the rebel forces had already withdrawn, even evacuating their wounded, accompanied by a good portion of the local population who also fled the city.

By the end of May, the second Shaba invasion was over except for scattered attacks by roving bands of insurgents that had remained in the area after the departure of the main FLNC force to Zambia. The Belgian force started to withdraw, leaving a battalion in Kamina, and the French Foreign Legion departed by the end of May.

At the Franco-African Summit in late May, Morocco (itself not a participant) offered to send its soldiers to Zaire again if it received the cooperation of other African states. By May 31, a Moroccan regiment had arrived in Kolwezi, followed a few weeks later by a Senegalese battalion, smaller units from Togo and Gabon, and a medical team from Côte d'Ivoire (Ivory Coast). These soldiers flew in on United States, French, and Belgian military aircraft, and France, the United States, and Saudi Arabia reportedly jointly financed this operation. This approach was a unique effort at peacekeeping outside the framework of an existing formal alliance or international organization. Most important, however, was its reliance on African forces to replace the departing Europeans.

During the post-Shaba II period, Mobutu again sought foreign assistance to remold his military. Thomas Callaghy notes that Zaire went so far as to post European NCOs, known as "godfathers," with Zairian units to ensure that the troops were paid and fed. In 1980 a French colonel, Maurice Mathiote, assumed command of the French-trained 31st Airborne Brigade. French officers essentially commanded the brigade down to the company level in peacetime, although they would not deploy with their units to combat. The Belgians trained the 21st Infantry Brigade in Shaba and remained as advisers to this unit. The Chinese were invited to train and equip the 41st Commando Brigade in Kisangani, and, after resuming diplomatic relations with Israel in 1982, Zaire requested and received Israeli military assistance focusing on training the Special Presidential Brigade, which expanded to a division in

1986—the Special Presidential Division (Division Spéciale Présiden-tielle—DSP). Despite this concerted international effort, the FAZ remained largely ineffective except for the airborne brigade and the presidential unit. Zairian regular units demonstrated their con-tinued inability to counter effectively the sporadic insurgent ac-tivities in eastern Zaire that continued in the 1980s (see Public Order and Internal Security, this ch.).

Public Attitudes Toward the Military

By the early 1990s, the FAZ's enlisted ranks represented much of society. However, members of President Mobutu's own Ngbandi ethnic group are disproportionately represented in the military and security forces, particularly at the highest levels. The Ngbandi over-whelmingly dominate the elite DSP. Mobutu has excluded certain areas of the country from recruitment in the military (in the past, the western half of the country had provided a majority of recruits). The army reportedly is dominated by soldiers from the Équateur Region, Mobutu's home region, as well as Haut-Zaïre. It has also been reported that soldiers from the regions of Shaba, Kasai-Oriental, Kasai-Occidental, Bandundu, Bas-Zaïre, Nord-Kivu, Sud-Kivu, and Maniema are discriminated against.

The military is highly visible in most areas of the country, but it is not an institution that most Zairians identify with or in which they have any pride or confidence. The FAZ, as a descendant of the colonial Force Publique, has retained an aura of separateness and, like the colonial force, is perceived, justifiably, as an instru-ment of repression. As such, the majority of the population sees the army as its enemy.

There is also discontent within the military itself. Low and ir-regular pay is the primary cause for depredations by the FAZ. Only the highest-ranking officers and the DSP receive pay sufficient to provide a basic level of subsistence. Most officers and other ranks receive wages that are inadequate to feed and clothe their fami-lies, and they often go unpaid for months (see Conditions of Ser-vice, this ch.). As a result, FAZ members often prey on the local community in an effort to make ends meet, and to enrich them-selves, which breaks down trust between the military and the Zairian population. In September 1991, unpaid paratroopers went on a rampage in Kinshasa, and widespread looting ensued. France and Belgium ultimately sent in troops to restore order and protect for-eign nationals. Another wave of military-led pillaging and looting occurred in early 1993 following the introduction of a new Z5 mil-lion (for value of the zaire—see Glossary) note that many merchants refused to accept from the military personnel who had been paid

297

with it. Lower-level, routine looting has continued; people who interfere or protest are often shot on the spot. As a result, fear of renewed military looting is widespread, inducing many citizens to pay the ''contributions'' that soldiers demand as the price of being left alone.

The FAZ has played a constructive role at times, in conducting occasional civic-action programs, but these may, in any case, have been largely window dressing for foreign advisers. For example, during a joint Zairian-American military exercise, Zairian engineer units built several bridges in Shaba Region, permitting vehicular travel between some towns for the first time in more than ten years.

Armed Forces Missions and Organization

The constitution states that the president is the supreme commander of the armed forces and is also responsible for formulating and executing defense policy. The Ministry of Defense and Veterans' Affairs assists him with these duties. Mobutu had served as minister of defense and veterans' affairs since his 1965 coup, relinquishing the position only in 1990, following his announcement of the Third Republic (see Proclamation of the Third Republic, ch. 4). During the 1977 Shaba crisis, Mobutu personally took over as FAZ chief of staff, in effect becoming the supreme commander, minister of defense, and chief of staff of the army, a staggering array of duties for a single person to assume. He holds the unique rank of field marshal in the FAZ.

Mobutu also heads the advisory National Security Council, which comprises the prime minister; the ministers of defense and veterans' affairs, external relations, interior and security, and justice and keeper of the seals; the administrators general of the National Service for Intelligence and Protection and the Military Intelligence and Security Service; the president's special adviser on security matters; and the chiefs of staff of the FAZ and the gendarmerie. Within the National Security Council, a Security Committee and a Secretariat were established in May 1982.

The official mission of the FAZ is to defend the country against all internal and external threats. But throughout its existence, the mission to protect Zaire against internal threats—as well as threats to Mobutu's rule—has been the military's primary task. The military's importance in propping up the Mobutu regime is amply demonstrated by the role military and security forces played in suppressing political opposition in the early 1990s. Mobutu has routinely deployed loyal military units to suppress popular demonstrations; to harass and intimidate political opponents and newspapers critical of his regime; to gain and retain control of key

Zaire's small navy operates along its short coast and on its numerous lakes and rivers, such as this one through dense jungle in Équateur Region.

government institutions such as state-run radio and television facilities and the central bank; to incite ethnic violence; and to obstruct the operations of the transitional government, including blocking access by members of that government to their government offices (see Subsequent Political Developments, 1990-93; Opposition since 1990, ch. 4).

Until 1988 the FAZ was organized into three military regions, but in August of that year, President Mobutu increased the number of military regions. They generally coincide with the country's administrative regions, but some military regions encompass more than one administrative region (see fig. 1).

Army

The 25,000-member army consists of one infantry division (with three infantry brigades); one airborne brigade (with three parachute battalions and one support battalion); one special forces (commando/counterinsurgency) brigade; one presidential guard division; one independent armored brigade; and two independent infantry brigades (each with three infantry battalions, one support battalion). These units are deployed throughout the country, with the main concentrations in Shaba Region (approximately half the force). The Kamanyola Division, consisting of the 11th Infantry Brigade, the 12th Infantry Brigade, and the 14th Infantry Brigade, operates generally in western Shaba Region; the 21st Infantry Brigade is located in Lubumbashi; the 13th Infantry Brigade is deployed throughout eastern Shaba; and at least one battalion of the 31st Airborne Brigade stays at Kamina. The other main concentration of forces is in and around Kinshasa: the 31st Airborne Brigade is deployed at Ndjili Airport on the outskirts of the capital; the DSP resides adjacent to the presidential compound; and the 1st Armored Brigade is deployed to Mbanza-Ngungu (approximately 120 kilometers southwest of Kinshasa).

The army is equipped with a wide variety of military equipment, most of which came from the United States, France, and China (see table 16, Appendix). In 1993 the FAZ's main military requirements included new military vehicles, jeeps, and communications equipment, as well as foreign assistance in repairing and maintaining equipment already in the inventory.

The maintenance status of equipment in the inventory has traditionally varied, depending on a unit's priority and the presence or absence of foreign advisers and technicians. A considerable portion of military equipment is not operational, primarily as a result of shortages of spare parts, poor maintenance, and theft. For example, the tanks of the 1st Armored Brigade often have a nonoperational rate approaching 70 to 80 percent. After a visit by a Chinese technical team in 1985, most of the tanks operated, but such an improved status generally has not lasted long beyond the departure of the visiting team. Several factors complicate maintenance in Zairian units. Maintenance personnel often lack the training necessary to maintain modern military equipment. Moreover, the wide variety of military equipment and the staggering array of spare parts necessary to maintain it not only clog the logistic network but also are expensive.

The most important factor that negatively affects maintenance is the low and irregular pay that soldiers receive, resulting in the theft and sale of spare parts and even basic equipment to supplement their meager salaries. When not stealing spare parts and equipment, maintenance personnel often spend the better part of their duty day looking for other ways to profit. American maintenance teams working in Zaire found that providing a free lunch to the work force was a good, sometimes the only, technique to motivate personnel to work at least half of the duty day.

The army's logistics corps is to provide logistic support and conduct direct, indirect, and depot-level maintenance for the FAZ. But because of Zaire's lack of emphasis on maintenance and logistics, a lack of funding, and inadequate training, the corps is understaffed, underequipped, and generally unable to accomplish its mission. It is organized into three battalions assigned to Mbandaka, Kisangani, and Kamina, but only the battalion at Kamina is adequately staffed; the others are little more than skeleton organizations.

The army's military capability is uneven, with some units more capable than others. For the most part, however, the Zairian army is not a combat-effective organization. The typical army brigade, such as the 21st Infantry Brigade in Lubumbashi, has virtually no offensive capability and only very limited defensive capability. The problems are manifold: ineffective leadership detracts from tactical and technical proficiency as well as morale; poor maintenance results in insufficient resources for mission accomplishment; and lack of funds limits the army's ability to purchase sufficient amounts of equipment or to pay soldiers a living wage. These conditions have long existed in almost all regular Zairian units and combine to keep capability at minimum levels.

The DSP, numbering between 7,000 and 10,000, is an exception to this rule. Members of the elite DSP have consistently received higher wages, been paid regularly, been well fed, and had better housing than soldiers in other units. These factors, and (in the past) the presence of Israeli advisers, have not only encouraged a better leadership environment but also produced more motivated soldiers.

There were, however, reports that even the DSP went for weeks without pay in late 1993. Only a subunit, Mobutu's personal guards known as Les Hiboux (The Owls), were paid regularly.

The situation in the 31st Airborne Brigade was at one time similar. Although paid the same basic salary as soldiers in other units, airborne personnel were once paid regularly. French advisers ensured that the soldiers of the 31st Airborne Brigade were well fed, trained, and clothed. Also, French command of the unit's logistics battalion meant that supply and equipment maintenance were effective. As a result, the unit was capable of conducting effective combat operations. The 31st Airborne Brigade demonstrated its effectiveness during Shaba II and the first occupation of Moba in 1984. That situation no longer prevailed by September 1991, however, when unpaid personnel from the 31st Airborne Brigade spearheaded mass looting and pillaging in Kinshasa.

In the chaotic political climate prevailing in the early 1990s, the loyalty and effectiveness of individual military units are open to question. Clearly, the looting and rioting by military personnel in September 1991 and in early 1993 were indicative of a serious problem. By contrast, the DSP apparently has continued to prosper relative to other military units. According to press reports, Mobutu ensured the loyalty of this key unit by continuing to pay its members, despite the scarcity of funds and the failure of the regime to provide regular pay to civil servants and other military personnel. The DSP has continued to support the Mobutu regime internally, both protecting Mobutu and serving as his primary instrument of control. The DSP's violent attack on students in Lubumbashi in May 1990 is the most vivid manifestation of its support of Mobutu, but far from the only one. The DSP also was used to suppress both the September 1991 and the even more destructive February 1993 incidences of military looting—although in 1993 the DSP is widely reported to have engaged in considerable vandalism itself before quelling the unrest. Its suppression of the violence reportedly included summarily executing hundreds of military looters. In addition, the DSP is reputed to have ransacked the offices and blown up the presses of *Elima,* the leading opposition newspaper, in October 1991; to have put down a ''coup attempt'' after some military personnel took over the state-run television station in February 1992; to have interrupted numerous public demonstrations, shooting unarmed demonstrators randomly; and to have been deployed to Nord-Kivu in mid-1993 to stop ethnic violence widely believed to have been instigated by government and security officials in the first place. In all of its dealings with the populace, the DSP has been accused of using undue violence and torture. Its fearsomeness was demonstrated graphically in February 1993 when its members went on a punitive rampage after civilians killed one of its members.

Some DSP personnel reportedly were also deployed to Angola in the early 1990s and to Rwanda in October 1990 to support the beleaguered Rwandan government. The DSP undoubtedly is the only Zairian military force loyal and capable enough to be deployed abroad.

Navy

Zaire's 1,300-member navy includes 600 marines and operates a small ocean-going force with larger river and lake flotillas. Because Zaire's Atlantic Coast is only about forty kilometers long, Lake Tanganyika is the largest body of water that the navy patrols, so the navy's primary mission is to control illegal entry into the country and to conduct antismuggling patrols as well. The navy has bases at Banana on the coast; at Boma, Matadi, and Kinshasa on the lower Congo; and at Kalemie, on Lake Tanganyika. A dry dock at Boma is used to repair the navy's patrol craft. The service reportedly has only a few vessels that can operate for short periods in the ocean. Its inventory includes small numbers of Chinese-made fast patrol craft (inshore) as well as three ex-North Korean torpedo boats, without torpedo tubes, which are normally only marginally operational (see table 17, Appendix). In addition, two United States-made coastal patrol craft, along with as many as eighteen French-built patrol craft, patrol the lakes and rivers (although their operational status is uncertain). Naval personnel receive basic training at the Banana Naval Base but in the past generally went to the United States, France, or Belgium for intermediate and advanced training.

Air Force

The air force consists of approximately 1,800 personnel and provides close air support, aerial reconnaissance, and transport support for the other services. To accomplish this mission, the air force is organized into one fighter squadron, one counterinsurgency squadron, one transport wing, one helicopter squadron, and a training element.

The air force has had little opportunity to demonstrate its capability; however, during the 1977 Shaba invasion, the air force's combat performance was reportedly no better than the army's. Western observers reported that Zairian pilots flying Italian trainers as fighter-bombers were particularly ineffective; their munitions usually landed harmlessly wide of the targets. During Shaba II, the FLNC destroyed four Aermachi MB–326K counterinsurgency aircraft, one Alouette helicopter, and an SA–330 Puma helicopter on the ground when its forces captured the airport at Kolwezi. The Zairians attempted to use their Mirage jets against the rebels, but to little effect. More recently, four Zairian air force pilots died when their jets collided in mid-air while returning from military exercises at Kamina in 1988.

Several factors have affected air force capability. Pilots are often inadequately trained to fly their aircraft; even when trained, funding is normally insufficient to provide an adequate number of flying hours for the pilots to maintain their proficiency. And because of poor maintenance over 75 percent of the aircraft are often nondeployable. The air force's major equipment includes Mirage ground attack fighters; assorted counterinsurgency aircraft; a variety of transport aircraft; military helicopters; liaison aircraft; and training aircraft (see table 18, Appendix). Future military requirements include additional transports and spare parts.

National Gendarmerie

In August 1972, the National Police was dissolved, and its functions were transferred to the National Gendarmerie (Gendarmerie

Nationale). In addition, oversight of the police was transferred from the Ministry of Interior to the defense portfolio. The 21,000-member gendarmerie functions primarily as a police force, but it also has a paramilitary mission, to form the first line of defense against an external threat (see Development of a National Police Force, this ch.). The 1972 transfer of oversight concentrated additional power in the hands of President Mobutu, while weakening the law enforcement role of municipal leaders at the local level who had previously exercised authority over a police detachment but now had to turn to local military commanders, who were often unresponsive, for assistance.

To accomplish its divergent missions, the gendarmerie is organized into two forces: a territorial force, the Territorial Gendarmerie (Gendarmerie Territoriale—GT) and a mobile force, the Mobile Gendarmerie (Gendarmerie Mobile—GM). The GT functions as the police component and the GM as a paramilitary organization. The gendarmerie is commanded by a chief of staff, who reports to the head of the FAZ and the minister of defense and veterans' affairs.

The gendarmerie is lightly armed with individual weapons and machine guns and is transported in jeeps and trucks. Although most of this equipment is often in disrepair, gendarmerie units in some parts of the country are better equipped than army units, which often have to borrow gendarmerie equipment to train or deploy. Nevertheless, the gendarmerie is normally not as well trained as army units and even less capable.

Armed Forces Manpower and Training
Recruitment and Retention

Military service in Zaire is voluntary, although the constitution does provide for conscription in the event of a national emergency. Zaire has a fairly large population in relation to the size of its military. For example, 1993 estimates indicated that Zaire had a potential military manpower pool (males fifteen to forty-nine years of age) of 8.9 million, about half of whom are fit for military service. Although this pool is in theory adequate to ensure a sufficient number of recruits, the FAZ has had problems attracting enough qualified personnel and retaining them in service. A major deficiency in this respect is that the FAZ has no formal recruiting organization, and prospective recruits often have to go out of their way to enter the military. Moreover, the service conditions inhibit many young people from electing to serve in the military and often make it difficult for the FAZ to convince them to make the service

Prior to the 1990s, some
Zairian officers received
United States military training,
including the air force
major (top left),
army captain (top right),
and army second lieutenant
(bottom right) pictured here.
Courtesy United States
Department of Defense

a career. The people who remain in the military are often not the best and most motivated soldiers, but rather those who have no alternative or are in a favorable position because of their ethnic affiliations.

An interesting aspect of Zairian military life is the fairly significant presence of women, both in enlisted and officer ranks. Although most enlisted women have insignificant roles and often owe their rank to sexual favors provided to senior officers, Zairian female officers usually perform legitimate roles in the military, in both command and staff positions. In 1987 three female captains graduated from the Command and Staff School, one of them among the top ten graduates. That result represented the first time women had attended and graduated from this elite institution and could signal the advancement of these women to field-grade ranks.

Conditions of Service

The conditions of service for most Zairian soldiers and officers are dismal. Even before the chaotic years of the early 1990s, in which the bankrupt government did not pay most troops regularly if at all, inadequate and irregular pay for the majority of personnel meant that they must have some outside source of income. Such income could come from a variety of interests, ranging from legitimate business enterprises to stealing and reselling government supplies and equipment. Such practices had an obvious negative effect on soldiers' morale and motivation but also seriously affected capability and readiness by forcing soldiers to spend much of their duty day attempting to make ends meet. As a result, training and other service-related matters assumed second priority.

In the early 1990s, most military units (except for the elite DSP) were paid so infrequently, and when paid were paid with worthless zaires, that they felt compelled to loot to survive. Aside from the two major military looting rampages in September 1991 and January–February 1993, smaller-scale banditry and looting continued routinely, both in Kinshasa and in other regions. In addition, military personnel often resorted to extorting money from the citizenry or made private arrangements with local and foreign businesses, who paid them to act as private guards.

In the past, the situation for some mid- and senior-level officers tended to be better. Starting with the rank of major or lieutenant colonel, some Zairian officers were able to secure outside sources of income, which permitted them to support their families. By the time an officer became a colonel, he had usually guaranteed himself an adequate income through involvement in business by exploiting his military position.

General officers traditionally were in the best financial position by far of all Zairian military personnel. First, they could profit from their duty assignments by skimming funds intended for the soldiers in their organizations, but they were also well placed to capitalize on contacts they made to establish business connections. For example, a former air force chief of staff was reportedly one of the wealthiest and shrewdest businessmen in Zaire. Even while he was chief of staff, he owned several companies, many of which did business with the air force and other government agencies. All these business interests, however, left little time to run the air force, which reflected this neglect.

Aside from pay, other conditions of service are also deplorable. Zairian units rarely are fed two meals a day, with most only fed once. In the past, the presence of foreign advisers often served to improve this situation somewhat. For example, at the Belgian-run Senior Military Schools Group, Zairian personnel received three meals daily, which was, however, exceptional. Many other benefits designed to offset low salaries either do not exist or are sporadic. Free medical care, for example, often depends on the presence of foreign advisers, and free medicine, although authorized, is rarely available. Housing is also usually inadequate to meet the basic needs of the soldiers. Most enlisted personnel are forced to live in squalor, and the situation, even for company-grade officers, is often not much better.

Military Schools

Military schools traditionally played an important role in Zaire's military, both as a means to provide assistance to other African countries and to train its own officers. The FAZ has the usual complement of military schools, such as the Officers Basic Training Course at Kananga (formerly Luluabourg), the Naval Officers Basic Course at Banana, the Armor Training School at Mbanza-Ngungu, and a variety of other basic and specialty schools. Two schools in particular stand out. The Command and Staff School is a course taught at the Senior Military Schools Group in Kinshasa. In the past, Belgian instructors, with limited Zairian assistance, conducted the course, which was designed to prepare senior company-grade officers to perform duties as battalion commanders and to function as staff officers at battalion level and higher. Although austere by Western standards, the training conducted in this course was professional, thorough, and accomplished its stated objectives.

The Commando Training Center at Kotakoli, in northern Kasai-Occidental, also did an excellent job of training personnel to conduct basic commando operations. Again, Belgian personnel supervised the majority of the training, which was divided into two programs. The first prepared personnel to serve as instructors at the school. This course was intensive, thoroughly trained personnel in individual survival and special operations skills, and at this level was equal to most Western schools of this sort. A second, abbreviated program trained units in commando operations. This instruction was shorter and less intense than the longer course. A significant shortcoming of the short course was that although it more than adequately trained personnel in individual skills, it offered no instruction in small-unit tactics.

Uniforms, Ranks, and Insignia

The uniforms and rank structure of the FAZ bear the mark of Belgian influence but also show evidence of long United States and French involvement with Zaire. Soldiers often wear fatigue uniforms, solid green in color or in a camouflage pattern. While dressed in fatigues, army personnel wear berets, the color of which denotes the branch of service. Personnel also wear combat boots and web or cartridge belts with this uniform.

Service uniforms are similar to those worn in the United States and several other countries. Army personnel wear a dark green uniform, the air force a light blue, the navy a dark blue, and the gendarmerie a forest green. Service uniforms are high collared and worn with visored caps, scarves rather than neckties, and low-quarter shoes. Officer rank insignia are worn on shoulder boards, enlisted rank insignia on the upper-left sleeve (see fig. 12; fig. 13).

Foreign Military Relations
Foreign Influences

In the years since independence, Zaire has benefited from a variety of foreign military assistance. President Mobutu was adept at playing one country against the other to gain increased aid. Nevertheless, by the early 1990s, Zaire was receiving less foreign assistance as Mobutu's hold on power became increasingly precarious. In addition, the end of the Cold War superpower competition was accompanied by a decrease in superpower involvement and interest in African affairs and thus in willingness to provide military aid to the region.

Belgian influence predominated within the ANC after independence. All the arms and equipment with which the new Congolese force began its existence were of Belgian origin, as were the training, organization, and military doctrine. During the early independence period, however, other Western influences became more important. After the withdrawal of UN forces in June 1964, the Congo established bilateral military assistance relationships with Belgium, the United States, Italy, Israel, and Britain. Much of the aid provided by these countries was in the form of grants, but some assistance was also provided by military technicians and advisers. The Congo's Western allies also made advanced and specialized training available to Congolese military personnel.

By the late 1960s, military assistance fit a pattern that continued into the early 1990s with slight modifications. Belgium directed its aid primarily to ground forces and military schools; Israel trained airborne personnel; Italy worked with the air force; and the United States provided logistics support. Subsequently, France replaced Israel for airborne training and Italy for the air force.

During the 1970s, China and the Democratic People's Republic of Korea (DPRK—North Korea) also began cooperation and training relationships with the FAZ. In the 1980s, China provided military equipment and spare parts to Zaire, assisted in repairing and maintaining Chinese-built T-62 medium main battle tanks and other armored vehicles, and maintained the navy's Chinese-built fast patrol craft. A Chinese military delegation arrived in Zaire in February 1990 to assess the work of Chinese advisers who had spent several years training soldiers of the 41st Commando Brigade, a rapid intervention unit of the FAZ in Kisangani. The North Koreans, who once maintained a 400-member mission in Kinshasa, withdrew during the mid-1970s, but military cooperation resumed in 1985 with the training of the Kamanyola Division. In October 1990, Zaire and North Korea discussed the possibility of upgrading the military cooperation between the two countries.

In late 1991, unconfirmed reports circulated that South Africa had undertaken the training of Zairian troops. Fifteen South African military instructors reportedly were in Zaire, at a military base near Kitona in Shaba. Some reports also suggested that South Africans were helping establish special units intended to harass Mobutu's political opponents.

By 1992 foreign military training relationships with Zaire's major allies had largely dissolved because of the country's deteriorating political situation. In the 1980s, Belgium had provided advisers to the 21st Infantry Brigade and ran the Officers Basic Training Course, the Command and Staff School, the Naval Officers Basic Course, and a variety of other schools. But by mid-1990, relations between the two countries had broken down over the Zairian government's human rights abuses, and by late 1990, there were no longer any formal military training relationships between Belgium and Zaire.

	SOUS-LIEUTENANT	LIEUTENANT	CAPITAINE	MAJOR	LIEUTENANT COLONEL	COLONEL	GÉNÉRAL DE BRIGADE	GÉNÉRAL DE DIVISION	GÉNÉRAL DE CORPS D'ARMÉE	GÉNÉRAL D'ARMÉE
ZAIRIAN RANK **ARMY**	SOUS-LIEUTENANT	LIEUTENANT	CAPITAINE	MAJOR	LIEUTENANT COLONEL	COLONEL	GÉNÉRAL DE BRIGADE	GÉNÉRAL DE DIVISION	GÉNÉRAL DE CORPS D'ARMÉE	GÉNÉRAL D'ARMÉE
U.S. RANK TITLES	2D LIEUTENANT	1ST LIEUTENANT	CAPTAIN	MAJOR	LIEUTENANT COLONEL	COLONEL	BRIGADIER GENERAL	MAJOR GENERAL	LIEUTENANT GENERAL	GENERAL
ZAIRIAN RANK **AIR FORCE**	SOUS-LIEUTENANT	LIEUTENANT	CAPITAINE	MAJOR	LIEUTENANT COLONEL	COLONEL	GÉNÉRAL DE BRIGADE AÉRIENNE	GÉNÉRAL DE DIVISION AÉRIENNE	GÉNÉRAL DE CORPS D'ARMÉE AÉRIENNE	GÉNÉRAL D'ARMÉE AÉRIENNE
U.S. RANK TITLES	2D LIEUTENANT	1ST LIEUTENANT	CAPTAIN	MAJOR	LIEUTENANT COLONEL	COLONEL	BRIGADIER GENERAL	MAJOR GENERAL	LIEUTENANT GENERAL	GENERAL
ZAIRIAN RANK **NAVY**	ENSEIGNE DE VAISSEAU 2ÈME CLASSE	ENSEIGNE DE VAISSEAU 1ERE CLASSE	LIEUTENANT DE VAISSEAU	CAPITAINE DE CORVETTE	CAPITAINE DE FRÉGATE	CAPITAINE DE VAISSEAU	CONTRE-AMIRAL	VICE-AMIRAL	AMIRAL	GRAND AMIRAL
U.S. RANK TITLES	ENSIGN	LIEUTENANT JUNIOR GRADE	LIEUTENANT	LIEUTENANT COMMANDER	COMMANDER	CAPTAIN	REAR ADMIRAL LOWER HALF	REAR ADMIRAL UPPER HALF	VICE ADMIRAL	ADMIRAL

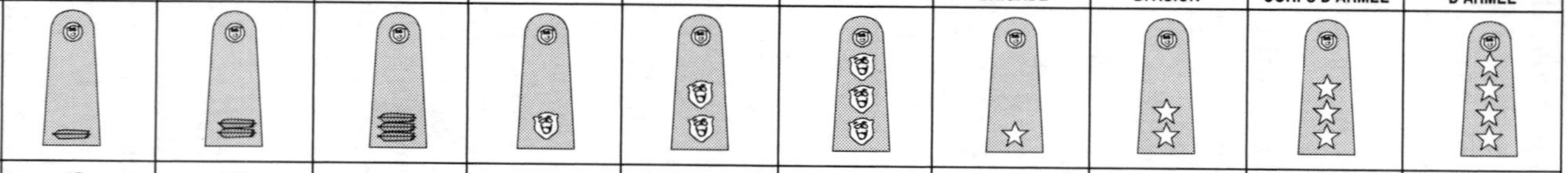

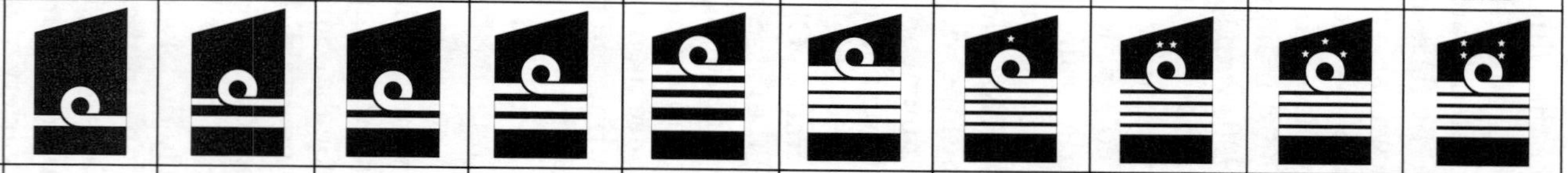

Figure 12. Officer Ranks and Insignia, 1993

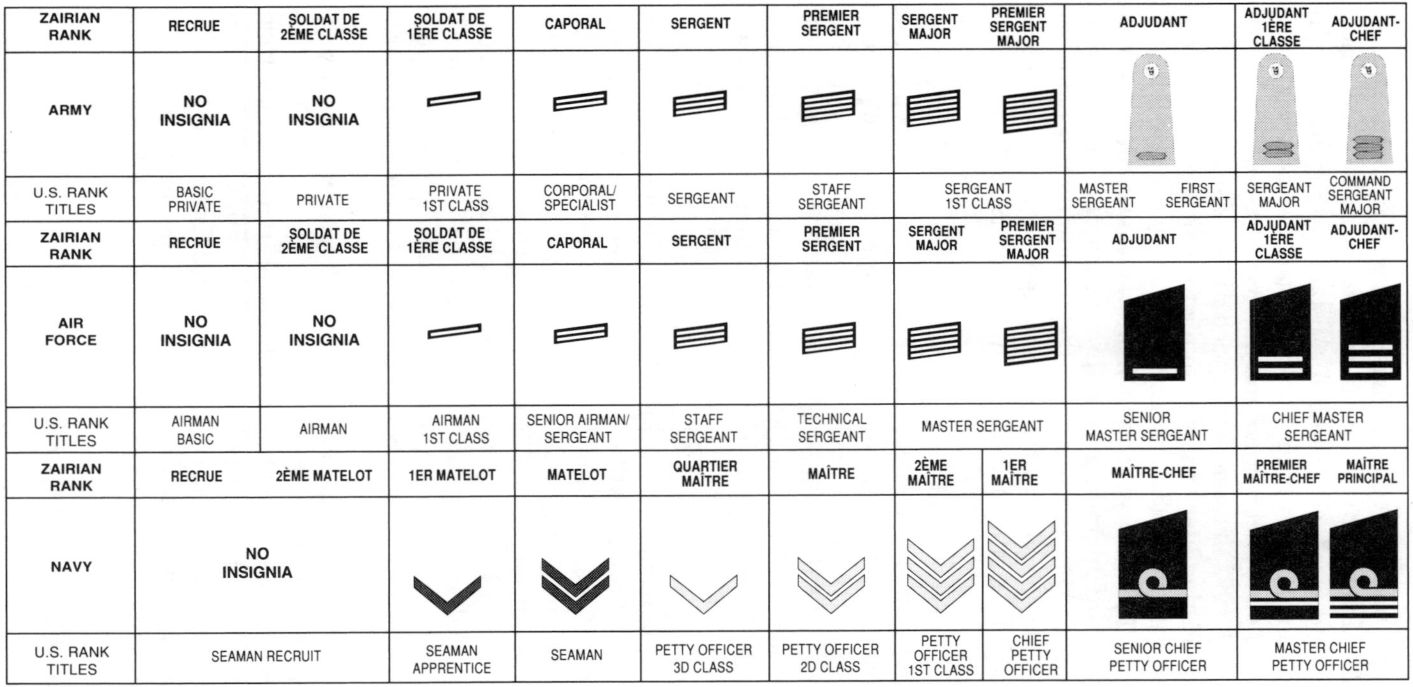

	RECRUE	SOLDAT DE 2EME CLASSE	SOLDAT DE 1ERE CLASSE	CAPORAL	SERGENT	PREMIER SERGENT	SERGENT MAJOR	PREMIER SERGENT MAJOR	ADJUDANT	ADJUDANT 1ERE CLASSE	ADJUDANT-CHEF
ZAIRIAN RANK — ARMY	NO INSIGNIA	NO INSIGNIA									
U.S. RANK TITLES	BASIC PRIVATE	PRIVATE	PRIVATE 1ST CLASS	CORPORAL/SPECIALIST	SERGEANT	STAFF SERGEANT	SERGEANT 1ST CLASS		MASTER SERGEANT / FIRST SERGEANT	SERGEANT MAJOR	COMMAND SERGEANT MAJOR
ZAIRIAN RANK — AIR FORCE	RECRUE — NO INSIGNIA	SOLDAT DE 2EME CLASSE — NO INSIGNIA	SOLDAT DE 1ERE CLASSE	CAPORAL	SERGENT	PREMIER SERGENT	SERGENT MAJOR	PREMIER SERGENT MAJOR	ADJUDANT	ADJUDANT 1ERE CLASSE	ADJUDANT-CHEF
U.S. RANK TITLES	AIRMAN BASIC	AIRMAN	AIRMAN 1ST CLASS	SENIOR AIRMAN/SERGEANT	STAFF SERGEANT	TECHNICAL SERGEANT	MASTER SERGEANT		SENIOR MASTER SERGEANT	CHIEF MASTER SERGEANT	CHIEF MASTER SERGEANT
ZAIRIAN RANK — NAVY	RECRUE — NO INSIGNIA	2ÈME MATELOT	1ER MATELOT	MATELOT	QUARTIER MAÎTRE	MAÎTRE	2ÈME MAÎTRE	1ER MAÎTRE	MAÎTRE-CHEF	PREMIER MAÎTRE-CHEF	MAÎTRE PRINCIPAL
U.S. RANK TITLES	SEAMAN RECRUIT		SEAMAN APPRENTICE	SEAMAN	PETTY OFFICER 3D CLASS	PETTY OFFICER 2D CLASS	PETTY OFFICER 1ST CLASS	CHIEF PETTY OFFICER	SENIOR CHIEF PETTY OFFICER	MASTER CHIEF PETTY OFFICER	MASTER CHIEF PETTY OFFICER

Figure 13. Enlisted Ranks and Insignia, 1993

311

The French had trained and advised the 31st Airborne Brigade and the 32d Airborne Brigade, ran an inter-African armor training course, and provided technical assistance to the air force. In early 1989, Zaire ordered French military matériel, including twelve VAB armored personnel carriers and thirteen rebuilt AMX–13 light tanks. But by 1992, France had ended aid to Zaire.

Israel provided military training in the form of advisers, instructors, and technicians, and some Zairian military personnel trained in Israel. In a 1983 five-year agreement, Israel was entrusted with restructuring and upgrading the military capability of the Zairian armed forces and began training and equipping the newly formed DSP. Israel also provided Zaire with weapons systems, including small arms. The status of Israeli military assistance in the 1990s was uncertain.

The United States had long provided Zaire with military assistance and grants, technical and training support, repair and maintenance of United States-supplied equipment, spare parts, as well as weapons. Between 1960 and 1991, Zaire reportedly received an estimated US$38.2 million in grants under the United States Military Assistance Program (MAP), an additional US$18.2 million under the United States International Military Education and Training (IMET) program (1,356 Zairian students were trained under this program), and US$144.7 million in Foreign Military Sales (FMS) agreements (US$132.7 million of that amount was in the form of Foreign Military Sales deliveries). Payment was waived for US$135.5 million of the FMS agreements. A number of joint American-Zairian military exercises were conducted in the late 1980s, according to published reports. However, in the late 1980s and early 1990s, American military assistance was increasingly threatened by congressional opposition to the Zairian government's violations of human rights, as well as widespread corruption and maladministration. As a consequence of the worsening repression in Zaire, in November 1990 the United States announced that it had decided to terminate all military and economic aid (except humanitarian aid) to Kinshasa.

Zaire and Egypt entered into a military pact in February 1980. Egyptian military instructors trained the Zairian Civil Guard, as well as units of the FAZ, and Egypt provided Zaire with Fahd armored personnel carriers and other Egyptian-manufactured military equipment. The status of this relationship in the early 1990s was, however, unclear.

Zaire as a Military Aid Donor

In addition to receiving military assistance from numerous

countries, Zaire aided other African countries, often in support of Western interests. Zaire's relationship with Chad was preeminent in this respect. In 1983 President Mobutu sent approximately 3,000 troops to Chad to help Chadian president Hissein Habré stop a Libyan-backed rebel offensive. France and the United States also aided Habré. Several Chadian commando battalions were trained at the Zairian Commando Training Center, and Chadian officers trained at Zaire's Armor Training School. In September 1986, Zaire sent two airborne companies to Togo to help Togolese president Gnassingbe Eyadéma stabilize his capital city after an attempted coup, and in late 1990 Mobutu sent elements of the DSP to help neighboring Rwanda fight an insurgency. Zaire also provided training at its Armor Training School for students from several other African countries.

Public Order and Internal Security

In the early postindependence days, the new nation was beset by regional and tribal factionalism, tremendous violence, chaos, and repression. After Mobutu's 1965 coup d'état, this unstable situation provided an excuse for the steady growth and entrenchment of Mobutu's personal authority. Yet in spite of the buildup of a massive, centrally controlled internal security apparatus, political and social dissent persisted. Moreover, this apparatus was itself responsible for exacerbating much of the public disorder that characterized modern Zaire.

As of 1993, no official statistics on crime had been published since 1959. Although general law and order and supremacy of central authority were largely restored under Mobutu, the incidence of crimes against persons has been consistently high, especially when general economic conditions deteriorate. Theft, robbery, murder, and rape have become increasingly common in and around the country's urban centers and along its main transportation routes, making travel dangerous. The police and security forces themselves commit many of these acts and frequently participate in armed banditry. Furthermore, both their ability and desire to protect the citizenry from common criminals are slight. In the early 1990s, crime was described as endemic in many areas of the country, including Kinshasa and both Nord-Kivu and Shaba, where ethnic violence was widespread.

Prior to the 1990s, public protest and civil unrest occurred periodically, although the events were usually localized and were on nowhere near the scale of 1960-65 (see Opposition to the Regime prior to 1990, ch. 4). The roots of such activity lay typically in economic hardships but were also sometimes sparked by overzealousness or impropriety on the part of the security forces. The regime's response was usually harsh and violent in discouraging more widespread protest. University students and teachers were among the more frequent demonstrators. In February 1989, for example, students in Kinshasa and Lubumbashi went on strike to protest IMF-inspired austerity measures and inadequate and costly transportation. The universities were temporarily closed and army units quickly sent in to quell the disturbances. In the process, several students were killed and others wounded. However, the episode was brought to an effective close only after President Mobutu had agreed to reduce the students' bus fares and had announced the initiation of court martial proceedings against the officers and troops responsible for the killing. In May 1990, students at Lubumbashi were killed by the DSP in an action widely characterized as a massacre.

Political resistance to the one-party regime was also accompanied by sporadic guerrilla activity. Guerrilla resistance centered on the activities of several insurgent groups. For example, on November 12, 1984, some 200 rebels belonging to the People's Revolutionary Party (Parti Révolutionnaire du Peuple—PRP), a force that had operated for years in the rugged mountains near Lake Tanganyika, temporarily seized and occupied Moba, a town on the shores of Lake Tanganyika. Elements of the 31st Airborne Brigade recaptured the town two days later. Again in 1985, the PRP briefly occupied Moba on June 17, but its forces were quickly dislodged. Although Moba possessed no strategic importance, its capture had significant psychological importance. It demonstrated that the Zairian government was still unable to exercise effective control over portions of the country. Even more important, the Moba incidents vividly demonstrated the incompetence of the front-line Zairian units stationed in the interior, notwithstanding the 31st Airborne Brigade's recapture of the town. The PRP was officially registered as an opposition party in late 1990.

Another organization, the Congolese Liberation Party (Parti de Libération Congolaise—PLC), also officially registered in late 1990, operated in northern Zaire during the mid-1980s. The PLC, formed in 1984 with the stated purpose of toppling the Zairian government, operated primarily out of bases in the Ruwenzori Mountains along the Zaire-Uganda border. It staged numerous attacks on towns, government forces, and installations along the Zairian side of the border. Although the PLC was unable to take and hold any terrain and posed no serious threat to the Kinshasa regime, the rebels demonstrated the government's lack of control of this area.

In the ostensibly multiparty era of the Third Republic in the early 1990s, opposition activity proliferated. The creation of political parties was tolerated for the most part (except for blatantly ethnic groupings), but military and security forces continued to suppress demonstrations, often with violent results.

The Civil Security Apparatus

In the early 1990s, Zaire had two so-called forces of order (*forces de l'ordre*) above the local level: the National Gendarmerie and the Civil Guard. In addition, several intelligence and security forces operated in support of the Mobutu regime. Their personnel arbitrarily arrest and imprison Zairians, although such responsibilities are not officially within their purview. Far from ensuring order, Zaire's forces of order and security forces have contributed to the disorder and lawlessness prevailing in the early 1990s. At his behest, security forces loyal to Mobutu—especially the Civil Guard, which reportedly was paid more regularly than most other units—continued to harass the populace and the transitional government. In addition, individual officials continued to prey on the populace, extorting money and meting out arbitrary punishment.

Development of a National Police Force

The development of police forces in Zaire has been anything but a steady, continuous process. Those elements that perform the police function in contemporary Zaire descend from a variety of colonial and postcolonial structures that have been reorganized, renamed, absorbed by other services, or disbanded altogether. Police duties are assigned to both military and civilian security organizations, often simultaneously, and have undergone alternating periods of centralization, decentralization, and transfer of authority. In all cases, however, the performance of the police has been mediocre at best and, at worst, completely dysfunctional and occasionally criminal.

From its founding in 1888, the Force Publique fulfilled the basic functions of both a police force and an army. This dual role caused tension within the organization and was a major factor in its poor discipline and lack of effectiveness. Because of the requirement to act as a police force, members of the colonial army were dispersed throughout the country, where they normally came under the control of local civilian administrators.

This dual role continued virtually unchanged until shortly after World War I, when the Belgian administration reorganized the force into two organizations: Garrison Troops and Territorial Service Troops. The Garrison Troops were intended to serve as a military force oriented against an external threat, while the Territorial Service Troops assumed the role of a gendarmerie or police force. Although the Territorial Service Troops remained an integral part of the Force Publique and could revert to the control of the commander, elements were deployed throughout the country under the operational control of the territorial administrators. Although this change theoretically created two distinct organizations, the separation of powers was not routinely applied. Garrison Troops gradually came under the control of the civilian administration and acted like a police force. In 1959 the Territorial Service Troops were redesignated as gendarmes, although their duties and responsibilities remained essentially unchanged. A year later, most of the gendarmes were incorporated into the ANC, totaling 6,000, out of a 25,000-member force. The remaining gendarmerie was a small, mostly rural police force.

In addition to the Territorial Service Troops, two other police forces existed during the colonial period. The Chief's Police, a rural force based in the local territories, maintained order and also functioned as messengers, jailers, and court attendants. This force served under the local chiefs and had no regional or national command structure. Although its members wore uniforms and maintained internal order, they did not carry weapons and received little training. At independence, this force totaled approximately 10,000 personnel.

The Territorial Police was a more structured organization, numbering between 6,000 and 9,000 personnel at independence. Created in 1926 and placed under Belgian administrators, this force performed numerous functions including maintaining order, running prisons, and guarding public buildings, as well as reinforcing the Chief's Police. After independence, each province maintained its own force, which was officered by former Belgian policemen. In some cases, during the immediate postindependence period, these forces became, in effect, private armies.

The chaos of the immediate postindependence period, along with the departure of the experienced officer corps, precipitated the disintegration of the constabulary forces. The UN restored a semblance of order, but the central government faced a long and tedious task of rebuilding its security forces. During the next four years, UN personnel and other foreign advisers instituted training programs in an effort to rehabilitate the police. Nigerian detachments established on-the-job training programs, and a limited number of Belgian police returned as advisers. The United States also initiated a broad assistance program to provide specialized training, arms, and equipment.

Rebellions continuing into the mid-1960s complicated the task of restoring coherence to police organizations. The increase in the number of provinces from six to twenty-one also exacerbated this process. As each new *provincette* achieved control of its provincial police force, it inflated its size, and these organizations began to resemble provincial armies. Mobutu's assumption of power in 1965 ended this trend, however. In December 1966, Mobutu removed the police from provincial control, standardized police organization and equipment, and centralized control under the Ministry of Interior (Ministry of Interior and Security in 1993). The 1966 law establishing the National Police gave it responsibility for regular police functions in both urban and rural areas. This new force, with an authorized strength of 25,000, absorbed many personnel from the overgrown provincial forces, while politically unreliable or undesirable elements were largely culled.

The reorganization was effective in reducing local paramilitary threats to the regime's authority, but it did not significantly improve the performance of basic police functions. Furthermore, the deployment of the National Police was limited, for the most part, to urban centers, with the responsibility for internal security and public order in the rural areas resting chiefly with the still extant gendarmes of the ANC.

National Gendarmerie

On August 1, 1972, President Mobutu dissolved the National Police and merged it with the largely rural gendarmerie into a single force, the National Gendarmerie. This move significantly increased the size of the national police force and made it an institutionally distinct component of the FAZ, hierarchically equivalent to the other services. By transferring the national police force from the Ministry of Interior to the Ministry of Defense (Ministry of Defense and Veterans' Affairs in 1993), Mobutu brought the police under his direct control. Key personnel from the police force were retained, and others were mustered out. Despite this reorganization, a large number of the local, or collectivity police, remained outside the national government's control, possibly totaling between 25,000 and 30,000.

Military authorities, rather than local civilian administrators, normally approve all significant deployments, including those required to perform typically civil police duties. This arrangement, combined with the National Gendarmerie's relatively poor training, discipline, and equipment, sorely limits the organization's capability to function as an effective police force. Furthermore, the typical gendarme is grossly underpaid, if he is paid at all, and so often uses his position to extort resources from the very people he is charged with protecting. As a result, the gendarmerie has contributed little to the maintenance of law and order in Zaire.

In August 1993, the chief of staff of the gendarmerie, on the twentieth anniversary of its founding, gave a speech in which he noted that the nation's roads are insecure because of widespread banditry, much of it perpetrated by gendarmerie personnel. He also acknowledged that members of the gendarmerie are involved in murder, the illegal possession of weapons, extortion, and armed robbery.

The Civil Guard

In part as an effort to improve the state's performance of the police function, and in part as a redistribution of power and influence, in 1984 Mobutu once again decentralized police powers and created a national civilian police organization, known as the Civil Guard (Garde Civile), to perform normal civilian police duties, as well as customs and border control. The guard's precise name is the General Elite Peace Force. The guard, trained and equipped by the Federal Republic of Germany (West Germany) and Egypt, appeared initially as if it might provide more effective and rational law enforcement than that which had been provided by the gendarmerie. However, it too has suffered, among other things, from insufficient pay and is just as ineffective and feared by the citizenry as the National Gendarmerie. Nevertheless, in the early 1990s the Civil Guard was regarded as loyal to Mobutu. In conjunction with the elite DSP, it was deployed to harass the opposition and transitional government on Mobutu's behalf and was generally paid—or at least paid more regularly than ordinary military and security units.

Although the Civil Guard was designated to take primary responsibility for police matters in Zaire, it probably had no more than 10,000 personnel in its ranks in the early 1990s, and its deployment was limited largely to the country's urban centers. The National Gendarmerie was still the prominent organization in rural areas and a competitor for dominance in most urban areas as well.

Local Police

At the local level, a large number of unarmed, untrained, and locally recruited Zairians still perform basic police tasks in support of local authorities. Their numbers totaled nearly 30,000 in 1993, according to some sources. Nevertheless, some local areas had virtually no police left because they lacked funding to pay them. Where police were present, their local activities typically were not coordinated with the national police elements, and they probably were neither capable of nor motivated to support national or regional security objectives.

Local and regional authorities have the power to arrest and impose fines, and in many cases they exercise these powers with the help of local police. But local police are underpaid (if they are paid at all) and tend to extort their living from the citizens.

The Intelligence Apparatus and Security Forces

In the tense and authoritarian climate prevailing in modern Zaire, intelligence and security agencies have provided President Mobutu with much of his support. All Zairian security organizations maintain their own prisons, networks of informers, and resources, much of the latter being the product of extortions and theft.

The Sûreté Nationale, a small, special-purpose police and investigative unit originally established by the Belgian colonial administration, continued after independence and was responsible for several diverse functions in the national security field. Prior to independence, the Sûreté's mission was to protect state security by controlling immigration, supervising resident aliens, and protecting key government leaders. Shortly after independence, the Sûreté came under the Ministry of Interior, but by mid-1961, the first director, Victor Nendaka, had turned it into a semiautonomous organization under his personal control. President Mobutu soon took steps to eliminate Nendaka as a power broker, however.

In 1969 the Sûreté became the National Documentation Center (Centre National de Documentation—CND). During the next few years, Mobutu played "musical chairs" with the directorship of this organization, as he attempted to maintain close personal control. During the early 1970s, the CND was reorganized into internal and external sections, and its agents reportedly had wide latitude in arresting, interrogating, and detaining people they considered a threat. Thereafter, Mobutu continually sought to improve his personal control over the intelligence apparatus and instituted several more reorganizations. In the early 1980s, the service gained the new title of National Documentation Agency (Agence Nationale de Documentation—AND). The national security service was renamed the National Service for Intelligence and Protection (Service National d'Intelligence et de Protection—SNIP) in August 1990.

The SNIP has separate branches for internal and external intelligence functions, with the internal role receiving a substantially higher priority. It is Zaire's primary intelligence service and, as such, provides liaison with foreign services. Although there is no information available to clarify further the organization or personnel strength of the SNIP, it almost certainly consists of a relatively small corps of agents who gain their information through a widespread network of informers and from other arms of the state apparatus. The SNIP communicates directly with the president. Its agents do not report to the local or regional administrators, nor are they subject to their authority. Indeed, other arms of state power such as the military and police forces are prime targets for surveillance.

In addition to gathering intelligence and conducting surveillance, the SNIP exercises almost unchecked powers of arrest, imprisonment, and interrogation. It has used these powers to intimidate individuals or groups posing a real or imagined challenge to the regime's authority. In the 1980s and 1990s, it played an important role in repressing political activists. In the past, the SNIP also had foreign agents operating in Europe to infiltrate anti-Mobutu exile groups. As with the other elements of the internal security apparatus, abuses are widespread and personal aggrandizement a primary motivator. It has been reported that the security services have engaged in extensive looting and plundering in the early 1990s.

The intelligence service is heavily politicized. Its assessments are not thought to be highly reliable, but it has been an effective if ruthless intimidator of potential opposition groups.

As well as the usual military intelligence roles, the intelligence arm of the FAZ, the Military Intelligence and Security Service (Service d'Action et de Renseignements Militaire—SARM), is tasked with internal surveillance and intelligence gathering on the general population as well as members of the armed forces themselves. It has not enjoyed nearly the prominence or freedom of action of its civilian counterpart, but it does possess a fairly sizeable and widespread network of informants among Zaire's soldiers, sailors, and airmen.

Other internal security agencies include the National Immigration Agency, which is responsible for border security, and in 1990 it was reported that a secret special operations force had been established within the security services to carry out abductions and other types of intimidation against political dissidents. The unit was popularly known as Les Hiboux (The Owls), which is also a name of a DSP subunit providing protection to Mobutu, but the existence of the force within the National Immigration Agency was not officially acknowledged by the government. There are additional intelligence units within the Civil Guard and the National Gendarmerie.

President Mobutu has also relied on various personally established networks to provide him with alternative intelligence and assessments that he can then fuse with information he receives from the official services. These operatives can also be used to spy on the services themselves. Little is known of these networks, but in the past they were reported to be large and well funded, given the president's tremendous personal wealth and unusual access to the Zairian treasury (see Patrimonial Politics and Corruption, ch. 3).

The Party Security Apparatus

Any discussion of Zaire's civil security apparatus would be incomplete without considering the Youth of the Popular Movement of the Revolution (Jeunesse du Mouvement Populaire de la Révolution—JMPR) and its disciplinary arm, the Corps of Activists for the Defense of the Revolution (Corps des Activistes pour la Défense de la Révolution—CADR). Although the JMPR was a spin-off of Zaire's single, ruling political party (until the legalization of multiple parties in the early 1990s), it played a role in state security, limited, however, by the poor quality of its personnel, who were typically unemployed youths. The JMPR's main tasks were maintaining party discipline and vigilance and providing information to the state. JMPR directors had arrest powers, which CADR members also exercised from time to time. CADR members could act alone or in support of local operations by the gendarmerie or Civil Guard. Municipal administrators sometimes called on CADR elements to perform in place of the often unresponsive gendarmes, who were part of the FAZ. At the same time, like the members of Zaire's other security elements, the typically unpaid and untrained young men of the CADR frequently used their positions to extract money and other resources from the local citizenry. The total strength of the CADR was unknown, but its presence was widespread, and elements of some size probably existed in nearly every municipal region prior to 1990.

Popular Attitudes Toward the Civil Security Apparatus

Given the predilection of the various internal security and police elements for preying upon citizens they are charged with protecting and their often negligible contribution to law and order, it is no wonder that Zairians hold them in low esteem, viewing them as no better than common bandits and thieves. Citizens fear to challenge their authority directly, although there have been numerous demonstrations and rioting against the Mobutu regime in the early 1990s. Extreme abuses by security forces also have resulted in occasional violent reprisals by angry villagers, especially against unarmed or poorly armed police elements. It is not apparent that any one service is uniformly more disliked than another. Indeed, the formal distinctions among them are often not readily apparent to the common citizen because of the lack of uniforms and the tendency of personnel engaged in illicit acts to misidentify themselves. The relationship is further complicated by the fact that criminals sometimes pose as members of the official services in order to induce fear and acquiescence in their victims.

The Legal and Penal Systems

Criminal Law and the Penal Code

Contemporary Zairian law still embodies most of the principles established during the Congo Free State and the Belgian Congo eras. These elements do not reflect a simple adoption of existing Belgian law but, rather, a unique combination of royal decrees, administrative and legislative ordinances, native customs, and a body of judicial decisions based on the above as well as "general principles of law equity." The various constitutions before and after independence for the most part recognized the continued legitimacy of earlier laws, except where they conflicted with more recently developed ones. Two important trends have, however, characterized Zairian law during the Mobutu era. First, the official role of non-Western "customary" law dwindled significantly in the process of centralizing and personalizing authority, although local custom and belief can still be considered in establishing punishment. Second, an often confusing and ill-defined body of codes emerged as a result of a 1972 ordinance giving all the public statements of President Mobutu the force of law. For the most part, however, these codes concerned only crimes against the state or the president.

The penal code adopted by the Congo Free State in 1888 remained in force until it was finally abrogated and replaced by the penal code of 1940. This later code was not abandoned at independence but has since undergone a variety of amendments, the most important of which was the creation in 1963 of a set of crimes concerning public order and state security. Unlike the penal codes of other French-speaking states, the nomenclature of the Zairian code does not distinguish among different classifications of criminal offenses and refers to all of them as "infractions."

It has been on the basis of political infractions that the state has most often invoked the death sentence and other severe penalties. By contrast, it has tended to be somewhat lenient in its punishment of common criminals, preferring, at least in theory, to attempt their rehabilitation. Special consideration is typically given to juvenile offenders, who are often remanded to the custody of the family in lieu of imprisonment.

The 1974 constitution imbued Zairian criminal law with certain fundamental principles, but in practice these principles are often violated, especially when other elements of the state apparatus are involved or interested. For example, although habeas corpus and bail do not exist, people arrested are supposed to be brought before a magistrate within forty-eight hours of arrest. This principle is rarely adhered to, however. Often, those arrested (frequently arbitrarily to begin with) are held for months without a hearing. People who can afford bribes buy their way out of detention without ever having been formally charged.

The Judicial System

Nearly the entire corps of the Belgian Congo's 168 European magistrates departed during the exodus that occurred in 1960. Native court clerks filled many of their positions and kept the justice system running, but the impact was severe and long-lasting. A fully functioning magistrature was never fully restored in Zaire. Magistrates have suffered generally from a lack of basic legal texts and documents, poor facilities, and insufficient transportation and staff support. These inadequacies led to a magistrates' strike in 1991, completely paralyzing the country's judicial system. Although the strike ended in December of that year, little was done to ameliorate the conditions giving rise to the work stoppage.

At independence, the new republic inherited a judicial structure comprising a dual system of courts—those that applied so-called customary law and those that applied the official codes (influenced by Belgian law). This situation persisted until the enactment in 1968 of a new Code of Judicial Organization and Competence that provided for the unification of the judiciary and the abolition of all customary courts. The magistrature itself was divided into distinct branches for the prosecution and judgement of cases. However, many Zairian magistrates moved freely between the two areas of responsibility, sometimes serving as public prosecutors and at other times as sitting judges.

The 1974 constitution established the national court structure that was, for the most part, still in existence in 1993 (see The Judiciary and the Courts, ch. 4). It consists, in descending order of importance, of the Supreme Court of Justice in Kinshasa; three courts of appeal in Kinshasa, Lubumbashi, and Kisangani, each of which has jurisdiction in several regions; a regional court in each of the ten regions and Kinshasa; and numerous urban and rural subregional tribunals with jurisdiction over trying most offenses. In 1987 President Mobutu also ordered the establishment of a system of juvenile courts, although the order did not appear to have been fully implemented. In addition, a Court of State Security handles crimes involving national security, armed robbery, and smuggling, while military courts try cases involving military personnel. In times of declared emergency or during military operations (such as in the first Moba crisis in 1984), the president can grant military courts jurisdiction over civilians as well.

In theory, defendants in Zaire are provided by the constitution with the right to a public trial and defense counsel; indigent defendants are to be provided with court-appointed defense counsel paid for by the state. In addition, the right of appeal is provided in capital cases, except for cases involving state security, armed robbery, and smuggling, all of which are to be adjudicated by the Court of State Security. There also is no appeal from military court decisions.

In practice, however, according to various human rights reports, these constitutional provisions are not evenly applied. Most citizens, for example, are not aware of their right to legal counsel or to appeal. In any case, Zaire does not have enough lawyers to provide adequate counsel to defendants.

The Zairian judiciary also lacks independence from the government and the presidency. Although it is a product of a colonial heritage of neutrality and independence, these qualities have diminished in a variety of ways since 1960. For example, the magistrature is by no means assured freedom from executive interference because the constitution empowers the president to appoint and dismiss all judges and to promulgate law. Furthermore, prior to 1990, all magistrates were automatically MPR party cadres and, as such, were responsible for promoting national party policy. District administrators were actually charged with submitting annual reports on the party "militancy" and loyalty exhibited by the magistrates in their area. The result was that although judges and prosecutors might perform independently and without political interference in the great majority of cases, in those of a political nature, or involving other members of government, property, or labor disputes, they were severely limited.

In addition, magistrates suffer from inadequate pay and are therefore susceptible to bribery and corruption. As a result, trials in Zaire are often far from fair by objective standards. People unable to pay bribes are disproportionately subjected to the full rigors of the judicial system.

The Prison System

The administration of prisons is the responsibility of the Ministry of Justice and Keeper of the Seals. Central prisons are located in the regional capitals and large urban centers, with district prisons, territorial prisons, detention centers, and informal lockups scattered among other towns and villages at lower administrative levels. In addition, some of the rural prison camps established to handle mass arrests and political detainees during the turbulence of the 1960s have occasionally been reactivated for similar purposes. A small number of juvenile detention centers exist, but they are not common, and most young offenders are released to their family's custody.

Prison facilities are grossly inadequate; living conditions are harsh and unsanitary, and prisoners are poorly treated. The system is marked by severe shortages of funds, equipment (including medicine and medical facilities), food, and trained personnel. Overcrowding and corruption are widespread. Reports of prisoners being tortured, beaten to death, deprived of food and water, or dying of starvation are common. Prison officials and guards typically steal from the often meager provisions of food and supplies available, and many prisoners are wholly dependent on family and friends for their survival. In 1993 there were reports that there was little food for inmates at the central prison in Kinshasa; the Red Cross was supplying some food to supplement the meager rations.

An "inspector corps" was formed by the government in 1987 to oversee prison conditions and operation. However, it lacks adequate manpower, transport vehicles, and government support to realize its mission. Also, it has no jurisdiction over the secret detention centers used by security forces for interrogation and imprisonment. Although persons arrested for political crimes traditionally have not been placed in prisons, they nevertheless are unlawfully detained by nonjudicial means, their cases are rarely brought to trial, and they are held incommunicado in detention centers or in internal exile.

Civil and Human Rights

Fundamental civil liberties, such as freedom of speech and press, peaceful assembly and association, and political rights, although nominally guaranteed to Zairians by the constitution, have been seriously infringed upon by the Mobutu regime. This deprivation has been compounded by the fact that the Zairian people have received very little information over the years concerning their civil and legal rights.

Several independent human rights organizations are active in Zaire, including the Voice of the Voiceless, the Zairian League for Human Rights, and the Zairian Association for the Defense of Human Rights. They are reported to operate freely, and generally have not been harassed by the government despite their critical reports documenting human rights abuses by the regime. Nevertheless, the Mobutu government has refused to permit governmental or private international human rights organizations to investigate cases of human rights abuses in Zaire. Complaints against the government have included political repression and imprisonment of the political opposition; curtailment of religious freedoms; intimidation, theft, killings, and other excesses by security forces; and inhumane treatment of prisoners. A 1991 report on human rights in Zaire by Amnesty International indicated that political imprisonment, security force violence, and other abuses were prevalent. The United States Department of State's 1991 publication on human rights practices reported that "Human rights in Zaire remained seriously restricted . . . . Zairians remained subject to arbitrary detention and physical mistreatment." According to that report, key sources of the problem include the authoritarian nature of the regime, the size of the security apparatus and its freedom of action, and pervasive and widespread corruption. The instruments of law and order are also the chief abusers of human rights, greatly diminishing their legitimacy. Another important factor is that although the armed forces receive their general authority from the central government, they are often not within its firm control, especially at the local level. Efforts by Mobutu to improve the human rights situation are typically in response to Western threats to diminish foreign economic or military aid and have generally been ineffective. This situation prevails despite the fact that Zaire is a signatory of the United Nations International Covenant on Civil and Political Rights and the African Charter of Human and People's Rights.

There had been some hope in the early 1990s that the human rights situation in Zaire would improve, following Mobutu's announcement in 1990 of political reforms, ostensibly intended to lead to a new constitution and multiparty elections. But in 1993 the political situation remained chaotic, with a beleaguered Mobutu clinging to power and continuing to repress dissent and block genuine progress toward political reform.

In March 1993, the United Nations Commission for Human Rights condemned Zaire's violations of human rights and basic freedoms. The commission's report cited in particular the widespread use of torture, inhuman conditions of detention, "disappearances," summary executions, and failure to ensure fair trials. It also deplored the regime's systematic and forceful repression of peaceful demonstrations and accused the regime of deliberately inciting ethnic violence in Shaba.

In September 1993, Amnesty International rated the human rights situation in Zaire as worse than it has been since the chaos following independence in 1960. In support of this assessment, it cited widespread deliberate violations of human rights by regional authorities loyal to Mobutu, ethnic murders in Nord-Kivu and Shaba instigated by government security personnel, the arrest and detention of the editor of an opposition newspaper, and the obstruction of transitional government meetings. Given the extent of random banditry throughout the country, Zaire in the early 1990s was a country in which lawlessness prevailed and human rights were systematically trampled.

*   *   *

Although no single book deals exclusively with Zaire's national security, several works serve as excellent sources of information on various aspects of national security. These include: *The Rise and Decline of the Zairian State* by Crawford Young and Thomas Turner; *The Dialectics of Oppression in Zaire* by Michael G. Schatzberg; and Thomas M. Callaghy's *The State-Society Struggle: Zaire in Comparative Perspective.* Several other studies recount aspects of Zaire's past national security environment, especially the immediate postindependence period. These include: *The Congo Cables: The Cold War in Africa—From Eisenhower to Kennedy* by Madeleine G. Kalb and Crawford Young's *Conflict in the Congo.* Also, annual editions of *Africa Contemporary Record: Annual Survey and Documents* provide useful information on recent developments within the armed forces as well as a detailed listing of military equipment. *The Military Balance,* published annually by the International Institute for Strategic Studies, also provides a detailed listing of military equipment, service strength, and military budgets. The magazine *African Defence Journal* provides a wealth of information about current developments in the Zairian armed forces. Current information on the internal security and police forces can be gleaned from George Thomas Kurian's *World Encyclopedia of Police Forces and Penal Systems,* as well as periodic and annual reports on human rights and judicial systems issued by Amnesty International, Africa Watch, and the United States Department of State. (For further information and complete citations, see Bibliography.)

Appendix

Table 1. Metric Conversion Coefficients and Factors

When you know	Multiply by	To find
Millimeters	0.04	inches
Centimeters	0.39	inches
Meters	3.3	feet
Kilometers	0.62	miles
Hectares (10,000 m²)	2.47	acres
Square kilometers	0.39	square miles
Cubic meters	35.3	cubic feet
Liters	0.26	gallons
Kilograms	2.2	pounds
Metric tons	0.98	long tons
....	1.1	short tons
....	2,204	pounds
Degrees Celsius	1.8	degrees Fahrenheit
(Centigrade)	and add 32	

Table 2. Population Estimates and Projections, Selected Years, 1940–2010 (in millions)

Year	Population
1940	10.4
1950	13.1
1960	16.2
1970	21.4
1980	27.4
1984 [1]	29.7
1986 [2]	31.5
1987 [2]	32.5
1988 [2]	33.5
1989 [2]	34.5
1990	35.6
1991	37.8
1992	39.1
2000	43.0
2010	54.1

[1] As per last census, July 1984; exact count was 29,671,407.
[2] Official mid-year estimate.

Source: Based on information from *Encyclopedia of the Third World* (4th ed.) (Ed., George Thomas Kurian), New York, 1992, 2134; United States, Central Intelligence Agency, *The World Factbook 1991,* Washington, 1991, 345; and United States, Central Intelligence Agency, *The World Factbook 1992,* Washington, 1992, 379.

Table 3. Average Annual Population Growth Rate, Selected Years, 1950-92
(in percentages)

Years	Growth Rate
1950-55	2.3
1955-60	2.4
1960-65	1.9
1965-70	2.1
1970-75	2.8
1975-80	3.3
1980-85	3.0
1985-90	3.2
1991	3.3
1992	3.3

Source: Based on information from *Encyclopedia of the Third World* (4th ed.) (Ed., George Thomas Kurian), New York, 1992, 2134; United States, Central Intelligence Agency, *The World Factbook 1991*, Washington, 1991, 345; and United States, Central Intelligence Agency, *The World Factbook 1992*, Washington, 1992, 379.

Table 4. Demographic Indicators, Selected Years, 1965-92

Indicator	1965	1975-80	1980-85	1985-90	1991	1992
Crude Birth Rate (per 1,000 population) ...	47.0	45.8	45.3	45.6	46.0	45.0
Crude Death Rate (per 1,000 population) ...	21.0	17.2	15.8	14.2	13.0	13.0
Infant Mortality Rate (per 1,000 live births) ...	140.0	n.a.	n.a.	103.0 *	99.0	97.0
Total Fertility Rate (Number of children born/woman)	n.a.	n.a.	n.a.	n.a.	6.2	6.1
Life Expectancy (in years)						
Males	n.a.	n.a.	n.a.	51.0 *	52.0	52.0
Females	n.a.	n.a.	n.a.	55.0 *	56.0	56.0

n.a.—Not available.
* Estimate for 1990 only.

Source: Based on information from United Nations, *World Population Prospects as Assessed in 1990*, New York, 1990; United States, Central Intelligence Agency, *The World Factbook 1991*, Washington, 1991, 345; and United States, Central Intelligence Agency, *The World Factbook 1992*, Washington, 1992, 379.

Table 5. *Area, Population, and Inhabitants per Square Kilometer, by Region, 1970 and 1984*

Region	Area (in square kilometers)	Population (in thousands)		Inhabitants per square kilometer	
		1970	1984	1970	1984
Bandundu	295,658	2,601	3,683	8.8	12.5
Bas-Zaïre	54,078	1,504	1,972	27.8	36.5
Équateur	403,292	2,432	3,406	6.0	8.4
Haut-Zaïre	503,239	3,356	4,206	6.7	8.4
Kasai-Occidental	156,967	2,434	2,287	15.5	14.6
Kasai-Oriental	168,216	1,872	2,403	11.1	14.3
Kinshasa	9,965	1,323	2,654	132.8	266.3
Kivu	256,803	3,362	5,188	13.1	20.2
Shaba	496,877	2,754	3,874	5.5	7.8

Source: Based on information from Federal Republic of Germany, Statistisches Bundesamt, *Länderbericht Zaïre 1990,* Wiesbaden, 1990, 24; and Zaire, Département du plan, Institut national de la statistique, *Le Zaïre en chiffres,* Kinshasa, 1988, 14.

Table 6. *Annual Population Growth Rates per Thousand, by Region, 1938–48 to 1970–84* [1]

Region	1938–48	1948–58	1958–70	1970–84 [2]
Bandundu	0.6	2.7	2.7	2.5
Bas-Zaïre	1.9	1.7	3.8	2.5
Équateur	0.2	1.2	2.3	2.7
Haut-Zaïre	− 0.4	1.0	2.1	2.1
Kasai-Occidental	− 0.4	1.7	2.7	2.3
Kasai-Oriental	− 0.4	1.0	4.2	3.4
Kinshasa	12.2	11.4	9.8	6.2
Kivu	1.6	3.6	3.2	3.4
Shaba	1.8	2.9	3.7	3.2
TOTAL ZAIRE	0.6	2.2	3.2	3.0

[1] Based on data from censuses of 1938, 1948, 1958, 1970, and 1984.
[2] Projected.

Source: Based on information from Joseph Boute and Léon de Saint Moulin, *Perspectives démographiques régionales, 1975–1985,* Kinshasa, 1978.

Table 7. Population of Major Cities, 1970 and 1985
(in thousands)

City	1970	1985
Bukavu	135	418
Kananga	429	938
Kikwit	112	346
Kinshasa	1,323	2,796
Kisangani	230	557
Lubumbashi	318	765
Matadi	110	216
Mbandaka	108	294
Mbuji-Mayi	256	625

Source:Based on information from Federal Republic of Germany, Statistisches Bundesamt, *Länderbericht Zaïre 1990*, Wiesbaden, 1990, 25.

Table 8. Number of Students, Teachers, and Classes or Institutions, by Level of Education, 1983–84, 1984–85, and 1985–86

Level	1983–84	1984–85	1985–86
Primary			
Students: Boys	2,663,903	2,736,515	2,810,707
Girls	1,990,710	2,084,051	2,182,816
TOTAL	4,654,613	4,820,566	4,993,523
Teachers	112,077	156,631	161,925
Classes	112,056	141,943	149,753
Secondary			
Students: Boys	1,541,526	1,864,117	2,528,000
Girls	610,374	756,258	940,051
TOTAL	2,151,900	2,620,375	3,468,051
of which			
Normal School	365,823	445,464	543,668
Technical and Professional	215,190	262,037	319,205
General	1,570,887	1,912,874	2,334,578
Teachers	43,459	47,086	47,952
Classes	27,609	26,844	29,213
Higher Education			
Students			
Universities	12,896	13,540	16,239
Teaching Institutes	10,670	10,338	10,928
Technical Institutes	14,814	14,778	13,711
TOTAL	38,380	38,656	40,878
Teachers	2,568	2,581	3,803
Institutions			
Universities	3	3	3
Teaching Institutes	14	14	14
Technical Institutes	18	18	18
TOTAL	35	35	35

* As published.

Source: Based on information from Zaire, Département du plan, Institut de la statistique, *Le Zaïre en chiffres*, Kinshasa, 1988, 19.

Table 9. Number of Health Facilities and Personnel by Region, 1985

Region	Health Facilities	Hospital Beds	Doctors	Other Medical Personnel	Beds per 1,000 Inhabitants	Inhabitants per Doctor
Bandundu	816	8,676	56	1,171	2.3	67,580
Bas-Zaïre	622	6,592	73	1,021	3.3	27,700
Équateur	850	8,646	80	944	2.5	43,590
Haut-Zaïre	792	9,829	117	758	2.3	36,866
Kasai-Occidental	441	5,026	54	731	2.2	42,906
Kasai-Oriental	249	3,405	63	743	1.4	39,075
Kinshasa	326	5,273	69	3,052	1.9	4,031
Kivu	710	7,593	96	717	1.4	56,124
Shaba	477	9,031	83	634	2.3	48,068
TOTAL ZAIRE	5,283	64,071	1,318	9,771	2.1	23,193

Source: Based on information from Zaire, Département du plan, Institut de la statistique, *Le Zaire en chiffres*, Kinshasa, 1988, 18.

Table 10. *Methods of Contraception Used in Urban Areas, 1984–87*
(in percentages)

Method	1984	1985	1986	1987
Pill	41	40	45	38
Injectable	24	25	23	17
Intrauterine device (IUD)	8	8	9	7
Condom	11	11	10	25
Sterilization	3	1	2	1
Spermicide	12	13	10	11
Other	1	2	1	1

Source: Based on information provided by the Project for Planned Birth Services (Projet des Services des Naissances Désirables—PSND), Bureau of Statistics, Kinshasa, 1988.

Table 11. *Agricultural Production, 1988–91*
(in thousands of tons)

Product	1988	1989	1990	1991
Grains				
Corn	816	846	870 *	906
Millet	30	31	31 *	31
Rice (paddy)	329	341	345 *	365
Sorghum	45	47	50 *	49
Wheat	35	35	n.a.	n.a.
Total grains	1,255	1,300	1,296 *	1,351
Tubers				
Cassava (manioc)	17,000	17,400	17,600 *	18,227
Potatoes	32	33	33 *	34 *
Sweet potatoes	368	373	375 *	377 *
Taro (coco yam)	37	38	40 *	42 *
Yams	265	266	280 *	300 *
Total tubers	17,702	18,110	18,328 *	18,980 *
Vegetables				
Cabbages	25 *	25 *	27 *	28 *
Onions (dry)	29	30 *	31 *	31 *
Peanuts	420	425	430 *	435
Pumpkins	40 *	40 *	40 *	42 *
Tomatoes	38	39	40	40 *
Total vegetables	552 *	559 *	568 *	576 *
Oils				
Cottonseed	50 *	50 *	50 *	50
Palm kernel	74 *	74 *	74 *	75 *
Palm oil	178	178	n.a.	n.a.
Total oils	302 *	302 *	124 *	125 *

336

Table 11.—Continued

Product	1988	1989	1990	1991
Fruits				
Avocados	44	45	45 *	46 *
Bananas	403	404	404 *	405 *
Grapefruit	12 *	13 *	13 *	14 *
Mangoes	205	208	208 *	210 *
Oranges	150 *	152 *	153 *	155 *
Pineapples	136	142	143 *	145 *
Plantains	1,799	1,800	1,800 *	1,820 *
Total fruits	2,749 *	2,764 *	2,766 *	2,795 *
Beverages				
Cocoa beans	6	7	5 *	4
Coffee (green)	99	107	120 *	102 *
Tea	3	3	3 *	3 *
Total beverages	108	117	128 *	109 *
Other				
Cotton (lint)	26 *	26 *	26 *	26 *
Rubber	17	24 *	10 *	10 *
Sugarcane	1,150 *	1,150 *	1,180 *	1,180 *
Tobacco	3	3	4 *	4 *
Total other	1,196 *	1,203 *	1,220 *	1,220 *

n.a.—not available.
* Estimate.

Source: Based on information from *Africa South of the Sahara, 1993,* London, 1992, 927; *Africa South of the Sahara, 1994,* London, 1993, 957; and *Europa World Yearbook, 1993,* 2, London, 1993, 3258.

Table 12. Trade and Current Account Balance, 1985–91
(in millions of United States dollars)

	1985	1986	1987	1988	1989	1990	1991
Exports *	1,853	1,844	1,731	2,178	2,201	2,138	1,500
Imports *	1,247	1,283	1,376	1,645	1,683	1,539	1,200
Trade balance	606	561	355	533	518	599	300
Current account balance	− 215	− 400	− 644	− 62	− 611	− 643	− 850

* Free on board (f.o.b.).

Source: Based on information from various issues of Economist Intelligence Unit, *Country Report: Zaire, Rwanda, Burundi,* London, 1987–92.

Table 13. Value of Principal Exports, 1990
(in millions of United States dollars)

Product	Value *
Copper and cobalt	1,001
Crude petroleum	227
Diamonds	240

* Does not include informal-sector exports and smuggling.

Source: Based on information from Economist Intelligence Unit, *Country Report: Zaire, Rwanda, Burundi,* No. 2, London, 1992, 3.

Table 14. Value of Principal Imports, 1988
(in millions of United States dollars)

Product	Value
Imports for Gécamines *	362
Petroleum products	169
Food, beverages, and tobacco	147
Transport equipment	95

* Gécamines—General Quarries and Mines (Générale des Carrières et des Mines).

Source: Based on information from Economist Intelligence Unit, *Country Report: Zaire, Rwanda, Burundi,* No. 2, London, 1992, 3.

Table 15. Main Trading Partners, 1990
(in percentage of total value)

	Percentage
Destination of exports	
Belgium/Luxembourg	56.0
United States	12.9
France	7.1
Germany	6.4
Other	20.6
Total *	100.0
Origin of imports	
Belgium/Luxembourg	27.6
France	12.3
Germany	10.8
United States	10.6
Other	38.7
Total *	100.0

* Totals may not add to 100 because of rounding.

Source: Based on information from various issues of Economist Intelligence Unit, *Country Report: Zaire, Rwanda, Burundi,* London, 1990–92.

Table 16. Major Army Equipment, 1993

Description	Country of Origin	Inventory
Main battle tanks		
T-62 medium	China	40
T-59 medium	-do-	20
M-60 medium	United States	10
AMX-13 light [1]	France	13
Armored reconnaissance vehicles		
AML-60 Panhard	-do-	30
AML-90	-do-	30
FERRET	Britain	28
Armored personnel carriers		
M-113/M-113A	United States	12
M-3A1	-do-	60
YW-531	n.a.	12
K-63	China	12
BTR-60	(former) Soviet Union	15
BTR-152	-do-	250
Fahd [2]	Egypt	n.a.
VAB [1]	France	12
Towed artillery		
75mm: M-116	United States	30
85mm: T-56	China	20
122mm: M-1938/D-30	(former) Soviet Union	20
T-60	China	15
130mm: T-59	-do-	8
Multiple rocket launchers		
107mm: T-63	China	20
122mm: BM-21	n.a.	10
Mortars		
81mm:	Belgium	n.a.
107mm: M-30	United States	n.a.
120mm: Brandt	France	50
Recoilless launchers		
57mm: M-18	United States	n.a.
75mm: M-20	-do-	n.a.
106mm: M-40A1	-do-	n.a.
Antiaircraft guns		
14.5mm: ZPU-4	China	n.a.
20mm:	n.a.	n.a.
37mm: M-1939/Type 63	China	40
40mm: L/60	Canada	n.a.
Surface-to-air missiles		
SA-7 Grail	(former) Soviet Union	n.a.
Surface-to-surface missiles		
SS-11 Gadfly	-do-	n.a.
AT-1 Snapper	-do-	n.a.

n.a.—not available.
[1] Ordered in 1989; status undetermined in 1993.
[2] Used by Civil Guard.

Source: Based on information from *The Military Balance, 1993–1994,* 1993, 221.

Table 17. Major Navy Equipment, 1993

Description	Country of Origin	Inventory
Fast Patrol Craft (Inshore)		
Shanghai II PFI	China	2
Huchuan	-do-	4
Torpedo Boats		
P-4	North Korea	3
Coastal Patrol Craft		
Swift MkII	United States	2
Arcoa	France	18

n.a.—not available.

Source: Based on information from *The Military Balance, 1993–1994,* 1993, 221.

Table 18. Major Air Force Equipment, 1993

Description	Country of Origin	Inventory
Fighters Ground Attack		
Mirage 5M	France	7
Mirage 5DM7	-do-	1
Counterinsurgency aircraft		
MB-326 GB	Italy	8
MB-326 K	-do-	6
AT-6G	United States	6
FTB-337 Cessna	-do-	20
Transport aircraft		
Boeing 707-320	-do-	1
Boeing 727-30	-do-	1
BN-2A Islander	Britain	1
C-46 Commando	United States	2
C-47 Dakota	-do-	8
C-130H Hercules	-do-	5
DHC-5D Buffalo	Canada	3
DHC-6 Twin Otter	-do-	1
C-54 Skymaster	United States	4
DC-6	-do-	2
MU-2J	Japan	2
Merlin III	United States	1
Mystère-Falcon 20	France	1
F-27 Friendship	Netherlands	3
Helicopters		
AS-332L Super Puma	France	1
SA-319 Alouette	-do-	4
SA-330 Puma	-do-	4
SA-321 Super Frelon	-do-	1
SA-350 Écureuil	-do-	n.a.
Bell 47G	United States	6

Table 18.—Continued

Description	Country of Origin	Inventory
Liaison aircraft		
Cessna 310R	-do-	6
Training aircraft		
Cessna 150	-do-	12
Cessna 310	-do-	3
SF–260MC/MZ Warrior	Italy	9

n.a.—not available.

Source: Based on information from *The Military Balance, 1993–1994,* 1993, 221.

Bibliography

Chapter 1

Anstey, Roger. "Belgian Rule in the Congo and the Aspirations of the Évolué Class." Pages 194–225 in L.H. Gann and Peter Duignan (eds.), *Colonialism in Africa, 1870–1960.* London: Cambridge University Press, 1969.

_____. *Britain and the Congo in the Nineteenth Century.* Oxford: Clarendon Press, 1962. Reprint. Westport, Connecticut: Greenwood Press, 1981.

_____. *King Leopold's Legacy.* London: Oxford University Press, 1969.

Ascherson, Neil. *The King Incorporated.* London: Allen and Unwin, 1963.

Birmingham, David. *Trade and Conflict in Angola.* Oxford: Clarendon Press, 1966.

Birmingham, David, and Phyllis M. Martin (eds.). *History of Central Africa.* (2 vols.) New York: Longman, 1983.

Bobb, F. Scott. *Historical Dictionary of Zaire.* (African Historical Dictionaries Series, No. 43.) Metuchen, New Jersey: Scarecrow Press, 1988.

Brausch, Georges. *Belgian Administration in the Congo.* New York: Oxford University Press, 1961. Reprint. Westport, Connecticut: Greenwood Press, 1986.

Bustin, Edouard. *Lunda under Belgian Rule: The Politics of Ethnicity.* Cambridge: Harvard University Press, 1975.

Callaghy, Thomas. *The State-Society Struggle: Zaire in Comparative Perspective.* New York: Columbia University Press, 1984.

Chomé, Jules. *L'ascension de Mobutu: du Sergent Joseph Désiré au Général Sese Seko.* Brussels: Éditions Complexe, 1974.

Curtin, Philip, Steven Feierman, Leonard Thompson, and Jan Vansina. *African History.* Boston: Little, Brown, 1978.

Dayal, Rajwshwar. *Mission for Hammarskjöld.* Princeton: Princeton University Press, 1976.

Ekwe-Ekwe, Herbert. *Conflict and Intervention in Africa: Nigeria, Angola, Zaire.* New York: St. Martin's Press, 1990.

Fabian, Johannes. *Language and Colonial Power.* Cambridge: Cambridge University Press, 1986.

Gérard-Libais, Jules. *Katanga Secession.* (Trans., Rebecca Young.) Madison: University of Wisconsin Press, 1966.

Gérard-Libais, Jules, and Benoît Verhaegen. *Congo 1960.* Brussels:

Centre de recherche et d'information socio-politique, 1961.

Gibbs, David N. "Dag Hammarskjöld, the United Nations, and the Congo Crisis of 1960–1: A Reinterpretation," *Journal of Modern African Studies* [London], 31, No. 1, 1993, 163–74.

_____. *The Political Economy of Third World Intervention: Mines, Money, and U.S. Policy in the Congo Crisis.* Chicago: University of Chicago Press, 1991.

Gould, David. *Bureaucratic Corruption and Underdevelopment in the Third World: The Case of Zaire.* Elmsford, New York: Pergamon Press, 1980.

Hodgkin, Thomas. *Nationalism in Colonial Africa.* New York: New York University Press, 1957.

Kalb, Madeleine G. *The Congo Cables: The Cold War in Africa— From Eisenhower to Kennedy.* New York: Macmillan, 1982.

Kalele-ka-Bila. "La culture obligatoire du coton au Congo belge," *Africa* [Rome], 47, No. 1, March 1992, 83–92.

Kamitatu-Massamba, Cléophas. *La grande mystification du Congo-Kinshasa.* Paris: Éditions Maspero, 1971.

Kanza, Thomas. *The Rise and Fall of Patrice Lumumba: Conflict in the Congo.* Cambridge, Massachusetts: Schenkman, 1977.

Kinder, Hermann, and Werner Hilgemann. *The Anchor Atlas of World History,* 2. (Trans., Ernest A. Menze.) Garden City, New York: Anchor Books, 1978.

Lefever, Ernest. *Crisis in the Congo: A United Nations Force in Action.* Washington: Brookings Institution, 1965.

Lemarchand, René. "The Bases of Nationalism among the Bakongo," *Africa* [Rome], 31, No. 4, 1961, 344–54.

_____. "Congo-Léopoldville." Pages 560–96 in James S. Coleman and Carl Rosberg (eds.), *Political Parties and National Integration in Tropical Africa.* Berkeley: University of California Press, 1964.

_____. "The Limits of Self-Determination: The Case of Katanga," *American Political Science Review,* 61, No. 2, 1962, 404–16.

_____. *Political Awakening in the Belgian Congo.* Berkeley: University of California Press, 1964.

Martens, Ludo. *Pierre Mulele and the Kwilu Uprising in Zaire.* (Trans., Michael Wolfers.) Atlantic Highlands, New Jersey: Zed Books, 1992.

Nguza Karl-i-Bond. *Mobutu ou l'incarnation du mal zaïrois.* London: Collings, 1982.

Nzongola-Ntalaja, Georges. "The Continuing Struggle for National Liberation in Zaire," *Journal of Modern African Studies* [London], 17, No. 4, 1979, 595–614.

Peemans, J.P. "The Social and Economic Development of Zaire since Independence," *African Affairs*, 74, No. 295, 1975, 422–35.

Ryckmans, Pierre. *Dominer pour servir*. Brussels: Éditions Nouvelles, 1948.

Rymenam, Jean. "Classes sociales, pouvoir et économie au Zaïre, ou comment le sous-développement enrichit les gouvernements," *Genève-Afrique* [Geneva], 19, No. 1, 1980, 43–53.

Schatzberg, Michael G. *The Dialectics of Oppression in Zaire*. Bloomington: Indiana University Press, 1988.

_____. *Politics and Class in Zaire: Bureaucracy, Business, and Beer in Lisala*. New York: Africana, 1980.

Slade, Ruth. *King Leopold's Congo*. London: Oxford University Press, 1962.

Stengers, Jean. "The Congo Free State and the Belgian Congo Before 1914." Pages 251–92 in L.H. Gann and Peter Duignan (eds.), *Colonialism in Africa, 1870–1960*. London: Cambridge University Press, 1969.

Thornton, John K. *The Kingdom of Congo: Civil War and Transition, 1641–1718*. Madison: University of Wisconsin Press, 1983.

Vansina, Jan. *Kingdoms of the Savanna*. Madison: University of Wisconsin Press, 1968.

_____. *Paths in the Rainforests: Toward a History of Political Tradition in Equatorial Africa*. Madison: University of Wisconsin Press, 1990.

_____. "The Peoples of the Forest." Pages 75–118 in David Birmingham and Phyllis M. Martin (eds.), *History of Central Africa*, 1. New York: Longman, 1983.

Willame, Jean-Claude. *Patrice Lumumba: La crise congolaise revisitée*. Paris: Éditions Karthala, 1990.

_____. *Patrimonialism and Political Change in the Congo*. Stanford: Stanford University Press, 1972.

_____. "La seconde guerre du Shaba," *Genève-Afrique* [Geneva], 16, No. 1, 1977–78, 87–89.

Young, Crawford. "The Colonial State and Post-Colonial Crisis." Pages 1–31 in Prosser Gifford and W. Roger Louis (eds.), *Decolonization and African Independence*. New Haven: Yale University Press, 1988.

_____. *Politics in the Congo*. Princeton: Princeton University Press, 1965.

_____. "The Politics of Separatism: Katanga 1960–63." Pages 167–208 in Gwendolen M. Carter (ed.), *Politics in Africa*. New York: Harcourt, Brace, and World, 1966.

_____. "Rebellion and the Congo." Pages 209–45 in Robert I. Rotberg (ed.), *Rebellion in Black Africa*. London: Oxford University Press, 1971.

Young, Crawford, and Thomas Turner. *The Rise and Decline of the Zairian State*. Madison: University of Wisconsin Press, 1985.

Chapter 2

Africa Contemporary Record: Annual Survey and Documents, 1988-1989. (Ed., Marion E. Doro.) New York: Africana, 1992.

Africa South of the Sahara, 1992. (21st ed.) London: Europa, 1991.

Africa South of the Sahara, 1993. (22d ed.) London: Europa, 1992.

Africa South of the Sahara, 1994. (23d ed.) London: Europa, 1993.

Berkeley, Bill. "Zaire: An African Horror Story," *Atlantic Monthly,* 272, No. 2, August 1993, 20-28.

Boute, Joseph, and Léon de Saint Moulin. *Perspectives démographiques régionales, 1975-1985*. Kinshasa: Zaire, Département du plan, 1978.

Boyle, Patrick M. "Beyond Self-Protection to Prophecy: The Catholic Church and Political Change in Zaire," *Africa Today,* 39, No. 3, 1992, 49-66.

Coquéry-Vidrovitch, Catherine, Alain Forest, and Herbert Weiss (eds.). *Rébellions-révolution au Zaïre, 1963-1965*. Paris: Harmattan, 1987.

Davis-Roberts, Christopher. "Kutambuwa Ugonjuwa: Concepts of Illness and Transformation among the Tabwa of Zaire." Pages 376-92 in Steven Feierman and John M. Janzen (eds.), *The Social Basis of Health and Healing in Africa*. (Comparative Studies of Health Systems and Medical Care, No. 30.) Berkeley: University of California Press, 1992.

Encyclopedia of the Third World. (4th ed.) (Ed., George Thomas Kurian.) New York: Facts on File, 1992.

Federal Republic of Germany. Statistisches Bundesamt. *Länderbericht Zaïre, 1990*. (Statistik des Auslandes Series.) Wiesbaden: 1990.

Feierman, Steven, and John M. Janzen (eds.). *The Social Basis of Health and Healing in Africa*. (Comparative Studies of Health Systems and Medical Care, No. 30.) Berkeley: University of California Press, 1992.

Goovaerts, Leo. "L'église et l'état au Zaïre à l'épreuve de l'authenticité," *Cultures et Développement* [Louvain, Belgium], 7, No. 2, 1975, 243-84.

Gould, David J. *Bureaucratic Corruption and Underdevelopment in the Third World: The Case of Zaire*. Elmsford, New York: Pergamon Press, 1980.

Guthrie, Malcolm. *The Classification of the Bantu Languages.* London: Oxford University Press, 1948.

Harms, Robert W. *River of Wealth, River of Sorrow: The Central Zaire Basin in the Era of the Slave and Ivory Trade, 1500–1891.* New Haven: Yale University Press, 1981.

Hart, T.B. "The Ecology of a Single Species-Dominant Forest and Mixed Forest in Zaire." (Ph.D. dissertation.) Ann Arbor: Michigan State University, 1985.

Hoffman, Dan C. "Zaire's Protestants in Search of Social Legitimacy," *Africa Today,* 39, No. 3, 1992, 69–76.

Jewsiewicki, Bogumil, and David Newbury (eds.) *African Historiographies: What History for Which Africa?* Beverly Hills: Sage, 1986.

Kabongo-Mbaya, Ph.B. "Protestantisme zaïrois et déclin du Mobutisme," *Politique Africaine* [Paris], 41, 1991, 72–89.

Léonard, Charles. *Profils de l'économie du Zaïre: Années 1955–1987.* Kinshasa: Zaire, Département de l'économie nationale et de l'industrie, 1987.

Matondo, Kunsunga. *Développement inégalitaire et disparités régionales dans les pays du Tiers-monde: Cas du Zaïre.* Kinshasa: Université de Kinshasa, Faculté des sciences économiques, 1986.

MacGaffey, Janet. *Entrepreneurs and Parasites: The Struggle for Indigenous Capitalism in Zaire.* Cambridge: Cambridge University Press, 1987.

_____. "Evading Male Control: Women in the Second Economy in Zaire." Pages 161–76 in Sharon B. Stichter and Jane L. Parpart (eds.), *Patriarchy and Class: African Women in the Home and the Work Force.* Boulder, Colorado: Westview Press, 1988.

_____. "Initiatives from Below: Zaire's Other Path to Social and Economic Restructuring." Pages 243–61 in Goran Hyden and Michael Bratton (eds.), *Governance and Politics in Africa.* Boulder, Colorado: Rienner, 1992.

MacGaffey, Janet (ed.). *The Real Economy of Zaire: The Contribution of Smuggling and Other Unofficial Activities to National Wealth.* Philadelphia: University of Pennsylvania Press, 1991.

MacGaffey, Wyatt. *Astonishment and Power.* Washington: Smithsonian Institution Press, 1993.

_____. "The Policy of National Integration in Zaire," *Journal of Modern African Studies* [London], 20, No. 1, 1982, 87–105.

_____. *Religion and Society in Central Africa: The BaKongo of Lower Zaire.* Chicago: University of Chicago Press, 1986.

Manwana Mungongo. "Les droits de la femme travailleuse au Zaïre," *Zaïre-Afrique* [Kinshasa], 163, 1982, 165–80.

Miracle, Marvin P. *Agriculture in the Congo Basin: Tradition and Change in African Rural Economies.* Madison: University of Wisconsin Press, 1967.

Mwene-Batende. "Le Kitawala dans l'évolution socio-politique récente: Cas du groupe Belukela dans la ville du Kisangani," *Cahiers des Religions Africaines* [Kinshasa], 10, 1976, 81–105.

Newbury, Catharine. "Ebutumwa Bw'Emiogo: The Tyranny of Cassava, A Women's Tax Revolt in Eastern Zaire," *Canadian Journal of African Studies* [Ottawa], 18, 1984, 35–54.

_____. "Survival Strategies in Rural Zaire: Realities of Coping with Crisis." Pages 99–112 in Georges Nzongola-Ntalaja (ed.), *The Crisis in Zaire: Myths and Realities.* Trenton, New Jersey: Africa World Press, 1986.

Newbury, Catharine, and Brooke G. Schoepf. "State, Peasantry, and Agrarian Crisis in Zaire: Does Gender Make a Difference?" Pages 91–110 in Jane L. Parpart and Kathleen A. Staudt (eds.), *Women and the State in Africa.* Boulder, Colorado: Rienner, 1989.

Newbury, David. *Kings and Clans: Ijwi Island and the Lake Kivu Rift, 1780–1840.* Madison: University of Wisconsin Press, 1991.

Nsondé, Jean. "Christianisme et religion traditionelle en pays kongo aux dixseptième-dixhuitième siècles," *Cahiers d'Études Africaines* [Paris], 128, Nos. 32–34, 1992, 705–11.

Nzongola-Ntalaja, Georges. "The Continuing Struggle for National Liberation in Zaire," *Journal of Modern African Studies* [London], 17, No. 4, 1979, 595–614.

Nzongola-Ntalaja, Georges (ed.). *The Crisis in Zaire: Myths and Realities.* Trenton, New Jersey: Africa World Press, 1986.

Packard, Randall M. *Chiefship and Cosmology: An Historical Study of Political Competition.* Bloomington: Indiana University Press, 1981.

Parpart, Jane L., and Kathleen A. Staudt (eds.). *Women and the State in Africa.* Boulder, Colorado: Rienner, 1989.

Roberts, Renée G. *Inducing the Deluge: Zaire's Internally Displaced People.* (U.S. Committee for Refugees, Issue Paper.) Washington: American Council for Nationalities Service, 1993.

Saint Moulin, Léon de. *Atlas des collectivités du Zaïre.* Kinshasa: Presses universitaires du Zaïre, 1976.

Schatzberg, Michael G. *The Dialectics of Oppression in Zaire.* Bloomington: Indiana University Press, 1988.

_____. *Politics and Class in Zaire: Bureaucracy, Business, and Beer in Lisala.* New York: Africana, 1980.

Schildkrout, Enid, and Curtis A. Keim. *African Reflections: Art from Northeastern Zaire.* Seattle: University of Washington Press, 1990.

Schoepf, Brooke G., and Claude Schoepf. "Food Crisis and Agrarian Change in the Eastern Highlands of Zaire," *Urban Anthropology,* 16, No. 1, Spring 1987, 5–37.

Schoepf, Brooke G., and Walu Engundu. "Women's Trade and Contributions to Household Budgets in Kinshasa." Pages 124–51 in Janet MacGaffey (ed.), *The Real Economy of Zaire: The Contribution of Smuggling and Other Unofficial Activities to National Wealth.* Philadelphia: University of Pennsylvania Press, 1991.

Scott, James C. *The Moral Economy of the Peasant: Rebellion and Subsistence in Southeast Asia.* New Haven: Yale University Press, 1976.

The Statesman's Yearbook, 1991–1992. (Ed., Brian Hunter.) New York: St. Martin's Press, 1991.

The Statesman's Yearbook, 1992–1993. (Ed., Brian Hunter.) New York: St. Martin's Press, 1992.

The Statesman's Yearbook, 1993–1994. (Ed., Brian Hunter.) New York: St. Martin's Press, 1993.

Thornton, John K. *The Kingdom of Kongo: Civil War and Transition, 1641–1718.* Madison: University of Wisconsin Press, 1983.

United Nations. *World Population Prospects as Assessed in 1990.* New York: 1990.

United States. Central Intelligence Agency. *The World Factbook, 1991.* Washington: GPO, 1991.

――――. Central Intelligence Agency. *The World Factbook, 1992.* Washington: GPO, 1992.

――――. Central Intelligence Agency. *The World Factbook, 1993.* Washington: GPO, 1993.

――――. Department of Commerce. Bureau of the Census. *World Population Profile: 1994.* (Report WP/94.) Washington: GPO, 1994.

U.S. Committee for Refugees. *World Refugee Survey, 1992.* Washington: American Council for Nationalities Service, 1992.

Vansina, Jan. "The History of God among the Kuba," *Africa* [Rome], 28, No. 1, 1983, 17–39.

――――. *Introduction à l'ethnographie du Congo.* Kinshasa: Éditions universitaires du Congo, 1966.

――――. "Knowledge and Perceptions of the African Past." Pages 28–42 in Bogumil Jewsiewicki and David Newbury (eds.), *African Historiographies: What History for Which Africa?* Beverly Hills, California: Sage, 1986.

――――. *Paths in the Rainforests: Toward a History of Political Tradition in Equatorial Africa.* Madison: University of Wisconsin Press, 1990.

――――. "Western Bantu Expansion," *Journal of African History,* 25, No. 2, 1984, 129–45.

Verhaegen, Benoît. "L'enseignement supérieur: Vers l'explosion," *Politique Africaine* [Paris], 41, 1991, 72–89.

Verhaegen, Benoît, Muamba Ngalula, and Kinsangani Endenda. "La marginalité, le mariage, et l'instruction à Kinsangani," *Canadian Journal of African Studies* [Ottawa], 18, No. 1, 1984, 131–37.

Vwakyanakazi, Mukohya. "Import and Export in the Second Economy in North Kivu." Pages 43–71 in Janet MacGaffey (ed.), *The Real Economy of Zaire: The Contribution of Smuggling and Other Unofficial Activities to National Wealth*. Philadelphia: University of Pennsylvania Press, 1991.

Willame, Jean-Claude. "L'automne d'une monarchie," *Politique Africaine* [Paris], 41, 1991, 72–89.

Witte, John. "Deforestation in Zaire: Logging and Landlessness," *Ecologist*, 22, March–April 1992, 58–68.

World Bank. *Social Indicators of Development, 1993*. Baltimore: Johns Hopkins University Press, 1993.

Young, Crawford. *The Politics of Cultural Pluralism*. Madison: University of Wisconsin Press, 1976.

Young, Crawford, and Thomas Turner. *The Rise and Decline of the Zairian State*. Madison: University of Wisconsin Press, 1985.

Zaire. Département du plan, Institut national de la statistique. *Le Zaïre en chiffres*. Kinshasa: 1988.

(Various issues of the following publications were also used in the preparation of this chapter: *African Affairs; African Studies Review; Africa Research Bulletin* (Political, Social, and Cultural Series) [London]; Amnesty International, *Urgent Action; Anthropus; Cahiers du CEDAF* [Brussels]; *Canadian Journal of Political Science* [Ottawa]; *Cultures et Développement* [Louvain, Belgium]; *Ethnology; Études zaïroises* [Kinshasa]; *Executive News Service;* Foreign Broadcast Information Service, *Daily Report: Sub-Saharan Africa; Journal of African History; Journal of African Religions; Journal of Modern African Studies* [London]; *Kongo ya Sika* [Kinshasa]; *Marchés Tropicaux et Méditeranéens* [Paris]; *Revue des Forces Armées Zaïroises* [Kinshasa]; *Revue Nouvelle* [Paris]; *Telex Africa* [Brussels]; and *Zaïre-Afrique* [Kinshasa].)

Chapter 3

Africa Contemporary Record: Annual Survey and Documents, 1988–1989. (Ed., Marion E. Doro.) New York: Africana, 1992.

Africa South of the Sahara, 1993. (22d ed.) London: Europa, 1992.

Africa South of the Sahara, 1994. (23d ed.) London: Europa, 1993.

Blumenthal, Erwin. "Zaïre: Rapport sur sa crédibilité financière internationale," *Revue Nouvelle* [Paris], 77, No. 11, 1982, 360–78.

Bobb, F. Scott. *Historical Dictionary of Zaire*. (African Historical Dictionaries Series, No. 43.) Metuchen, New Jersey: Scarecrow Press, 1988.

Callaghy, Thomas M. "The Ritual Dance of the Debt Game," *Africa Report,* September–October 1984, 22–24.

_____. *The State-Society Struggle: Zaire in Comparative Perspective.* New York: Columbia University Press, 1984.

The Europa World Year Book, 1993. London: Europa, 1993.

Federal Republic of Germany. Statistisches Bundesamt. *Länderbericht Zaïre, 1990.* (Statistik des Auslandes Series.) Wiesbaden: 1990.

Gould, David. *Bureaucratic Corruption and Underdevelopment in the Third World: The Case of Zaire.* Elmsford, New York: Pergamon Press, 1980.

Gran, Guy, and Galen Hull (eds.). *Zaire: The Political Economy of Underdevelopment.* New York: Praeger, 1979.

International Monetary Fund. *Zaire: Use of Fund Resources.* Washington: April 30, 1987.

International Petroleum Encyclopedia, 1992. (Ed., Jim West.) Tulsa, Oklahoma: Pennwell, 1992.

Kronsten, Gregory. *Zaire to the 1990s: Will Retrenchment Work?* (A Special Report of the Economist Intelligence Unit.) London: Economist, March 1986.

Léonard, Charles. *Conjoncture économique.* Kinshasa: Zaire, Département de l'économie nationale et de l'industrie, October 1987.

Leslie, Winsome J. *The World Bank and Structural Transformation in Developing Countries: The Case of Zaire.* Boulder, Colorado: Rienner, 1987.

MacGaffey, Janet. "Initiatives from Below: Zaire's Other Path to Social and Economic Restructuring." Pages 243–61 in Goran Hyden and Michael Bratton (eds.), *Governance and Politics in Africa.* Boulder, Colorado: Rienner, 1992.

MacGaffey, Janet (ed.). *The Real Economy of Zaire: The Contribution of Smuggling and Other Unofficial Activities to National Wealth.* Philadelphia: University of Pennsylvania Press, 1991.

Mokoli, Mondonga M. *State Against Development: The Experience of Post-1965 Zaire.* New York: Greenwood Press, 1992.

Morgan, George A., Kevin Connor, and Ben A. Kornhauser. *Zaire.* (Mineral Perspectives.) Washington: Department of the Interior, Bureau of Mines, 1985.

Peemans, J.P. "The Social and Economic Development of Zaire since Independence," *African Affairs,* 74, No. 295, 1975, 422–35.

Riddell, James C., Jeswald W. Salacuse, and David Tabachnick. "The National Land Law of Zaire and Indigenous Land Tenure in Central Bandundu, Zaire." (Research paper.) Madison: Land Tenure Center, University of Wisconsin, 1987.

Rymenam, Jean. "Classes sociales, pouvoir, et économie au Zaïre,

ou comment le sous-développement enrichit les gouvernements,''
Genève-Afrique [Geneva], 19, No. 1, 1980, 43–53.

Simons, E., B. Verhaegen, and J.C. Willame. *Transfert de technologie et emploi en Afrique, 2: Endettement, technologies, et industrialisation au Zaïre (1970–1981)*. Brussels: CEDAF, 1981.

Turner, Thomas E. "Decline or Recovery in Zaire?" *Current History*, 87, No. 529, May 1988, 213–16, 230.

United States. Department of State. United States Embassy, Kinshasa. *Economic Trends Report, Zaire*. Washington: June 1989.

_____. Department of State. *Investment Climate Statement, Republic of Zaire*. Washington: February 1988.

Vengroff, Richard. *Development Administration at the Local Level: The Case of Zaire*. Syracuse: Maxwell School of Citizenship and Public Affairs, Syracuse University, 1983.

Willame, Jean-Claude. *Zaïre: L'épopée d'Inga*. Paris: Harmattan, 1986.

Witte, John. "Deforestation in Zaire: Logging and Landlessness," *Ecologist*, 22, March–April 1992, 58–68.

World Bank. *Staff Appraisal Report: Zaire, Second Power Project*. Washington: June 1986.

Young, Crawford, and Thomas Turner. *The Rise and Decline of the Zairian State*. Madison: University of Wisconsin Press, 1985.

Zaire. Département du plan. Institut national de la statistique. *Le Zaire en chiffres*. Kinshasa: 1988.

(Various issues of the following publications were also used in the preparation of this chapter: *Africa Confidential* [London]; *Africa Economic Digest* [London]; *Africa Report; Economist* [London]; Economist Intelligence Unit, *Country Profile: Zaire, Rwanda, Burundi* [London]; Economist Intelligence Unit, *Country Report: Zaire, Rwanda, Burundi* [London]; Foreign Broadcast Information Service, *Daily Report: Sub-Saharan Africa; Marchés Tropicaux et Méditeranéens* [Paris]; *New York Times; Wall Street Journal;* and *Washington Post*.)

Chapter 4

Adelman, Kenneth Lee. "The Church-State Conflict in Zaire," *African Studies Review*, 18, No. 1, April 1975, 103–16.

_____. "The Political Party in Zaire as a Religious Surrogate," *Africa Today*, 23, No. 4, October–December 1976, 47–58.

Africa South of the Sahara, 1992. (21st ed.) London: Europa, 1991.

Africa South of the Sahara, 1993. (22d ed.) London: Europa, 1992.

Africa South of the Sahara, 1994. (23d ed.) London: Europa, 1993.

Amnesty International. *Political Imprisonment in Zaire: An AI Special Briefing.* New York: 1983.

Askin, Steve. "Amid Stench and Decay, Professors and Students in Zaire Struggle to Keep Their Impoverished University Alive," *The Chronicle of Higher Education,* 34, No. 20, January 27, 1988, A1, A42-43.

Asch, Susan. *L'église du prophète Kimbangu: De ses origines à son rôle actuel au Zaïre (1921-1981).* Paris: Éditions Karthala, 1983.

Badibanga, André. "Je suis le 'père de la nation,'" *Le Mois en Afrique* [Paris], Nos. 180-81, December 1980-January 1981, 103-16.

Bayart, J.F. *La politique africaine de François Mitterrand.* Paris: Éditions Karthala, 1984.

Berkeley, Bill. "Zaire: An African Horror Story," *Atlantic Monthly,* 272, No. 2, August 1993, 20-28.

Bianga, Waruzi. "Peasant, State, and Rural Development in Post-Independent Zaire: A Case Study of 'Réforme Rurale,' 1970-1980, and Its Implications." (Ph.D. dissertation.) Madison: University of Wisconsin, 1981.

Blumenthal, Erwin. "Zaire: Rapport sur sa crédibilité financière internationale," *Revue Nouvelle* [Paris], 77, No. 11, 1982, 360-78.

Brausch, Georges. *Belgian Administration in the Congo.* Westport, Connecticut: Greenwood Press, 1986.

Buana Kabue. *Citoyen président: Lettre ouverte au Président Mobutu Sese Seko . . . et aux autres.* Paris: Harmattan, 1978.

Bustin, Edouard. "The Foreign Policy of the Republic of Zaire," *Annals of the American Academy of Political and Social Science,* 489, January 1987, 63-75.

Buyseniers, Rob. *L'église zaïroise au service de quelle nation?* Brussels: Cahiers A.F.R.I.C.A., 1980.

Callaghy, Thomas M. *Culture and Politics in Zaire.* (Politics and Culture Series.) Ann Arbor: Center for Political Studies, Institute for Social Research, University of Michigan, 1987.

_____. "Internal and External Aspects of Repression by a Lame Leviathan." Pages 95-125 in George A. Lopez and Michael Stohl (eds.), *Dependence, Development, and State Repression.* Westport, Connecticut: Greenwood Press, 1988.

_____. "The Ritual Dance of the Debt Game," *Africa Report,* September-October 1984, 22-24.

_____. *The State-Society Struggle: Zaire in Comparative Perspective.* New York: Columbia University Press, 1984.

_____. *Zaire.* Boulder, Colorado: Westview Press, 1986.

Chomé, Jules. *L'ascension de Mobutu: du Sergent Joseph Désiré au Général Sese Seko.* Brussels: Éditions Complexe, 1974.

_____. *Mobutu et la contre-révolution en Afrique.* Waterloo, Belgium: Tiers-monde et révolution, 1967.

Comité Zaïre. "(Les) Syndicats belges et le syndicat du guide," *Info-Zaire* [Brussels], No. 34, January–March 1982, 3–20.

_____. *Zaïre: Le dossier de la récolonisation.* Paris: Harmattan, 1978.

Crabb, John H. *The Legal System of Congo-Kinshasa.* Charlottesville, Virginia: Michie, 1970.

De Vos, Pierre. *La décolonisation: Les évènements du Congo de 1959 à 1967.* Brussels: Éditions ABC, 1975.

Goovaerts, Leo. "L'église et l'état au Zaïre à l'épreuve de l'authenticité," *Cultures et Développement* [Louvain, Belgium], 7, No. 2, 1975, 243–84.

Gould, David J. *Bureaucratic Corruption and Underdevelopment in the Third World: The Case of Zaire.* Elmsford, New York: Pergamon Press, 1980.

Gran, Guy. *Development by People: Citizen Construction of a Just World.* New York: Praeger, 1983.

Gran, Guy, and Galen Hull (eds.). *Zaire: The Political Economy of Underdevelopment.* New York: Praeger, 1979.

Jackson, Robert H., and Carl G. Rosberg. *Personal Rule in Black Africa: Prince, Autocrat, Prophet, Tyrant.* Berkeley: University of California Press, 1982.

Jewsiewicki, Bogumil (ed.). *État indépendant du Congo, Congo belge, République démocratique du Congo, République du Zaïre?* Saint-Foy, Canada: SAFI Press, 1984.

Kwitney, Jonathan. *Endless Enemies: The Making of an Unfriendly World.* New York: Congdon and Weed, 1984.

Laïdi, Zaki. *The Super-Powers and Africa: The Constraints of a Rivalry, 1960–1990.* Chicago: University of Chicago Press, 1990.

Lemarchand, René. "The State, the Parallel Economy, and the Changing Structure of Patronage Systems." Pages 149–70 in Donald Rothchild and Naomi Chazan (eds.), *The Precarious Balance: State and Society in Africa.* Boulder, Colorado: Westview Press, 1988.

_____. "Zaire: The Unmanageable Client-State." Pages 145–64 in René Lemarchand (ed.), *American Policy in Southern Africa: The Stakes and the Stance.* (2d ed.) Lanham, Maryland: University Press of America, 1981.

Leslie, Winsome J. *The World Bank and Structural Transformation in Developing Countries: The Case of Zaire.* Boulder, Colorado: Rienner, 1987.

_____. *Zaire: Continuity and Political Change in an Oppressive State.* Boulder, Colorado: Westview Press, 1993.

"Lettre ouverte au citoyen président, fondateur du Mouvement

Populaire de la Révolution, président de la République par un groupe de parlementaires,'' *Politique Africaine* [Paris], 1, No. 3, September 1981, 94–140.

Mabi Mulumba and Mtamba Makombo. *Cadres et dirigeants au Zaïre: Qui sont-ils? Dictionnaire biographique.* Kinshasa: Éditions du C.R.P., 1986.

MacGaffey, Janet. "Initiatives from Below: Zaire's Other Path to Social and Economic Restructuring." Pages 243–61 in Goran Hyden and Michael Bratton (eds.), *Governance and Politics in Africa.* Boulder, Colorado: Rienner, 1992.

MacGaffey, Wyatt. "The Policy of National Integration in Zaire," *Journal of Modern African Studies* [London], 20, No. 1, 1982, 87–105.

Makau wa Mutua and Peter Rosenblum. *Zaire: Repression as Policy—A Human Rights Report.* New York: Lawyers' Committee for Human Rights, 1990.

Naipaul, V.S. "A New King for the Congo: Mobutu and the Nihilism of Africa." Pages 183–219 in V.S. Naipaul (ed.), *The Return of Eva Peron, with the Killings in Trinidad.* New York: Random House, 1981.

Nguza Karl-i-Bond. *Mobutu, ou l'incarnation du mal zaïrois.* London: Collings, 1982.

Nimer, Benjamin. "The Congo in Soviet Policy," *Survey* [London], 86, No. 1, Winter 1973, 184–210.

Nzongola-Ntalaja, Georges. *Class Struggles and National Liberation in Africa: Essays on the Political Economy of Neocolonialism.* Roxbury, Massachusetts: Omenana, 1982.

_____. "The Continuing Struggle for National Liberation in Zaire," *Journal of Modern African Studies* [London], 17, No. 4, 1979, 595–614.

_____. "Mobutu's Dirty Tactics," *West Africa*, No. 3979, December 27, 1993–January 9, 1994, 2345.

_____. *Revolution and Counter-Revolution in Africa: Essays in Contemporary Politics.* London: Zed Books, 1987.

_____. "United States Policy Towards Zaire." Pages 225–88 in Gerald J. Bender, James S. Coleman, and Richard L. Sklar (eds.), *African Crisis Areas and U.S. Foreign Policy.* Berkeley: University of California Press, 1985.

Nzongola-Ntalaja, Georges (ed.). *The Crisis in Zaire: Myths and Realities.* Trenton, New Jersey: Africa World Press, 1986.

Odier, Jeannick. "La politique étrangère de Mobutu," *Revue Française d'Études Politiques Africaines* [Paris], No. 120, December 1975, 25–41.

Pachter, Elise Forbes. "Our Man in Kinshasa: U.S. Relations with

Mobutu, 1970–83, Patron-Client Relations in the International Sphere.'' (Ph.D. dissertation.) Washington: School of Advanced International Studies, Johns Hopkins University, 1987.

''Pile et face: Bilan de la coopération belgo-zaïroise,'' *Revue Nouvelle* [Paris], Special issue, March 1989.

Rymenam, Jean. ''Classes sociales, pouvoir, et économie au Zaïre, ou comment le sous-développement enrichit les gouvernements,'' *Genève-Afrique* [Geneva], 19, No. 1, 1980, 43–53.

Schatzberg, Michael G. *The Dialectics of Oppression in Zaire.* Bloomington: Indiana University Press, 1988.

_____. ''Ethnicity and Class at the Local Level: Bars and Bureaucrats in Lisala, Zaire,'' *Comparative Politics*, 13, No. 4, July 1983, 461–78.

_____. ''Military Intervention and the Myth of Collective Security: The Case of Zaire,'' *Journal of Modern African Studies* [London], 27, No. 2, 1989, 315–40.

_____. *Mobutu or Chaos? The United States and Zaire, 1960–1990.* Lanham, Maryland: University Press of America, 1991.

_____. *Politics and Class in Zaire: Bureaucracy, Business, and Beer in Lisala.* New York: Africana, 1980.

_____. ''Zaire.'' Pages 283–318 in Timothy M. Shaw and Olajide Aluko (eds.), *The Political Economy of African Foreign Policy: Comparative Analysis.* New York: St. Martin's Press, 1984.

Schoepf, Brooke G. ''Man and Biosphere in Zaire.'' Pages 269–90 in Jonathan Barker (ed.), *The Politics of Agriculture in Tropical Africa.* Beverly Hills, California: Sage, 1984.

Shaw, Timothy M. ''Beyond Neo-Colonialism: Varieties of Corporatism in Africa,'' *Journal of Modern African Studies* [London], 20, No. 2, 1982, 239–61.

Simons, E., B. Verhaegen, and J.C. Willame. *Transfert de technologie et emploi en Afrique, 2: Endettement, technologies, et industrialisation au Zaïre (1970–1981).* Brussels: CEDAF, 1981.

Stockwell, John. *In Search of Enemies.* New York: Norton, 1978.

Turner, Margaret A. ''Housing in Zaire: How the System Works and How the People Cope.'' (Ph.D. dissertation.) Madison: University of Wisconsin, 1985.

Turner, Thomas E. ''The Case of Zaire: Is Mobutu a Corporatist?'' Pages 129–47 in Julius E. Nyang'oro and Timothy M. Shaw (eds.), *Corporatism in Africa.* Boulder, Colorado: Westview Press, 1989.

_____. ''Chiefs, Bureaucrats, and the MPR of Zaire.'' Pages 370–91 in Kay Lawson (ed.), *Political Parties and Linkage.* New Haven: Yale University Press, 1980.

_____. ''Decline or Recovery in Zaire?'' *Current History*, 87, No.

529, May 1988, 213–16, 230.

_____. "Mobutu's Zaire: Permanently on the Verge of Collapse?" *Current History,* 80, No. 463, March 1981, 124–27, 130.

_____. "Zaire: Stalemate and Compromise," *Current History,* 84, No. 501, April 1985, 179–83.

Tutashinda, N. "Les mystifications de l'authenticité," *Pensées* [Paris], 175, May–June 1974.

United States. Congress. 102d, 1st Session. Senate. Committee on Foreign Relations. Subcommittee on African Affairs. *The Situation in Zaire.* (Hearing, November 6, 1991.) Washington: GPO, 1992.

_____. Congress. 102d, 2d Session. Senate. Committee on Foreign Relations. *Emergency Situation in Zaire and Somalia.* (Hearing, February 5, 1992.) Washington: GPO, 1992.

_____. Department of State. *Country Reports on Human Rights Practices for 1991.* (Report submitted to United States Congress, 102d, 2d Session, House of Representatives, Committee on Foreign Affairs, and Senate, Committee on Foreign Relations.) Washington: GPO, 1992.

Vanderlinden, Jacques (ed.). *Du Congo au Zaïre 1960–1980: Essai de bilan.* Brussels: Centre de recherche et d'information sociopolitiques, 1980.

Vansina, Jan. "Mwasi's Trials," *Daedalus,* 111, No. 2, Spring 1982, 49–70.

Verhaegen, Benoît. *L'enseignement universitaire au Zaïre: De Lovanium à l'Unaza, 1958–1978.* Paris: Harmattan, 1978.

_____. "Les mouvements de libération en Afrique: Le cas du Zaïre en 1978," *Genève-Afrique* [Geneva], 17, No. 1, 1979, 173–81.

Weissman, Stephen R. "CIA Covert Action in Zaire and Angola: Patterns and Consequences," *Political Science Quarterly,* 94, No. 2, Summer 1979, 263–86.

Willame, Jean-Claude. *L'automne d'un despotisme: Pouvoir, argent, et obéissance dans le Zaïre des années quatre-vingt.* Paris: Éditions Karthala, 1992.

_____. *Patrimonialism and Political Change in the Congo.* Stanford: Stanford University Press, 1972.

_____. *Zaïre: L'épopée d'Inga.* Paris: Harmattan, 1986.

Wilson, Francille Rusan. "Reinventing the Past and Circumscribing the Future: *Authenticité* and the Negative Image of Women's Work in Zaire." Pages 153–70 in Edna G. Bay (ed.), *Women and Work in Africa.* Boulder, Colorado: Westview Press, 1982.

Young, Crawford. "Elections in Zaire: The Shadow of Democracy." Pages 187–212 in Fred M. Hayward (ed.), *Elections in Independent Africa.* Boulder, Colorado: Westview Press, 1987.

_____. "Ethnic Politics in Zaire." Pages 163–215 in Crawford Young (ed.), *The Politics of Cultural Pluralism.* Madison: University of Wisconsin Press, 1976.

_____. "Zaire and the Soviet Union." Pages 202–24 in Dennis L. Bark (ed.), *The Red Orchestra, 2: The Case of Africa.* Stanford, California: Hoover Institution Press, 1988.

_____. "Zaire: The Unending Crisis," *Foreign Affairs,* 57, No. 1, Fall 1978, 169–85.

_____. "The Zairian Crisis and American Foreign Policy." Pages 209–24 in Gerald J. Bender, James S. Coleman, and Richard L. Sklar (eds.), *African Crisis Areas and U.S. Foreign Policy.* Berkeley: University of California Press, 1985.

Young, Crawford, and Thomas Turner. *The Rise and Decline of the Zairian State.* Madison: University of Wisconsin Press, 1985.

Zartman, I. William. *Ripe for Resolution: Conflict and Intervention in Africa.* New York: Oxford University Press, 1985.

(Various issues of the following publications were also used in the preparation of this chapter: *Africa Confidential; Cahiers du CEDAF* [Brussels]; *Current History;* Economist Intelligence Unit, *Country Profile: Zaire, Rwanda, Burundi* [London]; Economist Intelligence Unit, *Country Report: Zaire, Rwanda, Burundi* [London]; Foreign Broadcast Information Service, *Daily Report: Sub-Saharan Africa; Jeune Afrique* [Paris]; *Le Monde* [Paris]; *New York Times;* and *Washington Post.*)

Chapter 5

Africa Contemporary Record: Annual Survey and Documents, 1988–1989. (Ed., Marion E. Doro.) New York: Africana, 1992.

Africa South of the Sahara, 1992. (21st ed.) London: Europa, 1991.

Africa South of the Sahara, 1993. (22d ed.) London: Europa, 1992.

Africa South of the Sahara, 1994. (23d ed.) London: Europa, 1993.

Africa Watch. *Zaire: Two Years Without Transition.* New York: July 1992.

Amnesty International. *Amnesty International Report, 1991.* New York: 1991.

_____. *Amnesty International Report, 1992.* New York: 1992.

_____. *Amnesty International Report, 1993.* New York: 1993.

_____. *Human Rights Violations in Zaire.* London: 1980.

_____. *The Ill-Treatment and Torture of Political Prisoners at Detention Centers in Kinshasa.* London: 1980.

_____. *Political Imprisonment in Zaire: An AI Special Briefing.* New York: 1983.

_____. *Report on Cases of Nineteen People Tried by the Court of State Security in Kinshasa, June 1982.* London: 1982.

_____. *Student Arrests in Zaire During the First Half of 1980.* London: 1980.

_____. *Summary of Concerns in the Republic of Zaire.* London: 1987.

_____. *Zaire: Amnesty International Concerns Between January 1987 and January 1988.* New York: 1988.

_____. *Zaire: Reports of Torture and Killings Committed by the Armed Forces in Shaba Region.* London: 1986.

Berkeley, Bill. "Zaire: An African Horror Story," *Atlantic Monthly,* 272, No. 2, August 1993, 20–28.

Bobb, F. Scott. "Another Rescue Operation," *Africa Report,* March–April 1979, 16–20.

Callaghy, Thomas M. *The State-Society Struggle: Zaire in Comparative Perspective.* New York: Columbia University Press, 1984.

Coquéry-Vidrovitch, Catherine, Alain Forest, and Herbert Weiss (eds.). *Rébellions-révolution au Zaïre, 1963–1965.* Paris: Harmattan, 1987.

Crabb, John H. *The Legal System of Congo-Kinshasa.* Charlottesville, Virginia: Michie, 1970.

Fungula, Fumu Ngondji. "Une réflexion sur l'opposition politique zaïroise." Pages 115–24 in Bogumil Jewsiewicki (ed.), *État indépendant du Congo, Congo belge, République démocratique du Congo, République du Zaïre?* Saint Foy, Canada: SAFI Press, 1984.

Gérard-Libais, Jules. *Katanga Secession.* (Trans., Rebecca Young.) Madison: University of Wisconsin Press, 1966.

Gildea, Tara. "A Case Study of Zaire's Foreign Policy: Shaba I and II." (M.A. thesis.) Geneva: Institut universitaire de hautes études internationales, 1990.

Gould, David J. *Bureaucratic Corruption and Underdevelopment in the Third World: The Case of Zaire.* Elmsford, New York: Pergamon Press, 1980.

_____. "Patrons and Clients: The Role of the Military in Zairian Politics." Pages 465–506 in James Isaac Mowoe (ed.), *The Performance of Soldiers as Governors.* Columbus, Ohio: University Press of America, 1980.

Grundy, Kenneth W. *Guerrilla Struggle in Africa: An Analysis and Review.* New York: Grossman, 1971.

Hoare, Michael. *Congo Mercenary.* London: Hale, 1967.

International League for Human Rights. *Zaire's Human Rights Record: Comments on the Government of Zaire's Official Report to the Human Rights Committee.* New York: 1987.

Jackson, Robert H., and Carl G. Rosberg. *Personal Rule in Black Africa: Prince, Autocrat, Prophet, Tyrant.* Berkeley: University of

California Press, 1982.

Jewsiewicki, Bogumil. "Pour une histoire comparée des révoltes populaires au Congo." Pages 130–57 in Catherine Coquéry-Vidrovitch, Alain Forest, and Herbert Weiss (eds.), *Rébellions-révolution au Zaïre, 1963–1965*. Paris: Harmattan, 1987.

Kalb, Madeleine G. *The Congo Cables: The Cold War in Africa—From Eisenhower to Kennedy*. New York: Macmillan, 1982.

Kengo-wa-Dondo. "Le pouvoir judiciare sous la deuxième république zaïroise," *Studia Diplomatica* [Brussels], 28, No. 5, 1975.

Kilch, Ignacio. "Israel Returns to Africa," *Middle East International*, No. 176, June 4, 1983, 11–12.

Kitchen, Helen (ed.). *Footnotes to the Congo Story*. New York: Walker, 1967.

Kurian, George Thomas. *World Encyclopedia of Police Forces and Penal Systems*. New York: Facts on File, 1989.

Lawyers' Committee for Human Rights. *Zaire: Repression as Policy: A Human Rights Report*. New York: 1990.

Lefever, Ernest. *Crisis in the Congo: A United Nations Force in Action*. Washington: Brookings Institution, 1965.

_____. *Spear and Scepter*. Washington: Brookings Institution, 1970.

Malu, Malutamidi. *The Shaba Invasions*. Fort Leavenworth, Kansas: United States Army Command and General Staff College Press, 1988.

Mangold, Peter. "Shaba I and Shaba II," *Survival* [London], May–June 1979, 107–15.

Meason, James E. "African Navies South of the Sahara," *U.S. Naval Institute Proceedings*, March 1987, 56–64.

The Military Balance, 1993–1994. London: International Institute for Strategic Studies, 1993.

Miller, Charles. *Battle for the Bundu: The First World War in East Africa*. New York: Macmillan, 1974.

"Mobutu's Battle for Survival," *Africa* [London], 91, March 1979, 16–20.

"Mobutu's Secret War," *New African* [London], No. 191, August 1983, 11–14.

Mockler, Anthony. *The New Mercenaries: The History of the Hired Soldier from the Congo to the Seychelles*. New York: Paragon House, 1987.

O'Brien, Connor Cruise. *To Katanga and Back: A U.N. Case History*. New York: Simon and Schuster, 1962.

Odom, Thomas P. *Dragon Operations: Hostage Rescues in the Congo, 1964–1965*. Fort Leavenworth, Kansas: United States Army Command and General Staff College Press, 1988.

_____. *Shaba II: The French and Belgian Intervention in Zaire in 1978*. Fort Leavenworth, Kansas: United States Army Command and

General Staff College Press, 1992.

Ogunbadejo, Oye. "Conflict in Africa: A Case Study of the Shaba Crisis, 1977," *World Affairs,* Winter 1979, 219–34.

Paulus, Jean-Pierre. *Droit publique du Congo belge.* Brussels: Université libre de Belgique, 1959.

"Republic of Zaire," *Journal of Defense and Diplomacy,* October 1986, 28–37.

Salacuse, Jeswald W. *Introduction to Law in French-Speaking Africa.* Charlottesville, Virginia: Michie, 1969.

Schatzberg, Michael G. *The Dialectics of Oppression in Zaire.* Bloomington: Indiana University Press, 1988.

_____. "Military Intervention and the Myth of Collective Security: The Case of Zaire," *Journal of Modern African Studies* [London], 27, No. 2, 1989, 315–40.

Shaw, Bryant P. *Force Publique, Force Unique: The Military in the Belgian Congo, 1914–1939.* Madison: University of Wisconsin Press, 1987.

Turner, Thomas E. "Decline or Recovery in Zaire?" *Current History,* 87, No. 529, May 1988, 213–16, 230.

_____. "Zaire's Armed Forces," *Journal of Defense and Diplomacy,* October 1986, 38–41.

United States. Agency for International Development. *Economic Development vs. Military Expenditures in Countries Receiving U.S. Aid.* (Report submitted to Congress, 96th, 2d Session, House of Representatives, Committee on Foreign Affairs, and Senate, Committee on Foreign Relations.) Washington: GPO, 1980.

_____. Department of Defense. Security Assistance Agency. *Foreign Military Sales, Foreign Military Construction Sales, and Military Assistance Facts.* Washington; September 1991.

_____. Department of State. *Country Reports on Human Rights Practices for 1989.* (Report submitted to United States Congress, 101st, 2d Session, House of Representatives, Committee on Foreign Affairs, and Senate, Committee on Foreign Relations.) Washington: GPO, February 1990.

_____. Department of State. *Country Reports on Human Rights Practices for 1990.* (Report submitted to United States Congress, 102d, 1st Session, Senate, Committee on Foreign Relations, and House of Representatives, Committee on Foreign Affairs.) Washington: GPO, 1991.

_____. Department of State. *Country Reports on Human Rights Practices for 1991.* (Report submitted to United States Congress, 102d, 2d Session, House of Representatives, Committee on Foreign Affairs, and Senate, Committee on Foreign Relations.) Washington: GPO, 1992.

Verhaegen, Benoît. "La rébellion muleliste au Kwilu: Chronologie des évenements et essai d'interprétation (Janvier 1962–Juillet 1964)." Pages 120–46 in Catherine Coquéry-Vidrovitch, Alain Forest, and Herbert Weiss (eds.), *Rébellions-révolution au Zaïre, 1963–1965*. Paris: Harmattan, 1987.

_____. "Le rôle de l'ethnie et de l'individu dans la rébellion du Kwilu et dans son échec." Pages 147–67 in Catherine Coquéry-Vidrovitch, Alain Forest, and Herbert Weiss (eds.), *Rébellions-révolution au Zaïre, 1963–1965*. Paris: Harmattan, 1987.

Wagoner, Fred E. *Dragon Rouge: The Rescue of Hostages in the Congo*. Washington: National Defense University, 1980.

Weiss, Herbert, and Adrienne Fulco. "Les partisans au Kwilu: Analyse des origines sociales des membres et cadres des équipes de base." Pages 168–81 in Catherine Coquéry-Vidrovitch, Alain Forest, and Herbert Weiss (eds.), *Rébellions-révolution au Zaïre, 1963–1965*. Paris: Harmattan, 1987.

Weissman, Stephen, R. *American Foreign Policy in the Congo, 1960–1964*. Ithaca: Cornell University Press, 1974.

_____. "CIA Covert Action in Zaire and Angola: Patterns and Consequences," *Political Science Quarterly*, 94, No. 2, Summer 1979, 263–86.

Willame, Jean-Claude. "Political Succession in Zaire or Back to Machiavelli," *Journal of Modern African Studies* [London], March 1988, 37–49.

Wright, John B. *Francophone Black Africa since Independence*. (Conflict Studies Series.) London: Institute for the Study of Conflict, 1981.

_____. *Zaire since Independence*. (Conflict Studies Series.) London: Institute for the Study of Conflict, 1983.

Young, Crawford. *Conflict in the Congo*. Princeton: Princeton University Press, 1965.

_____. "Elections in Zaire: The Shadows of Democracy." Pages 187–212 in Fredrick M. Hayward (ed.), *Elections in Independent Africa*. Boulder, Colorado: Westview Press, 1987.

_____. "The Portuguese Coup and Zaire's Southern African Policy." Pages 195–212 in John Seiler (ed.), *Southern Africa since the Portuguese Coup*. Boulder, Colorado: Westview Press, 1980.

_____. "Zaire and Cameroon." Pages 120–49 in Peter Duignan and Robert Jackson (eds.), *Politics and Government in African States*. Stanford, California: Hoover Institution, 1986.

Young, Crawford, and Thomas Turner. *The Rise and Decline of the Zairian State*. Madison: University of Wisconsin Press, 1985.

(Various issues of the following publications were also used in the preparation of this chapter: *Africa Confidential* [London]; *African*

Defence Journal [Paris]; Amnesty International, *Urgent Action;* British Broadcasting Corporation, Monitoring Service, *Summary of World Broadcasts, Pt. 4: The Middle East, Africa, and Latin America* [London]; *Christian Science Monitor; DMS Market Intelligence Reports: Middle East/Africa;* Foreign Broadcast Information Service, *Daily Report: Sub-Saharan Africa; Military Technology; New York Times; Washington Post;* and *World Defense Almanac.*)

Glossary

abacost—Name for the male attire favored by Mobutu and promoted as part of the authenticity (*q.v.*) campaign, consisting of a short-sleeved suit worn without a tie. The word *abacost* is derived from the French *à bas le costume,* or "down with the suit."

authenticity—An official state ideology of the Mobutu regime that emerged in the late 1960s and 1970s. Emphasizing the value of authentic Zairian culture, authenticity was a reaction against the lingering vestiges of colonialism and the continuing influence of Western culture. As implemented, the policy resulted in numerous changes in both public and private life; for example, the name of the country was changed to Zaire, and Zairian names were given to cities, regions, streets, bridges, boats, and other public facilities. Individuals were encouraged to drop Western, Christian names in favor of Zairian names; to adopt the *abacost* (*q.v.*) and its female equivalent in place of Western attire; and to address each other as "citizen" instead of using the standard French *monsieur* or *madame.* The policy began to wane in the late 1970s.

clan—A group whose members are descended in the male line from a putative common male ancestor (patriclan) or in the female line from a putative common female ancestor (matriclan). Clans may be divided into subclans organized on the same principle or into lineage (*q.v.*) groups believed to be linked by descent from a remote common ancestor.

descent group—A group having political, economic, or social functions. Formation of the group is based on actual or putative descent through persons of one sex from a common ancestor of the same sex, and therefore called a unilineal descent group (clan—*q.v.* or lineage—*q.v.*), or through persons of both sexes from a common ancestor of either sex (cognatic descent group).

évolué—A French term (literally, "evolved," or "developed") used in the colonial era to refer to Africans who had "evolved" through education or assimilation and accepted European values and patterns of behavior. *Évolués* spoke French, usually held white-collar jobs, and were primarily urban.

fiscal year (FY)—In Zaire, the calendar year.

gross domestic product (GDP)—A measure of the total value of goods and services produced by a domestic national economy during a given period, usually one year. Obtained by adding the value contributed by each sector of the economy in the form of profits, compensation to employees, and depreciation (consumption of capital). Only domestic production is included, not income arising from investments and possessions owned abroad, hence the use of the word *domestic* to distinguish GDP from the gross national product (GNP—*q.v.*). Real GDP is the value of GDP when inflation has been taken into account. In countries lacking sophisticated data-gathering techniques, such as Zaire, the total value of GDP is often estimated.

gross national product (GNP)—The total market value of all final goods and services produced by an economy during a year. Obtained by adding gross domestic product (GDP—*q.v.*) and the income received from abroad by residents and then subtracting payments remitted abroad to nonresidents. Real GNP is the value of GNP when inflation has been taken into account.

immatriculation—In the colonial era, the process by which an *évolué* (*q.v.*) was given the same legal status as Europeans.

import substitution—An economic development strategy that emphasizes the growth of domestic industries, often by import protection using tariff and nontariff measures. Proponents favor the export of industrial goods over primary products.

International Monetary Fund (IMF)—Established along with the World Bank (*q.v.*) in 1945, the IMF is a specialized agency affiliated with the United Nations that is responsible for stabilizing international exchange rates and payments. The main business of the IMF is the provision of loans to its members (including industrialized and developing countries) when they experience balance of payments difficulties. These loans frequently carry conditions that require substantial internal economic adjustments by the recipients, most of which are developing countries.

lineage—A group whose members are descended through males from a common male ancestor (patrilineage) or through females from a common female ancestor (matrilineage). Such descent can in principle be traced. Lineages vary in genealogical depth from the ancestor to living generations; the more extensive ones often are internally segmented.

Mobutism—An official state and party ideology encompassing and glorifying the thoughts, visions, and policies of Mobutu. Includes such major Mobutu initiatives as Zairianization (*q.v.*) and authenticity (*q.v.*).

parastatal—A semi-autonomous, quasi-governmental, state-owned enterprise.

Paris Club—The informal name for a consortium of Western creditor countries (Belgium, Britain, Canada, France, Germany,

Italy, Japan, the Netherlands, Sweden, Switzerland, and the
United States) that have made loans or have guaranteed export credits to developing nations and that meet in Paris to discuss borrowers' ability to repay debts. Paris Club deliberations
often result in the tendering of emergency loans to countries
in economic difficulty or in the rescheduling of debts. Formed
in October 1962, the organization has no formal or institutional
existence. Its secretariat is run by the French treasury. It has
a close relationship with the International Monetary Fund (*q.v.*),
to which all of its members except Switzerland belong, as well
as with the World Bank (*q.v.*) and the United Nations Conference on Trade and Development (UNCTAD). The Paris Club
is also known as the Group of Ten (G–10).

patrimonialism (adj., patrimonial)—A traditional political system
in which government is personal, and government administration is an extension of the ruler. In such a system, the individual national leader controls the political and economic life
of the country, and personal relationships with the leader play
a crucial role in amassing personal wealth or in the rise and
decline of members of the political elite.

retrocession—The official name given to the policy of reversing
Zairianization (*q.v.*). Under the policy, announced on December 30, 1974, up to 40 percent of ownership of Zairianized
properties could be returned to foreign owners. The proportion was increased to 60 percent in late 1975.

special drawing rights (SDRs)—Monetary units of the International
Monetary Fund (*q.v.*) based on a basket of international currencies including the United States dollar, the German deutsche
mark, the Japanese yen, the British pound sterling, and the
French franc.

World Bank—Informal name used to designate a group of four
affiliated international institutions that provide advice and assistance on long-term finance and policy issues to developing
countries: the International Bank for Reconstruction and Development (IBRD), the International Development Association (IDA), the International Finance Corporation (IFC), and
the Multilateral Investment Guarantee Agency (MIGA). The
IBRD, established in 1945, has as its primary purpose the provision of loans at market-related rates of interest to developing countries at more advanced stages of development. The
IDA, a legally separate loan fund administered by the staff of
the IBRD, was set up in 1960 to furnish credits to the poorest
developing countries on much easier terms than those of conventional IBRD loans. The IFC, founded in 1956, supplements

the activities of the IBRD through loans and assistance designed specifically to encourage the growth of productive private enterprises in the less developed countries. The president and certain senior officers of the IBRD hold the same positions in the IFC. The MIGA, which began operating in June 1988, insures private foreign investment in developing countries against such noncommercial risks as expropriation, civil strife, and nonconvertibility of currency. The four institutions are owned by the governments of the countries that subscribe their capital. To participate in the World Bank Group, member states must first belong to the International Monetary Fund (*q.v.*).

zaire (Z)—Zairian currency unit, introduced on June 24, 1967, replacing the Congolese franc. Consists of 100 makuta (sing., likuta), designated by the symbol k. From June 24, 1967, through March 11, 1976, Z1 equaled US$2. On March 12, 1976, the zaire was pegged to special drawing rights (*q.v.*), thereby establishing an effective value of Z1 equaled US$1.15. The rate between the zaire and the dollar was subject to market forces thereafter. In recent years, the zaire has been devalued numerous times (e.g., 1983, 1988, 1989, and 1991), and its value has plummeted. In terms of the dollar, the average annual exchange rate declined from Z50 in 1985 to Z719 in 1990, to Z15,587 in 1991, and Z645,549 in 1992. In early 1993, the exchange rate was estimated at Z8 million to the dollar, and in December 1993, Z110 million equaled US$1.

Zairianization—Name given to the policy, announced in November 1973, requiring the transfer of foreign enterprises in strategic sectors of the economy, such as agriculture, commerce, and transport, to Zairians. The inefficient management of the enterprises thus transferred led to a partial retrocession (*q.v.*) of ownership to original holders beginning in 1975.

Index

abacost, 50, 212

Abako. *See* Alliance of the Kongo People

ACPC. *See* Association of Coffee Producing Countries

acquéreurs, 98, 144

acquired immune deficiency syndrome (AIDS), liv, 128

Actualités Africaines, 45

Adamawa-Eastern language family, 80–81

Adoula, Cyrille, 25; as prime minister, 38

Adoula government, 38–39; opposition to, 39; revision of districts under, 38–39; resignation of, 37–38, 42

Afco. *See* Association of Women Merchants

African Charter of Human and People's Rights, 326

African Development Bank, 191

African Solidarity Party (Parti Solidaire Africain—PSA), 33

Agence Nationale de Documentation. *See* National Documentation Agency

agricultural production, 150; quotas for, 17, 75–76, 102, 108, 140, 174

agricultural products (*see also under individual crops*), 171–74; bananas, 5; cash crops, 110, 139, 167, 172; cereals, 5; for export, 102, 196; imported, 168; oil palm, 5; smuggling of, 167, 168; subsistence, 167; yams, 5

agriculture, 167–76; Chinese advisers in, 197; colonial, 139–40, 168; corruption in, 168; enterprises, 168; inputs, 167; as percentage of gross domestic product, 156, 167; portion of budget allocated to, 162; potential of, 167, 168; precolonial, 5, 94, 138–39; privatization in, 150; slash-and-burn, 167, 175; subsistence, 167, 168; women in, 110–12, 172; work force in, 167; under Zairianization, 167, 168

Agrifor: privatization of, 150

AIDS. *See* acquired immune deficiency syndrome

air force, 277, 303; capabilities of, 303; matériel, 303; mission, 303; number of personnel in, 277, 303; organiza-

tion of, 303

airlines, 108, 192

Air Transport Union (Union de Transports Aériens—UTA), 192

Air Zaïre, 108, 192; government ownership of, 152; management of, 192

Alliance des Bakongo (Abako). *See* Alliance of the Kongo People

Alliance of Patriotic Forces, li, 215–16

Alliance of the Kongo People (Alliance des Bakongo—Abako) (*see also* Association for the Maintenance, Unity, and Expansion of the Kikongo Language), 3, 22, 23–24; in elections, 24; manifesto of, 23; recognition of denied, 247

Alur people, 82

Amin Dada, Idi, 279, 280

Amnesty International, 279, 326, 327

ancestors, 121

AND. *See* National Documentation Agency

ANC. *See* Congolese National Army

Angola: armed forces of, 281; involvement in, xlvii, 265–67, 291–92; migration to Zaire from, 71; refugees from, 71, 73; refugees to, 293; relations with, 267–69, 279, 281–82; support for invasions of Shaba, 281; troops deployed to, 302

Angolan civil war: Cuban intervention in, 278; Zairian intervention in, 55–56, 278, 281

ANL. *See* National Liberation Army

Armée Nationale Congolaise. *See* Congolese National Army

Armée Nationale de Libération. *See* National Liberation Army

Arabs, 77; trade with, 9–10, 14, 139, 283; military campaigns against, 14, 283

armed forces (*see also under military*), 277; in Angolan civil-war, 55–56; attitudes toward, 297–98; buildup of, 278; civic-action role of, 298; under colonial rule, 282–86; conditions in, 304, 306–7; control of, by Mobutu, 232–33; corruption in, 279, 306; development of, under Mobutu, 288–90; discontent in, 297; discrimination in, 297; evolution of,

369

Frente Nacional de Libertação de Angola. *See* National Front for the Liberation of Angola

Frente para a Libertação do Enclavo de Cabinda. *See* Front for the Liberation of the Enclave of Cabinda

Front for the Liberation of the Enclave of Cabinda (Frente para a Libertação do Enclavo de Cabinda—FLEC), 291

Front for the National Liberation of the Congo (Front pour la Libération Nationale du Congo—FLNC) (*see also* Black Arrows), 56; discipline in, 295; invasions of Shaba by, 57, 278, 281, 292, 294, 295–96; number of personnel in, 295; origins of, 56; strategy of, 294; support for, 281

Front pour la Libération Nationale du Congo. *See* Front for the National Liberation of the Congo

Fundamental Law (Loi Fondamentale), 28, 29, 221; judiciary under, 227; legislature under, 224

Furiiru people, 84

Gabon, 296

Garde Civile. *See* Civil Guard

Garrison Troops (Troupes Campées), 315–16; established, 284

Gbadolite, 205; development of, 231; summit in, 282

Gbadolite Declaration, 282

Gbemani, Albéric, 44

Gbenye, Christophe, 39, 213; exiled, 42

GDP. *See* gross domestic product

Gécamines. *See* General Quarries and Mines

Gemena: development of, 231

gendarmerie (*see also* National Gendarmerie; Territorial Service Troops), 285

Gendarmerie Mobile. *See* Mobile Gendarmerie

Gendarmerie Nationale. *See* National Gendarmerie

Gendarmerie Territoriale. *See* Territorial Gendarmerie

General Act of Berlin (1885), 14

Général des Carrières et des Mines. *See* General Quarries and Mines

General Elite Peace Force. *See* Civil Guard

General Holding Company of Belgium (Société Générale de Belgique—SGB), 140, 178

General Motors, 182–84

General Property Law (1973), 171

General Quarries and Mines (Générale des Carrières et des Mines—Gécamines), 151, 159, 177; bankruptcy of, liii, 177; copper production by, 177–78; electricity consumption by, 187; employees of, 166; formed, xliv, 141, 152; funds diverted from, 177; health care by, 130, 132; imports for, 194; as source of revenue, 162, 196; turnover in, 100–101

General Secretariat of the Presidency, 222

General Union of Congolese Students (Union Générale des Étudiants Congolais—UGEC), 48, 207–8

gens d'eau (water people), 6

geographic regions, 67–68

geography, 64–70; land area, 64

Germany (East): relations with, 262–63

Germany, Federal Republic of: aid from, 191, 197; currency printed in, 163, 165; investment by, 198; military assistance by, 318

Gizenga, Antoine, 33, 287; dismissed, 32

GM. *See* Mobile Gendarmerie

gold, 180; artisanal mining of, 180; earnings from, 180, 194; export of, 177, 180, 194; illicit mining of, 108; mining of, 141, 177, 180; production of, 180; smuggling of, 108, 180

Goma, lv, lvi

Goodyear, 182–84

Gould, David, 106

government: bankruptcy of, 163; centralization of, 52; control of business by, 18, 151; corruption in, 64, 74, 152, 153; de facto decentralization of, lv; during decolonization, 28–29; economic regulation by, 146; human rights abuses by, 326; involvement in energy, 184; official languages of, 76; portion of budget allocated to, 162; restructuring of, 47, 52; revenue, 137, 147, 153, 177; rotation of posts in, 205; structure of, 220–32

government, local, 21, 228–32; autonomy of, 231; under colonial rule, 229–30; under First Republic, 229; function of, 228–29; reform in, 18, 19

government, provisional, 33

government, transitional. *See* Tshisekedi government

government agencies: foreign personnel in, 97

Government Council, 28

government of national salvation. *See* Birindwa government

government spending, 197; excessive, 149; untraceable, 162

Great Rift Valley, 64

Greece: business enterprises of, 96–97; foreign residents from, 96; judges from, 227

gross domestic product (GDP), 155–56; decline in, 146, 151, 155; growth of, 148, 155; increase in, 155; regional, 156; sectoral composition of, 156

gross domestic product fractions: agriculture, 156, 167; budget deficit, 149; debt, 163; informal economy, 158; manufacturing, 182; mining, 156; per capita, 130, 155; service sector, 156

GT. *See* Territorial Gendarmerie

Guevara, Ernesto "Che," 288

Gulf Oil, 186, 196

Habré, Hissein, 313

Haiti: judges from, 227

Hammarskjöld, Dag, 31, 36; killed, 27

Haut Conseil de la République. *See* High Council of the Republic

Haut-Katanga cluster, 85

Haut-Shaba Subregion, 85

Haut-Uele Subregion: ethnic groups in, 81

Haut-Zaïre Region: agriculture in, 171; ethnic groups in, 81; malnutrition in, 130; mining in, 179, 181; population density in, 73; refugees in, 73, 74

HCR. *See* High Council of the Republic

health care: access to, 129; for armed forces, 307; colonial, 140; immunization, 127; for internal refugees, 74

health care professionals, 129; strikes by, 166

health care system, liv, 64, 126–32; portion of budget allocated to, 162

health facilities, 102, 129; closed, 64; of missions, 63, 112; private, 130

Hemba cluster, 85

High Council of the Republic (Haut Conseil de la République—HCR), 203–4, 217, 218; created, 226; rejected by Mobutu, 218; role of, 218

High Council of the Republic-Parliament of the Transition (HCR–PT), xlix, lii, 226

highlands, 67, 68; economic conditions in, 110; ethnic groups in, 81–82, 84–85; livestock in, 176; logging in, 69; occupations in, 84; political organization in, 84; population density in, 73

Hitler, Adolf, xxxvi

housing: for armed forces, 307

human rights, 25–27

human rights abuses, 59, 309, 325, 326; by army, 288; under colonial rule, 14–16; by French Foreign Legion, 295; under legal system, 324; in Moba, 279; under Mobutu, 197; opposition to, 312

hunting: precolonial, 138, 139

Hutu people, 74

identity cards, 229

Ileo, Joseph (*see also* Ileo Nsongo Amba), xlviii, 25, 213; as prime minister, 32

Ileo government, 33

Ileo Nsongo Amba, Joseph (*see also* Ileo, Joseph), 213, 216

IMF. *See* International Monetary Fund

immatriculation decree (1952), 21; provisions of, 21

imports, 150; of food, 150, 167–68, 176; of oil, 145; value of, 194

import substitution, 141, 182–84

income (*see also* wages): per capita, 146, 151; of teachers, 125–26; of workers, 101, 108

independence: Belgian declaration of intent for, 24; crisis related to, xxxv, 28–37; date of, 29; effect of, on economy, 141–42; factors behind, 21

India: foreign residents from, 96

industrial development: exploitation of mineral wealth for, 141; investment in, 154

industrialization, xlv, 137; plans for, 141

Industrial and Mining Development Company (Société de Développement Industriel et Minier de Zaïre—

63, 76–79; choice of, 78; indigenous, 78–79; multilingualism, 78; officially recognized, 76–78
League of Young Vigilantes (Ligue des Jeunes Vigilants), 207
Lebanon: judges from, 227
Leele people, 88
legal system (*see also* customary law), 322–23; attempts to reform, 227; bribery in, 323; penalties in, 322
Legislative Council (*see also* Colonial Council), 28; member of, 28
legislature, 224–26; under constitution of 1964, 224–25; under Fundamental Law, 224; under Transitional Act, 226
Lengola language, 84
Léopold II (king), xxxvi, xxxvii, 13, 116, 282
Léopoldville (*see also* Kinshasa): ethnic associations in, 22; founded, 13; Mobutu government in, 33; riots in, xxxix, 24, 28
Léopoldville Round Table (1961), 38
Lia people: political systems of, 83
Liboke Iya Bangala (Arm of the Ngala), 52
Libya: relations with, 271–72
life expectancy, 71, 126
Ligue des Jeunes Vigilants. *See* League of Young Vigilantes
lineages, 79
Lingala language, 76, 77–78; expansion of, 77–78
literacy rate, 122, 123
livestock, 168, 176; cattle, 176; goats, 176; pigs, 176; precolonial, 138; sheep, 176
living standards, 63, 137, 156; decline in, liii, 145, 150; factors determining, 63, 155
Livingstone, David, xxxvi, 13
Lobala people, 6
Loi Fondamentale. *See* Fundamental Law
Lomongo language, 77
Lomotwa people, 86
Lovanium University, 114, 124
Lualaba River, 67
Lualaba Subregion, 85
Luba kingdoms, 7; occupations in, 139; organization of, 9
Luba people, xxxviii, l, 6, 79; discrimination against, 27; ethnic conflicts of, 91; expelled from Shaba, 74, 91, 92,

247–48; influence of, 91; language of, 77, 86; massacre of (1960), 32; traits of, 90–91
Lubumbashi: armed forces deployed in, 300; mining in, 179; population in, 75; student massacre, xlvii, 164–214, 302
Lulua people, 86; ethnic conflicts of, 91
Lumumba, Patrice, 25, 213; assassinated, xxxviii, xxxix, 33; conflict of, with Kasavubu, xxxix–xl; conflict of, with United Nations, 32; dismissal of Kasavubu by, 32; dismissed, 32; and Mobutu, 46; placed under house arrest, 33; as prime minister, xxxix, 25, 29, 286, 287; travel by, 32
Lumumba government, 31; martial law declared by, 32; opposition to, 31; policies toward secessionists, 31–32; problems of organizing, 31
Lunda Bululu, 214
Lunda cluster, 88
Lunda Empire, 7, 85, 85, 89; indirect rule under, 7; succession in, 7
Lunda Kingdom, 7–9; expansion of, 7–9, 89; occupation of, 9
Lunda people, 6, 79; ethnic conflicts of, 91, 247–48; occupations of, 139; political activities of, 27
Lunda Region: ethnic groups in, 85–86
Lundula, Victor, 30, 46, 286, 287
Luntu people, 86

MacGaffey, Janet, 106, 110, 111, 129, 158
MacGaffey, Wyatt, 89
Makanda Kabobi Institute, 50
malnutrition, liv, 111, 127, 131
Malula, Joseph (cardinal), 114; exiled, xliii, 114
Mamvu people, 81
manganese, 177, 179
Mangbetu people, 6, 79, 81
Mangutu people, 81
Maniema Region: creation of, 232; population density, 73
Manifesto of N'Sele, 49, 51, 208
manioc. *See* cassava
manufacturing: capacity, 184; cessation of, 184; neglect of, 156; obstacles to, 182; as percentage of gross domestic product, 182; products of, 182

Published Country Studies

(Area Handbook Series)

550-65	Afghanistan		550-87	Greece
550-98	Albania		550-78	Guatemala
550-44	Algeria		550-174	Guinea
550-59	Angola		550-82	Guyana and Belize
550-73	Argentina		550-151	Honduras
550-169	Australia		550-165	Hungary
550-176	Austria		550-21	India
550-175	Bangladesh		550-154	Indian Ocean
550-170	Belgium		550-39	Indonesia
550-66	Bolivia		550-68	Iran
550-20	Brazil		550-31	Iraq
550-168	Bulgaria		550-25	Israel
550-61	Burma		550-182	Italy
550-50	Cambodia		550-30	Japan
550-166	Cameroon		550-34	Jordan
550-159	Chad		550-56	Kenya
550-77	Chile		550-81	Korea, North
550-60	China		550-41	Korea, South
550-26	Colombia		550-58	Laos
550-33	Commonwealth Caribbean, Islands of the		550-24	Lebanon
550-91	Congo		550-38	Liberia
550-90	Costa Rica		550-85	Libya
550-69	Côte d'Ivoire (Ivory Coast)		550-172	Malawi
550-152	Cuba		550-45	Malaysia
550-22	Cyprus		550-161	Mauritania
550-158	Czechoslovakia		550-79	Mexico
550-36	Dominican Republic and Haiti		550-76	Mongolia
550-52	Ecuador		550-49	Morocco
550-43	Egypt		550-64	Mozambique
550-150	El Salvador		550-35	Nepal and Bhutan
550-28	Ethiopia		550-88	Nicaragua
550-167	Finland		550-157	Nigeria
550-155	Germany, East		550-94	Oceania
550-173	Germany, Fed. Rep. of		550-48	Pakistan
550-153	Ghana		550-46	Panama